The good life for Molly Weir is to be kept busy writing and acting, and it is no wonder her TV producer in Aberdeen remarked, 'Aye Molly, there you are, still spinning like a peerie'. It really does sum her up. And instantly became the title for this book.

MOLLY WEIR

Spinning Like a Peerie

Happiness is the exercise of one's vital abilities.
Greek Saying

LOMOND
BOOKS

This edition published in 1999 for
Lomond Books Limited
36 West Shore Road
Granton, Edinburgh EH5 1QD
by Diamond Books
77-85 Fulham Palace Road
Hammersmith,
London W6 8JB

Published by Grafton Books 1986

First published in Great Britain by
Gordon Wright Publishing 1983

ISBN 094-7-78234-6

Printed and bound in Great Britain by
Caledonian International Book Manufacturing, Glasgow

Set in Times

To the 'Dear Departed', those friends and colleagues
who have so enriched my life, but are now, like
The Flowers o' the Forest, A' wede awa'.

There's a cure for a'thing but stark deid.

Scots Proverb

Love is not changed by death,
And nothing is lost.
And all in the end is Harvest.

Edith Sitwell

CHAPTER ONE

A lyric from an old Fred Astaire film has stuck in my mind right down the years, and I can see that lopsided grin as he sang up there on the silver screen:

> Nothing's impossible I have found
> And when your chin is on the ground,
> Just pick yourself up,
> Dust yourself off
> And start all over again!

Well, my chin wasn't exactly on the ground, but for the first time for ten years I was actually unemployed! And without the faintest hope that any acting jobs would come my way in the foreseeable future. There was also the matter of an overdraft for FIVE THOUSAND POUNDS. At today's values, that would be equivalent to around fifty thousand pounds. I, who had never owed a penny in my life, had gone mad and coaxed Sandy into buying a wildly expensive house. I had blithely assumed, wrongly as it turned out, that the gravy train of *Life With the Lyons* which had carried me to prosperity for a decade, would run on a smooth track forever.

It didn't.

It stopped suddenly, with a jolt which left me and the rest of the cast gasping with shock.

In the time it took all of us to read the headlines in

the evening papers which somebody handed to us during the tea-break, we were out of work actors!

'LIFE WITH THE LYONS COMES TO AN END', the banner headline read. And underneath was another. 'BEN LYON TAKES TEN THOUSAND A YEAR POST WITH ASSOCIATED TELEVISION'.

Still we didn't understand. Why weren't we just going to record the show that night, go on holiday as planned, and come back in the autumn as usual? Surely if Ben was now going to occupy a senior executive position he could just give himself permission to take time off to do our shows? We were, after all, among the top comedy series on TV and on radio. Everybody loved our scatty family. It *couldn't*, simply couldn't finish as suddenly as this, with none of us being told a word of this dramatic news until we read it in the newspapers.

But it could.

And it did.

It was not ethical, apparently, for Ben in his new post to employ himself or any of his family as actors. In silence we listened to him spell it out.

And that was that.

We recorded the show, not allowing our sick sense of shock to affect our professional pride in doing our best, and we gave what we now knew was our very last performance with the Lyon family.

For ten years I had been completely identified in the public mind as Aggie, the cook-cum-housekeeper-cum-friend of the entire madcap family, in a family show which had become as much a part of the British comedy scene as the Goons. Our gimmick was that it was a real family. Ben and Bebe Daniels were really husband and wife. Barbara was their own daughter. Richard was their adopted son. And the rest of us had

8

been their staff, their bank manager, their neighbours through eleven radio series, six TV series, two films and a stage run.

Like every actor who's had the luck to be in a long-running series, I knew the built-in danger of being too strongly identified with a single character. No casting director will look at you, in case it unbalances his show. I felt sure I would never work again.

In the event, I didn't get a single nibble of gainful acting employment for thirteen months.

Sandy, my husband, doesn't believe me when he hears me say this. 'I can't remember a single week in your entire life when you weren't working like a beaver,' he protests. 'You've never been out of work.'

But I know better.

How else could I be so exact, and *know* without a shadow of a doubt that it was every day of thirteen months?

A starving man knows to the hour the last time food crossed his lips.

An unemployed actor can measure the days which followed his last job as accurately as a prisoner marking off the calendar in his prison cell.

Not that I was in prison, not even the prison of despair by this time, a despair which had paralysed my will following my mother's death. I was now plunged into the joyous activity of making our newly purchased expensive 'folly' of a house as perfect as my hands and talent – and cash – would permit.

Thank goodness, not knowing that the show-business cheques would cease so dramatically, we'd gone over-board and had the whole house decorated from top to bottom, and had actually spent a small fortune ordering shrubs and trees for the garden so that we could spend the summer out of doors getting our 'estate' to rights!

9

Had we known how hard up we were going to be, we'd never have dared to be so extravagant, employing a veritable army of craftsmen to do all this expensive work for us. Ignorance was indeed bliss, and all was mixed with mercy, for thanks to having had such experts exercising their skills throughout the house, we didn't have to part with a penny on decorating for years. Quality always lasts, we told ourselves, looking at our empty bank books. And we were right.

The only thing missing was a carpet for the sitting room. The bare boards there were a reproach each time we looked in. It was a bit like the staff quarters in posh hotels, when one leaves the carpeted stairs which have cushioned the feet to the third landing, to find only cold stone treads leading upwards to where the hired help sleeps!

True, there was that overdraft, but we had to have a carpet some time, and suddenly I knew just where I was going to buy it.

I wasn't the only one who had had to accept the challenge of a future devoid of greasepaint. Bebe also had to face up to this. It was all very well for her husband, Ben. He had his new job and was up to the eyes in it. But she, who had earned her living as a young Hollywood actress since the age of thirteen-and-a-half, simply had to find a new interest. It wasn't in her nature or training to sit at home as a housewife, divorced from some sort of show business activity. She also felt a compulsion to provide a livelihood for their son Richard. She knew how insecure an actor's life could be, and she felt that whatever happened to his future prospects in the profession, it would be a great comfort to have a second string.

Behind those enormous eyes of Bebe's a shrewd and lively intelligence was always at work. Antiques were

10

the 'in' thing in London. She and Ben had excellent taste in furniture, porcelain, pictures and décor, and more than a fair knowledge of values. The family name wouldn't hurt either. There could be a nice cachet in being associated with the esoteric world of antiques and fine art. She would open a shop, and run it with Richard. So, when the right premises in the right part of Kensington came on the market, Bebe bought them.

It was a new part for her to play, and she threw herself into it with her usual enthusiasm and zeal. She was having the time of her life.

Richard, I could see, was to be cast in the rôle of antiques buyer, learning as he went along. He was to attend the house auctions, study the markets, and in the fullness of time he would be entrusted with assisting any customers who had interior decorating problems.

At this point, I cast myself in the rôle of a customer. I had, after all, earned most of my money working in *Life with the Lyons*, so it seemed only right and fitting that I would help to launch the new shop by buying our new sitting room carpet there. Bebe knew exactly how hard up we were, so she wouldn't encourage us to spend too recklessly.

When I arrived at the shop, I stood back to admire the sign above the door. In beautifully executed lettering, sign-writers had painted the words, 'BEBE DANIELS-RICHARD LYON LTD' – Fine Old Furniture and China. Interior Decorators.

I pushed the door open, and it was like stepping into a TV set for an episode of *Life with the Lyons*.

Bebe sat with a pencil stuck through her hair, working out sums on a piece of paper. Ben brought in a tray of salad for her, and she looked faintly surprised that it was Ben who did this and not me. I am sure she was so immersed in her part as an antique dealer, that

11

she didn't see me as a customer at all, but as Aggie her cook and fellow conspirator in her ploys against Ben. Ben urged her to stop working and eat her salad. If people hadn't put food down in front of Bebe, she would have quietly starved to death. She never knew what time of day it was unless somebody told her. Such practical trivialities didn't concern her. Work and show business totally absorbed her. It was always a source of amusement to me that she had actually compiled a cookery book, for I never knew anyone less interested in food or anyone who bothered less about eating.

Richard, hearing my voice, flew through from the back shop to show me round. Jean, the secretary, followed him with a pile of envelopes and samples which were to be sent off. Barbara, true to form, rang for a taxi.

It was all movement and colour and activity, and I was delighted to be with them all again, and to admire the lovely items which filled the shop and which were displayed with such casual effect. I instantly swooped on a short sample length of flame-coloured velvet with a narrow white stripe running through it. 'Oh Richard,' I said, 'could you use this to cover a wee folding chair for me?' It was a spare sample, so he laughingly put it aside, and said he'd measure the chair when he came to measure the room for the carpet. 'These Scots are always out for a bargain,' he said with a wink to the others.

Sandy would tell you that every item in our house has its own special story, and the wee chair is no exception. I had bought it for two shillings, with some other items from an office colleague who was leaving Glasgow.* The chair had belonged to her grannie, and

* Best Foot Forward

had stood in the kitchen for years, and it later graced the first room I had all to myself following a nervous breakdown. An upholsterer pal of my mother had re-covered it for us in cut brown velvet for nothing, using a piece of left-over material from another job, and he'd carried the chair on his head through Springburn to work on it in his own tiny workshop at the back of the house. I was as proud of it as though it had been made by Chippendale. I couldn't part with it. It is a treasured reminder of grannie, of my mother, and the make-do-and-mend days of Springburn and childhood. I may add that when Richard did finally give it its elegant new flame and white velvet covering, he had to drape it under a piece of sacking in the shop where it stood ready to be delivered, because so many customers fell upon it with cries of delight and wanted to buy it! Wouldn't my mother have been pleased? She always loved confirmation of her own good taste, from those she regarded as 'toffs'. Today it stands in our bedroom, and it is the first thing I see when I open my eyes in the morning, and in the eye of memory I also see it carried upside down through the streets of my childhood on the head of a generous wee craftsman, who was kind to us because he appreciated that my mother knew a good worker when she saw one.

But before the chair had its new covering, there was the serious business of choosing the colour and texture of our new fitted carpet. Richard, very business-like, produced swatches of colours, patterns, and textures from various carpet-makers, and after a palpitating hour swithering over first this one, and then that one, I threw caution to the winds and chose a shade the exact tone of our golden privet hedge.

Sandy nearly had a fit when I showed him the sample I brought home with me for his approval, and was gloomily certain we would never keep it clean, and I'd thrown away a fortune on a carpet which would have to be renewed in no time.

But, like my mother before me, I recognized hard-wearing quality when I saw it and it is still down as I write. I have Richard's estimate in front of me. How modest it seems, by comparison with today's prices.

To:	Supply 19 sq yds York Wilton Broadloom	£61–15–0
	Supply 5½ yds of 27 in York Wilton to match	14–11–6
	Supply 15 yds of UD4 underfelt 54 in wide,	15–15–9
	making up of same and carpet. Laying smooth edge	£92– 2–3

Please note. This estimate includes 12½% purchase tax on all carpet, plus 10% cutting charge.

When it was laid, Richard came out here to check that his fitters had made a proper job of it, just to ensure that we were completely satisfied. No wonder we talk of the good old days! Richard laughed at my saying the new colour scheme made it look as though the garden had strayed into the sitting room, but he agreed that the contrast with all my dark blue Bristol glass and other colour touches made a most attractive impact against the golden tone of his expertly laid carpet.

He couldn't stay for lunch, but he *did* enjoy a handful of little cold new potatoes which were lying in a dish in the kitchen. My heart gave a lurch as I remembered my mother used to do just the same thing – she never could resist a cold potato, especially a new potato, and when she was with us there were very few ever left over for frying. Oh how I wished she could have known that this was another taste she shared with Richard. She was very fond of him and he of her, and I wished too that she could have been there to admire his supervision of the laying of the fine new carpet.

But the carpet laying was a very sedate affair compared with the laying of the lino tiles in the hall, landing and upstairs lavatory.

The two Scotsmen we'd engaged to do this work had also agreed to adapt some carpets and linoleum from our old house. They were great fans of the Lyons, and were enchanted to find themselves working for 'Aggie', to whom they had listened for years cheeking up to Ben every Sunday, so when they turned up to lift the floor coverings, they brought their cine-camera with them. This was a chance they couldn't miss, they told us. Before a stroke of work was done, they were determined to record the entire performance for posterity.

First I was 'directed' to meet each of them in turn, and we shook hands at the gate, with much hamming and bowing as though we were Japanese businessmen! Then we walked back and forth to the car, and were filmed loading up the vehicle with the floor coverings they'd now lifted. The final dramatic shot from the old house saw us driving into the 'sunset' towards a new life!

Up at the new house, the camera was set up, and we re-enacted our arrival. Now they took it in turns to be shown round the new garden by me. There was hardly a thing to be seen, for our shrubs hadn't arrived, but I waved my arms about like Lady Bountiful and they clasped their hands in delight as they bent to admire the empty borders, one dashing to the cine-camera while the other 'acted'.

Unknown to me, I discovered later they had also filmed me trying to back the car out of the new gates, with Sandy suicidally throwing himself on to the boot to stop me destroying both the car and the gates.

They were far more interested in making home movies than in doing anything so tedious as laying floor tiles, and all this took hours. It wasn't far short of midnight before two tired Scotsmen sat at the bottom of the stairs and smiled with weary pleasure as we drooled over the beauty of the kitchen floor with its pale grey background and 'random' squares of carefully chosen contrasting colours.

After all they had had quite a day, those two chaps. They'd been actors, cinema directors, removal men, and lino layers! And it showed!

When they came back at the end of the week to do a few finishing touches here and there, they brought a young son with them, and the projector, screen and camera were set up. After supper, we all sat down to see the show.

We might have been heard laughing up in Scotland.

The Keystone Kops weren't in it. We all moved like lightning, arms and legs going as though we'd been wound up like clockwork toys. My hands moved and mimed with the speed of a racing tic-tac man, and my tongue wagged non-stop. The men rushed in and out of the house with carpets and bundles of linoleum as though the place was on fire. There was a wild frenzy about the whole scene which had us clutching our sides with laughter. At one point, the smaller Scotsman 'brought the house down' by falling full-length over the grass verge with a huge roll of carpet, and almost disappearing under the car wheels. None of us could even remember that happening at the time.

Then we watched it all over again, more calmly this time, taking in the beauty of the colour and the details of the gardens. I was delighted with their camerawork, and Sandy said I was far better at this fast-moving stuff because it is perfectly natural to me. He was shouting with laughter over his dramatic saving of the car from harm, and at the look of joy on my face when I finally got the car safely through the gates.

I am quite certain that very few lino laying sessions finish on such a hilarious note. We sometimes meet those men with their wives when we're walking over the golf course, and when we do, we all explode with laughter. I'm sure passers-by must wonder what shared memory makes us unable to keep our faces straight, and would stare at us disbelievingly if we told them it was all concerned with laying lino tiles in our kitchen.

All these happenings were grist to the mill for my writing of the weekly article for the Scottish *People's Journal*, my one small source of income since *Life with the Lyons* finished.* This was the one door which had opened for me following my mother's death, and after a lot of thought I had decided to make my contribution in the form of a weekly letter as though to her.

Looking back, I can see that my mother's death was a turning point in my life.

It was after that traumatic experience, writing would come to occupy a larger and larger portion of my working days, until I was uncertain whether to describe myself as an actress who wrote, or a writer who acted.

At the time though, the *Journal* column was a great therapy for me, which softened the terrible finality of

* One Small Footprint

17

that bereavement, and for a long time I was able to carry on the pretence to myself that I was still writing to my mother and that she was still in living touch with my news. I poured out my feelings in such a personal way, that *Journal* readers felt that I was truly writing for their ears alone, and letters arrived in shaols, each and every one wanting an individual reply! It was a lovely, quite unexpected, and flattering reaction, but it made personal mail almost an occupation in itself, and posed quite a problem in postal expenses when we were so hard-up!

Indeed, financial problems had become so pressing that I was inspired to have a grand sale of a wild assortment of household goods which could safely be regarded as superfluous to our needs. Carpets, curtains, a Ewbank cleaner, a length of stair carpet, a mattress, carpet clips and underlay, lampshades and a small table. We certainly needed the cash more than we needed them. I advertised them in the local paper, and I must truly have sold them at giveaway prices for the house hummed like an ant-heap the following Saturday.

With stunning timing, the morning's post brought with it a £25 prize from Ernie!

We'd hardly finished our waltz of joy round the kitchen over the £25 win when the door-bell started ringing. The bargain-hunters had arrived. People rushed out the back door clutching their possessions, as others rang the front bell. There was ceaseless furious activity as buyers roped or strapped their purchases on top of their cars. To me that was almost the most surprising thing which happened that morning – practically every one of our customers drove up in a spanking expensive car! My mother would have been

18

flabbergasted. To her, the possession of a car meant that you shopped 'doon the toon' for everything!

As the thought crossed my mind, a man arrived whom I mistook for a buyer, but who turned out to be a marooned Scot, down on his luck, who wanted to borrow five bob to see him on his way! I don't know how he knew where to find us. Maybe he just followed the crowd and chanced his arm, but I handed him the silver I'd just received from the sale of a couple of lampshades and he went down the road whistling. I think he probably felt he was lucky to get anything, as it was clear we were reduced to selling our household possessions to keep body and soul together.

Ecstatic over the £25 Premium Bond win, we recklessly added our wedding present vacuum cleaner to the sale goods, added the few pounds we got for it to our prize money and later bought a spanking new vacuum cleaner which would do justice to the new sitting room carpet. The buyer of our Hoover didn't even want to try to see if it worked, so anxious was he to get it to his car before I changed my mind. He had obviously decided I was one of those impractical women who knew the value of nothing. But not content with his bargain, the rascal made off with the three-pin plug. *That* was why he was in such a hurry. I was furious, for even with a brand new cleaner, the cost of the plug was extra. I didn't grudge anybody a bargain, in fact I rejoiced in their pleasure, but the petty meanness of pinching a new electric plug dented my faith in mankind a trifle.

When they had all gone, Sandy and I looked at one another with sparkling eyes. What a success our sale had been. Everything we had advertised had been sold. We had a nice little pile of notes to spend as we liked, and plenty of room to display future purchases.

I was beginning to realize there were great compensations in not being gainfully employed. I could throw myself with enthusiasm and energy into all such ploys, without giving a thought to being tired, or straining my voice, or 'saving myself' for a late performance, and I positively bloomed with the complete relaxation from show business tension. When people told me how well I looked, and asked me if I'd been on some marvellous holiday, I used to laugh and say, 'The answer is in one word – unemployment.' It's perfectly true. The working actor is fulfilled in many essential ways, but he's leaner, tenser, and aware of every bodily imperfection in a way unknown to the 'resting' actor. When you know you have a responsibility to the other members of the cast, much less to a waiting audience, every sniffle is a tragedy. When you're only responsible for keeping your house clean and your garden tidy, the most vicious bacteria can attack, and you can blithely take to your bed, knowing nobody is suffering but your solitary self. For ten years I had been part of a team of top entertainers, and the guarding of one's health had become a major occupation. The relief when this pressure ended was as glorious as it was unexpected. The bank balance was feeling the strain, but I was, in the words of Muhammed Ali 'floating like a butterfly', and it was a lovely feeling.

For the first time for years, I could actually take time to get to know the neighbours properly and be neighbourly myself.

We seemed to be surrounded by old ladies. So much so, that I was highly amused to be told later by the youngish couple across the way that they had actually had their house up for sale before we arrived, because the wife couldn't stand the elderly hush, and longed for a bit of contemporary life. The moment she saw us arrive, she took the house off the market, feeling that 'young' life had returned! What a nice compliment.

As for me, I loved the old ladies. I've always had an affinity with older folk because of the closeness of the relationship with my grannie, and I revelled in the peace and quiet of having three huge gardens almost to myself. On our left was a tall old lady, in her eighties, with dark eyes and dark hair, one of those creatures whom nature has blessed by giving her the sort of hair pigment which never goes grey. I used to admire the way she bent right over from the waist when she was weeding or picking up anything in the garden, and she told me seriously, 'You see I'm like a rogue elephant. When I go down on my knees I can't rise again. So I have to bend right over to reach the ground.' Definitely a card, and we hit it off right away. Once I saw her bending over and popping something into the ground, then moving off and doing the same thing a little further along. What could she be doing, I wondered? When I asked her, she informed me she was planting potatoes. By the side of the lawn, if you please. It was a habit she'd acquired during the war, and she couldn't give up the secure feeling it gave her to have a little food in her own ground. 'How many are you planting?' I enquired, stifling my giggles. 'Seven,' she replied solemnly. 'Oh well,' I said, 'when you are harvesting them, perhaps I may put my name down as a customer?'

With dead-pan expression, she said, 'You realize I deal only in bulk?'

What a treasure, and what a delicious sense of humour.

She scorned the slothfulness of wearing a dressing gown, and never appeared out of doors other than fully dressed, even to collect the early morning bucket of coal. She hadn't the strength to lift it, but she pushed it with her feet until she reached the back door, and then heaved it indoors in a single movement. She always wore her wrist watch in the garden, so that she would know the exact moment to down tools and go inside to listen to *The Archers*, whom she adored.

This admiration for her favourite radio programme had stood her in good stead one autumn evening years before, she told me, when someone came to the door and she'd unthinkingly carried the rake into the kitchen where she'd left it leaning against the back door while she answered the front door caller. By the time he'd gone, it was the magic hour for *The Archers*, so she sat down to listen, and when that was over it was growing dark so she just left the rake where it was until morning.

During the night, she was wakened by an almighty crash and a muffled cry, followed by complete silence. Wisely she decided not to investigate, although personally I'd have been terrified, but she just turned over and went to sleep.

In the morning, the rake was lying across the kitchen, and an assortment of pots and pans littered the floor. A small window in the kitchen was smashed, and it was obvious somebody had tried to break in.

When the police were called, they patted her shoulder and told her she couldn't have set up a better burglar deterrent if she had tried. The intruder, in the dark, had stood on the teeth of the rake, which had of course shot up and smacked him in the face, sending him staggering into the pots and pans, which he'd brought down with such a clatter it had frightened the life out of him. So he'd vanished without taking a thing. I've since listened to broadcasts from thieves, and each and every one admits he's as nervous as a cat when he's 'on the job' and that the one thing which sends his nerves on end is any sort of unexpected noise, or unusual obstruction.

And my dear old neighbour, because of the coincidence of a late caller and a favourite radio programme, had supplied the perfect alarm by behaving uncharacteristically and not tidying her tools away. Wasn't it marvellous that she was less disturbed at her great age, than the young tearaway who had thought he could get easy pickings? I was most impressed by this story and her courage.

On our other side were two darling old ladies who shared a bungalow. They were 'ladies' in the true sense of the word. The older, a tiny bird-like creature, had been 'finished' in Switzerland, had toured Europe in her youth, with the younger woman as her companion, and the bungalow had in fact been designed and built by the father of the companion. They were quiet and beautifully spoken, as I found when I at last made contact with them in the garden. The younger lady, the companion, had her hair done up in old-fashioned 'ear-phones', and wore the most beautiful hand-knitted suits. A grand piano almost filled one side of the lounge, and I learned from another neighbour that the younger woman had in her youth sung for King George V, and her accompanist had been the talented pianist known to all of us later as Dame Myra Hess!

We had a great barter system. They gave us trays of their beautiful apples, some for apple pies and some with red polished skins for dessert, and we gave them plates of our own tomatoes. We didn't see a great deal of them, but we sensed their quiet presence in the garden, for they loved to do a little weeding and tidying when the weather was fine.

The older lady, Miss B., was very timid, and never ventured out of the bungalow, leaving any necessary shopping to her companion. When I suggested they might like to come round for tea one afternoon, and see over the house, my invitation was accepted on the strict understanding that it would depend on whether Miss B. felt up to the visit.

On the appointed afternoon, all was in readiness when Miss C. called to me from her side of the tree-lined hedge. 'I'm sorry,' she said quietly, 'Miss B. got as far as the front gate, but her courage failed her, and she just couldn't venture out into the lane.'

It had been so long since she had been out of doors, that she simply could not manage the dozen yards to reach our front door.

'All right,' I said cheerfully, 'what about *not* going out to the front. What about squeezing through that little space between the spruce and our garage. You're both so slim, if I can get through it, you can.'

She disappeared to consult her friend, and returned smiling.

'We will arrive by the spruce,' she said, 'even if it does seem a little ill-mannered not to use the front door.

I breathed a sigh of relief, hiding my amusement. I hadn't wanted all that home baking to go to waste, or to have the bother of doing it all again at some later date in case I was busy. The actor always expects the sudden call to action!

Five minutes later, they arrived, wearing their visiting clothes. Beautifully knitted suits, with gold brooches at the neck, dress rings sparkling on their thin fingers, shod in lovely fine leather shoes with a high polish which reflected the sunshine.

I had laid the tea-things in the garden, and after

they had enjoyed the scones with home-made strawberry jam, the shortbread, and the sponge cake they had a little tour of the garden. Their own bungalow was only on the other side of the hedge, but you'd have imagined they were visiting another town altogether. 'What a lovely view you have,' said little Miss B. gazing round admiringly at the frieze of trees, as though she'd never seen them before. 'You're *very* secluded,' she added, making me stifle a laugh, for their own garden was so overgrown I had christened it 'the enchanted forest' as it was so difficult to catch sight of either of them through the foliage.

They were interested in every shrub, every flower, every newly planted tree. They rejoiced to see rose trees where potatoes had been grown before our arrival, and they were so glad we hadn't cut down the golden forsythia whose brilliance they could just see from the bungalow. They were like children, examining everything in minute detail and it took us more than an hour just to go round two borders and a rock garden!

Indoors, they were enchanted with the changes we had made. They kept clasping their hands and gazing at one another in amazement, 'Oh what would Miss S. say if she could see it now,' they kept saying to one another. 'It is so bright. It is so colourful. It seems so much bigger.' I must say they were a marvellous audience, and not a thing escaped their attention.

They were so enraptured with the novelty of being in another house and garden, that they forgot all about their polite provisos earlier that they must be home by five o'clock. They had arrived at three, and they were just on the point of leaving when Sandy arrived home at seven! And when I went outside to collect the tea things which we'd left while we were doing our tour of the house, it was to find a cheeky squirrel devouring the shortbread and the sponge cake! The tinkling laughter of the two ladies rang out with pleasure at the sight, and they disappeared through the space by the spruce like two creatures from a fairy tale.

The excitement was almost too much for Miss B. who stayed in bed all next day, but our friendship was well and truly cemented with this visit, a friendship which lasted until the end of their days. And when the second old lady died, I was touched beyond words to find that she had left me £100 in her will. It was utterly unexpected, and moved me to tears. I bought a gold necklet from our local jeweller with the money, and every time I wear it I have a picture of that afternoon tea party, and their delight and amazement at the 'view' from our garden.

One of the saddest things when a show comes to an end, is that you're suddenly cut off from the companionship and friendship of colleagues with whom you've been in the closest contact for years. The curtain comes down on the last show, everyone goes his own way, and sometimes you never see any of them again.

In *Life with the Lyons*, I had kept in touch with the family, especially over the purchase of our carpet, but the others had gone their separate ways and I hadn't heard a syllable from any of them. Until the telephone rang one day, and it was Tom Ronald's office at Aeolian Hall, that magic centre of the Light Entertainment world of the BBC where I'd first seen Tommy Handley of *ITMA*. Tom had been our producer for *Life with the Lyons*, and he was telling me that darling old Horace Percival had died. Horace, beloved of all *ITMA* fans, whose phrases were on everyone's lips then, and are quoted even today. 'After you Claude.

26

No, after you Cecil.' And as Ali Oop, 'Excuse please. You buy saucy postcards? Very grimy. Oh blimey!' Even the Queen Mother echoed his 'I go, I come back' when they did a concert for the Royal Family at Windsor Castle. And there was the lugubrious 'Don't forget the diver, Sir. Don't forget the diver. I'm going down now, Sir.' The latter copied by every wise-cracking liftman in London.

In *Life with the Lyons* he had played Ben's neighbour Mr Wimple, father of an enormous family, one of whom was played by me as daughter Ethel. I played quite a lot of other characters, apart from my main one as Aggie, and I particularly enjoyed the fact that listeners didn't realize that the adenoidal little Cockney kid was me.

I had known Horace ever since I'd come to London, and I was very fond of this gentle, humorous, talented actor. I was shattered to learn that he had died in a home for elderly actors not far from our new house, and I had been completely unaware of his proximity or his frailty and so hadn't gone to visit him.

While I had been absorbed in my own concerns, he had been dying in a Home less than three miles away.

I felt I must atone for this in some way, and as he had no relatives of his own and would be buried in a local cemetery, I decided I would offer hospitality to the mourners after the funeral in the traditional Scottish way.

It had been a bitterly cold winter, and there were severe coal shortages owing to some rail dispute, so we could have only the smallest of fires in the dining room. It was impossible to light a fire in the sitting room, for there wasn't another particle of fuel in the house.

We were still as hard up as ever, but the morning of

27

the funeral dawned so damp and freezing that I went down to the off licence and with my last £2 bought a bottle of gin in case anybody would want spirits to warm them.

I had baked little savoury puffs filled with bacon and cheese, and a batch of shortbread. In the fridge I had a magnificent cheese cake, baked and given to me by the Jewish President of a synagogue where I'd done a free charity opening the previous week. I didn't actually think anyone would eat anything so rich in the morning, but at least it was there.

When we reached the church, one after another Ben, Bebe, Carleton Hobbs, Tom Ronald, Doris Rogers, Hugh Morton came over and said quietly that they wouldn't come back to the house after all. They had decided they would just go straight to town after the service at the graveside, for they hadn't realized it was so far out and they wanted to get back for lunch and attend to their afternoon commitments.

However, after we'd tramped through an icy field of clay to get to the newest part of the cemetery, and teeth began chattering like castanets, when the service was over they came to me again, one after another, and this time said, 'I think we'll come back to your place after all, if it's all right with you, for we don't want to catch pneumonia.'

'Of course, of course,' I said, 'I want to do this for Horace, and I want you to see the house.' And I turned to the Lyons, 'Especially you, for you'll want to see the carpet now that it is in place.'

We were all a little hysterical remembering the delay on the way to the cemetery, when the entire funeral procession had been held up by an enormous dust-cart which refused to let us pass. It was pure *Life with the Lyons* and we all felt Horace would have enjoyed it as

28

much as anyone. Just as he would have relished the scene when we all arrived at Primrose Cottage.

Everyone's feet were encased in sticky Middlesex clay, and I trembled for my nice clean carpets and brand new floor coverings. But I hadn't the courage to mention anything so mundane as material possessions at such a time.

Not so Ben. He took one look at his own shoes and said, 'Jeez, I think I've brought half of Horace's grave with me on my feet. I'm going to take my shoes off.'

In a moment, everybody else was doing the same.

It was like a Japanese house.

Solemnity vanished as eleven pairs of shoes were placed neatly on the papers I put down in the hall, and everybody walked about in their stockinged feet. Ben said he was very glad he'd worn the socks without a hole in the toe!

Everybody clustered round that miserable little smoking fire, for although I'd now switched on the few electric fires we possessed, the house was like an iceberg. We had no central heating, and the walls exuded the sort of cold which bricks hold after weeks of frost. To my amazement, nobody wanted gin. They *all* wanted scalding hot coffee. Doris Rogers quickly filled the two percolators and a kettle. Barbara and I got out the wedding china and tiny silver spoons. The savoury puffs were heating in the oven. Ben kept bossing me, as always, and shouting, 'Goddammit, you should have had all this done before we arrived.' 'I thought you would only want gin,' I yelled back. Bebe sat serenely, gazing round her, deciding just where she wanted the little antique brass candlestick to go. She'd brought this with her as a 'first visit' present, and it was lovely. A little hound lying on a brass base, with a decorated holder for the candle, and it stands today in the same spot where she placed it, with its pure white candle, on top of the fitment by the fireplace.

Richard rushed through to the freezing sitting room to see what the carpet looked like, and everybody followed him, and approved the colour scheme, until the smell of coffee drew them all back at a run to the dining room. Carleton Hobbs said it was the maddest funeral party he'd ever attended, as he carried the cups of hot coffee out to the drivers of the various cars, with pieces of shortbread.

It was lovely to watch the colour stealing into their faces as the hot coffee warmed them, but I was petrified to find they had devoured all the savoury puffs and every bit of shortbread with the first welcome cup. My mind went blank with fright, as I filled the percolators again. What on earth was I to give them now? They were obviously starving. Suddenly, I remembered the cheese cake in the fridge. Was it too rich for the morning? I knew that Ben used to have one sent over every Thanksgiving Day from the famous *Sardi's* restaurant in New York, and it was a highlight of the celebratory meal. But their meal was in the evening.

Would they eat such a thing in the forenoon?

Tentatively, I asked if anyone would care to try it.

Ben, the connoisseur, roared with laughter at my offering cheese cake. Why the finest cheese cake was produced in the States. What would I, a Scot, know about cheese cake? Nothing at all, I had to admit.

Truth to tell, I didn't even like it very much, and couldn't have told a luscious one from a dud one. But I did know that the lady who had specially baked this beauty for me was a *Cordon Bleu* cook, and that her cheese cakes were famous throughout the Jewish community.

Without another word, I brought the cake to the table, handed Ben a knife and asked him to cut it.

He cut twelve slices, and there was silence as the first bites were savoured.

Ben's mouth fell open in sheer disbelief.

'Honey,' he said softly, 'this is even better than *Sardi's*. Where'd you get it? Don't tell me you baked this. I don't believe it.'

When I told him, he laughed. 'I knew you couldn't bake a cake like this in Scotland. Haggis, yes. But not American cheese cake.'

As the last crumbs vanished, we all echoed Ben's 'God bless old Horace.'

In true Scottish tradition, what had been a sad occasion had become a party, all because a little charity appearance of mine had been acknowledged with a cake which had transformed my modest catering into a feast. And because we truly were as close as any family.

When they had all gone, I looked steadily at that bottle of gin which hadn't been opened. And I looked at my empty purse. Next day, taking my courage in both hands, I returned the gin to the off licence, and asked for my money back. I certainly couldn't afford to lock up £2 in liquor, when it was needed for proper food.

I was outraged when the owner held the bottle up to the light to check that it was really gin, and not water. What cheek!

'Do you really think I would hand you a bottle of water and pretend it was gin?' I asked indignantly. 'I know I'm a good actress, but I don't flatter myself I could carry off such a deception in one of my own village shops. Nor would I try to defraud anyone, especially a grocer who I regarded as a friend.' I practically choked with injured innocence. 'I'm used to being *trusted*,' I gulped. 'I don't tell lies.'

I could see my £2 vanishing into thin air under his suspicion.

Hastily he laid the bottle down. 'No, no, of course you don't tell lies,' he said soothingly, 'it's just a matter of training. It's second nature to check.'

He handed me my £2. I smiled my forgiveness, glad to be solvent again, and headed for the butcher, where I blued half of my recovered wealth on a tiny pot roast.

CHAPTER TWO

In the thirteenth month following the end of *Life with the Lyons*, I got my first job. A film. My very favourite side of show business. You can't believe the surge of energy which rushes through an actress's being when she realizes she is still part of the acting world. She hasn't been forgotten. Somebody, in some casting office, has actually remembered she exists and *wants* her.

The film was entitled *Wot a Whopper*, and starred Adam Faith. Adam had been a brilliantly successful pop star, and was at last being allowed to make the transition from the world of pop to the world of acting, for which he yearned. The film's plot revolved round the Loch Ness Monster, and I was to play the part of a prim wee schoolteacher, supposedly taking my class of girls on a country walk.

As it was to be shot 'on location' I fondly imagined I'd have my fare paid all the way to Inverness, or to Loch Ness itself, and even as the casting director was discussing possible dates I was mentally packing my case with walking shoes, anorak and enough clothes for a week's holiday. Nothing could have been further from the truth. It was shot at a lido not twenty minutes' drive from our new house, and the entire scene was completed before lunchtime!

But it was great fun all the same. In spite of the location being so close to our house, I still had to go all the way to the film studios at 7 A.M. for the make-up. There I had a hilarious reunion with my old chum Hattie Jacques, who was sitting in the make-up chair next to mine. As my girl wasn't quite ready, I flew to the end room, made a pot of tea for everyone, and handed round cigarettes and sweeties to ward off the pangs of hunger. All actors are hungry all the time. Hattie said, 'How is it the Scots get a reputation for meanness? I've *never* understood it, for they're among the most generous people I know.' 'Och,' I said, 'it's just a story put out by the Scots themselves to encourage the tourist trade.'

It was a beautiful summery day, but I had decided my pepper-and-salt suit would be right for the character I was playing (I supplied my own clothes), and willingly sweltered in the interests of my 'art'. But I envied Terence Longden, with whom my scene was played, when he appeared clad in blue jeans and nothing else! Marie France and Carole Lesley, the glamour girls, wore lovely summery clothes, and Adam Faith kept nice cool knees in his kilt. He had a very pleasant attractive personality, and from the short scene I watched him play, he showed every promise of being a good actor.

As usual, the moment I arrived on the set, it was time for the morning tea break, so we all queued up for hot dogs before a stroke of work was done. By the time the cameras started turning, I felt I'd known all of them for weeks. That's one of the nicest things about show business, the instant sense of friendship that exists between actors. There's no time to break the ice, or to adopt a wary attitude until one assesses character. We have to work together as soon as we are introduced, for the play's the thing, and we're all striving to do our very best, so there's no indulgence in shyness or self-consciousness. It's 'Scene 1, take 1', the clapper-board boy leaps clear of the camera, and we're off!

The director was a Scot (I wonder if he was the one who had asked for me?) and he seemed pleased with my work, and especially delighted we'd got it 'in the can' before lunch. In films, it is more popular with directors and producers to be a fast and accurate actor than to be a genius. Unless, of course, you are Marilyn Monroe! Time is money, and you'll never be forgotten if you get it right first time.

Lunch was served from a caravan trailer. I, who at home would have been happily content with an egg or a piece of cheese, found myself getting through steak and vegetables, fruit salad and cream, and excellent coffee! Location work can be awful. Draughty streets or pouring wet alleys, but that day was idyllic. A sparkling lido, hot sunshine, good company and wonderful food, and I was getting paid for it! It was a lovely welcome back to the film world, and I felt it was a good omen for the future.

The next film part I was offered sounded as though it would be fun to do, because the star was James Robertson Justice, that huge bearded figure who struck terror into the hearts of the young medical students in the *Doctor* films. The director wondered if I could possibly look seventy-five years old on the screen. I

34

looked anxiously at my face in the mirror beside the telephone for signs of swift old age, was fairly reassured, but on the principle that an actor never says anything is beyond him (or her), I assured him that with suitable lighting I felt certain I could look as ancient as he wished.

It was then I discovered I was to play James Robertson Justice's mother!' 'Oh yes, I'm *sure* I can look seventy-five,' I repeated, for I felt it would be hilarious, 'but I'll do it only on one condition.' 'What's that?' asked the director, no doubt wondering what lunatic he had on the other end of the telephone. 'I'll do it provided I can dandle James Robertson Justice on my knee!' His laughter practically shattered my eardrums. 'It's a deal,' he said.

When Sandy came home, and I told him about the film, he took one look at me in my shorts and sun-top, and said, 'Don't be daft. You could never look like James Robertson Justice's mother in a thousand years. Ring them up and tell them you've changed your mind.'

But before I could do any such thing, *they* rang *me* back. The men with the moneybags took cold feet when it was discovered I would have to look nearer *eighty-five* to play the mother character, and that, they thought, was a bit much to expect.

Wasn't it a pity though?

The very next day, while I was filled with gloomy regret over having lost the film with Robertson Justice, and mutinously mentally arguing with the film moguls that of course I could look eighty-five, the 'phone rang. I sprang to answer, and I was all ready to look a hundred if need be, but it was another casting director altogether. Could I come along to the studios to be considered for the part of a bird-woman for one of the

Carry On films? Could I not! I switched off the washing machine, leaped upstairs and changed into my best suit, burbling with joy that I had been right in feeling that *Wot a Whopper* had been a good omen. I was well and truly back where I belonged, among the acting fraternity.

I saw the director and the producer, and to my joy they liked me on sight. I was just what they wanted, and they sent me along to wardrobe there and then so that we could arrange what a woman who was fond of birds would wear. We had a high old time raking through rails and rails of clothing, and in the end decided a droopy, faded crêpe-de-chine garment of genteel shabbiness would be perfect, worn with a long cardigan on top, and, as a final touch to make her look fairly eccentric and pixielated, lots of earrings and bangles and beads. I promised I'd bring all the bits and bobs of jewellery from my own collection of 'character' baubles, and drove home in high spirits, to await the call later in the month when they would be ready to shoot my scenes.

I enjoyed every minute of that little part. The best bit was that I wasn't called until 9 A.M. for although I love films, I hate the usual 7 A.M. start which means getting up practically in the middle of the night. I am deeply thankful I have never been a romantic actress, for I simply couldn't summon up the enthusiasm for any love scene at that hour.

Thanks to this late call, I was able to enjoy my 'beauty sleep', and didn't have to leave the house until after 8 A.M. to drive myself to Pinewood. Between us, the hairdresser and I decided we'd try for a bird's-nest coiffure, seeing that I was playing a bird-woman, and we piled my longish hair on top, letting wisps and tendrils escape, and the effect of this with the crêpe-de-chine dress, and the beads and earrings and bracelets seemed to please the director.

I was escorted to make-up, and, once I was ready for the cameras, was then taken to a lovely dressing room complete with cretonne-covered chairs and divan, with an elegant dressing table and wardrobe, private toilet and wash-room, and blissful central heating. Then somebody brought me a nice cup of steaming coffee and a piece of home-made cake baked by one of the studio attendants.

You wouldn't believe how pampered you are in films, once they get you there in the morning! It is very hard and concentrated work, and very costly once you're in front of the cameras, so everybody who isn't actually acting or part of the camera crew, helps in every possible way to save the strength and energy of the performers. You're dressed and undressed like a lady, clothes are hung up, escorts provided to take you to the set or to the canteen, make-up girls stand by ready with powder puff or lipstick, hairdressers keep a watchful eye on your hair, so that all *you* have to worry about is your performance and your interpretation of the lines.

My scene was with Bill Owen, a fine actor, who was at that time married to my friend Edith Stevenson from Glasgow who had shared all those wartime concerts and revues we did for Moultrie Kelsall.* I was fairly looking forward to meeting him, and to working with him. We got on like a house on fire from the word 'go'. A worker, like me, he was more than willing to go over and over our little scene until we knew it outside in. We had a wee debate as to whether I

* A Toe on the Ladder

should play my part as a wide-eyed trusting creature, or as a bit frightened and nervous. After trying it both ways, we decided I should be frightened, and that's how it was done

We were free to work like this until lunch time, because the director was busy with a frantic scene involving Kenneth Connor and a bevy of Chinese girls, and when this was completed we all met in the canteen for a scrumptious lunch.

The 'set' which was supposed to be my living room was delightful. It was furnished in Victorian style, and was full of birds, alive and stuffed. Canaries, budgies, an Indian Mynah bird, a parrot, some brilliant tiny coloured birds whose name I didn't know, all chirping and twittering away. There were the usual delays while they lit the set and got everything ready, and I was highly amused by two of the Chinese girls who came back and stood beside the set to watch me at work. For the film they had dressed in those slit-skirted silk Cheong-sams with high Mandarin neck-line, but for leisure they now appeared in tight trousers and roomy Italian pullovers, black hair streaming down their backs. They were fascinated by my hair because it was so light and fluffy. They had very black, heavy, lank hair – beautiful but very different from the Anglo-Saxon texture. They ran and fetched me cups of tea during the afternoon and twittered like the birds with delight over my Scottish accent. When I asked them why they weren't anxious to go home, now that their scene was finished, they said, 'All in family working today. If we go home, we must do cooking and wash dishes. So we no go home.'

Girls! They're the same the whole world over.

They had learned early the truth of the saying which

I used to quote to make my dear ma-in-law laugh, 'You don't get mink standing at the sink!'

We finished our scenes by a quarter-to-six, and then I had to face the ordeal of driving home cross-country, in the dark, for the very first time. All my film work seems to lead to my having new driving experiences. The very first time I ever drove alone was for a film test* and here I was about to face night driving after a long day in the studios.

The car was white with frost, and being ignorant of the magic of de-icers at that time, I had to use my car keys to scrape off a clear space to enable me to see through the windscreen. I kept my eyes firmly on the hedgerows so that I wouldn't be blinded by the oncoming headlights, and there was a hint of fog to keep me alert and stop me from wondering how my scenes would come over. Sandy had got home just ahead of me, and was very relieved that I had managed my icy, foggy, dark drive without mishap!

There was a letter waiting for me, signed by the Marchioness of Lothian and the George Cross heroine Odette Hallowes, inviting me to attend the Woman of the Year Lunch at the Savoy as an honoured guest. Well! You could have knocked me over with a feather. How on earth had they thought of me? The aftermath of the Lyons' show was still keeping me in demand for Exhibition openings, not to mention bazaars and fêtes for which I charged no fee, and which practically emptied the housekeeping purse buying things I could no longer afford, but the Woman of the Year Lunch was something else indeed. This was attended by around five hundred of the top women from all the professions, women who had achieved distinction in

* One Small Footprint

their own right and not through either inheritance or via their husband's position. The speakers were ladies of great renown, and the tickets were greatly coveted and could not be bought for gold. It was by invitation only.

And here was I, invited to attend such a lunch, whose proceeds were to go to the Greater London Fund for the Blind.

Thank goodness I had a practically new lightweight wool and terylene tartan dress, which I'd had made for me for the launching of my cookery book the previous year, and which I'd hardly worn since. That would do fine, for who would notice me especially, among five hundred top ladies? So long as I looked right for the Savoy, and fitted the general scene, that was all that mattered.

On the Friday evening before the lunch, the telephone rang. A voice informed me that Lady Lothian wished to speak to me, and would I please hold the line. All sorts of thoughts flew round my head as I waited. Had they realized they'd made a mistake and the invitation hadn't been meant for me after all? Did they want me to sell programmes? Thank goodness I hadn't rushed out to buy anything new, if I was now to be told I wasn't going.

It was far worse than any of these possibilities. I practically fainted when her ladyship at last spoke and said in honeyed tones that she and the committee had had another look at their list of speakers, and felt they would all treat the theme strongly and seriously, and they'd agreed it would be a lovely idea to finish up on a note of light comedy and so they were inviting me to *speak* at the lunch!

The theme for the lunch was 'Success'.

The other speakers were Dame Ninette de Valois,

Governor of the Royal Ballet, Miss Angele Delange, top member of fashion design, Miss Mary Grieve, the Editor of *Woman* Magazine, the Rt Hon Patricia Hornsby-Smith, MP, Mrs Janey Ironside, Professor of Fashion, and Dame Anna Neagle! And me!

Lady Loathian refused to take 'no' for an answer. She just *knew* that I would be splendid. She would look forward to seeing me on Monday, and of course I would now be sitting at the top table beside Anna Neagle. And she hung up. It's a fact of life that everybody, except the speaker herself, knows she will be perfect.

I hardly had a wink of sleep. I tossed and turned, thinking up ideas, phrases, stories, jokes, and my stomach whizzed and churned with terror as I thought of myself standing up there in the biggest reception room in the Savoy, addressing five hundred high-powered ladies. It would be far worse than a theatrical first night, for I would have nobody to share my moments of torment. I would be standing up entirely alone when my turn came, with five hundred pairs of ears waiting to hear what pearly words of wisdom would fall from my lips. And my dress wasn't even new. But my shoes were. Thank goodness I had managed to get a pair at the sales. When my feet felt elegant, the rest didn't matter.

All weekend, I was marching up and down memorizing my merry quips, muttering to myself, my legs turning to jelly every time I thought of the 'all-star' bill who would precede me. For I had been told I was to speak last.

Monday morning dawned bright and sunny, and bone dry, with not the slightest hint in the atmosphere of damp or drizzle, so my hair wouldn't drop all over my shoulders. Thank the Lord for small mercies, for my 'page-boy' would remain reasonably neat under my mink-trimmed velvet beret (the newspapers described it as a 'tammy').

The Savoy was buzzing with elegant ladies when I arrived, and the preliminaries passed in a haze of nerves. I shook hands, I smiled, I suppose I must have chatted, but I remember little of anything before I found myself seated at the top table. Every time I looked along the table, and saw famous face after famous face, I practically died of fright at the mere idea of having to get up to speak. I was seated between Anna Neagle and Dame Anna Stephens of the WAAF. Further along were the then Prime Minister's wife, Lady Dorothy Macmillan, next to her Lady Attlee, then came Lady Georgina Coleridge, and beside her the heroine of the French Resistance, Odette Hallowes. Audrey Russell, who used to give all those marvellous commentaries when the Queen was doing anything important, was nearby and she advised me to eat some sugar to steady my stomach, for she saw that I was hardly eating a bite. It was a waste of a superb lunch, for I couldn't taste a thing. Anna Neagle did the sensible thing, and ate one course, the fish, so she had a nice lightly-cooked dish in her tummy. I had a spoonful of soup, a forkful of fish, a bite of meat, and coffee, which did nothing to fill me or comfort me.

When the Rt Hon Pat Hornsby-Smith rose to speak, I thought, 'Well, it's pretty easy for her. She, after all, is used to addressing Parliament.' And then, to my horror, I saw her give a smile of sheer relief when she had finished her speech, forget she had pushed her chair back, and go sprawling full length on the floor, elegant hat rolling out of sight!

'Oh Lord God,' I thought, 'if she can do a thing like that, what's going to happen to me?'

42

Anna Neagle, all through the lunch, kept taking off one long pale suede glove, smoothing all the fingers, laying it down in front of her, and then putting it on again. I recognized all the signs of nerves, and through my own terror was amazed that a great star like Anna seemed as petrified as I was.

She spoke beautifully, and gave a sigh of utter bliss when she sat down, and a whispered word of encouragement to me not to worry, I would be fine.

Janey Ironside spoke next, and then the microphone was brought and placed in front of me by the toastmaster, who announced in ringing tones 'Pray silence for Miss Molly Weir'. I had never been announced by a toastmaster in my entire life. This was the great Ivor Spence, whom I got to know so well later, and who said for years afterwards each time he met me, 'Ah! Miss Weir, that speech!' and cast his dark eyes eloquently to heaven.

The Savoy staff had stolen in and were ranged round the back of the room. The theme, as I have said, was 'Success' and I had decided to concentrate on my small domestic successes, for how could I compete on any other level with such an audience? The first laugh I got was something I made up even as I rose to my feet and noticed that the waiters, the chef, and others were there. So after my opening words, I said, 'In passing, the chef of the Savoy has scored no mean success himself today, in making five hundred women entirely forget they're on a diet!'

The chef was delighted, and the staff roared their approval and this was so unexpected after the tone of the previous speeches that it was accorded far more laughter than it deserved.

I told them about our tandem bicycle, and how to make potted hough for sixpence, and how pleased I

43

was when I changed a plug on our old wireless set. I also told them how I made a hat for 1/4½d (about 6p), from the hem of my coat when I couldn't find a matching hat. Odette Hallowes said it was the funniest speech she had ever heard and she wanted me to do it all over again. Anna Neagle wrote 'my congratulations' on my programme. And Ivor Spence, when he came to remove the microphone, beamed upon me and whispered, 'Marvellous speech, Miss Weir, quite marvellous.'

It was a wonderful compliment, and a blissful feeling that something which I had dreaded had come off so well. It had been a challenge and a terror, and I thanked the Good God from the bottom of my heart that I hadn't made a fool of myself, and also for the fact that I would never never be asked to make a speech at the lunch again, for nobody is ever asked twice. I did become a member of the Committee and a Hostess, which I am still, as I write, but I bask in the knowledge that I will never again be asked to speak at that particular event.

When I went to bed that night, after telling Sandy all about it, chapter and verse, I could hardly sleep for excitement..I was so glad I hadn't let the Committee down and had managed to speak well for Scotland. But fancy wee Molly Weir from Springburn sharing a table with the Prime Minister's wife! My mother should have lived to see the day!

Speaking of Prime Minister's wives, the most amusing aftermath of that speech was that from then onwards, Lady Attlee regarded me as an authority on hats. Every year afterwards, she sought assurance from me that her hat was just right for the lunch and the occasion. 'You're such an expert on hats,' she would say, gazing anxiously into my eyes, and pressing my hands. 'If you say it looks all right, then I know it is.'

Shortly after my Savoy début, I was invited to speak to the Ladies Press Club. My dear friend, Dorothy Laird the writer, a Scot, asked me if I would do this as part of a Scottish evening she had arranged. We had eightsome reels, and pipers. We ate haggis and chapped tatties and neeps, and the English members were enthralled with this 'Taste of Scotland'.

Dorothy had suggested I tell them about my childhood in Glasgow, for she felt I always spoke on the radio of those tenement days with warmth and affection, and without a sign of a chip on my shoulder. When I looked round the room and saw a galaxy of representatives of the 'glossies', and other sophisticated members of the Press, I couldn't believe my memories of Glasgow would be of the slightest interest to them. I was sure the whole thing would be a flop. Poor Dorothy — her friends would think she was really scraping the bottom of the barrel. And I would die the death! They probably wouldn't even understand my accent.

All I could do was launch desperately into the speech I had prepared, so I spoke of the old Glasgow tramcars, of the swimming baths, of my grannie's old sayings, and of my mother's wee single-end, as a Glasgow apartment is called north of the border. To my amazement, not only did they understand every word, they shouted with laughter, and seemed to fall in love with my mother at first hearing. So I told them how my mother used to read Neil Munro's *Para Handy* every summer when she came to stay with us, and how she had loved the story of the wee wife who made 'chuckie soup'. She always said grannie could make soup out of an old boot, so she was more than ready to accept that

45

another thrifty wife could make soup from stones, or 'chuckies' as we say in Scotland.

This wee anecdote of the 'chuckie soup' got a small round of applause and I only discovered later that the daughter-in-law of the great Neil Munro was in the audience! I didn't realize writers were mortal like everybody else, and that I would actually be able to tell this lady that not only had I been brought up on the humour of *Para Handy*, but *The Daft Days* was a treasured School Prize.

Looking back, I believe it was on that night when I spoke to the Ladies Press Club that the seeds were sown which later germinated and resulted in my becoming an author. For, in spite of myself, I was impressed when they came to me afterwards, those ladies who wrote and edited the top glossy magazines and who worked for the Press barons, and said in urgent tones, 'But you *must* write a book about your childhood, and get all those fascinating memories between hard covers.' At the time, I laughed at the very idea that the memories of my tenement youth were the stuff that books were made of. I put it down to English exaggeration. But I remembered their words all the same, and, like Mary in the Bible, I pondered them in my heart.

Later, Lady Georgina Coleridge, who edited one of the top glossies at that time, and whom I'd met at the Woman of the Year Lunch, invited me to lunch, and informed me that if ever I did write such a book, she wanted first serial rights. Not only was I ignorant of what 'first serial rights' were, I had no idea of the compliment she was paying in bidding for such rights for a book which wasn't even contemplated. I didn't appreciate that most writers have to chase magazine editors for such golden promises, not the other way round. I just felt, somewhat uneasily, that I was being propelled towards writing disciplines for which I wasn't quite ready, and was assumed to have skills I wasn't even sure I possessed. However, I gave her my solemn promise that if ever I did write a book, she would certainly have those mysterious 'first serial rights', and then I shelved the whole idea while I pursued a Will-o'-the-wisp sideline suggested to me a long time before by my old friend and drama producer Moultrie Kelsall.

Moultrie had advised me that if ever I was hard up and needed a job, I was to go into the Players' Theatre and introduce myself. He said the money was infinitesimal, but the experience would be invaluable, and it was much better to be working than not. The Players' Theatre is unique. It is a replica of the old theatre of the times of Queen Victoria, and a picture of the old Queen herself is on the backscreen behind the stage. Candles are lit on the stage, the music is supplied by a piano, and the whole evening is under the control of a colourful Master of Ceremonies, dressed in Victorian costume. Television has copied it to some extent, in *The Good Old Days*, but this is the original, and indeed the television version uses the Players' chorus singers and dancers because their expert style of movement and gesture sets exactly the right tone for a Victorian entertainment.

In the theatre, unlike the TV version, it's only the performers who dress in Victorian costume. The audiences are composed of ordinary Londoners or tourists, wearing their ordinary clothes. A coffee counter runs along one side of the theatre, and there's a bar at the far end, so the audience can drift about and buy refreshments during the performance. Small tables between the seats make eating and drinking comfortable while watching the show. Chorus sheets are sold instead of programmes, and everyone joins lustily in the singing, the performers on stage taking the verses. A toast is drunk to Queen Victoria, and latecomers are heckled mercilessly by the quick-witted Master of Ceremonies. It's noisy and exuberant and the greatest fun. Americans love it for its quaint old-fashioned sense of ceremony, for although one has to be a member to get in, one can take friends, and tourists are given guest membership.

I went to one of the performances with a friend, just to get the feel of the place, and the whole exciting music-hall zing of the show so impressed me that I felt I'd never have the nerve to attempt to join their list of splendid artists.

Not only did I have a fairly small singing voice, I didn't even have an 'act', and it was obvious this home of Victorian Theatre was not only very specialized, but extremely polished and professional.

However, wandering down Villiers Street some weeks later, after a disappointing interview with a casting director, I found myself standing outside the Players' Theatre in the middle of the forenoon. Should I go in? What would I do if they asked me to do a 'turn'? I bit my lip in uncertainty. I half turned away. Then I thought of Moultrie's words again, which echoed my old boss Ben Lyon's own philosophy, it was much better to be working than not, or as Ben used to put it, activity breeds activity.

That did it. I pushed the door open, and I walked in. I heard voices at the far end of a long narrow auditorium, and I walked towards the sound. A group of men were discussing music, and one detached himself. He introduced himself as Don Gemmell and I knew I was speaking to the Scotsman who at that time ran the enterprise. When I introduced myself, and mentioned Moultrie, his face lit up at the sound of my Scottish voice, and he welcomed me with open arms. 'Oh what a lovely accent,' he exclaimed. 'I've practically lost mine, I don't get home nearly often enough.' Every Scotsman calls Scotland 'home' even if he hasn't seen the land of the bens and the glens for decades.

Then we got down to discussing what I could do. He knew I wasn't really a variety artist, but he stoutly declared that 'they' would love me whatever I did. He was sure I had a song somewhere that would do for their sort of Victorian entertainment and I was to come back the following week and do an audition for them. He pooh-poohed my fears that my voice wouldn't be big enough to withstand the competition from the trains which rattled overhead at regular intervals out of Charing Cross Station. When I first heard the tumult as we talked, I thought it was thunder! As I looked round the theatre, which in fact wasn't unlike a long railway tunnel, I was seized with apprehension and felt certain that nobody at the back would ever hear a word I said or sang. 'Don't worry,' Don clapped me on the back, 'Maria Charles has the tiniest voice you ever heard, and every syllable is clear as a bell. Go home now and find that song. We'll see you next week.'

I chose the song I had once auditioned for Jack Buchanan as a teenager in Glasgow, *The Laird o' Cockpen*, but this time I had the sense to take sheet music with me for the pianist, who was quite marvellous and gave me the confidence I greatly needed. He and Don decided I had a small but true sweet voice, and I wasn't to worry about it carrying. It would be fine. I did a little piece of Scottish gibberish, devised years before by Moultrie for one of our revues, and pretended this was a lesson in the Scottish language.

Don was delighted with this. I was to dance on, hands upraised, to the tune of *A Hundred Pipers*. And that was my act.

Don then informed me I could start as soon as I liked.

I swallowed half-a-dozen times in sheer terror at the thought of an audience, a paying audience, being offered this modest offering, took a deep breath, and said, 'Right, the sooner the better.' 'Tonight?' queried Don. 'Tonight,' I agreed. I knew if I took too long to think about it, I'd get cold feet, for this was different from anything I'd ever done. But it was a challenge which I felt I must meet.

I was sent along to a nearby theatrical costumier and fitted out with a lovely tartan dress, with wire cage bustle underneath the skirt, and a pad inserted to add to my curves over the hips. White tights looked like white stockings, and I had my own little scarlet flat slippers which I'd taken along for dancing comfort, and which looked just right.

That first performance was like a dream. I had rung Sandy to tell him what was happening, but whether he was in the audience or not, I had no idea. I stood in the wings, listening to the toastmaster announce to the audience, 'And *now*, the newest of the new Joys. Your *own*, your *very own* – *Molly Weir!*' The music started up, and with a loud skirling *hooch*, my hand raised in the classical position for the Scottish dance, I found my feet carrying me forward in a skipping *pas-de-bas* to interested, welcoming applause, which died down when I launched into my gibberish lesson in the Scottish language! I heard neither laughter nor applause. Only the beating of my own terrified heart sounded in my ears, and made me deaf to all outside noises. I didn't even hear the trains. The pianist caught my eye, gave me an approving wink and broad grin, and I realized he was repeating the opening chords of *The Laird o' Cockpen*, which I hadn't heard, but on his nod I gave *The Laird o' Cockpen* everything I had. I threw my arms wide, I tossed my head, I did the lot in fact, to illustrate the story and help them to understand the broad Scots, for I knew it would all be double Dutch to most of the audience.

When I'd finished (thank God, I'd remembered all the words), I danced off, and before I could collapse in the wings from sheer relief that it was all over, the toastmaster smilingly invited me back to take a curtain call.

I had done it! And I hadn't got the bird!

Nobody who isn't a performer can believe how nervous everyone is who has to walk out on to a stage. That night I was probably more palsied with terror than anyone else, for they had all worked at the Players' for years, off and on, but I was quite comforted to find signs of nerves among them just the same.

It was only on the second night that I was able to hear laughter and applause, and any sort of reaction to my performance. And I began to be relaxed enough to sit and chat with the other girls, who seemed to me so impressively confident. I discovered that it was quite usual for them to go along to the Players' any time they were out of work, and to be fitted into any performance as an added attraction. The wages were little more than pocket money, so the budget wasn't shattered if one more appeared on the bill, and anyway people were always dropping out or popping in, and that was part of the charm of *Late Joys* for the audience.

I found it a most fascinating set-up. There was one long narrow dressing room for the ladies, and another somewhere for the gentlemen. We all sat in front of our tiny bit of mirror at a long narrow shelf, make-up arranged on its allotted space, and our costumes hung on the hooks behind us.

We ate supper in the restaurant at a long table, and were privileged to eat at 'wholesale' prices because we were performing. At the interval we were allowed a cup of coffee and a sandwich free! But, to my amusement and slight chagrin, because I love them, there were no prawn sandwiches for actors. Too expensive! Just for paying customers.

It had a sort of touring company atmosphere, with an added taste of Priestley's *The Good Companions* because we all ate and dressed together, and I enjoyed the whole thing enormously. I felt pleased to have met the challenge with reasonable success, and to have added something new to my experience. I couldn't hope to meet the expertise of the established favourites, and I envied them their swaggering confidence, and their ability to eat huge meals, play cards, and cheek the audience without turning a hair once the first night uncertainties had been overcome.

By my second week, though, I found enough nerve to answer the customers when they called out their wisecracks. I was learning fast! They loved doing this, for the audience at the Players' is truly part of the show and they are encouraged to shout out their approval or otherwise, just as they did in the days of the old music-hall. It's all taken in good part, to shouts of uproarious laughter.

If there were Scots in the audience, I was sure of a good cheer on my entrance, and on the Saturday night when some Scottish sailors occupied the front row, I had to take *three* curtain calls, which was a satisfying improvement on the single call I had taken at Monday night's quieter house.

Those Victorian costumes made me appreciate that I live in a more modern age. There were dozens and dozens of hooks and eyes, and there was a constant fever of activity as we all hooked each other into our clothes, terrified of being late for an 'entrance' because of those complicated fastenings. There wasn't a zip between the lot of us!

The liveliness of the dressing room was a tonic to me, and I loved the extrovert behaviour of the girls. One girl was plunged into the depths of despair because she was sure she'd failed an important audition that afternoon, and she made up her mind she was going to have a prawn sandwich at the interval, and to hell with poverty!

Another arrived exhausted, flopped wearily into her chair and closed her eyes, and moaned that she had been flat-hunting all day and hadn't seen a thing to suit her, and the wedding was only a few weeks off! Little did she know that a day would dawn when to have a choice of flats would be unbelievable luxury, and the mere whisper of a flat to let would be kept as closely guarded as a state secret. In those days one could actually be choosy, and feel certain that the right rented accommodation would turn up eventually.

The nice girl who sat next to me was dimpling with delight because she had found her ideal flat, and had successfully moved in the day before. I gave her a stainless steel potato peeler as a wee 'hanselling' gift, as we say in Scotland, and she bought my cookery book, and took my telephone number so that she could ring me if she got into cooking difficulties! I assured her this 'after-sales' service would be a pleasure!

I found it quite touching that although they all took

acting talent for granted, they were most impressed because I had written a cookery book. They all rushed out to buy copies, which I autographed, and they found they now took quite a new interest in the culinary art.

At the end of my fortnight's engagement, Don Gemmell told me to have another offering up my sleeve, as they would almost certainly want me back, so I racked my memory for something Victorian, and finally from the distant recesses of my mind came the words of an old Cockney ballad heard in a show in Glasgow when I was taken to the theatre as a youngster. It was sung with a sort of violent despair as a pseudo-dramatic number, and was called *Don't 'ang my 'Arry, For he is my only Son,* and was certainly in the right mould of Victorian melodrama.

I fitted it to a remembered tune, and two months after my first Players' appearance, there I was in full spate as a Cockney mother. The outfit was most elegant. It really was a dressy period in good Victoria's reign. I wore a long dark green fine woollen skirt, with three narrow rows of velvet at the hem, a grey and black taffeta blouse with a high neckline piped with black lace, lace cuffs, pale grey gloves, black shawl, delicious little black bonnet tied with ribbons under my chin, black stockings and long-legged boots with serge tops. The last time I wore long-legged boots was at school, but I found I hadn't lost the knack of doing up the laces at top speed. My hair was piled on top of my head under the bonnet, and I had a false bun pinned firmly at the nape of my neck to keep the bonnet on.

I was delighted to be accepted as a Cockney, and quite elated to find they had printed the words of my re-discovered song on the chorus sheet, so that the entire audience joined in when I reached the wailing *Don't 'ang my 'Arry.* Nobody could do this with *The Laird o' Cockpen,* but a Cockney ditty was right up their street, and I truly felt part of the Players' with the audience soulfully belting out the choruses with me.

Funnily enough, the thing which impressed most of my own friends who came to see the show was what a splendid wee old wife I made. And here was I fondly imagining that everyone knew I was a character actress.

Because most of them had only heard me on radio, or seen me on TV and hadn't seen me in the theatre, they were amazed to find I could walk on to a stage like a sad little old wife so convincingly, and that I could look and sound so different from their accepted image of me.

Mind you, it was very comforting for me too to find that I could still do character work acceptably, after such a long spell working before the mikes and in front of the cameras.

I now knew I could go back to Don Gemmell whenever I wanted to work at the Players', and I hugged myself with pleasure that I had been truly accepted as one of the regular *Late Joys* and had graduated from my earlier status as a *New Joy.*

Actually I didn't go back for another year, for a variety of reasons, not least because I felt I didn't have another number which seemed right for me. Then, on a visit to Glasgow, where I was working with Lavinia Derwent, a writer of children's stories and a broadcaster, and Ian Gourlay the pianist and arranger with the BBC variety orchestra, I suddenly had an idea. 'How about you two writing a number for me for the Players'?' I suggested over our tea break. They both knew the Players', of course, everybody in show business did, and they were aware of the style of the work which was required. They also knew that Sandy and I whizzed all over Britain and the Continent on our tandem bicycle, so they came up with *Bella the Bicycling Queen*. Lavinia wrote the words, and Ian the music. It had a nice rollicking air and it had also the merit of being an original number, even if the audience couldn't join in the chorus.

I took it along to Don Gemmell, who liked it, and I was kitted out with navy blue serge bloomers, black button boots, black gaiters, the lot, and a large real bicycle. Handling the bicycle was the worst part, for although I rode a tandem for years, I've never been able to ride a solo bicycle, nor could I even walk alongside one without falling over it. By the end of my fortnight's engagement I was black and blue, my ankles were skinned, and so were my fingers.

But the number was pleasantly received, and it was as always a joy to be in touch with a real live audience again, to smell the greasepaint once more and to sit beside the girls and listen to all their patter. Patsy Rowlands was on the bill this time, and stunned me by strolling in about twenty minutes before she was due to go on, eating a mouth-watering hamburger, imparting all the gossip of the day as she changed into her Victorian outfit without the slightest appearance of haste, and fastening the last button as her opening music was played!

How different from the panic and nervous flutterings I endured before I went on, for although I was now much more used to being a 'turn', I still had whole armies of butterflies fluttering in my tummy as I waited in the wings. Even on the odd occasion when champagne was being shared round, in celebration of a birthday or some other special occasion, I couldn't swallow a drop until after I'd done my number. The girls used to beg me to take just half a glass, for the sheer devil of it, to see what it would do to my performance! But I never did. My old voice teacher's ghost would have risen to confront me. 'Never take a drink before going on stage, my child,' she would say. 'You may think you are giving a better performance. But the audience will know better!' So the voices of my temptresses fell on deaf ears!

But nervous as I always was, I was convinced it was a good idea to keep all facets of any acting skills I possessed well exercised. It was a very good discipline to have to work hard for my effects and my laughs, and doubly rewarding to fit into the bill as an entertainer in a real theatre full of people out to enjoy themselves. On radio and TV, you never know just how your performance has come over. In the theatre, you know without a doubt whether you're a hit or a flop, and there's nobody to help you when you're out there on your own. It's a great exercise in standing on your own two feet, and the most testing theatrical experience I know.

The next time I visited the Players' was as a member of the audience, when, with Sandy, I went to see Sandy Wilson's *Divorce Me Darling*. We were right in the front row, practically under the fiddler's elbow, so didn't miss a word or a note. It was a lovely clean show, and such a pleasure to enjoy really good singing from principals who could truly use their voices and who, unlike me, found it no trouble to soar out over the rattle of those infernal trains! How I envied them this singing talent!

To celebrate being a member of the audience and

not a performer, I had prawn sandwiches and coffee in the interval!

CHAPTER THREE

One of the highlights of the year for actors was the TV Ball. I had been roped in to help right from the start, for it was launched with great style, with hundreds of autographed programmes on sale at the first of the balls. I spent an entire afternoon with Mary Malcolm, the famous TV announcer, signing non-stop, and mobilizing other actors as they drifted in and gave us an hour or so of their precious leisure before dashing off, with yelps of alarm as they noticed the time.

I'd been brought to the notice of the organizers, for as a member of the *ITMA* team, I had taken part in the first 'Tommy' awards after the death of Tommy Handley.

The real purpose of the ball of course, was to celebrate excellence on television by making awards to everyone connected with this exciting medium. The Coronation had set the seal on television as the most popular entertainment in the country, and the people who would receive the awards would be of far greater interest and be much more familiar names and faces to the general public than the stars and personalities of the theatre. With a few exceptions of course! Everybody knew Olivier, Dame Edith Evans, Margaret Rutherford and such luminaries of stage and cinema, but the supporting players and writers were an unknown breed to the man in the street.

On Television, on the other hand, everyone from the smallest character part to the top star, had been in everybody's living room nightly, and were as friendly and familiar to the public as the family next door. And so the TV awards had a tremendous appeal and interest far beyond that of the theatre.

As I was to be a programme seller, I would be running around among the great ones and could hardly hide my light under a bushel, so the nail-biting worry was *what to wear* for such a glittering occasion.

By great good fortune, I discovered that one of the top couturiers was having an end of season sale. Normally I'd never have had the nerve to cross such a threshold, but I thought there might just be something I could afford and which would look suitably dazzling as I moved around shaking my little box, coaxing as much cash as possible from the stars for their 'lucky' programmes.

It had been a day of bitter winds and driving rain when I left Pinner, and I saw the doorman flinching slightly as he caught sight of my short mud-splashed boots as I mounted the carpeted stairs to the salon. My camel coat had been chosen more for warmth than style, and I felt about as elegant as a tinker as a tall slender saleslady led me to a pale grey velvet settee, invited me to be seated, and with a snap of the fingers proceeded to present a mannequin parade. For me alone! I hadn't in my wildest dreams imagined such a thing. I had thought of riffling with a fair amount of excitement through a rail of beautiful clothes, more or less unnoticed, until I found something I could privately take to a dressing room and try on.

Now I saw a swooningly beautiful model glide towards me, wearing an off-the-shoulder midnight blue velvet ballerina-length dress, and to my horror it was at that precise moment I remembered I was wearing a *vest*. I couldn't hide my admiration of the blue velvet creation, but how could I try it on and let those sophisticated sales girls see me taking off such an old-fashioned item as a semmit! They weren't to know my grannie would have risen to haunt me if I'd cast a single clout before May was 'oot', or that instant bronchitis would be my fate if my bosom was unprotected from winter's chill during the hours of daylight.

'Do try it on, Madam,' they were urging, 'it is just your size.'

Oh it was, indeed it was. I tried to put on an act of indecision. I bit my lip. I put my head on one side, wondering aloud if the colour was *quite* right for me. It was the *vest* and the thought of their reaction which haunted my every breath.

I needn't have worried. When it came to it, they were tact personified.

They hung up the old camel coat as if it were mink.

They produced a pair of high-heeled shoes, the better to judge the dress length. (Fancy them having a pair of high-heeled size threes at the ready!) They raised manicured hands and removed the despised vest with the words, lightly uttered, 'I think we'll have this off so that you can see the shoulder line properly.' They had clearly been well trained never to cause the slightest discomfort to a prospective buyer. I loved each and every one of them at that moment, and for the first time recognized what true sophistication was.

I stepped into the dress. The zip was pulled up, the shoulders eased into position and they all stepped back to look. 'Madam,' breathed the youngest, 'it is *perfect*. It could have been made for you.' I stared into the mirror. The midnight blue did everything for my pale skin. Warm and flattering, it swooped from the point of my shoulders to a deep V front and back, and this edging was finished with a narrow collar of shocking pink satin. The two colours were exquisite together, and bore the unmistakable hallmark of haute couture. The skirt buttoned back in a full fold like a riding skirt, and the waist fitted like a glove.

The other girls crowded in to look. Like me, they couldn't believe that the wee muddy-booted creature in the camel coat had been so magically transformed. I don't think it was just to sell the dress they were so flatteringly approving. I do believe it was the contrast, for I'm sure they all knew about my vest!

One of them murmured laughingly, 'Cinderella, you *shall* go to the ball!'

I drew a deep breath.

It was forty-eight pounds – a fortune then. I'd have had to work for a month at the Players' to have earned such a sum, gross.

The couturier himself arrived at this psychological moment. 'Oh madam,' he said, 'you *must* have it. It fits you and it suits you even better than our model. I couldn't sell it to anyone else after seeing you wearing it.'

That did it.

I bought it and carried it home in its beautiful box, which had the couturier's name artistically scrolled all over its pale grey surface. I enjoyed the sidelong glances at the famous box from the typists in the train. Not so enjoyable, though, as they took in my muddy boots and old coat, was their obvious conclusion that I must be delivering it for somebody posh! Little did they know!

My feet hardly touched the ground as I raced up the road from the train. Sandy wasn't home yet, and I sang like a lintie as I peeled the potatoes and scrubbed the carrots for our dinner. As I looked down at my apron, I realized I had quite a lot in common with that childhood heroine, Cinderella!

I managed to find a pair of long satin gloves which exactly matched the shocking pink collar, and when Sandy saw me emerge from the ladies' room at the Dorchester wearing my model gown with its matching accessories, not forgetting the latest in Italian coiffure styling, he said I was without a doubt the belle of the ball. He said it felt like having two wives – one the wee skivvy in the kitchen, and the other this fashion-plate in glorious technicolour! He (and I!) reckoned that it had been forty-eight pounds well spent.

I enjoyed that ball from first to last. I was fairly drunk with the excitement of it all. I decided that being chosen to sell programmes was the best thing that could have happened to me, for it gave me the perfect opportunity to speak to everybody, without looking as though I were gawping like a star-struck fan. Which of course is exactly what I was.

I could hardly believe it when I found myself selling a programme to Jeannie Carson, who had been married that very morning. A vision in parchment satin, with yards and yards of matching stole, she and her new husband were the bonniest pair of redheads I'd seen for many a long day. I got £1 for that programme! I whirled from one table to another, selling programmes to our own Stanley Baxter who never gave the smallest hint that he was one of the award-winners. Then on to David Nixon, who introduced me to his new wife, who turned out to be the daughter of my old colleague Eric Robinson, the popular orchestra leader. Hugs all round, before chatting with Ben Lyon's old friend, Val Parnell, the power behind the London Palladium. I even had a heart-to-heart with Dame Edith Evans, who would be presenting the awards. We had last met in the Hoffnung Festival where we were both appearing*, and we rejoiced in the fact that we didn't have to worry about any speeches or performances at the ball, but just concentrate on enjoying ourselves.

Sandy and I found ourselves at the same table as quite a few old friends, and Sandy was delighted to be sitting next to Sid James. Sid guessed, shrewdly, that Tony Hancock must be getting an award or he wouldn't have turned up, for he usually avoided big functions like the plague. Sure enough, when the time came to present the awards, Hancock was up there on the receiving line. Tony was already beginning to get restless over the lack of challenge in his professional life, for although he was grateful that his *Hancock's Half Hour* was so popular, he wanted to stretch his talents in the theatre, and in films, to judge how he matched the giants in those demanding fields of entertainment.

Sid sighed. 'I'd go on doing these half-hours with Tony till the cows come home,' he said. 'I love 'em. The money's good, the public love them, so what more do we want?' He laughed ruefully. 'But then I'm just happy to be working. I haven't Tony's genius – I can leave challenges out of it.'

Oh if only Tony had managed to share Sid's sensible outlook, what a happy man he could have been. He was admired and loved by everyone, and he was, above all, an actor's actor. Appreciated by all of us who recognized his unique talent. And yet in the end, the restlessness of genius led this great comic to a lonely death in Australia, when his sense of failure had brought him to despair. How could he know that even today, in the eighties, his shows are unmarked by time

* One Small Footprint

63

and are included in every anthology of classic comedy. Like many a genius before him, Tony Hancock's best was never good enough for him.

I was sitting beside Eleanor Summerfield and her husband Leonard Sachs, and Leonard was enjoying what he thought was a short stint as Master of Ceremonies at Old-Time Music Hall from Leeds. It goes on till this very day, and he is now almost an institution himself.

We danced to Jack Parnell's orchestra, and a hilarious Gay Gordons at 1 A.M. wakened everybody up. It's on the dance floor you see all the starry talents you've missed till that moment. As we skipped and stepped and turned, every face which floated into vision was a famous one. Jessie Matthews, light as a feather, Honor Blackman of *The Avengers* in sparkling gold, Eamonn Andrews and his wife, Richard Dimbleby and Dilys, Spike Milligan, Warren Mitchell (your actual Alf Garnett), Alan Whicker, Hermione Gingold, Rupert Davies (Maigret himself) – I tell you, you couldn't have thrown a teaspoon without hitting a celebrity.

Earl Mountbatten was our new president and chief guest and he was an absolute riot. He captivated the entire audience of celebrities with his witty, sparkling speech, and brought the house down by sheer force of personality. I didn't envy the other speakers who had to follow him, stars though they were. I was right. He was undoubtedly top of the bill, by general consent.

At the end of the evening when I pulled on a cardigan to keep my arms cosy under my fur coat, a lady at the next dressing table eyed it in amazement and said drily, 'Back to reality, I see.'

I almost told her that there would be kitchen sink reality next day, with a washing to be tackled, but I decided this might have been too much for her delicate nerves!

Maybe it's because I'm a Pisces that I adapt equally readily to the demands of domesticity, or the heady delights of show business. The contrast charms me. Everything in life is a bonus when you've been born and brought up in a poor background, with a family who could find abundant riches in providing its own fun and its own opportunities. Not for me the life of hand-outs. Just the resilience and enthusiasm to suck all the juice from life's orange.

Sandy and I stayed in town overnight, to save the long journey back to Pinner, and it was bliss to be in bed within half-an-hour of leaving the Dorchester.

I was far too excited to go to sleep though. I lay still as a mouse, the events of that wonderful evening whirling before my eyes like a continuous film. I could hardly believe I had met Peter Sellers at last. He and I had been the 'voices' for a Lyon's ice-cream commercial months before, but we had recorded our pieces separately and until the night of the ball had never met face to face. He laughed when I reminded him of our playing the adenoidal kids, and our little song which Ben Lyon made me sing for weeks before every recording to give them a good giggle.

At that time Peter was a nice serious plumpish man, almost shy in his manner, but already on his way to becoming a big star. His head hadn't yet been turned by working with top names like Sophia Loren, nor had he become a fanatic about food, and obsessed with his weight and his diet. In later years, when I saw that lean face with the gleaming wolfish smile I hardly recognized the chubby-cheeked smiling man I'd joked with at the Dorchester.

I was so absorbed with my re-run of the evening's

incidents, I found I'd forgotten to breathe and was gasping like a fish out of water! That reminded me of my conversation with Hermione Gingold in the dressing room. Hermione told me that when she worked in the theatre in Denver, Colorado, they had rows of oxygen cylinders at the side of the stage, and whenever an actor came off at the end of a scene, he or she immediately inhaled reviving draughts of oxygen. This was essential, because of the altitude, for Denver is about a mile above sea level. Not for me, I fancy. Ordinary nerves are bad enough for robbing one of vital breath, as I've discovered many times; to add a real lack of oxygen in a place at an altitude like Denver would knock me flat on my back. Maybe that's why she put off for life any thoughts of my working in America.

At last I fell asleep, and we were able to stay in bed till after eight o'clock next morning because Sandy was within twenty minutes of the office. I had joined this club when I was in the Lyons, to give me somewhere to put my feet up when I had to be in town all day, with an evening recording ahead of me, and no time to dash back to Pinner between engagements. My mother was amazed when I took her there for tea. She had 'never heard of a wumman belangin' tae a club – she thought that wis fur auld men!' But even she soon realized how tiring it could be to be walking around the capital all day, and how essential it was to be able to relax somewhere to be in sparkling form for an audience in the evening.

I seldom had any need to sleep there, but on gala nights like the TV ball, it was worth its subscription in gold, for I could dress there, and we could both use it like a private hotel afterwards. Sandy hated it, because it was a ladies' club. He always felt ill at ease going down to breakfast next morning, imagining the rather elderly members suspected he had been up to no good! He said he always felt he ought to have had our marriage lines pinned to his lapel!

I must say I got some pretty queer glances myself when I left for home in the middle of the forenoon, carrying my ball dress in its cellophane covering over my arm. It looked as if I had been out all night on the tiles, and was getting home well after the milk.

But I didn't care. I was still on cloud nine after one of the most exciting and enjoyable nights of my life, when almost every famous name and face in show business had been my buddy.

Who could have thought then that an event which started off so joyously would in the end become touched with so much tragedy that it almost seemed as though a jinx was determined to provide a spectre at each feasting.

I have only to look at the TV ball-dresses hanging on the rail in the loft to remember each and every tragedy to which they were linked. Like Miss Haversham in *Great Expectations*, I can't bear to throw them out.

Looking back, I think it started with the Suez crisis. As I handle the pale yellow satin ballerina-length dress with its sparkling French diamanté shoulder straps, I feel again the tension of that evening. Rumours of troops and invasion sent hearts skittering with alarm. Most of us remembered all too vividly the recent war, and were unable to plunge into the gaiety of TV awards with any enthusiasm. The fine savour had all drained away and merriment was quenched, and although we danced a little, there was no enjoyment.

The creased gold lamé I try in vain to smooth, had given me the jitters at the ball the next year because the front of the skirt had resembled the deep grooves of an old-fashioned washing-board. Even as I tried to adjust a stole to cover the worst creases, the sirens of fleets of ambulances wailing through the fog told us that there had been a disaster in the capital. It was the night of the terrible train crash at Charing Cross, involving hundreds of commuters, with dead and dying demanding every rescue service London could mount. We went on with our award ceremony, but it was a very muted occasion, and it felt wrong somehow to go on to dancing afterwards.

The next year found us all very nervous, but it passed without incident, except that for Sandy and me we had the added pleasure of having, for the first time, the company of our old friends Franklin Engelmann and his wife Tynee. Incredibly, they had never been asked on previous years, although Jingle, as everybody in the business called Engelmann, was such a big name, and they were delighted when I said it could easily be arranged. I did the twist for the very first time that night, my narrow tartan skirt keeping me on an even keel, and supporting me like a pair of splints.

I told Jingle, in fact, that he must take wee toty steps when he was dancing with me, on account of my tight skirt, for he was over six feet tall, but he said I need have no fear. I was dancing with a very old gentleman, and they would be the totiest wee steps I ever took. He was right! About the steps anyway!

Even now I shudder when I look at the green velvet sheath I wore the following year.

That was a dreadful night.

The mere memory reminds me of that famous poem which describes the night before the Battle of Waterloo, 'There was a sound of revelry by night'.

Jingle and Tynee were with us again, their second visit to the ball.

Although Jingle was at the ball because I'd steered the invitations in the right direction, he knew practically everybody there was to know. He'd been an announcer, a link man, a correspondent, and indeed everything in the presentation line. All directors and producers knew him, and so the moment we entered the foyer and headed for the cocktail bar, he was greeted and pulled aside to meet this one and that, and the last I saw of him he was down on his knees in mock obeisance to a director who had just asked him to take over the chairman's job in *Gardeners' Question Time*, a job which was to last for years and was to take him to every corner of the country.

As Tynee, Sandy and I headed for our table when the dinner was announced, I noticed Cliff Michelmore hurrying into the room, looking very flushed and very perturbed. A little knot of men, including Jingle, were nearby and Cliff must have asked them where he could find Richard Dimbleby, for I saw them point to where Richard was standing. I also saw the men looking at each other in what appeared to be stunned silence.

Jingle made his way through to us at the table, and as he reached us, he whispered or rather mouthed to me, 'Kennedy's been shot'.

I stared at him uncomprehendingly.

'Kennedy?' I echoed. 'President Kennedy?'

He nodded.

Somehow I imagined in my bewilderment that there had been an accident, that he had been slightly grazed out shooting. Nothing more than that.

The next moment Richard Dimbleby was calling for silence and asking us all to stand, as he had an important and serious announcement to make.

And that was how we all learned that President Kennedy had been assassinated.

They say everyone can remember exactly where he or she was when they heard the news. Well the time, the place and the circumstances were certainly engraved forever in the hearts of all of us at the Dorchester on that fateful night.

Practically the entire television network were present under that roof. It was, after all, the night of the television awards. All the 'outside' cameras were on duty to cover such a glittering occasion. Interviewers, writers, camera-crews, editors, advisers, producers, directors, scenic artists, sound crews – everyone in fact of any importance in the television world.

Only a skeleton crew had been left at the Centre, and Cliff Michelmore was on duty almost on his own when the dreadful news had broken. Richard Dimbleby as the senior announcer and personality left the Dorchester almost at once, and some luckless stand-in took his place.

We ate our meal in almost hypnotic, trance-like silence. We couldn't begin to speculate what had happened or what it would mean to the world. All that seemed to penetrate was that Kennedy was dead, and the dreadful word 'assassinated' echoed and buzzed in my brain with sickening insistence.

The awards' ceremony had to take place, and it did. The applause was genuine but restrained, and it must have been a nightmare for those who had to make speeches, wondering how they could cut the jokes and still have anything left to say. After some indecision, the orchestra started playing. Nobody danced at first.

People stole out and tried to buy newspapers, to see if there was anything else we could learn about this tragedy. It seemed that some late editions had indeed been rushed out, for one or two men returned carrying newspapers, and it was the strangest sight to watch them standing in knots, in full evening dress, faces grave with anxiety as they read the sparse details of that terrible murder.

Their wives sat nervously tapping their toes, no doubt wondering, like us, when they could decently leave and go home. The music continued to play to an empty dance floor.

And then, as though at a pre-arranged signal, we rose in little groups and left the ballroom.

It was good to ride home in the comfort of Jingle's Citroen, and to sit quietly over a cup of tea together in our house after the shocking drama we had all shared. We didn't say much, but we found comfort in just being together.

When the time came round for the next TV ball, Sandy decided he didn't want to go. 'You go,' he said. 'You can easily find one of your actress friends to go with you. You know everybody, and it's fun for you. I've been to enough of those balls to last me a lifetime. Anyway Jingle has told us he won't be going, so that lets me out.'

'Are you sure, Sandy?' I asked.

'I'm sure,' he said. 'I'll come and meet you at the end and take you home. If I get there around half-past one that should give you a good chance to see and speak to all your cronies.'

I'd recently done a TV play with Wilfred Pickles, and had become very friendly with a delightful actress called Anna Turner. Anna had been a noted West End actress, and I'd taken Miss Chree to see her in the play based on the Thomson-Bywaters murder, called *People Like Us*, a play which made a tremendous impression on both Miss Chree and myself. Miss Chree was enchanted to see it from the stalls, and I never forgot it because from that close proximity to the stage I nearly jumped out of my skin with fright when a gun was fired, and I actually screeched aloud, to my shame!

In the TV play I discovered what a likeable personality Anna had, and she and I got on like a house on fire. She was one of those people whom you scarcely notice in a room at first. Small, and a bit old-fashioned at first glance. But the more you looked at her face, the bonnier it became. A pale luminous skin. White lovely teeth. Deep blue eyes, almost violet, and very dark curling hair slightly silvering at the temples. You will appreciate I do not exaggerate her beauty when even the blasé doormen at the rehearsal rooms used to say to me, 'Your little pal's late this morning – you know the one I mean, the one with the lovely face', as though there was only one of us who could fit that description. Which indeed there was.

Anna looked after an aged mother, which meant she didn't get out very much apart from her work, and she was quite overcome by the prospect of going to the Dorchester and being with all her acting colleagues, something she hadn't thought of for years. Not only was she a beauty, but she was clever with it, and for that special occasion, as she hadn't an evening outfit worthy of the name, she ran up a black velvet dress whose simple elegant lines showed off her lovely colouring to perfection. I may say that I, whose abysmal performance with a sewing machine is on record*, was filled with envy and admiration at the nonchalance with which Anna told me she'd just 'run up something' which would look all right, and wouldn't cost too much! I'd have looked for a medal if I'd been able to do such a thing with such obvious ease!

* Best Foot Forward

One of the worst aspects of going to the TV ball every year, and being in the limelight as a programme-seller meant that I simply could not wear the same rigout in that same starstudded company twice. The more eye-catching the outfit, the more easily it was remembered. And in those days of couture sparkle and style, nobody could get by with a chain-store dress. Originality was all.

I had gradually slipped down-market after the first fine careless rapture over the midnight blue velvet affair, to home-made 'goonies'. I had been able to do this because on most occasions I could call on the services of a marvellous Pinner dressmaker, whose skills were lovingly and faithfully put to good use in following all my creative ideas. This year, however, she wasn't able to do any sewing as she had hurt her hands, and I couldn't face chasing through shops for materials and patterns, much less trying to find a dressmaker to equal Georgie.

I gloomily resigned myself to traipsing through miles of showrooms trying to find something to fit my small proportions, but thought I'd just have one more shot at seeing what a classy shop in the next district could produce. As usual, at that time of the year, it was a perishing cold day and I had to shed boots, trousers and sheepskin jacket before I could try on a thing.

The assistant trotted out several dresses which were either too big or too bare, and when I said I liked a more 'covered-up' look she disappeared and brought back a most unusual outfit. The sort which looks peculiar on the hanger but can look great on the right torso! And mine was the right torso!

I fell in love with it immediately, for it had a long matching coat with gold clasp fastenings. When the fitter came to make one or two small adjustments, she said, not having seen me in the boots, breeks or sheepskin, 'Madam, you look just like a film star.'

For less than half the price of my one and only couture gown, there was the same reaction from fitter and salesgirls. So of course I bought it.

When I look at it now, I wonder why no premonition warned me of what was to follow. At the time all I could think of was how to adorn it as tastefully as possible. I felt certain that nothing could happen which would be so terrible as Kennedy's assassination. That surely had been the final tragedy.

The outfit was so striking in its colour and pattern that it would have been too much to wear a necklace, but the fashions at that time absolutely demanded a hint of jewellery somewhere. I thought I'd see what I could devise to adorn the high ring collar. I fancied myself as a bit of a creative jeweller, having just won half a guinea from a glossy magazine for my pattern for a 'gold' collar crocheted from 'gold' braid and stitched with pearls. To lend a helping hand I roped in my friend Maureen Burnett, a fine journalist who is the wife of Alastair, the famous TV news-reader, and we flew in and out the big London shops in search of something to gild the lily!

Maureen has the sort of knowledge of London stores that can save hours of leg-weary hunting. We pounced with glad cries upon a short sample length of beaded braiding, studded with amber-cut stones, just waiting for us in a counter display case in one of Oxford Street's most famous stores. The girl was aghast at the mere idea of parting with it, as it was the only piece in the shop. We wheedled her into opening the case and allowing us to look at it more closely. Maureen's eyes met mine. We both knew there wasn't a hope of an order going through in time for the TV ball. We were ruthless! We wouldn't hand our treasure back. The girl was mortified by our refusal to pay the slightest attention to the shop's rules. She only recovered when I whispered that every actor and actress in London would see it, and would be told where I had bought it. For good measure I also bought 1½ yards of expensive brown and gold trimming.

Afterwards, our peals of laughter ran round the coffee room.

A pair of determined Scots can achieve almost anything, especially when they have cash and common-sense to back their arguments!

When I'd sewn the amber-studded braiding and the gold trimming round the ring collar, completely covering it, it stood above the collarless coat like a solid jewelled band. It was *far* more opulent than my prize-winning half-guinea collar, and looked like something out of the *Arabian Nights*. The little sample was exactly the right length to go round my neck – it was lucky I wasn't any fatter!

In the cloakroom of the Dorchester, Barbara Kelly said, 'Don't take the coat off, Molly, even if you're boiling! It looks like a million dollars.'

I took her advice, and swanned around with my programmes, and chortled with laughter every time someone admired my 'gorgeous Eastern collar', when I remembered snatching our prized sample from a salesgirl who, I am sure, thought she was dealing with a pair of nut-cases.

Anna and I found one another at the cocktail bar when I was free of my programme duties, and headed for our table. Anna's off-the-shoulder black velvet was lovely, but she pooh-poohed my admiration, and just said, 'Oh well, black velvet is always useful – it was such an easy pattern, you couldn't go wrong.' 'Oh yes,

I could!' I told her. We shared a table with Fenton Bresler, the legal eagle who expounds the rights and wrongs of 'you and the law' in a Sunday newspaper, Martin Benson, a fine actor whose work we knew well, an anaesthetist friend of his, and of course their wives, plus a couple of technicians.

After an excellent meal we were all in merry mood, bubbling with curiosity to see who had won the awards in all the various categories behind and in front of the cameras. There would be awards too, for those who worked long exhausting hours creatively at their own desks, far from the limelight, but whose stories, and plays and series were the foundations on which the actors built careers and reputations. Television's demands on writers were insatiable and they were fast becoming the aristocracy of this demanding medium.

Kenneth Horne, a great favourite and a lovely man, was announcing the awards. He was in great form, having made a splendid recovery from a fairly serious illness a few years previously. His voice rang round the ballroom with a richness and strength which were impressive, and his familiar underlying chuckle brought an answering smile to everyone's face.

His cheeky 'plug' for his own radio show *Round the Horne* had us all shouting with laughter and applause.

As the laughter simmered down, he started to announce the winners of . . . He never reached the end of the sentence.

He crashed from the stage like a felled oak.

The explosive sound as he hit the floor brought the room to its feet.

There was a moment of utter silence.

Then, for the first time in real life I heard the words, 'Is there a doctor in the house?'

But I knew in my soul he was beyond help.

76

Death had struck swiftly and surely, and its wings had brushed all of us.

Dr Hill, the famous radio doctor, was at the top table but appeared so stunned that I think he must have forgotten he *was* a doctor, for he did not move.

In the shocked silence, as we still stood, hardly able to comprehend we had seen what we had seen, the question was repeated. 'Is there a doctor in the house?'

It was left to the man at our table, the anaesthetist, to offer his services as a medical man, though not a doctor, and as he moved towards the still form lying on the floor in front of the stage, he was joined by Dr Hill.

Willing hands carried the lifeless figure from the ballroom, and both doctor and anaesthetist went in the ambulance. The anaesthetist told me afterwards they had applied the kiss of life with desperation, although they both knew it was no good.

We were told a little later that it was all over.

If a director had tried to show such a scene in a TV play, it would have been thought a contrived piece of drama, too far-fetched to be acceptable. And yet it happened just as I have described it, for I will never forget the drama and horror of the death of Kenneth Horne.

The floodlights of the TV cameras trained on Kenneth, standing beside Earl Mountbatten. The winners moving to receive their awards. Then the crash as he fell from the stage in a single toppling movement, not even an out-thrown hand to break the impact.

A frozen moment, as though it were a tableau.

And afterwards the silence.

A marvellous exit for any actor, but a terrible grief for his poor wife sitting there among us. And for us, who were his friends, and who loved him.

It was decided, yet again, to go on with the ball. Everyone said this would have been Kenneth's wish. People nodded mechanically in agreement, but faces wore a look of shocked disbelief, and the sound of dance music was incongruous.

Anna and I were 'solo', so there was no compulsion for us to put a brave face on it, and get up to dance.

I found the 'phone box in the foyer and broke the news to Sandy. He couldn't take it in at first. He simply couldn't believe that once again tragedy had quenched the laughter at the Awards' ball. 'There is surely a jinx on the television ball,' he said at last. 'I'll collect you as soon as I can get to the Dorchester.'

That finished the TV balls as we had known them.

They were abandoned in favour of a sort of 'Oscar's award ceremony', held first at the Albert Hall I think, and later at the Wembley Conference Centre. But I never attended any of the ceremonies thereafter.

The only reminders I have of all those glittering occasions are a row of ball gowns and a collection of souvenir programmes.

And my memories of how a most glamorous period of my life ended in almost Shakespearean tragedy.

CHAPTER FOUR

It was Franklin Engelmann who first told me about the Talking Books for the Blind, and as one who loves to be 'read out to', even although I fortunately can see perfectly well for myself, I thought this was a wonderful idea, to help to open up the world of books to the blind and the partially sighted, who hadn't perhaps mastered the art of Braille, or who simply wanted the blissful relaxation of sitting back and listening to a whole book unfolding on tape.

Jingle suggested I might like to offer my services, with my well-known broadcasting voice, but warned me it was more or less a charity task, as resources were small, but if I had any spare time I might like to think about it.

The whole idea was so appealing that I went along to their offices at once, arranged to do an audition for them, and when I had done that, they said they would keep an eye open for just the right book on their list which required my Scottish voice.

This turned out to be Jane Duncan's lovely story *My Friends the Miss Boyds*. I had already read and loved the book, and as it was about a wee girl, her grannie and her cronies, I felt it was truly meant for me, and I was going to enjoy every minute of it.

In the event, I found it absolutely exhausting! I had no idea that I, being more familiar with five, ten or fifteen minutes' talks for the BBC, would become dizzy with fatigue and concentration tackling half-an-hour at a time without pausing. And there were *four* half-hours to a session!

Jingle wasn't at all surprised when I told him what a broken reed I was turning out to be. He found the whole exercise so tiring, or soothing, depending on how you looked at it, that he sent himself sound asleep in the midst of recording, and had to be wakened by the engineer in charge, who wondered why the tape was whirring round and not a sound coming from Jingle next door!

However, everything grows easier with practice (except of course getting up in the morning!), and by the end of the book I could face the four half-hour stints per session without flinching. Mark you, I did require a reviving cup of coffee after the first hour, but so did all the other readers, they told me.

I found the next books for myself, when I suggested Lillian Beckwith's *The Hills is Lonely* followed by *The Sea for Breakfast*. The sound engineer laughed so uproariously over my reading that he had to draw the little curtain over the window between our studios, so that his reactions wouldn't put me off my stroke!

He wasn't the only one to be convulsed and almost hysterical with those marvellous books. In the fullness of time I had a splendid letter from Australia, from a Scandinavian lady. She had been on a world tour, but alas, had taken a heart attack in Sydney, and had to be left behind. Complete rest was essential, and as she was registered as partially sighted, the hospital authorities decided a Talking Book would help her to get over the disappointment of her lost holiday, and keep her quietly entertained without any sense of strain. The tape they chose was my reading of *The Hills is Lonely*. She told me the ward sister had had to take it away from her until she was stronger, because she had laughed so much they feared she would have another heart attack.

She wrote that this gave her a great incentive to get well as quickly as possible, and when eventually she did manage to finish the whole story, she just had to write to tell me that not only was this one of the funniest books she'd ever listened to, but she couldn't imagine Lillian Beckwith could have been better served than by my interpretation and my 'lovely Scottish voice'.

To say I was pleased with this tribute is putting it mildly. This book reading was a new venture for me, and to have such an unsolicited pat on the back from the very type of person for whom it was intended was a great encouragement. And it led to my friendship with Miss Beckwith, for I sent the letter on to her. This started a life-long correspondence between us, and eventually we did personal appearances together at the book-signing sessions, and later shared a table at the Woman of the Year Lunch, where I had nominated her as a guest.

Oh but I was jolly glad when those particular recordings were completed. Not that I minded the actual work, which I was getting used to, it was just the commuting in high summer when London is packed with tourists was torture. I began to appreciate my mother's reaction on being told that Sandy travelled on those packed, rocking underground trains daily, 'Dae ye dae this every day, Sandy? My Goad, ye deserve the Victoria Cross!' He did too!

On the day of the final recording of *The Sea for Breakfast*, I tottered out of the studio after a three-hour reading session. We'd extended it to three hours to get it completed before the holidays. The Underground looked like a football match coming out. I managed, eventually, to squeeze myself into a train so packed that if we had been cattle, the RSPCA would have gone into action to improve such inhumane conditions. If a purse had been dropped, it would have been impossible to bend to pick it up.

The lady beside me leaned so heavily on my arm, that I was pins and needles from finger-tips to shoulder, and she couldn't move so much as an inch to relieve the pressure until somebody got out at the next station.

The only laugh I had was in observing one of the tight-trousered brigade of hippy, who had been squashed so tightly in his seat (he was sitting, of course!), that his packet of chewing gum had been prised out of his pocket by the press of bodies, and lay abandoned on the seat when he got up to leave. He'd been showing off so noisily to his two girlfriends that not a single tired commuter raised a voice to tell him of his loss.

I picked it up and later gave it to a youngster who liked chewing gum. It had never even been opened. Well, it's no' lost what a freen gets!

After all this studio work on the Talking Books, I was more than ready for a holiday and we had a glorious fortnight on the romantic island of Elba. As I don't like flying, we went by trains and boats, and I began to feel, like Napoleon himself, as if I was going into exile. There was a tremendous thunderstorm the evening we arrived, and the funniest sight was of a parrot, the hotel pet, spreading its wings to their fullest extent and holding up its beak to the heavens, giving every appearance of ecstasy as the rain fell on its feathers. The hotel manager said it had been the first rain for months, and signalled cooler weather. I groaned in dismay. Surely at the end of that long and exhausting journey we deserved better than the sort of weather we could easily have found at home!

However we soon found to our delight that the Italian idea of 'cooler weather' is quite different from ours. All it meant was that the temperatures didn't roar up to the high seventies until the afternoon, and so the cooler mornings and comfortable evenings allowed us to explore the whole island under perfect conditions. The proprietor specialized in Tuscany cooking, which was what had attracted us in the first place, but we only realized how lucky we were when we met other holidaymakers who'd chosen different resorts on the island and who were very dissatisfied with the food. We bumped into them on our island walks, and swapped experiences. The youngsters found the portions mean, and the older ones complained of poor cooking and uninteresting menus.

We praised our cuisine so lavishly and so enthusiastically that a crowd of the complaining ones came over to our hotel for a meal, and they were furious with themselves for not realizing the plain little unadorned picture they'd passed over in the brochure had disguised four-star quality.

'You must have the second sight,' they said to me wonderingly.

'So she has,' agreed Sandy. 'I always leave choice of restaurant or hotel to her – she smells out quality.'

I coughed to disguise a smug smile. Sandy is always magnanimous with his praise once we're safely established, but he does his fair share of muttering and protesting when I stand with pursed lips in front of a possible hotel or restaurant and shake my head. 'No, I don't like the look of it – let's try somewhere else.'

The rebel at my heels then is a very different chap from the one who purrs contentedly when I am proved to be right! Men!

Actually the reason for my choice of the Elba hotel had been governed by the very simplicity of the picture. I reasoned that if the owners had the confidence to be so modest in the midst of the flamboyance of the other photographs which filled the brochure, then they were secure of their skills in the kitchen and of their reputation. And so it proved. It was a marvellous holiday, and the weariness of the hard-working year sloughed off both of us like an old skin.

Elba was just at the beginning of its popularity then, and few people knew much about it. Consequently Sandy and I later astounded acquaintances and friends by recognizing the names of every resort they were considering. I felt almost as ecstatic as the parrot that the 'cooler' weather had allowed us to discover every corner of the island's beauty during those enchanted two weeks. Other friends down our lane had visited Elba in August, when it had been so palpitatingly hot they had moved no further than the beach or the hotel bar. When they saw our colour slides, they couldn't believe they had missed so much.

Elba is one of the places I would really love to visit again, but there is always a danger in returning to the spot where you once found perfection.

Before that visit to Elba we had only been to mainland Italy and that holiday had turned out to be an exercise in mathematical wizardry, for it was the year when our Government was up to the eyes in currency problems, and holidaymakers were only permitted to take £50 with them on foreign jaunts. We actually chose a walking holiday, with rucksacks on our backs, thinking it would be more economical to live in simple rooms. It wasn't, but it did wonders for my Italian vocabulary, arguing with landladies and waiters, trying to stretch that £50 to cover two weeks' food and shelter.

However, thanks to my grannie's training and Scottish prudence, I found I could actually maybe afford to have my hair shampooed and set before we set off for home. Two weeks' wandering under the Mediterranean sunshine and daily dips in the briny had left my hair a sticky lifeless mess, and as we were going through Paris on the way home, I felt the least tribute I could pay to France's capital was to have clean hair. I would certainly be no fashion plate, for we carried every stitch we wore, apart from what we stood up in, in our rucksacks.

I counted up the lira in my purse, examined the prices in the window of a small unpretentious shop, said cheerio to Sandy, who was going to have a wander down by the harbour, and went inside. Before I dared to sit down, I asked the price of an oil shampoo. Eight hundred lira, the girl said. Those two weeks' haggling in Italy, mentally converting every price to sterling had given me the dexterity of an adding machine. So that made it roughly 9/- or 10/- with tip, or in today's currency, 45p to 50p. It was the very end of our holiday. I could just manage it, and not a lira more.

I was a bit worried about the sight of some very prosperous-looking Americans drifting in and out of the various cubicles as I waited. 'Och,' I reassured myself, 'they *said* 800 lira. I can't and I won't be roped in for any extras.' I knew perfectly well that, travelling independently as we were, there wasn't a soul in all Italy who could have guaranteed a cheque from us, even if we'd had one. I don't know how I had the nerve even to consider the luxury of having my hair done, but it really was a disaster area, and there's something about the feeling of clean shining hair which makes everything else seem irrelevant.

I was ushered into a cubicle and a tall willowy Frenchman, with hair nearly as long as my own strolled in. French! That was a surprise. He lifted a strand of my hair and shuddered delicately. 'Ugh! The hair is *very* dry. Madame must have our very special friction – eet ees 1600 lira for Italians,' and he smiled conspiratorially, 'but for ze English, 1400 lira.'

I jumped with alarm. 'I'm not English. I'm a Scot,' I began. His shoulders rose expressively, and his lips curled round the breathed whisper, '*Scotch!*' I could practically see the thoughts forming like a bubble over his head. 'Not only a miserable £50 allowance, but *Scotch!* She'll probably hang on to every last lira.'

'Yes, *Scots,*' I corrected him, 'not *Scotch!*'

His eyebrows rose.

'I only require an 800 lira shampoo and set – an 800 lira *oil* shampoo and set,' I said firmly, 'I want nothing else.'

'But madame,' and his eyes rolled in disbelief that I could refuse such an offer, 'with our friction the hair is soft, soft like silk.'

'I daresay,' I said. 'But silk or no silk, you'll just have to do your best for 800 lira, for it's all I've got.'

Believe it or not, after all that, a girl appeared and began to divide my hair into strands, obviously preparing it for a friction. Panic rose in me. I seized her wrist so fiercely, she squealed with fright. 'Stop!' I commanded in my best Italian, '800 lira shampoo only.'

She gazed at me, stunned, and then disappeared. I heard a fierce, whispered consultation going on next door. To show my nonchalance, I hummed a few bars of 'Clopin, Clopin', a very popular tune at that time, and, like magic, the manageress of the shop whisked in. Bending down and gazing into my eyes, she whispered urgently, 'You are artiste?'

'We-ll,' I smiled in some confusion, 'I suppose I am, in a way. I work a bit for the BBC.' I wasn't bending the truth too much, for I *had* after all done a radio revue series where I sang a song each week.

She threw back her head in delight, expanded her nostrils, and to my astonishment burst into song. 'Ah, you are surprised? Madame, I am Russian singer, but my husband, he is Italian and very jealous. So now I only teach how to sing. Come here.'

She drew me to my feet and shooed me into a back room. Pointing to her plump cheeks, she said: 'When you sing, Madame, think only of the cheeks, nevair of this,' and with a contemptuous gesture she pointed to her diaphragm.

'Oh I will, I will,' I promised without hesitation. I had always hated all that emphasis on the diaphragm which would never behave itself as it ought, not even in those RADA classes.

'Think of the cheeks, and open the nose – so! And smile, always a smile. Start with a leetle sigh, a leetle yawn, and open the nose so! And *smile!*'

She puffed out her cheeks, flared her nostrils, yawned most realistically and once more burst into song. The effect was so comical, and so incongruous in such a setting that I could control my laughter no longer. 'You're a comedienne, Madame Polovski,' I giggled, instantly christening her with the name of the beautiful spy of the song.

'I am Madame Vicki,' she began, and then stopped trying to explain, mystified by my laughter. She was flattered by my rapt attention, though, and we went through the whole routine together, sighing, and yawning and smiling, and she didn't even notice the two Americans who peeped round the door to investigate the origin of the unexpected aria.

She was clearly delighted by the enthusiasm of her unexpected pupil, for she bent down and whispered, 'Because you are an artiste, you get everything for 800 lira. Friction, everything. And some day, when you are permitted to bring lots of money to Italy, you come back to us and we are pleased.'

She smiled slyly.

'And when your artiste friends come here, you tell them of us, eh?'

'Oh yes,' I promised my Russian songbird recklessly, 'they shall all come to you.'

I was frictioned. I was oiled. I was shampooed and I was set, and when I was combed out the entire staff assembled to admire the silk of my hair. 'Ceeta Poora,'

I said in my finest Italian. They were delighted with my feeble joke, for I had deliberately used the words in all the advertisements for the best Italian silks.

'Nylon,' shouted an assistant, fondly imagining this was even more flattering.

Never had ten bob been better spent. A dry bird's nest had been transformed into a mane of shining glory. I'd had an argument in French, one in Italian, and a hilarious singing lesson from a Russian, all because I had hummed a few bars of music, and with becoming 'modesty' had admitted I was an 'artiste' who worked for the BBC! It was the first time I learned, to my profit and amusement, how great was the power of the mere mention of my first employer in the world of entertainment, the British Broadcasting Corporation.

I also realized, with some surprise, that I'd never have had so much fun if I hadn't been so hard-up. All is truly mixed with mercy.

When Sandy cast an eye over the silken tresses, he was suitably impressed. He had had a great time wandering round the sea-front and harbour taking the last of our photographs. He shook his head, laughing in baffled admiration that I'd managed to get all that attention *and* a free singing lesson for the equivalent of ten shillings.

It was after the Elba holiday that I began to build up a small reputation as a speaker. I'd never seen myself at all as a public speaker, although I could talk the hind legs off a donkey in private life. However, a neighbour who lived the lush life of private clubs and elegant dinner parties, and who moved in the world of advertising and so knew I'd spoken at the Press Club, decided I was just the person to speak at a friend's Ladies Luncheon Club in Cheshire. 'But Isobel,' I protested, 'what can I talk about?' It was one thing speaking at a Club on Burns' night when everybody expected a Scots voice speaking on Scottish subjects, but in Cheshire what on earth would interest them?

Isobel brushed all objections aside. 'You can speak about anything you choose,' she said. 'They'll love you whatever you tell them.' I have noticed when anyone wants you to do anything, they are absolutely certain you will be a brilliant success, while you, the person who has actually to do the thing, are quietly dying with fright.

I had to travel the day before, and I stayed overnight at the beautiful little privately owned hotel, whose owner was organizing the lunch next day. I was fascinated by the old-world atmosphere, the wrought-iron hanging flower baskets, the lovely black and white exterior, and the miles of open countryside which made a perfect setting for the hotel. The hand-domed ceilings were of solid oak, and the furnishings exquisite. No shortage of cash there!

I had intended to have an early night, after my longish journey, to give me a quiet restful sleep to prepare me for the ordeal next day, but the local photographer turned up for some pictures. We all adjourned to the 'garden room' where the lunch was to be held so that I could be photographed against the flower-bedecked tables. The waiter, fully alive to the importance of the occasion and the local publicity brought in a champagne bottle and flourished it over our empty glasses for the photograph. However, the hostess would have none of this miming. 'If you're showing champagne,' she said, 'then we'll drink champagne!' Next moment we were all quaffing bubbly. Then her husband and a friend arrived, and it was

2 A.M. before I could decently retire to bed. So much for my sedate plans!

The husband's friend, it seemed, owned a local lingerie factory and I was warmly pressed to visit it next morning before the lunch. I was on the point of refusing, on the grounds that there wouldn't be time. *When*, I thought wildly, was I ever going to have a calm moment to think of my speech? I'd only once before spoken at a Ladies Lunch, and that was the Woman of the Year Lunch at the Savoy, and as you know I found that terrifying. I required some time of quietness to pull my thoughts together, and steady my nerves. The hostess, however, brushed aside my misgivings. 'Of course we'll come,' she said cheerfully. 'There's plenty of time. We've the whole morning.'

Well, if she felt there was time and she had a whole lunch to organize, how could I be so craven as to say a half-hour speech was beyond my capabilities unless I had an entire forenoon to myself?

I asked to be called at 8.30, but they allowed me to sleep till almost ten o'clock. The lunch was at 12.30!

After a light breakfast, the hostess appeared in a dazzling white outfit, obviously kitted out for the lunch. Blasé she may have appeared when consenting to visit a factory on such a morning, but she was astute enough to realize there would be no time for changing into her glad rags when we returned. I was in my everyday travelling clothes! To me, special occasion garments are for special occasions, and I never dreamed of wearing my 'public appearance' dress to visit a factory.

It was miles outside the town – bright and clean and modern, with beautiful quality undies. They had nothing small enough for me, and for the first time ever I was measured for two petticoats, which would be made specially to fit me. My mother would have thought they were mad. 'Whit would have been wrang wi' takin' a wee hem up?' she'd have said. 'Fancy them goin' tae a' that bother for a petticoat.'

But it was a touch of class I rejoiced in. I chose a straight white slip heavily encrusted with embroidered lace, and a midnight blue with full skirt intersected with bands of fine lace. I loved them from the moment they arrived, and I have them to this day. Through all the changing dress lengths, I refused either to take up a hem or cut anything off, for I wouldn't sacrifice a centimetre of lace on the altar of fashion. And so they have come into their own through the years, the only undies I ever possessed which were made for me alone.

All this choosing and measuring took far longer than we anticipated, and it was a mercy the roads were quiet when we zoomed back all those miles to the hotel. The guests were already going in when I raced from the car and flew up to the bedroom to change in to my 'lecture' dress. No time for panic about the speech. No time for anything except getting out of the clothes I was wearing and into my other outfit so that the food wouldn't be kept waiting – or the guests! When I rose to speak, I hadn't the slightest idea what I was going to say. I found myself telling them about the Woman of the Year Lunch at the Savoy when I had been asked to speak for the first time, and of making my hat out of the hem of my coat for 1/4½d, and the laughs came so spontaneously and so encouragingly that before I knew it the half-hour was over, and I was being applauded for a speech which literally came out of the top of my head. I was very relieved and glad that it had gone well, but I wouldn't want to repeat that sort of sense of unpreparedness very often. Bebe would strongly have disapproved, and I wasn't too mad about my behaviour myself! Still, maybe we can allow ourselves one small diversion from the disciplined paths, especially if we survive!

I was no sooner back from Cheshire, than I was invited to go to Blackpool to speak as guest of the National Book League. I was booked to do two 'lectures', one at night, and other other the following afternoon. The location was a big Exhibition held at Olympia, and my usual nerves were heightened by the knowledge that I would have to lure the audiences away from the temptation of free food and drink samples! When I thought back to the big Kelvin Hall Exhibitions of my childhood, I knew that nothing short of a lasso would have prised us away from the doughnut stand, or the delicious little tit-bits spread with special meat roll, or cheeses, or even chocolate. However, either the Blackpool audiences were better fed, or just glad of a place to rest their feet, but suffice it to say that the hall was packed and I managed to entertain them with enough lively stories and anecdotes to bring heart-warming applause at the end, and great relief to my own heart!

It had been ten years since I had done the season in Blackpool with the Lyons*, and I was amazed when I walked into my favourite antique shop to be greeted with 'Hullo Miss Weir, how nice to see you again' – just as if I'd been there the previous week.

It was a little china group in the window which had drawn me into the shop. It consisted of three Chinese children, gazing spellbound at a 'top' or as we Scots say a 'peerie', which had just been thrown by the centre figure. It was modelled in that highly-glazed white porcelain called 'Blanc-de-Chine', and was clearly the Chinese version of our back-court games

* Walking into the Lyons' Den

with our peeries. It was irresistible. I bought it, hoping Sandy would approve, and he did. It looked lovely in our sitting room with a dark blue plate forming a contrasting background, although it's now to be seen on the tiled ledge on the staircase window, where the angle of the pose is even more expressive when we catch sight of it on the way downstairs.

I love shopping in various towns and cities, finding unusual souvenirs of my various jobs, and I was lucky in my leisurely stroll in Blackpool. Not only did I find the peerie ornament, but I found something I'd been chasing for months in Glasgow and London without success. I'd broken the silver-mounted comb of my dressing table set, and discovered to my dismay that hardly any shop will sell such an item separately. However, Blackpool was my lucky spot. I found a shop which was selling part of a dressing table set, and there in the window was an exact replica of my broken comb. I was in and out of that shop in minutes, and carried home my prized replacement in triumph.

I was constantly amazed by the demand for speakers, by all sorts of unexpected organizations. I didn't regard this activity even as a sideline. To me it was just a fluke, but I now discovered organizers were hot on the scent, the moment they got wind that somebody was able to get up on her hind legs and *speak*. It was like the old Springburn days when I used to find myself asked here there and everywhere to do elocution pieces. I could have been out every night during the concert season in Scotland, and had to learn to resist the flattery of their invitations or I'd never have had any time for homework or any other interests.

And so it came about that before I knew it, I was on the list of the National Association of Youth Clubs, and invited to the various centres where girls went on courses of character-building and study. These courses were called McAllister Brew, and I was amused to discover the original McAllister who'd started the courses had a cat which she called *Tattie* after my character in *ITMA*. This was particularly inappropriate, when I have a phobia about cats and am absolutely terrified of them!

The first time I spoke at such a course, I was almost as terrified to face a roomful of girls all gazing at me, notebooks in hand to jot down the pearls of wisdom they awaited to fall from my lips!

The 'guest speaker' was the highlight of the week's course, and much was expected of her. They had been instructed in the arts and crafts, taught the disciplines of social life, engaged in various forms of physical exercise, been encouraged to express themselves in class, indulge in public speaking, play their part in serving the food, in clearing up, in washing up, and arranging all such rota themselves. It was a marvellous week of assuming true responsibility for their actions, and learning to think and speak for themselves.

They were also by now well equipped to judge the quality of their speaker, and I felt as though I were auditioning for a board of governors, to justify my qualifications as entertainer and public speaker! I was not only facing the girls, but their instructors, who had also entered the room and formed a backcloth of adult experts. It was even worse than speaking at the Savoy, for they were all much closer to me, and I could judge every reaction immediately. I was glad I had remembered to swallow my ever-reliable wee Phosferine tablet, that good old-fashioned guarantor of steady nerves, and once I had persuaded them to arrange their chairs in a semi-circle rather than in rows, I settled down to tell them of all the challenges I personally had met on my way to acceptance in the world of entertainment.

There was almost immediate rapport, when they discovered we had so many points of shared experience, for they came from all sides of industry and commerce. Those who worked in offices gasped on hearing of my shorthand speeds, and were full of questions afterwards as to how I had achieved them. The cyclists hooted with laughter on being told I couldn't ride a bicycle, so went everywhere with Sandy on our tandem. They were all amazed that I could still feel nervous, and laughed at the mere idea that I could actually be nervous of *them*.

They enjoyed knowing that I too had to save for all special treats, and one girl spoke up and confessed that she took far better care of the wee transistor she had saved for and bought for herself, than of anything she had been given.

They were staggered to learn of the demanding disciplines of the theatre, and admitted they'd never thought a sore throat could be a major tragedy to a working actor.

The questions came thick and fast at the end, and even over our bedtime coffee and biscuits they went on and on, until the instructors had to rescue me and declare it was everybody's bedtime.

In time I came to enjoy those talks, and found it very rewarding to be with such worthwhile lasses. They had all been chosen by their employers for those subsidized courses, because they had shown qualities of character and leadership which could derive great encouragement and benefit from mixing with girls from varying backgrounds from all over the country. The instructors told me it was amazing how they blossomed out, after the first initial shyness, and how the general level of excellence was the greatest stimulus to their imagination and creativity.

I went all over the country on those talks. To Kilmory Castle in Scotland, to Avon Tyrrell in Dorset, to Wales, and was even asked to address a special lunch at the NAYC headquarters in London. This latter one was fairly staggering, for I found I was to address a mixed audience. I was so used on all those courses to be talking to girls and women, that I had expected the usual hens' convention, and was stunned to be introduced by a chairman who described me, in the words of Colonel John Glenn, as 'A Ball of Fire'. After that introduction, I just *had* to pull out all the stops, and luckily for me they were in a good mood (after a delicious lunch) to be amused by my tales of life behind the scenes, and of the difficulties and stresses of show business.

I was then invited to a special meeting of 'celebrities' and well-wishers chaired by Angus Ogilvy, the husband of Princess Alexandra, who was one of the top names associated with the NAYC and it was at that meeting I met Lulu for the first time. Now she really is a ball of fire, if ever I met one, from the top of her lovely red hair to the tip of her dainty tootsies. Funnily enough, I'm always being told how much I resemble her, or she resembles me, and when we actually met face to face I could see the resemblance myself. We clicked from the word 'go' and we always enjoy a laugh whenever we see one another or speak on the telephone.

That meeting was to think up special activities in connection with the Diamond Jubilee Year of the NAYC, and one of the very special events, as far as I was concerned, was an invitation to a reception in St James's Palace in the Gracious Presence of Her Majesty Queen Elizabeth, the Queen Mother! In the

Throne Room, if you please! All the rules and regulations were printed on the back of the invitation, so that we would all know exactly what to do and what to wear. 'Afternoon wear' was advised.

So, what to put on? Something to keep warm enough and dry enough for the journey into London on a dreich November afternoon, and yet look reasonably in keeping with a Royal personage and a Royal Palace.

I find there are some clothes which earn their keep over and over again. Such an outfit is my navy blue Shetland coat-dress, with gold buttons and gold belt-buckle. It's plain, but as my mother would have said, 'Aye looks good', and I can vary the accessories to suit the occasion.

I decided an emerald green silk scarf tucked into the mandarin neckline and emerald green Leghorn *Thoroughly Modern Millie* cloche would be right for the Palace. My beige raincoat and an umbrella would be enough protection if it poured.

I had a date at the National Portrait Gallery first, where two actor friends of mine were narrating at a lunch-time concert on 'Peoples Past and Present', produced by a BBC producer friend. I had promised to be there, and couldn't let them down, and there would be plenty of time to keep both engagements. There was, though, no time for a proper lunch and I prudently packed a piece of cheese and a slice of buttered wholemeal bread, which I nibbled while waiting for the concert to begin. My actress friend said it was small wonder people regarded me as eccentric! I wonder why?

The funniest thing was, that because I usually dress so casually, none of my friends recognized me in my Palace get-up. I laughed at their start of surprise when I greeted them, and they exclaimed, 'It's Molly! Get that hat!' And of course it was a splendid piece of oneupmanship when I replied, 'Well, I'm having tea this afternoon with the Queen Mother!' When they looked at me to see if I was joking, I added, 'Me and about 700 others!' They were very impressed just the same.

At the Palace, I discovered there were about half-a-dozen reception rooms being used, and the colour of the ticket indicated which room one had to head for. I was in the Throne Room which I found to be beautifully proportioned, with ceiling-high mirrors down one side, and on the other wall magnificent portraits of Queen Victoria, Prince Albert, George IV, and two lesser Royal persons.

A long buffet table ran down one side, with silver urns for boiling water, silver teapots, and all the china, sandwiches, cakes and scones we'd require for our tea.

We all stood about and chatted until the flash of the photographers' cameras in the ante-room told us that the Queen Mum was about to arrive.

She came in with Angus Ogilvy and Sir John Hunt, and she looked absolutely lovely in a delicate blush pink wild silk coat, with three-quarter length sleeves, over a matching dress. Her feathered hat was in the same delicate pink, mixed with darker-striped feathers, and she wore gunmetal grey long gloves with matching high-heeled shoes. My mother used to say, 'Hoo does she manage tae staun aboot in thae peerie-heels?' They were peerie-heels right enough, and there was never a hirple to indicate the slightest discomfort. I was filled with admiration for such elegant feet.

She is so pretty. Lovely pink and white skin, clear blue eyes, those famous well-marked brows, and a warm and lovely smile for everyone presented to her.

I wasn't presented, but her wee corgi, Billy, made

straight for my shoes, no doubt sniffing my passion for footwear, and proceeded to lick them with enormous vigour. He could of course have caught a whiff of Katie's scent, the fox terrier across the lane, which I often took for walks at that time. Anyway I tickled his ears and neck, and gave him Katie's regards, and the Queen Mother turned and waved to us, and called to Billy, then disappeared into the next room to mingle with another lot of guests.

The tea was delicious, and then Lulu, Jimmy Saville and I did a brisk bit of autograph-signing. Everyone seemed to want our signatures on the back of their invitation cards. I imagine they fancied having a complete souvenir of such an exciting occasion. I must say it's not every day I sit signing autographs in a Royal Palace, and I thought of how my mother would have gloried in the whole occasion. She would have loved the scarlet-coated orchestra sitting in a corner of one of the rooms, playing in the background, and the sight of all the fashionably dressed guests wandering from room to room, free to look at everything and even chat to the orchestra between numbers. 'Ah like a good baund,' my mother used to say enthusiastically, and that was indeed a good band.

When the Queen Mother came through the Throne Room again on her way to her own apartments, she met a few other people. Not me, I regret to say, but Billy had another lick at my shoes! Then we had our last glimpse of our bonnie Queen Mum as she turned and waved to us, called to Billy, and was gone.

It was a lovely afternoon, and one I remembered for a long long time.

CHAPTER FIVE

Although I was delighted to be picking up all sorts of little jobs from various sources, the odd lecture, a little part with Arthur Askey in an Alan Melville revue, and on one memorable day, *three* broadcasts booked in the space of a single hour, I hadn't heard anything from the Lyons for months. Just when I was contemplating ringing the shop to find out how they were all surviving, the telephone rang and it was the BBC. Could I come along to Broadcasting House to discuss something which they thought would interest me?

Of course I could.

And when I got there, I discovered they were going to feature Ben in *This is Your Life*.

It would be lovely to be with them all again, and I could just imagine Bebe's joy in plunging into all the secret arrangements attendant on such a show, and organizing all the details like a battle. I was most impressed with the thoroughness of the BBC in maintaining absolute secrecy. They actually swapped theatres to make sure Ben would suspect nothing, for they reasoned he would be well aware of the theatre from which they normally did *This is Your Life* and so they booked him for what he thought was an appearance with a comedy show, in the Light Entertainment theatre.

We all went to the BBC separately for the early briefing, which was well ahead of the *This is Your Life* performance, and I had a little chat with the producer and we decided what my contribution would be from the multitude of incidents which we'd enjoyed through eleven years of working together. I was given my little 'piece' to say out of vision, and told they would contact me again later.

On *the* day, we all made our way separately to the theatre, like a spy operation, and were swiftly allocated to our various dressing rooms. We had make-up of course, and hairdressers, and I was wearing my hair up on top of my head in a bun for the first time in public. Sandy always preferred my hair up, so I'd just let it grow until I could wind it round a bun, and the family were quite taken aback at my changed appearance. I also wore a pale green cocktail dress, instead of the usual cashmere and skirt 'Lyons' Aggie outfit', and felt no end of a swell!

As always, wherever I am there is an association with food. We were all getting to the teeth-chattering stage with nerves, awaiting the arrival of Ben, which wouldn't be for over an hour, and we had already gone through the details of where we would stand, where the mikes would be, and the order in which we would come on. This was the moment, I decided, when food would settle our fluttering stomachs, and warm us up. Nerves either have you freezing cold or gasping with heat. It was March, and we were freezing.

It didn't take ten minutes to get it organized, and almost before I knew it, my dressing room had become a running buffet. Everybody crowded in. Secretaries, hairdressers, Vic Oliver, Doris Rogers, Anna Neagle, Janette Scott, Barbara and Richard, and the unexpectedness of the party atmosphere enabled all of us to relax and enjoy one another's company. Vic Oliver told us how much he was appreciating the variety of his professional life just then. What with conducting orchestras, doing his act in variety, and performing the odd play he had a full and busy life, and the use of each facet of his acting prevented his ever feeling that he was getting stale. How I agreed with him. Variety is truly the spice of life, and it's lovely when one gets the chance to extend all one's talents in every possible direction. Bebe used to tell me that Vic Oliver felt he was unemployed if he didn't have at least three engagements per day. Just as Sir Ralph Richardson declared he must have his 'daily fright', tearing around London on a powerful motor bike, Vic had to have a crammed diary before he felt he was living. A pace which was to kill him in the end, in a country far from home. But that was a long way ahead.

Bebe of course didn't join us for food. She was far too busy studying the sheets giving the running order, holding them in hands which shook, and I was alarmed at how thin, and nervy and jumpy she was. Barbara too looked very gaunt, and Richard, with two abscesses in his mouth looked like death. Doris Rogers was just recovering from pneumonia and was half her usual size. In fact when Sandy saw us all later, he said Ben and I were the only two healthy-looking people in the entire cast.

The show itself was an enormous success. The audience fairly made the rafters ring when Eamonn appeared, and confronted Ben at the stage door, with the famous red book. Ben had thought he was appearing with Anna Neagle, to do an interview! We saw it all on the monitors and then leaped to the wings to be ready to say our introductory phrases out of sight. Bebe chose to say, 'BEN LYON THIS IS YOUR WIFE'.

The audience oohed and aahed when Richard's wife Angela came on with their first baby, and I must say the photographs later showed everyone in sparkling form. When I came on, Ben, who hadn't ever seen me with the bun on top of my head, took my hands and said 'Gee, Aggie, you look cute – that hair is a great idea, it'll get you work.' How right he was, although I didn't take it in just then. I was far too excited to be on the same stage with Anna Neagle, Vic Oliver, and the whole Lyon family, and to be seeing Bebe shedding all her nervous tension and basking once more in the warm applause of an adoring audience. Ben was thrilled to the core to be the centre of *This is Your Life*, and at the party afterwards he was in great form, laughing and joking and teasing everybody.

Bebe whispered to me that the BBC were planning for us all to come back in the autumn in another family show *The Lyons at Large*, and they were working out the details. When I told Sandy this, he looked very doubtful. 'Well,' he said, 'the rest of them will have to do somethng about getting their health back. Apart from you and Ben, they all look as if a month's convalescence wouldn't do them any harm.'

Two months later, Bebe was working in the shop with the others. It was lunch-time, but as usual she hadn't any idea that it was time to break for a meal. Ben, always attentive, had brought up a plate with a lovely salad, and had said, 'Now stop working, Bebe, and eat that – I'll bring up some coffee later.' When he came up a few minutes afterwards, she had fallen forward on to the table with a cerebral haemorrhage.

Nobody expected her to live. She was taken to the National Hospital at Queen's Square, where she lay in a coma for days, and she was given the last rites. Ben never left the hospital. He was either at her bedside or in the waiting room, day and night, and only when the miracle happened and she began to show slight signs of recovery was he persuaded to go out for a meal just to get away from the hospital atmosphere.

103

He told me that the first tiny ray of hope was when one of the specialists touched the soles of her feet and she reacted. 'There is hope,' the specialist said, 'the nerves are not dead.'

I don't know what *their* house must have been like, but our door knocker went all that first day, and the telephone never stopped ringing. The coalman, the postman, the grocer, the milkman – everyone wanted to say, 'Wish her well.'

When I told Ben this later, he said 'All that goodwill got through, Molly. She has still a long way to go, but we are happier about her today. Show-biz can be tough and cruel, but when illness strikes and you have such positive proof that the whole country is wishing for your recovery, it makes our profession the most rewarding in the world in terms of human friendship.'

They had bouquets of flowers from all over the country, some without names, some with famous signatures, and one which touched Ben very much just said, 'From the taxi drivers of London.' Prayers were said for her in churches, and there were front page bulletins in all the newspapers. The whole country seemed willing her to get well, and the placards read one night, 'BEBE – LATEST', a tacit acknowledgement that such bulletins were awaited by everybody.

Her recovery was very slow, and she had some curious and at times quite hilarious tricks of memory. She told Ben quite seriously one lunch-time, 'Gary Cooper came by this morning, and George Burns wants to see you when he comes in this afternoon.' Her memory had gone right back to her Hollywood days.

She could remember that Richard had two children, but the wedding itself was completely blotted out. 'Barbara,' she had whispered to her urgently, 'Richard has two children, but he isn't married. Isn't that terrible? Don't tell Daddy.'

And then, at long last, she was allowed to go home, and we could all breathe again. She had to have day and night nursing, of course, but it was Ben who was the tower of strength. I rang the house regularly, and he said he would tell me when I could come to see for myself how well she was getting on. He knew it would be a long slow job, and he devoted himself completely to getting her fit again. That was when he told the BBC that the new series *The Lyons at Large* was out of the question.

'Bebe's health comes before everything,' he told me, 'and I will not allow her to do any more radio or TV shows.'

Knowing Bebe as we did, and how she threw herself into the script-writing and planning of all our shows, she would have had to be 100 per cent physically fit to tackle all the strains involved in a new TV series. Ben was so right to protect her from this taxing work. For she would never have saved herself.

When Ben rang to say I could come along to see Bebe, I felt quite nervous, dreading to find how changed she might be after such a severe stroke. I needn't have worried. Apart from the fact that she was sitting in a cosy arm-chair and not at her desk, and was possibly a trifle heavier than of yore, she was very recognizably the old sparkling Bebe Daniels. Those magnificent dark eyes were bright, and her smile was radiant as she called out to me, with all the old vibrancy of voice, 'Hullo Aggie (she always called me Aggie). Gee, it's good to see you.'

I handed her the little basket of our own tomatoes which I'd taken along as a wee present. I knew she would be surrounded with fresh flowers, and I also knew she always loved anything which had been grown or nurtured specially by the giver. 'Are they your own-grown tomatoes, honey?' she asked, and when I nodded, she picked one up and sniffed the minty stalk enthusiastically, 'Look, daddy, aren't they beautiful?' and she held them out for Ben to sniff. 'We'll have them for lunch tomorrow.'

It was the liveliest convalescent room you could wish for. The two poodles Skeeter and Toby frisked around, the postman delivered another load of cards and letters from well-wishers, and we tucked into tea and mince pies, pies which had just been sent by a 'fan' from Wales, home-made in her own kitchen, as she had emphasized in her 'get well' note. I saw from the way that Bebe tucked into them that Ben spoke the truth when he told me that she was enjoying her food. Although they had domestic staff, Ben prepared every meal for her himself, and, like cooks the world over, was delighted with her good appetite. Her skin was smooth, and the tranquillity of her expression reflected nights of refreshing sleep.

She had to learn to walk all over again, and Ben's constant encouragement kept her own courage high. It was most moving to see her utter dependence on him for support, and to watch the dark eyes light up with laughter when he teased her about not holding her bottom in when she essayed a few painful steps. 'Get the can right back, Bebe,' he instructed her. 'You know where it is – get it back.' 'Isn't he awful?' she giggled, and took one more step forward.

His tender watch over her every movement, his pride in her miraculous return to life, and her own responsiveness to his humour touched me almost to tears.

He was thinner, and quieter in his manner towards

106

me, but the old gaiety flashed out when we started talking of the theatre season we had done in Blackpool* and then of the TV episode when the chimpanzee had made such a fuss and wouldn't let Ben out of its sight. Bebe leant forward in her chair, drinking in every word, and it was a joy to see her losing herself completely, remembering the scripts and the stories she had helped to devise. At such moments, she could easily forget the complete paralysis which had gripped her for so many months.

Ben and I exchanged glances of triumph over the success of our diversionary tactics, and I could well understand his feelings. I myself had witnessed a small miracle on a recent visit to hospital where I'd been having heat treatment on an arm which had been giving me a spot of bother.

As I waited for a cubicle, two wee coloured girls sharing an invalid chair were wheeled in to have their exercises. They were about eight or nine years old and both were spastics.

I teased them to make them laugh and said they were very lucky to be wheeled about in such style, and I was dying to watch them doing their exercises. Norma, her little thin legs twisted, feet turned in, gazed at me with great chocolate-brown eyes. 'I like you,' she said simply.

I was moved by her childish candour. 'All right, Norma,' I said, 'I like you too. Now show me how you can walk.'

She took a pair of specially constructed supports and, with the nurse holding her shoulders, tottered uncertainly towards me, gave up, and sat down on a chair to rest.

* Walking into the Lyons' Den

Meanwhile Maxine, the other little spastic, took up *her* support and tried to walk. As I encouraged Maxine, Norma's lip puckered, vexed that I wasn't paying her any attention. Next minute she'd thrown away one of her supports, transferred the other to her right hand, and *walked* right across the ward, all by herself, without a nurse anywhere near her. Then she sat down on a bed and gazed at me triumphantly.

The nurses stared, amazed. They called the chief physiotherapist, and the poor little twisted spastic walked across the ward again.

'She's been here for months,' the chief said to me in a low voice, 'and that's the first time she has walked. She'll improve from now on.'

If I never did anything else in my life, I'll never forget the rewarding feeling which suffused me from head to toes when my eyes met the sparkling triumph in that wee spastic's eyes as she looked at me to see if I was pleased.

As for the nurses, they declared they were going to recruit me into the service right away!

Oh yes, I could truly understand Ben's feelings with every sign of progress Bebe showed.

On my next visit to the house, Bebe and the nurse were deep in a card game, each quite sure she was about to win the next shilling stake money! Bebe always loved cards, and she had lost none of her enthusiasm for a good game. It was splendid therapy for her when she had of necessity to spend so much time indoors in a chair, and it helped her memory greatly. She still had odd lapses, which Ben and I 'cured' by bringing the conversation round to whatever it was she had forgotten. As we chatted over tea on this visit, and remembered how Wilfred Brambell had been in one of our shows, I discovered she had missed a very funny episode of *Steptoe* earlier in the week. The next minute Ben and I were re-enacting the entire episode for Bebe and the nurse. They made a great audience! Bebe's laughter pealed out spontaneously and led us to wild extremes of comedy, and the nurse had to wipe the tears of laughter from her eyes.

Who could have thought the day would dawn when Ben and I would team up to put on a 'double act' to entertain a chair-bound Bebe and a nurse, and feel so well rewarded by the laughter of an audience of two.

When Ben showed me out he said, 'Eight months and nine days since she took ill. God has been very good. Doesn't she look wonderful?'

I could say with sincerity and honesty that she did, with her serene expression and smooth cheeks.

The most amazing thing to me, was her patient acceptance of being more or less chair-bound, and her sunny enjoyment of the things she *could* do.

They moved to a flat in Dolphin Square some time after this, which became a mecca for all their friends from show-biz. It was much easier for Bebe, for it had no stairs of course, and she gained daily in strength, and soon found courage to go out with Ben for the occasional meal and even to a theatre. Anna Neagle was thrilled and delighted when Bebe chose *Charlie Girl* for her very first theatrical outing, and the whole theatre rose in tribute when Anna announced that Bebe and Ben were in the audience. They were all old friends, and Bebe had always loved musicals, so it was an enchanted evening and a great reunion.

She actually did a broadcast where I was one of the panel in *Sounds Familiar*. She was introduced as the 'mystery celebrity', and when I told a little story to illustrate her discipline and her integrity, she listened intently and at the end said, simply and naturally, 'Oh!

that was nice, Aggie.' Her instinctive use of my name as the 'Aggie' character sent a ripple of delighted laughter through the audience, and Bebe turned in slight bewilderment wondering what she had said that was so funny. It was the only time I ever saw her surprised by audience laughter.

There were eight bonus years before Bebe collapsed again.

When it happened I was up in Glasgow, doing my last recording as Effie the garrulous little post-office wifie in *High Living* for Scottish Television, a part I loved. I never went out for lunch so they knew there was no danger of my seeing any newspapers or placards. They kept the news from me until I had returned to my dressing room to change to go home. I was pulling on my jersey, when two good friends knocked on the door, and told me that Bebe Daniels had died that morning.

Everyone in the studio had known but me.

Sandy and I spoke briefly on the telephone. It was the day before my birthday and he knew he would see me then, and say the things which would bring comfort and some consolation.

I was touched by everyone's thoughtfulness, even if my heart gave a great lurch at the full realization that I would never again see that well-loved face.

With a pang I also realized that no longer would I hear people say, after a first greeting, 'How's Bebe?'

This question had been put to me by everyone, from the dustman to our MP ever since her first illness.

On the morning of the funeral, in the great Catholic church in Finchley Road, the cast of *Life with the Lyons* was together for the last time.

Bebe lay in front of the altar in a flower-covered coffin. Ben's tribute of gladioli, red and pink roses, orchids, pink and crimson carnations and tiny irises covered almost its entire length.

Leaning against the bier stood a wreath from the RAF.

Her family, friends and fans filled the church. The famous and the unknown mourned together. How many memories we shared with that still figure lying before us.

Across the aisle sat Jack Hulbert, and my thoughts went back to the stage session we had done in Blackpool eighteen years previously, when he had produced us. After five hard-working weeks of rehearsals before we opened, we had done a punishing season of twelve shows a week.

I remembered that wild adagio dance of Bebe's performed twice nightly, and which she had refused to cancel even after a severe dental operation. She merely rinsed out her mouth and said, 'I'll live!' For such a star we would all have crawled on to the stage.

Dickie Henderson was there, and nearby sat Stanley Black, our old orchestra conductor.

Pat Hilliard, who had been head of Light Entertainment at the BBC during our radio series had come to pay tribute to his old friend, and there was also Michael Brook who used to announce us and whom Ben teased unmercifully. Beside him was John Dyas, who produced me in *Sounds Familiar*. As I caught sight of John, I realized that it was on his show I had seen and worked with Bebe for the last time, in the self-same theatre and on the same stage where we had done *Life with the Lyons* for over ten years.

If I am legendary now for punctuality, it is because of my ten years' training with one of the most professional families in the world of entertainment.

If I can give a 'performance' at the very first reading

111

of a script, it is because that was our way in *Life with the Lyons*.

And if I know what is meant when it is said 'two hearts beat as one' it is because I saw so often Ben's restlessness when Bebe was a little later than he expected, and that look change at once to relaxed gaiety the moment she appeared.

They were never far apart, those two, either in body or spirit.

His was the last face she saw in this life.

Ben! What would he do without her? I wondered in panic.

And suddenly he was there, walking down the aisle with Richard by his side, and Barbara looking helpless in her grief. She looked so vulnerable that the tears which I had been able to stem until that moment rushed forth.

Anna Neagle read the first lesson, a piece from *The Song of Solomon*, and Richard Attenborough read the second lesson, from *St Paul's Letter to the Corinthians*.

It had been a dull March morning, with a piercing wind, but suddenly as we sang, 'Through Cloud and Sunshine, Lord, Abide with me', on the very word 'sunshine' the sun blazed over the coffin like a stage spotlight, and lit catafalque and flowers with startling brilliance.

I lifted my head in wonderment, and I saw Ben do the same.

It was such a miraculous moment, so filled with promise that it calmed the heart.

Sometimes the words of the ordinary listener are far more moving than those which we, who were so close to Bebe and Ben, could bring to express our feelings.

One such letter was sent to me from Glasgow.

'We British owe them such a lot for "seeing us

112

through the war" and those who lived near the danger zones will never forget them. Their *High Gang!* was the highlight of the week.

'Theirs was a true love marriage, and both of them loved by so many people.

'God bless them. We won't ever forget what they did.'

It always amazed me that Bebe, who did so much for our entertainment in this country in times of peril and in times of peace was never awarded any public honour.

But the avalanche of telegrams, letters and cables which poured into the flat in Dolphin Square after her death was eloquent testimony that she had her honoured niche in the hearts of the nation and of the world.

I prayed that Ben would be sustained by the love and sympathy of the millions to whom they had brought so much laughter.

It was heartbreaking that Bebe never lived to see Barbara's little son Bruce. My heart ached that she missed the joy of being a grandmother by two short months. Barbara had a very bad time, but Bruce's arrival helped in some measure to ease the icy grief which had gripped Ben, and in future years he was to say that Barbara had done well to name her son after a Scottish hero, for the wee lad talked nearly as much as I did!

He is a dear little boy, very loving, and with much of Bebe's magic in his eyes and personality.

Bebe would have thought it a fine omen that on my birthday I met an Irish priest who saw me wearing a little buttonhole of shamrocks, and came over to wish me a Happy St Patrick's Day. The shamrocks had been sent by a fan, and as our beloved Queen Mum always presented shamrocks to the Irish Guards on that special day, I thought I would show that it was also special for me. It was after all my birthday, and my mother's birthday too come to that – both of us Presbyterians and both born on an Irish Saint's day.

It was indeed a good omen, for almost immediately afterwards I was approached by the BBC and asked if I would like to read the Sunday Story on television on four consecutive Sundays. The stories were to be from Isobel Cameron's 'Doctor' books, very well-known and very popular in Scotland and especially in the Aberdeen area, and I would be produced by a minister, John Elphinstone-Fyffe. He turned out to be a charmer, but stunned me by having complete confidence that I would be able to work with autocue without the slightest trouble.

'But I've never worked with autocue,' I said in dismay. 'I'd have to learn how to do it. And I'd have to rehearse it.'

'Oh you don't rehearse or learn with autocue,' he said cheerfully. 'There are only about two things you have to know. Don't look as if you're obviously reading and don't *rush*! You don't follow the autocue, it follows you!'

And that was my coaching!

Mark you, it was an enormous relief not to have the nightmare of memorizing a whole story, or of doing it live, but it would be no picnic either, acting out four stories and disguising the fact that I was reading. Could I dare to move my head, I wondered, and venture to look away, or glance around in the mood of the action?

I'd never had such VIP treatment, for I'd never done this type of solo performance. No canteen snack for this engagement. I was ushered into a private room, all crimson carpets and excellent furnishings and we

114

sat down to a beautifully served meal. After telling my delightful minister-producer that I didn't each much before going before the cameras as I was too nervous, I cleared the plates! He must have wondered what sort of appetite I have when I'm hungry!

Later, for the first time, I had an entire studio and about a dozen men all working to put 'my' programme out. I was led to a lovely blue upholstered chair set on a dais, as though I were about to conduct a service, and after a little soothing chat with the minister, I was away. The moment we started, and I absorbed the first half-dozen words on the autocue, I was all right. The minister declared himself very pleased when I'd finished and, like Vic Oliver, I was more than happy that I'd added another little accomplishment to my list of new experiences. I could now truthfully say I could use autocue! Wouldn't my grannie have been pleased if she'd heard me tell those stories. She always said I was destined to be a minister, and this was certainly the nearest I'd got to fulfilling her prediction!

Another nice thing that happened because of those Sunday Stories was that I came to know the great Gaelic singer and scholar, Jimmy McPhee. There was a wee bit of Gaelic in the 'Doctor' stories, and, having met Jimmy briefly at a Burns' celebration earlier in the year, I dared to ring him and ask for expert coaching in the exact pronunciation. He made me repeat the phrases until his ear was satisfied, and that single 'phone call established my reputation with everyone who knew and understood Gaelic. When they heard who had been my teacher, they nodded sagely, 'Ah lassie, you couldn't have gone to a finer Gaelic speaker – Jimmy is an expert.' Even my brother Tom was impressed and that's saying something! But almost the most heart-warming approval came from the Gaelic-speaking secretary of the producer of the Gaelic programmes in Glasgow, whom I hadn't even met. She came over to me in the canteen when I was up in my native city doing a broadcast and she said to me in her lovely soft Highland tones, 'You did a fery good chob on the "Doctor" stories, Miss Weir. You're the first person I've effer heard from Glasgow who could manage a decent Highland accent. And you managed it, I think, because you didn't over-do it.' As you can see, I've treasured that compliment and remembered it word for word to this very day. There's probably a disproportionate feeling of pleasure when something one has never done before turns out well. For, as they say, it's better than a poke in the eye with a burnt stick!

As a result of the success of these stories, and their popularity with the viewers, I was asked if I could suggest something myself, and I decided to have a shot at adapting the story of Mary Slessor, that brave Scottish lass who became one of the most famous and most influential missionaries in darkest Africa, and who had long been a childhood heroine of mine. I didn't realize what I was taking on, for in the end I had to devour at least half-a-dozen books from all sources before I felt I was steeped enough in every aspect of her life and work to put down a single word.

Then the minister and I nearly came to blows because, after I'd had the stories accepted and been over the moon with joy, he asked me to re-write every single one, because I'd spread the tale of this wonderful pioneering spirit over too many weeks! 'But I *can't* cram all that history into five weeks,' I wailed. 'Oh yes you can,' came the minister's cheerful voice over the telephone. 'They'll be all the better for being crisper and more direct.' When I continued to argue rebelliously, he said, 'Now Molly, five weeks are fully long enough to expect any audience to follow a continuous story. Any longer and they'll give up, because they'll have other things to do.'

He was right, of course.

We decided I would record them all in one full session just after Christmas. And just after Christmas somebody 'up there' had other ideas, it seemed, for I was felled by my *bête noire,* bronchitis and 'flu! One minute I was right as rain, and the next I was fighting for breath.

I rang John (the minister and I were on Christian name terms by this time – Grannie would have been outraged by such familiarity!), and he nearly had a fit when he heard my croaking. They couldn't postpone the recording, he told me. It would have to be complete cancellation if I really couldn't do it. The schedules had already been arranged for the forseeable future.

There was still another day of the Christmas holiday to go, so I recklessly promised that my 'crash course' could effect a miracle cure and I would be ready. 'What's the crash course?' asked John dubiously. 'Oh Friar's balsam and boiling water, plus linctus, throat tablets, rum and honey. And of course the whole of the next day in bed.'

We both agreed it would be a real blow if we had to cancel the series, after all the hard work we'd put in. All those rewritten scripts! I couldn't bear it.

John said he would ring next night to see how I sounded.

When he did ring, he said I sounded marginally better, and added hastily that of course he agreed with me, I would be even better after a good night's sleep, and be almost as good as new on the morning of the recordings. He organized the whole thing like *Emergency Ward 10*. Cars fetched and carried me to the studios, heater going full blast. Warm rugs enveloped me from ears to feet. The driver was under strict instructions not to speak to me, to discourage me from using my voice.

In the studio, hot drinks were provided all day to keep me going, and I began to feel like the tragic heroine Camille as I coughed into tissues and dropped them into overflowing baskets, which were held at arm's length, and removed from the studio at regular intervals. John exhibited a truly Christian spirit by staying close to me all day, risking infection, giving me his support and strength, and encouraging me by his enthusiasm for the story-telling. I prayed I wasn't passing on my germs to the entire crew.

The lighting man did a marvellous job and even managed to produce a sort of 'halo' effect with my Friar's-balsam-steamed hair, but even so I looked perfectly ghastly. By the time we reached the final episode, my voice had dwindled almost to vanished point, and gave great conviction to the tired broken tones of the dying and overworked Mary!

After the first episode went out, I had quite a bit of fan mail, and all of them commented on how ill I looked, but added, 'You'll probably have thrown off your chill when the next episodes are shown.' Little did they know there would be no improvement. I'd recorded them in a single day, and in the end would almost begin to resemble the dying Mary Slessor!

But 'say not the struggle naught availeth', it was a good series, and it was well received, and somehow it was felt that my own fragility lent an air of pathos which underlined Mary Slessor's courage. I had a most interesting letter from a Helensburgh man afterwards, and he told me that when he was a wee boy Mary Slessor had stayed at their house. His father was a minister, and they were well used to entertaining visiting missionaries who had served in the foreign field. She had brought back with her two of the black babies rescued from twin murder. Twins were regarded as evil spirits in that part of Africa at that time, and the parents threw them out to die.

Apparently, the small baby girls developed a passion for baking powder, and were always sneaking into the kitchen in search of it. He said he never forgot how funny it struck him seeing them wetting their fingers, then dipping them into the baking powder and sucking it off, eyes rolling in ecstasy. He was entranced to observe how startlingly white the fingertip looked against the jet-black of the rest of the finger. I was fascinated to share this memory from the distant past, a memory which linked me to an old man who had actually been alive and a boy under the same roof which had sheltered Mary Slessor.

Another envelope brought a host of memories, and a pang of sadness. My Christmas card was returned from Elgin, the home of my old school-teacher Miss McKenzie, with the message written in ink 'Miss McKenzie died a few weeks ago.' We always exchanged cards, and her pride in my achievements was a great warmth to me, just as her unshakeable belief in me as a schoolgirl had terrified me for fear I wouldn't be as good as she thought I was.

Dear Miss McKenzie, how I admired and respected her. She was my good angel, and I have much to thank her for. She taught me the value of disciplined study, and I hope my success and my acknowledgement of the part she played in it repaid her in some small measure for all her hard work as a teacher. She was truly one of the old school, who knew every pupil's strength and weakness, and who understood when to admonish and when to praise. May she rest in peace. She left me one unexpected little legacy. My hand-writing is exactly like hers.

Another unexpected missive was from the BBC in Manchester and they wondered if I would like to come up to do a recording with Jimmy Clitheroe, playing the part of Great Aunt Flora opposite Jack Laurie as Great Uncle Angus. Would I not! I'd never met Jimmy before, although I'd always listened to his programme and I loved his explosive impersonation of the Scottish accent. Some people can set the teeth on edge, mistakenly imagining they are expert at 'taking off' the Scottish voice. Jimmy had no such airs. He let it burst out of him and it sounded hilarious.

He was absolutely delightful to work with. Full of humour, with no side at all in spite of being such a success. He not only queued with the rest of us at the canteen, but made a game of it, rushing about serving the rest of us with cups of tea and toast which hadn't been ready when we'd collected our main course.

When I was being introduced to the audience he called out to me, 'Give them a recipe, Molly!' He told me later he listened to me doing my shopping flashes, and followed my recipes with keenest interest. Like Ben Lyon, he was fascinated by my always knitting when I wasn't actually at the microphone, and if I happened to lay down the needles for a minute, he would urge me on with cries of, 'Come on noo Molly – get knitting! There's nae time to sit idle.' He was truly a coughdrop. Patricia Burke did patchwork so I was glad to be in the company of someone who also believed in the therapy of busy hands.

It was great too to renew working acquaintance with

my old friend from ITMA and the Charlie Chester show, Deryck Guyler. The last time I'd seen him was ten years previously, also in Manchester, when we did a documentary programme. Peter Sinclair was also in Clitheroe, and altogether it was a very happy show. The stammering boyfriend, Danny, was a wonderful comic, and his scenes with the young sweetheart brought the house down.

Deryck always said that I, as Great Aunt Flora, was the one sane voice in a mad world!

I hadn't worked with John Laurie before, and we got on like a house on fire. When we had finished our recording, I said goodbye, thinking it would just be a single 'guest spot' for John and me, but we were asked back again and again until I grew almost as familiar with the Manchester studios as I did with those in London and Glasgow. Our producer was the son of the great Jimmy James, and he was highly amused when I told him I'd worked with his dad in the Glasgow Empire when I was one of Henry Hall's guests, following my appearance as a Carrol Levis discovery*. James Cassidy (our producer) could do a great impersonation of his father which was so true to the original that I could see myself once more standing in the wings of the Glasgow Empire, watching the genial comic at work, that little bent cigarette dangling from his lips, as he struggled to find the right key to start off his song.

Patricia Burke was the daughter of the great Marie Burke, and I felt I was truly part of theatrical history to find myself working with this lovely lady. She had a flat in Greece, which she at that time rented out to holidaying friends, but regretfully I had to refuse to

* A Toe on the Ladder

avail myself of the offer, tempting as it was, because those terrible Colonels were mis-ruling the country and I refused to encourage them with the smallest sum from my pocket. 'I know my wee bit of holiday money can't make much difference, Pat,' I said, 'but it is a matter of principle.' She cast her eyes heavenwards, 'I didn't know they were going to take over the blooming country, Molly,' she said, 'and I still have to pay my rates!'

It was the same with Spain. I wouldn't go there either when they started behaving outrageously over Gibraltar. Sardinia too blotted its copybook with me when they didn't stamp down hard enough on the bandits at that time. Sandy said, laughingly, 'You're turning the world into an "out of bounds" area!' He looked at me thoughtfully, 'I'm not surprised folk think you're eccentric.'

'Well, I don't mind that,' I said, 'I like eccentrics.'

I always remember seeing a play starring Gladys Cooper, and she had shocked her young daughters by pulling down her stocking in a shop and dabbing a bite with soothing lotion. 'But mother,' said one, 'you are definitely getting eccentric, it's awful. Don't you mind people thinking you're eccentric?'

'No,' said Gladys Cooper joyously, 'I love being eccentric. Eccentrics have a *wonderful* time. They can do exactly as they like.'

I was amazed to find a playwright who could express through a character precisely how I felt, and I've allowed myself to behave entirely naturally ever since, without fear of conventional criticism.

I can't tell you what a help this has been during many sticky moments in my life. And sticky was the word on a very hot day in London when the heat and a brand-new pair of shoes combined to make an agonizing blister on my left heel. I was dressed to the nines, having had to keep a rather grand appointment, and there I was in pale beige silk shift, posh white 'bazaar-opening' hat, beige gloves, and white handbag, both shoes dangling from one hand! I had taken my shoe off to examine my blister, and the blood seeping through my stocking convinced me I'd never put that shoe on again. So off came both, and I travelled home that way. Two old ladies sitting resting their own feet at the top of Pinner High Street, stared at me in amazement, and then clucked in sympathy when they glanced down at my gory stocking. Now if I'd been worried about people's reactions, I'd have hirpled home in agony, whereas I strode out vigorously, rejoicing in the cool pavements beneath my stockinged feet.

On my way through the 'snicket', the tiny passageway connecting the two lanes from the station, I caught up with another Pinner character, who could truly be regarded as an eccentric because he had such pride and enthusiasm for his job, and scorned those who thought only of the pay packet and of doing as little as possible in return. He was our local road-sweeper and he and I shared many a merry chat. We both shook disapproving heads over broken glass lamps, and I was always kept fully informed of his immediate plans for keeping 'his' lanes spick and span. Neat as a new pin, in light navy denim jacket and trousers, his was the face of a contented man as he surveyed with satisfaction his well-swept territory, and he envied no man. He told me he visited the chiropodist regularly for, as he put it, 'The feet are very important in my job.'

He fully approved my wearing trousers for cold days, but when he caught sight of me all dressed for town, he would call over quietly, 'Petticoats today?' with no

123

familiarity, but a lovely old-fashioned appreciation of the correctness of the attire for the occasion.

He made me laugh when he told me that his wife, instead of accepting a box of chocolates on Mother's Day, persuaded him to put the five shillings on three horses of her choosing for the Grand National, and they were the first three! So he was able to bring home nearly £5 and put it in her lap. His face crinkled with amusement at her cleverness when he told me this story.

He was always on the go, and when Pinner had the benefit of his care and energy our lanes would have been fit to receive Royalty any time they cared to call. He was a rare chap – truly irreplaceable, and after he retired no successor equalled his cleaning skills. He only lived a few months after retirement, and when his wife wrote to me breaking the sad news, she told me how much he had valued my friendship, and how pleased he had been when I had paid a small tribute to him in my *People's Journal* column. How glad I am to have been able to give public expression to such integrity as I found in this man. As my dear ma-in-law would have said, 'There were no many like him in a pun.'

Just as the splendid road-sweeper liked my casual friendliness, I myself am always amused by this characteristic when I go north of the Border. I remember a visit we paid to Largs during a touring holiday, and on a lovely Sunday morning we parked the car beside the kerb. A young lad called over, 'Hey, you'll get arrested if ye stey there!' When Sandy pointed out that the restricted times were 10 A.M. till 6 P.M., and it was just after 9 A.M., he said, 'Och aye, ye'll hae a guid half-oor then. Make the maist o' it.' Which we did. It's just such brief encounters which make me laugh, and say with delight to myself, 'My ain folk. They're ma ain folk, and there's naebody like them.'

Of course in Glasgow, conversation with everybody is a way of life. I remember one wet morning on my way to rehearsal at the BBC, I suddenly felt a pair of hands gripping my shoulders. I turned round to find a wee man who whispered in my ear, 'Dae ye know ye've goat a ticket hingin' doon fae yer scarf, hen?' Then, as he took a closer look, he muttered, 'Ma Goad, it's a silk label!' He was gone before I could thank him for his interest, and I laughed every time I thought of his friendly word that it could have been a price ticket hanging for all to see. In London you could be walking about without a skirt, and not a soul would dream of uttering a word of warning!

The difference between the Londoner and the Glaswegian was never more clearly demonstrated than on a very hot August day when I was travelling home in a train packed with commuters. One business type, with brief case and dark suit removed his bowler and placed it on the luggage rack. Heat and perspiration had glued the leather lining band to his forehead, and he sat all the way to Pinner without a single person in that packed compartment mentioning it. Or even smiling. I had a job to hide my amusement, and I thought to myself, Now if that had been in Glasgow, somebody would have given instant voice to make the poor chap aware of what had happened.' I could almost hear the words, 'Hey Mac, you've loast the feather oot o' yer heid-band. Ur ye playing Rid Indians?'

In Glasgow, everybody present would have had a good laugh, including the victim. In London, there was only silent embarrassment, and a blushing exit for the poor perspiring traveller who'd sat for half-an-hour, completely unaware of the fact that he had given an unwitting impersonation of Big Chief Running Water.

CHAPTER SIX

I had a speaking engagement on a bitter February evening to those girls on the McAllister Brew course, and I had arranged to meet Sandy next day in town for lunch. It would break my journey between Dorset and Pinner and we could exchange all our news. My train was due to arrive around Sandy's lunch-hour and I was to ring him from Waterloo when I got in.

It was a morning of snow and ice, and when I tried to close the train door my feet had slipped on the frozen step and I'd tumbled down on to the platform, my mink coat gathering the slush and snow as I rolled! I had more of a fright than anything else, for of course the train wasn't moving, but when I got to Waterloo (late because of the weather), and rang Sandy, and started to tell him of my mishap, giggling over my Tarzan leap from the train door, he seemed strangely distrait and disinclined for conversation. It seemed he couldn't get away from the office after all, and I was to go straight home and he'd see me in the evening. I wondered if he was irritated because I was so late, but I didn't mind going home at once, for I wanted to make sure my coat would dry and clean up properly, and I had a lot of writing to do.

When Sandy came home in the evening he just picked at his food, and, unbelievably, he didn't tell me off for falling out of the train! I couldn't believe I wasn't getting my usual cautionary lecture about *not* rushing, and making sure next time to *look* where I was going. There was definitely something amiss with our Sandy.

And then, after our meal, as I carried the dishes to the sink he put his arms around me and said, 'I have something to tell you.' My heart leaped into my mouth. 'What is it?' I whispered, and struggled to free myself. I always feel claustrophobic at the merest hint of bad news. Sandy put his arm round my shoulders again. 'Miss Chree is dead,' he said.

'She can't be, she can't be,' I shouted, and then burst into uncontrollable sobbing. I always feel that nobody I love can possibly die without my being there to try to hold them back from that great divide. How could Miss Chree, my darling A.J. as I always called her, my first friend in all of uncaring London,* be dead? I had spoken to her only ten days ago. She worked for a group of doctors, as housekeeper, and I had let the 'phone ring out and out, for I wanted to make sure she would take time to wrap herself in a warm shawl before she came upstairs from the basement into that icy passage to speak. 'Are you warm enough now?' I asked. 'Aye lassie, that I am. I ha'e my Paisley shawl roon' ma shouthers.' She could speak pure Queen's English, but she liked to fall into the couthy accents of her youth when she spoke to me. We talked for a good half-hour, for I felt she was in a mood to reminisce, and we took our time and roamed over incidents from her childhood, when her mother was driven to the point of tears, almost, with Miss Chree's habit of losing herself in a book. 'When your father comes in, I'll tell him to put that book on the back of the fire.' Miss Chree's voice had soared with laughter at the very idea of her good and caring

* A Toe on the Ladder *Stepping into the Spotlight

127

mother's threat, and then we went on to 'Father', and his clever hands, and the auntie and uncle who had 'terrible fechts' and to whom a visit was a great source of hushed wonder. 'Mither,' Miss Chree would say when she and her sister returned from such a visit, 'they were roarin' oot and a'thing.' I had only ever met her nephew Michael, when he came down to London from Aberdeen to watch test cricket, but I felt I knew the entire family almost as well as I knew my own.

Miss Chree used to say if we saw each other every day for a month, we'd never get in the half of the things we wanted to say. She possessed neither radio nor television, but loved the newspapers, the London markets, and above all, discussion and debate. She and I were completely and utterly in sympathy. She had few worldly goods, but was abundantly rich in every way that mattered. In intellect, in enthusiasm, in kindliness and in sheer goodness.

As we talked long and intimately that night, I could sense that she was unusually happy that I had rung. She made a small protest about the cost of the call, which I brushed aside. I never count the cost of 'phone calls to friends – they are always cheaper than a train journey, and they're as good as a visit to lift the heart and the spirits of the lonely. Thank God there has always been sufficient 'roughness' in my purse to enable me to do this. And now that Sandy was forcing me to believe this terrible news, my mind rushed back to that last long talk we'd had together and I rejoiced in my heart that I had picked up the 'phone on that icy February evening. 'Aye we've had a grand "speak", lassie,' she had said before we bade each other 'Goodnight'. 'We have,' I answered, 'now mind and keep

128

warm, for this weather is bitter.' 'Yes dear,' she said, 'it is positively dangerous.'

It was more than dangerous for my poor A.J. It turned out in the end to be lethal. It appeared she had taken a heavy cold on the Friday following our conversation, and had promised the doctors for whom she worked that she would rest up over the week-end, to give herself a chance to get rid of it. When the doctors had arrived on Monday morning, she was lying, collapsed, at the top of the stairs on her way to open the surgery. It was bronchial pneumonia, and the next day she was dead.

It was completely typical of her unswerving sense of duty that she would attempt to crawl upstairs to open that surgery when she was, quite literally, dying. Other folk might have stayed in bed, only too glad of an excuse in such bitter weather, but not Miss Chree.

I was filled with the most overwhelming grief that I would never again hear that vibrant voice. Never again see those blue eyes light up with enthusiasm as we roamed from one topic to another in fierce discussion or argument. She loved the fact that the rows we had were academic and that we were friends immediately afterwards. 'Here was I shouting oot last night,' she would say, 'and here we are this morning yarning over a cup of coffee. Isn't it *good*?' It was indeed good.

She came to us every Christmas, and I knew with certainty that our Christmasses would never be the same without her. How would I be able to listen to *All in the April Evening* without seeing her blue eyes fill with tears, and hear her whispered 'Beautiful!' at the finish. She was a Scot all Scotland could be proud of, for she carried the traditions of duty and truth to every task she performed, and everyone she worked for described her as a 'cast iron certainty, utterly reliable, always faithful'.

They had found my telephone number with my last letter in her desk, and had rung Sandy to tell him the shocking news. Michael and his mother, Miss Chree's sister, had come down to clear up that little basement room where we had last seen her when we had gone to collect her to bring her back to Pinner to spend that last, so recent, Christmas with us. It was a glorious hotch-potch of newspapers, nicknacks and books. Like me, she couldn't bear to throw out a thing, and like me, she was always hoarding old articles she wanted to consult again, and so the newspaper stacks grew like small columns in every part of the room. The Paisley shawl lay like a bright flag over the end of the bed, purely so that she could enjoy its colour every time she came into the room, and be reminded of her early days in Aberdeen. Her sister had been appalled at the disorder, and when Sandy had thought of the nightmare task of clearing it up he said to me, 'Don't die before me. Please don't. I couldn't bear to have to go through such a collection. For you're just as bad.'

'I didn't care about the mess,' I said, 'I loved her, and that apparent untidiness was part of her.'

There were four of us at the crematorium. Her sister, her beloved nephew Michael, Sandy and me.

'You are so white, Molly,' said her sister.

I was desolate. I miss her still, and when I see the way the world is going nowadays, I often wonder what she would have made of it all, and I long for her wisdom.

She never married. She was, in the words of the wee spinster who used to write to me, 'an unclaimed treasure'. This poetic description of her own state always made her laugh.

It took a long time for me to get over the loss of my darling A.J. and I showed a distressing tendency to burst into tears, no matter where I might be, whenever I thought of her lonely end. My neighbour's little son went white to the lips the first time I did this in the midst of a perfectly normal conversation, and this incident confirmed my feeling that I must *do* something to shake myself out of this emotional instability. As always, work is the great cure, so when I found another RADA refresher course was about to start, I enrolled for a month's voice and movement classes.

I had hardly even begun to tackle the problem of breathing properly, than I was offered a tiny snippet of a part in the Terry Scott–Hugh Lloyd series *Hugh and I*. It would involve only a few days' absence from class, so I was able to carry on for most of the month with my self-imposed task of sending deep breaths right down to my diaphragm, while keeping my ram-rod shoulders relaxed! Ordinary mortals may believe breathing is a natural process. Actors know otherwise. Anyone watching us sitting in a circle, bottoms on the edge of our chairs, feet firmly on the ground, concentrating on keeping our spines straight and relaxing our shoulders at the same time, would have imagined we were curing ourselves of some painful ailment with a spot of physiotherapy. As for the mouth exercises, these were quite hilarious and sent Fenella Fielding and me into uncontrollable giggles when we caught each other's eye, and this in turn sent our breathing all to pot. We had to let our jaws hang, then purse up our lips like rabbits, and finally swivel our heads right round till our eyes popped. This last exercise proved to be a great ice-breaker at a Christmas party I attended later, when all the guests were so intrigued by my description of the RADA classes that they decided they'd prove just how easily they could breathe and vocalize without sound, and ended up gasping and howling with laughter. The hostess declared it was the most unusual and successful party she'd given for years!

Similarly, when I went along for the *Hugh and I* rehearsals, I was enthusing over the 'movement' classes, and the next moment the entire cast was on its feet, arms and legs swinging like pistons, rehearsals forgotten as they laboured to get all the muscles working. When the coffee trolley arrived, the man in charge gazed at us as though he thought we had all gone quite mad. Then he decided to join us, and was elated to find himself moving with the grace of a ballet dancer! Everyone loves a challenge, and all actors love to prove that everything they will require for their performance is in good working order.

One of the most terrifying things I ever did happened while I was attending those classes. John Fernald, the king-figure of the Royal Academy of Dramatic Art for ten years, had resigned, and the whole affair had been fraught with drama. As a part-time student, I of course didn't know the ins and outs of RADA politics, but I did know that the students, past and present, were so determined to show appreciation and loyalty to him that they had organized a big party at the Vanbrugh Theatre. Everybody who was anybody in the world of theatre turned up, from Miles Malleson to Richard Briers, the former a tried and true Thespian, the latter a brilliant newcomer. And there were all shades of experience and talent in between. Robin Ray, Ted's son, took me under his wing and I joined his party for a while, thoroughly enjoying dancing with my fellow-students and exchanging 'hullos' with well-known faces from the newer world of television. Jack Hedley, then the current heart-throb from the TV series *The World of Tim Frazer* was greeted with adoring sighs from the younger students.

There was to be a cabaret at midnight, and Sandy was coming to meet me around 1 A.M. for although I didn't really want to stay so late, I felt it would be rather ungracious to leave before the cabaret. I heard someone ask Susannah York if she would do something for them to add a touch of glamour to the cabaret but she refused with horror, 'I *couldn't*, I simple *couldn't* get up in front of so many actors. I should die of fright.' I sympathized with this reaction, although I was slightly surprised that a successful young beauty felt much the same as I did about such appearances.

About a quarter past eleven, carefree and irresponsibly enjoying myself, I found myself being introduced to the man who had organized the cabaret, and when he asked me, jokingly as I thought, why I wasn't in it I, like a fool, said 'Nobody asked me.'

To my horror, I heard him say, 'Well, you're in it now!'

'But I *can't*,' I stammered in panic, 'I *can't*. There's nothing I could do in a cabaret.' If Susannah York was terrified, I would positively die the death.

'Oh yes you can,' came the cheerfully vigorous voice, 'You can be in the VIP auditions.'

This was the first time I'd heard of them!

Everyone has to do an audition to get into RADA, so they had devised a sketch where as many established players as possible would enter into the spirit of the party, and pretend they were auditioning for RADA for the first time as hopeful would-be students.

To say I was petrified at the mere idea of getting up on that famous stage to perform for such an audience is the understatement of the year. Especially when I hadn't a clue what I was going to do, or what was expected of me. For two pins I'd have run out of the theatre. I was given no opportunity to escape, for the fiendish organiser kept tight hold of me and took me straight backstage to join the other actors for the VIP audition sketch.

I saw half-a-dozen famous faces through a blur of sheer terror, while the words of half-remembered poems and ditties raced through my head. Oh how I wished I hadn't enjoyed that fruit punch so much. I couldn't remember a single complete verse. And then, suddenly, to the surface of my consciousness floated the daft bit of Scottish gibberish I used at the Players' Theatre to introduce my *Laird of Cockpen* number. Feverishly I went over the words. One line escaped me, vanished in the terror of the moment. As the cabaret was announced with a roll of drums, the line came back. 'Thank you, God,' I breathed, 'thank you,' perspiration trickling down my back. I would do my gibberish. They wouldn't understand a word, but it didn't matter. The main thing was that it was short, and it would certainly be different. I would pretend that I was terrified (that wouldn't be difficult!), straight from the Hielans, the broadest of broad Scots.

I heard my name announced. I tip-toed on to the stage as though frightened to make a sound, gazed round me fearfully, answered questions as to my name and my audition piece in a whisper, and then with a roar launched into my Double Scotch, fixing 'the house' with a wildly dramatic eye. The students roared and whistled their appreciation, and I could hardly hear the applause for the blood singing in my ears. My back was patted all the way to the cloakroom, where I threw on my coat with shaking hands. Susannah York

134

breathed 'Marvellous!' as I passed her, and I knew the heady sensation of having conquered fear.

When Sandy met me at the front door, I squeaked, without even a nod in the direction of breath control or voice-tone, 'I've been on in the *cabaret*. No rehearsal. No nothing. But I've been *on!*'

When he heard the full story, Sandy decided I deserved a decoration for valour. So, I may say, did I!

I didn't get a decoration, but I did get a small bolt from the blue in the shape of a telephone call. A call to me not at home, as I might have expected, but at RADA. We were in the midst of our breathing exercises when someone knocked on the classroom door and said there was a call from Glasgow for Molly Weir. The teacher nodded permission, eyebrows raised in some surprise, and I flew downstairs wondering who could want me so urgently as to have taken the trouble to trace my whereabouts. Could it be illness? Could brother Tommy have had a climbing accident? Was somebody dead? It was none of these things. It was Jimmy Logan, a famous name in the ranks of top Scots comics. I knew him well and admired him greatly. I always went to see him when I was in Glasgow, whenever he was appearing in the hilariously funny family shows at the old Metropole Theatre. I had been his landlady in the first film he ever made, and he had brought his new bride out to Pinner to see us.* I knew he had recently taken the plunge and bought the old Empress Theatre near St George's Cross in Glasgow, which he had re-named the Metropole, and whose policy he was changing from twice-nightly variety to drama and comedy plays. 'Jimmy!' I cried in surprise, 'What can I do for you?'

* Stepping into the Spotlight

He was highly amused to find me polishing up my breathing and movement techniques, for he was casting *The Lums*, the first play for the newly re-furbished theatre and he wanted me to take the part of the predatory widow Maggie Buchanan. John Grieve, a splendid Scots comedian was to play the local undertaker, the object of Maggie's passion, and her rival in love was to be that great comedienne, Renee Houston. I gasped and stammered in sheer amazement that such an offer should come out of the blue like this. They were planning a three month's run of the play, and there would be two to three weeks' rehearsals in Glasgow. Mentally I was saying to myself, 'That means about four months away from home and from the garden. I'd miss not only Sandy but the entire spring blossoming!'

Meanwhile Jimmy was saying he would send down the play for me to read, and suggesting we discuss salary.

I put back the receiver in a daze, and the class were enthralled to learn that I had just received an offer to do a play. All actors feel that news of anyone getting a job is lucky. It means jobs are going, and the next one might well be for any of them. Hope surges anew, and it's this eternal optimism which keeps all of us going in this overcrowded profession.

I couldn't have taken my classes at a better time. This offer was proof, if proof were needed, of the truth of Ben Lyon's oft-quoted maxim that 'activity breeds activity'. Or, as that lovely Scottish actress Meg Buchanan put it, 'A gaun fit's aye gettin'.'

As soon as the play arrived, I dived into it and discovered Maggie's was a gem of a part. All wide eyes and admiring squeaks every time the undertaker was within flirting distance, but maintaining a modest

136

demeanour, befitting her status as a respectable widow. Renee's part, as the rival Martha McTaggart, was enormous and I didn't envy her one little bit having to memorize all those pages, nor the length of time she would have to spend on stage establishing the plot. I wasn't too keen on having to wait backstage for over an hour before my own first appearance, for that is extremely nerve-racking, but Maggie as a character part was irresistible.

But what salary should I ask? I had no idea. So I went to my friend and mentor, Ben Lyon. Ben had been engaging actors for years, and knew the market outside in, and what exactly a name and a performance was worth. He paced back and forth, thinking aloud. 'Don't forget you'll be away from home for almost four months, honey,' he said, 'so that means that Sandy will eat more expensively.' I hadn't thought of that. 'You'll also have to take care of his expenses when he comes up to Glasgow,' he mused, 'and you'll have the extra cost of a flat up there.' He did a swift piece of calculation, while I threw in the fact that the low price of theatre tickets in Glasgow compared with London meant weekly takings for Jimmy couldn't be as high as down here, and the fares for me wouldn't be so costly in my native city. I didn't want to ruin Jimmy! So we arrived at a figure which Ben decided was fair to everyone, and I sent this off with my acceptance of the part. Sandy was elated to discover he would be visiting Glasgow almost every weekend, and was full of plans for going to Saturday football matches, and stravaiging over Scotland together on Sundays. All his original dismay over the length of my absence vanished like snow off a dyke in the excitement of such busy spring adventures ahead.

When the RADA classes came to an end, we were

all invited to do our 'party pieces', just to demonstrate that we could do other things besides merely moving and breathing. Remembering the success, in its small way, of my Scottish gibberish at the RADA cabaret and knowing full well I could never compete with our talented class in the world of Shakespeare and Milton, I decided to do Rabbie Burns' *Address to the Haggis*. I knew it would sound like a foreign language to their ears, and its very strangeness would preclude any serious criticism of my performance! As Barbara Lyon was wont to say when she took no chances, 'I'm no fool!'

So there we were, listening to speeches from Henry VIII's much-abused Queens, from the daughter of Lear, from Portia's plea for justice in *The Merchant of Venice*, from *Twelfth Night*, from *As You Like It*, and then, from yours truly, using a ruler for a dagger, Rabbie's *Address to the Haggis*. The class was mesmerized. It could have been double Dutch, for all they understood. But the *sound* of all those rolling rrrs, and the swift violence with the ruler pretending to be a dirk as I plunged it into the imaginary haggis, 'trenching your gushing entrails bright like ony ditch' left them gasping with admiration of our National Bard and his vivid language. I don't think the haggis has been addressed in a stranger setting, but it allowed me to discharge my duties with honour, and allowed no invidious comparison with the language of Shakespeare and Milton!

There was just time amidst all my preparations for Glasgow to go along to the Mermaid Theatre to see and meet my fellow-actress Renee Houston. The Houston sisters were the pin-ups of all Scotland at one time, but I had never seen them. So I determined I must meet Renee before we started rehearsals for the

Metropole. Renee was starring in *The Marriage Broker*, and Sandy and I enjoyed the performance from the front row. I knew three of the others in the cast, so I popped round backstage later to see them, and to say 'Hullo' to Renee. Sandy waited outside, in case Renee would be tired and want a little rest before the next performance which was due to start within the hour.

She was indignant at my treatment. 'Fancy leavin' yer man ootside,' she snorted. '*Of course* I'm no' too tired. Go and bring him in this minute.' It might have been my mother speaking. I burst out laughing when she instantly greeted Sandy with the old Glasgow welcome, 'Hullo son. Come in and sit doon.'

He, for his part, was quite mesmerized at the way Renee and I darted about the dressing room, assembling her clothes and props with never a pause in the conversation.

As the call-boy shouted 'Five minutes, please', she said to Sandy, 'Turn your back,' picked up her Russian hooked jacket and said to me, 'Fasten me into this, pet.' I had to run with her into the wings to do up the last hook as she swept on to the stage. I had never seen anyone, apart from Patsy Rowlands at the Players', use a stage so casually.

I could see there wasn't going to be a dull moment with her during *The Lums*.

A quick visit to Glasgow to be part of a judging panel for STV allowed just enough time to fix a flat for my Metropole season. I had a list of addresses, and I flew up and down endless flights of stairs, looked at moth-eaten carpeted floors, reeled back in dismay at smelly kitchens, and felt the onset of claustrophobia in attics with tiny windows about the size of a hard-back novel.

So when I saw a flat close to the BBC in a nicely situated terrace, all I noted were the clean new furnishings, the huge windows showing trees across the road, and the modern bathroom. I never even thought to examine utensils or blankets. I paid three months in advance, and left for London with a light heart.

A week later the neighbours waved me off from Pinner, and I had a long last look at them, then at our house, and then I closed the door on memories and determined to concentrate on the job in hand and to enjoy everything as it came.

At Euston Sandy and I were amused to find that the entire sleeping coach, apart from my compartment, was occupied by Russians. The list on the door showed names like Irlunski, Vorlok, Britneiva, Naruski, and we had a wee joke that I must be in the Siberian section. 'See you at the week-end,' Sandy called, and turned away.

We spoke truer than we knew of Siberia, for when the train arrived in Glasgow, those Russians really had snow on their boots – Glasgow was deep in sparkling winter dress, and looked like a Christmas card. A porter, who informed me he'd been in my class at school, took care of my luggage while I flew to the telephone box to let my friend Lavinia Derwent (of *Tammy Troot* fame) know that I had arrived. I invited her to join me for breakfast, and as my taxi drew up at my digs, I saw her hurrying over the bridge laden with electric kettle, an extra pair of sheets and pillow cases to supplement the ones I'd brought with me, and a lovely pot plant to make me feel at home.

Up and down the snowy steps we ran, carrying suitcases and parcels, and when all were safely stowed away, Lavinia and I sat down to bacon, eggs, tea, bread and butter brought from Pinner, and finished up

140

with a sample taste of my home-made marmalade. Lavinia declared it was the biggest breakfast she'd eaten for years. I could safely and truthfully say the same thing. There's nothing like a two-hour delay and biting cold to give one an appetite.

The door bell rang, and when nobody seemed troubled to answer it, I went and opened the door. On the mat stood the biggest of the Russians who had travelled on my train. We stared at each other in amazement. 'I haf seen you someveres beefore,' he said.

'You have,' I said solemnly, and slowly. 'On the train last night.'

'You too,' he said. 'You haf joost come?'

His face split in a huge grin, and I burst out laughing.

It was a million to one chance, but there they were, the entire sleeping coachload of Russians waiting outside to get into the self-same house where I was to be for three months. It turned out they were a trade delegation, and the man who rang the doorbell was the only member who could speak English. I discovered this within five minutes, when the hall 'phone rang with an inquiry about 'the Russians' and I ran to the top of the house to find someone. I was confronted with several large Russian ladies. 'Parlez-vous Français?' I asked.

Shake of the head was the only response.

'Sprechen sie Deutsch?'

No good.

So I seized the nearest pair of hands and uttered the single Russian phrase at my disposal, 'Dobra dinn', which, roughly translated, means 'How do you do?'

Good relations thus being established, with smiles all round, I fled downstairs.

I was to discover later, to my cost, that my position

141

on the ground floor made me the unofficial caretaker of the building. Although there were eight bells to be pressed, everyone rang mine. I let in the electricity man for all the flats. The mail for the whole house was handed to me. Furniture deliveries were signed by me. Milk boys rang my bell, and announced tersely each Friday, 'Mulk Money'. Prospective tenants demanded details of the flats from me. I answered the hall telephone, and even when the occupants of the flat were not present, the callers were quite amiably happy to talk to me instead, having recognized my voice as that of Molly Weir. Of the landlord there wasn't a sign. It was just as well, perhaps, for I'd have requested he pay *me* for my services, instead of my having paid him for my room.

And I'd certainly have had more than a few words to say to him about his blankets and utensils. Blankets which were grey and thin and, to quote my mother's words, 'Biled within an inch of their lives'. There wasn't a particle of heat in them. There was no eiderdown, and the thin mattress held no warmth. The teapot was big enough to have supplied tea for the Russian delegation, and the unsavoury frying pan was scoured and uneven. None of these did I see on my first visit when I took the flat, for they hadn't been installed. The proportions of the room had dazzled me, and naturally I had thought the domestic items would match this elegance, especially with the rent demanded. I had to borrow a fluffy double blanket from my sister-in-law, which I wrapped round me like an Indian brave, before sliding between my own sheets, while a hot water bottle bought around the corner added greatly to my comfort.

Rehearsals for *The Lums* were under the direction of my old friend and colleague Eddie Fraser, now head

142

of Light Entertainment with the BBC. He it was who taught me to tap dance, and who played Benny to my Susan in *Desert Song* when I was with the Pantheon. Having acted together and known each other over the years, we got on like a house on fire, and I could try out all sorts of comedy without feeling any sense of embarrassment or self-consciousness.

On the very first day of rehearsals, as I climbed the stairs to the rehearsal rooms at the top of the theatre, a voice called out to me, 'Not a dampt drop of hot water – what do you mean by it?'

I clucked in sympathy with the unseen complainer, for it was a freezing day, and said, 'Oh what a shame!'

Out shot a male figure from one of the dressing rooms, clad in singlet and kilt, hand clapped to his mouth in dismay. I recognized one of the Alexander Brothers!

'Oh, I'm sorry,' he said, 'I thought you were one of the cleaners!'

Every time I see those talented brothers, I think of that first meeting, which somehow set the tone for all the fun we had during our rehearsals.

It took me weeks to get used to the backstage geography of the Metropole. I have absolutely no sense of direction, and I vastly amused the stage manager one day when I called out from a long empty staircase, 'Where should I be?' It was just a piece of luck that he happened to be on his way to make the tea and heard me. And this was after I'd been working there for four or five days. My private nightmare was that one night, after we'd opened, I'd rush down the wrong staircase and miss the stage altogether when I ought to be on it. There were literally hundreds of stairs to go up and down, and Jimmy Logan's dad was convulsed with laughter when I announced the exact

143

number I had to traverse at every performance. 'She actually counted them,' he told somebody. 'Naebody else would dream of doing such a thing.'

'Aye they would, Jack Short!' I told him. 'Avril Angers did that very thing during the run of *Little Me* when she had five hundred stairs to negotiate nightly!'

'Ach that's where ye learnt yer tricks, is it,' he grinned, 'in London!'

Eddie worked out a great piece of 'business' for me one day during rehearsals. The undertaker and I were seated side by side and having a completely cross-purposes conversation. He was speaking of the romance of the cinema, while I imagined he was leading up to a proposal, and Eddie wondered if it would be possible for me to leap into John Grieve's arms. He thought it could be very funny, with John in his mourning clothes, complete with black tile hat, and me in auburn wig, scarlet jacket and pale pleated skirt. Eddie knew I was pretty supple, but even he was surprised, I think, by the success of this suggestion. One moment I was sitting starry-eyed beside John, and the next, from a sitting position I had sprung into his arms. The shock was so sudden, that John leaped to his feet, while I clung to him like a limpet, as he staggered about the stage trying to get rid of this unwanted appendage.

The cast shouted with laughter, and Eddie was delighted. John and I knew we'd struck gold!

This 'lover's leap' brought the house down at every performance, and John had to keep staggering about until the laughter had subsided, minutes later. And yet, in spite of the success of this arranged piece of comedy, some of the best effects can come about quite by accident, and are often the most fun to do. One night, after John had managed to get rid of my clinging arms, and was backing towards the table pursued by me, I saw that he was going to miss the table and I was afraid he would fall clumsily and hurt his back. So, instead of letting him do his own fall, I pounced on him and threw him back across the table and nearly landed on top of him!

The roar of the audience at his reaction of shock and horror, and mine of triumph, told us we'd found the perfect ending for Act II, and we kept it in for every performance thereafter. It had always been difficult to follow my 'lover's leap', and the scene as written had ended fairly tamely.

Now, with this accidental 'seduction', the comedy peaked to almost hysterical level and when John and I left the stage, the curtain fell to gales of laughter and a storm of applause.

It is the most marvellous feeling to build up comedy like this, and to hear an entire theatre shouting with true uplifting laughter. John and I gazed at each other with glee, perspiration running down our faces.

Renee was out on the landing, hands on hips, toes tapping.

'Imphm,' she snorted in mock confrontation, '*whit* hiv you two been up to? Naebody could follow *that*!'

The audience were still laughing when we reached our dressing rooms on the third floor.

Sandy used to come in every Saturday he was in Glasgow just for that one scene, and he said it made him laugh every time he watched it. Another ballet-dancer friend used to come in regularly to see if she could work out how I managed that leap through the air from a sitting position. Even as a dancer she didn't know how I did it. Neither did I! I just willed myself, and it happened! But I would never have thought of it myself. It took Eddie Fraser to suggest it, and that's the sort of skill which distinguishes a good director from the other sort.

Renee amazed me by her ability to speak under her breath during laughter or applause. We had to go through to the Lyceum Theatre in Edinburgh for a week, while the Metropole was being made specially beautiful for a charity visit by Princess Alexandra. This was very early in the run, and in spite of my voice exercises I had found projecting my delivery to the huge Metropole very difficult after years of radio, films and television.

One night at the Lyceum, as I was uttering a sure-fire laugh line, 'Ah've been up a' night wi' the bile,' I suddenly became aware of my voice ringing round the theatre with the sureness of a well-struck bell. Under the audience laughter, Renee said approvingly, 'You've found your range, hen.' I was so amazed by her coming out of character and speaking as herself that I nearly forgot my next line! What an enviable facility to be so completely at home on a stage that she had the poise and confidence to behave naturally without a shred of fear.

Tom Fleming came round to see us all after the first night in Edinburgh. He was about to take over the management of the Lyceum very shortly, and he was very complimentary and said he hoped for such packed enthusiastic houses when he was putting on a series of plays.

I couldn't persuade Moultrie Kelsall, my old drama producer from BBC Glasgow, to come along to see us though. 'Molly,' he had said, 'much as I love you, I just couldn't watch *The Lums* again.' As a one-acter it had been the stand-by of every amateur dramatic company throughout the length and breadth of Scotland in the drama festivals, and Moultrie must have had to sit through it a hundred times, as an adjudicator. Indeed it was because of its enormous success that it had been expanded to three acts for the theatre, and the reason why the part of Maggie, which I was playing, was so strong, was because it was the kernel of the one-acter. The reset was padding and extra plot, and although the whole piece was well-crafted and well-acted, the meat was concentrated on the strong plot of the rivalry between the two women for the undertaker, which had been the substance of the one-act original play.

We were back in Glasgow again at the Metropole when I celebrated my birthday. Somebody in the cast must have got hold of the date, for the entire cast sang on stage, at the end of the performance, 'Happy Birthday to you', with the audience joining in, and there were bouquets and presents. I made my first-ever curtain speech, thanking all of them, and was deeply thankful for all the experience I've had in opening bazaars and fêtes, or I'd never have dared to make such an impromptu speech. I threw a party in the dressing room afterwards, intending it to be entirely a surprise that it was my birthday. They had stolen my thunder by knowing the date, but my party was a great success all the same. I was so glad I had arranged not only drinks, but sausage rolls, biscuits and little savouries to give a nice tasty foundation. Everyone was so amazed to have food provided, you'd have thought I had invented it! By coincidence, friends from Pinner had turned up, and they joined the celebrations and were thrilled to meet Jimmy Logan, the theatre owner, in person. I laughed when the St John's Ambulance man said, drinking my health, 'Aye it's great tae hear a hale theatre laughing. This is the kind o' stuff that pits ye aff television!' He was right. It was really marvellous to play to packed enthusiastic houses.

CHAPTER SEVEN

Sandy was growing used to commuting between London and Glasgow, although he took a poor view of that rubbishy creaking bed in the so-called 'luxury flat'. He usually travelled by the overnight train from Euston, arriving in Glasgow in time for breakfast on Saturday mornings, so he only had to endure the frail divan-type bed on Saturday nights. It took just two sleeps for the matchstick legs to collapse! I was covered in confusion and embarrassment when I knocked on the door of the ground-floor flat, which I knew was occupied by a group of trainee shop-assistants. I wanted to know where I could contact our invisible landlord. After I had stammered out my problem, they waved an arm in the direction of the end wall, and there, ranged under the window were *fourteen* broken beds! Some were from the heavyweight Russians, some belonged to the boys, and the rest to the nurses who lived in the basement! The general opinion was that the rotten beds had been constructed by the landlord from matchwood! My broken item was added to the stock, to await collection at some unspecified date. They gave me a telephone number. At long last, I found myself dialling that landlord. I had a list of bones I wanted to pick with him!

When he answered, I felt like a detective who has successfully tracked down a suspect! And just like a shifty suspect, he was slippery as an eel. He had no idea when he would have time to call. Yes, yes, he would see that a replacement bed was supplied. (I noted he expressed no surprise that it *had* broken!). When would the bed be delivered? He wasn't sure. Some time today. He was astonished when I went on to itemize the other shortcomings. Nobody else had complained about the thin well-boiled blankets, or the Sunday-school trip sized kettle, or the grotty frying pan. 'But the flat is brand new,' I said. 'You told me so when you showed me round. So naturally I assumed all the contents would be new.' 'Who do you think you are?' he snarled, 'We have other flats. We're not just attending to you.'

With blinding clarity I saw it all! They simply re-routed those grisly utensils and bed coverings, some of which must have been in use since the First World War. It made no difference whether they were to be put into a luxury flat or a slum. He had three months' rent in advance, and I could like it or lump it.

After a ding-dong slanging match, when I threatened to write an article for the *Glasgow Evening Times* exposing the 'fittings' he had supplied for his 'luxury flat', complete with photographs, I wrung from him a promise to supply a smaller tea-pot and small saucepan. I had already supplied, at my own expense, a non-stick frying pan, for nothing would have induced me to insult an egg by placing it in the filthy rocky horror he had provided. I ended by instructing him to hire a fridge for me. He thought this was the final proof of my eccentricity! Fancy anybody objecting to food being kept in the room where they slept, or worrying about having to go daily shopping! But if I wanted to throw away good money on such fancy gadgets, he would get it for me. I could almost hear the wheels whirring in his shifty brain. The next tenant would be informed that the flat was 'complete with refrigerator' and charged accordingly.

I am convinced it was only the thought of the extra cash due to him for the fridge which brought him back to the house, but like the replacement bed, he arrived while I was absent and so confrontation was avoided.

In spite of the battles and disappointments over the flat, we didn't allow them to spoil our reunions at week-ends. We had some marvellous times exploring a wintry Scotland, and somehow managed to pack an enormous amount of sight-seeing into my single completely free day. On one never-to-be-forgotten Sunday we caught an early train and managed to get through to visit brother Tommy and his wife Rhona at Loch Lomond in time for a quick coffee, as arranged. The picnic food was soon packed into the boot of the car, and within the half-hour we were off, into countryside which was a frozen Christmas card. The nearer mountains showed dark streaks through the snow, and the distant peaks rose white and glittering. Mile after mile of magnificent countryside opened out before us, and I was dazzled by the brilliant green of the conifers in brilliant contrast against the whiteness of the surrounding scene. It was a world away from the theatre and the digs.

It was a dream world, a pageant specially arranged for our special enjoyment as we bowled along empty roads. But my brother is not the sort to allow you to sit in a car too long. Every now and again we were ordered out to descend a slippery track, negotiate a narrow bridge, or ascend an almost perpendicular rock ladder. Having organized us satisfactorily, he then found a favourite rocky outcrop on which he could test out his skills in rock-climbing, finding handholds and footholds which confirmed that muscle, eye, and judgement were all in good trim. He never missed an opportunity to pit his climbing experience against a tricky challenge and I have seen him stop the car, with a muttered 'Just a minute – that rock looks very interesting,' and before any of us could say 'Which rock?' he was stretching from one hold to the next, nimble as a mountain goat, and was back in the car before we knew it. The only comment might be, 'Ah that was very good. It was too wet the last time I passed it.' It never failed to impress me how natural such exercises were to him, or to amuse me that he was on such intimate terms with practically every rock in Scotland!

The main purpose of our excursion that day was to visit Glen Lyon, one of Tommy's favourite glens, and we looked forward to seeing it for the first time under his guidance. It opened in most dramatic fashion, one moment almost hidden and the next swallowing us up as though it meant never to let us find our way out again. We left the car and slithered on foot under a bridge, then up by a chilly waterfall, and at one point where my legs weren't equal to stretching to the next foothold, Tommy and Sandy each held out a hand and up I flew like a bird. Rhona doubled up with laughter. She said my legs never touched the rocks, and I appeared over the top of the bridge as though from a catapult. I was glad of all the exercise I had running up and down all those stairs backstage at the Metropole, for we walked and scrambled up hill and down dale for miles that Sunday.

In spite of the bitter cold, it was lovely to be able to have our picnic meal under the trees. We were all properly dressed for the weather, and had a great appetite for the hot soup, and the bread and meat we had brought with us. We didn't linger long over it though, for we were pressing on to Loch Daimh while the light held. I hadn't seen a frozen loch since the days of childhood when I spent a wintry convalescence at Kilmun after grannie died*, but this grey loch now reminded me of pictures of the frozen lakes of Norway. There was hardly any colour, and the ground under our feet was like iron. 'With Peary to the Pole,' I shouted, as Tommy took a picture of me complete with lined suede coat, extra socks and scarf, and woollen hat, and I may say when we saw that photograph later, it could easily have been mistaken for an Arctic background.

We had gone only a little way when Tommy lowered the car window and put a finger to his lips. We all fell silent, and Sandy and I heard for the first time the strange sound of two buzzards *mewing*. A hovering kestrel caught our attention, unmistakable in its manner of remaining airborne and almost still, before diving to transfix its unwary prey. But the supreme ornithological treat of this special day, without a doubt, was when Tommy, with some excitement in his voice, said, 'Look. Over there. See it?' We did see it. Soaring above us, in magnificent flight, was a golden eagle! It was breathtaking to observe this wild and free creature spreading great wings over the snowy wastes of Glen Lyon, providing a spectacular ending to our first visit to one of Scotland's loveliest glens.

As we drove back, Sandy said, 'All this will seem like a dream when I'm walking down St Mary Axe to the office tomorrow.'

If I was amused by Tommy's intimate knowledge of the Scottish rocks, I was equally amazed by his expert

* Best Foot Forward

awareness of the whereabouts of birds' nests. On a week-day visit to Loch Lomond, Tommy had shown me a brown owl's nest, which contained two large white eggs. I would have passed that tree without a second look, but he knew, from observing the parents' habits, that there was a nest. When Sandy and I went down to spend the following Sunday at the Loch, the nest now held two white fluffy owlets, lying as though in drunken sleep, eyes closed, and beaks which seemed parted in a smile. They were lovely, but I shuddered when I spied the corpse of a poor wee willow-warbler their fond mother had massacred for their dinner! I wonder how those campaigners who would preserve the life of every living species could convince mother owl that her fledglings' appetites and future survival are of no consequence? The animals know by instinct that the balance of nature must be preserved, cruel though it seems, for there could never be enough sustenance for all that hatch out successfully.

It was a most rewarding walk that morning, revealing not only a thrush's nest, and a chaffinch's nest full of gaping beaks, but a roe deer among the foliage of the young trees. The greatest excitement for me, though, was to *see* a cuckoo for the first time in my life. It was sitting on a tall tree and cuckoo-ing for all it was worth. Tommy showed me how to adjust the binoculars, and I was amused to see that the bird actually burped the sound out like a hiccup, the head popping forward with each *cuck*. While I had the glasses in my hand, I swung them round on a pair of herons, to admire them in close-up, when lo and behold a shoveller duck swam into sight as if saying, 'Have a look at my lovely colouring – faur better than yer grey herons!'

Sandy and I found it marvellously rewarding to visit the country with someone who knows it as well as my brother does. Little did we dream then that the day would dawn when Tommy would take thousands of people with him on similar journeys, via the television screen, in series after series of *Weir's Way*. And who could have foreseen that eventually he would become, by popular consent, top TV personality of the year in Scotland?'

'Aye, how does it feel to have a TV star in the family?' I was asked by a slyly-smiling director in a Glasgow TV canteen. It was clear he hoped to needle me by his inference that I'd been knocked off my perch! Wasn't I, after all, the Weir celebrity of the family? Or had been until Tommy's unexpected rise to the top of the charts!

I smiled serenely into the watchful eyes. 'I think it's *lovely*,' I said. 'He well deserves the honour. It's so rewarding to see such recognition for a man who presents a programme which reminds Scotland of its beauty and its heritage. And it's all his own!'

Collapse of snide party! I meant every word, and he knew it. There has never been any rivalry between us. Tommy, I may say, has never quite believed in his own TV success or in the brilliance of his programmes. Like all perfectionists, he always feels he could have improved on them here and there. But he has had to accept acclaim, his personal privacy vanished. A high price to pay for a man who always preferred the quiet places and the peace of the high mountain tops. He knows now why I tend to sneak away to self-catering cottages for my holiday breaks with Sandy, and to avoid public restaurants and big hotels whenever possible. Tommy's 'disguise' when he has business in town and is in a hurry, is to wear a conventional suit. If he were to wear his preferred plus-fours and pullover, topped with woollen bonnet, he wouldn't get a dozen yards without a conversation from 'fans'. Lovely, but exhausting when one has work to do, or is in a hurry, or just plain weary.

For me there is no such disguise. Whether in bikini, shorts, ballgown, or gardening clothes, I am instantly recognizable, and always regarded as available to the public. Sandy hates going shopping with me for this reason, for he says every purchase involves at least half-an-hour's post mortem with strangers or neighbours on the feebleness of Telly nowadays, or the bad language, and what am I going to do about it?

It's nice to be popular, but it doesn't exactly go hand in hand with a tranquil life.

In Glasgow, it was great fun at first to revel in the unique flavour of its humour. It was all around me, and it was expressed in all its variety everywhere. One night on my way to the theatre, a fully-loaded fire engine passed me and the whole crew roared out, 'How are you, hen? How's the Wee Red Lums? Mind you don't set them on fire!'

Another day, when I'd washed my hair and left it streaming down under my scarf to dry in the sun, a coalman called to his mate, 'Hey Erchie, look at the lovely wee blonde!' Then he twisted round as the horse plodded sedately on, 'Aye, you're a bonnie wee thing!'

I am nothing of the sort, as a closer look would have told him, but it was guaranteed to warm the cockles of my heart to be complimented in the very words of Rabbie Burns himself.

And on Sunday morning at The Barrows, known locally as 'ra barras', Glasgow's famous Sunday morning market, it was pure pantomime. We stood transfixed before vendors who were born comics. One pair, selling bedding, called out in perfect unison:

155

Bargains here worth every penny,
Hurry up noo, or ye'll no' get any!

They were encouraged and delighted by my laughter, for of course what was an old story to the other Glaswegians was, to me, back from the South where I'd been living for years, hilarious.

Fixing me with a hypnotic gaze, the pair produced a double-bed quilt and called over to me, 'Now Madam, can ye juist imagine this on top o' yer bed the night – wid it no' be juist perfect cuddlin' doon under this lovely quilt?'

They obviously expected no repartee, and jumped when I called back, 'No it wouldn't, for I sleep in a single bed.'

The crowd roared (by this time I had been recognized), and the two jokers fell on each other's necks crying, in mock dismay, 'She's goat us bate. She sleeps in a single bed!' I moved off before they grew more inventive!

In the taxi, I merely uttered the district 'Botanic Gardens', and the driver swung round to look at me. 'Oh heh,' he said, 'is that Mother's Pride ah've goat in ma cab? Hiv ye brought ony breid wi' ye?' This was a reference to an advert for Mother's Pride bread where I did the 'voice' of the little cartoon character.

In a tearoom one Saturday, when Sandy came up for his week-end visit, he was startled when a man sitting two tables away from us started off with 'Aye, no' a bad day,' and ended up giving us chapter and verse about his bad eyesight and his visits to the eye hospital. Sandy could hardly keep his face straight, but I was getting used to Glasgow's confidential style again, and could respond in full voice across the width of two tables without the slightest embarrassment. That's something that could never happen in London!

In the bakers' shops, when I was buying my mutton pies, potato scones and pancakes, everything came to a halt while my saleswoman announced to the heavens, 'Wid ye look at her? Hauf the size o' tuppence and buyin' a' that stuff. Where dae ye pit it a'?' 'Right enough,' a comfortably padded wifie echoed, 'it's no' fair, so it's no'. I've only goat tae look at a scone, an' Ah pit oan hauf-a-pun'.' This was delivered in the same breath as her order for 'Six pies. Hauf-a-dizzen doughnuts, hauf-a-dizzen pancakes, a dizen tottie scones, an' six aipple tarts.'

To aid and comfort the stout good-natured customer, I explained that it was my metabolism which accounted for my ability to consume all those carbohydrates and stay as thin as a whippet. 'It's like a fire with the damper out,' I said, 'I burn it all up.' And, warming to my theme, I said, 'Now if you have a *slow* metabolism, it's like a banked-up grate, there's no draught to burn up your food. So it stays with you as fat.' 'Oh, so *that's* whit it is, is it?' said the well-upholstered wee woman. 'Och Ah don't feel sae bad noo. It's no ma faut at a'. It's ma damper. Just wait tae Ah get hame an' tell ma man.' Then, turning back to the counter she said, 'Right missus, Ah'll have a walnut loaf for masel'. Ah've been tryin' tae cut that oot, but if Ah've nae draught in ma metal-bizzum Ah might as weel enjoy masel'.'

I felt, somehow, that my lecture had gone slightly adrift!

I didn't dare confess that my own weight was going down alarmingly, and my appetite required constant coaxing. It's hard for the public to realize what a strain it is working in the live theatre, in spite of all the fun we have. Renée lost over a stone, John Grieve lost five or six pounds, and I lost half a stone I could ill afford.

We poured with perspiration night after night, as if we were in a Turkish bath. It has nothing to do with fear, although that plays its part, it is the tension of appearing on top of our form week in, week out. It doesn't matter how tired an actor may feel or how off-colour, the public sits waiting to be entertained, and to appear always sparkling, always tireless, takes a tremendous toll of health and energy. The one essential re-charger of the batteries is sleep. Which in my case grew harder and harder to enjoy, with every night I spent in that noisy house.

It took me quite a while to realize mine was the only flat occupied by one person. Because the landlord found few individuals who would lash out such high rents for his 'luxury' apartments, and because he didn't live on the premises himself and was far removed from consequent noise, he didn't care how many shared each flat. His only interest was hard cash. There were never fewer than four trainees living in the flat next to mine. In the basement, four or five nurses shared a flat. They were all on the loose, as it were, and with no caretaker to supervise comings and goings, and no rules of behaviour laid down by the invisible landlord, it was bedlam. I don't think the youngsters gave a single moment's thought to the comfort of anyone else in the house. It was like living in a holiday camp.

The nurses had irregular shifts, as might have been expected, and the front door, which was by my bed-head, was slammed into the wee sma' hours of the morning. There was no attempt to close it quietly. Night after night I was shot into wakefulness as it crashed against my ear-drums.

This was bad enough, but the girls sneaked boy

friends home with them, and because of some freak in the ventilating system their giggling and chattering came straight up the shaft, and they could have been sitting on my pillow doing their courting! When there were no boy friends, they washed their hair, or had baths, and the gurgling and knocking of the pipes was like Chinese torture and made sleep impossible. All this went on at 2 A.M. and 3 A.M. as if it was the middle of the afternoon, which I suppose is what it seemed like to them.

When I spoke to them about it, they smiled and said they hadn't realized I could hear them, and carried on as before.

The boys in the back room held bottle parties three or four nights a week! I thought at first I had coincidentally arrived when several birthdays were being celebrated, and things would soon settle down. I was to discover that this was their normal life style. They were revelling in living away from parental discipline, free as birds. Their 'luxury flat' was the mecca for all the local trainees who met there during the course of their work. They came, like troubles, not in single spies, but in battalions! I grew to dread the sight and sound of cans and bottles of beer being delivered. The record player and the tape recorder shattered the ear-drums when I got home from the theatre, and it was often 4 A.M. and even 5 A.M. when the last guest staggered out. They used the hall telephone opposite my door to ring for a taxi. This was followed by the inevitable crashing of the front door by my head, and then the slamming of car doors under my window.

When I complained and begged for quiet, the boys seemed genuinely amazed that the music and the shouting could possibly be heard through *their* closed door and *my* closed door. And they could hardly credit that a 'wild actress' would actually want to go to sleep quietly, and alone!

How they ever worked with clear heads after such regular binges, I don't know. What I did know was that they were turning me into a sleepless nervous wreck, hardly able to find appetite to finish a boiled egg. Where would I find the strength to meet the demands of seven shows a week? My mother used to say 'sleep's meat to anybody that's no' weel.' Well, I was getting neither sleep nor meat, and my body knew it.

To add to the mayhem downstairs, the couple in the flat above me seemed very sociable, judging from the constant stream of male visitors coming and going all day. I decided not to speculate too closely as to what might be going on up there. I hadn't actually spoken to them, but when the 'husband' was involved in a noisy brawl under my window one morning around 1.30 A.M. it was the last straw. I wasn't going to give anyone the chance to tell me that such a noise wasn't disturbing me and keeping me off my sleep. I rose in righteous wrath, pulled on a dressing gown, and crossed to the telephone to dial 999. Next moment, three of his male friends seized my arm. 'Don't ring, hen,' they urged me, 'you'll juist get him into trouble, wi' the polis. We'll quiet him doon, so we wull. Away back tae yer bed, hen.'

I hesitated. I didn't really want to get anyone into trouble if it was just a flare-up which they could stop. They saw I was weakening. 'Aye, away back to yer bed. We'll sort it oot.'

I was hardly into bed when the row started up again, both protagonists yelling at the top of their voices and it went on until 2.30 A.M. Up I sprang once more, like an avenging fury. *This time,* I hissed, 'I *will* ring the police. If I don't get my sleep, I'll go stark staring mad.'

They saw I meant it. 'A' right, a' right, hen,' they said soothingly, turning me back towards my room, 'we'll get him up tae his bed, so we wull. Away you back an' get yer sleep.' For good measure they added, 'It's no' right, so it's no'.'

Well, they certainly got him to go up to his room, but the fight continued over my head for another hour!

I lay listening to the shouting, wide awake. It was a madhouse. I had landed in a madhouse among people who needed no proper rest at night. There was never any sense of quiet or night silence. Or was I the one who was mad? I was doing seven shows a week. I looked and felt a wreck. In the daytime I walked about like a zombie, and my weight was down to six stones. I began to get the strange disorientated feelings I had after grannie died, and although commonsense told me that I ought to move, rent or no rent paid in advance, I knew I hadn't the strength to look for another room or to pack my cases.

Strangely enough, Sandy experienced none of this noisy behaviour, for everyone seemed to go home at week-ends and he was only with me on Saturday nights. I put on a good act for him, for I knew he would worry. I couldn't disguise my thinness, but this he put down to the tensions of the theatre!

Complaints to the landlord met with the bland response (over the telephone of course – he was never more than a disembodied voice) that I must be very sensitive to noise, as I was the only one to complain. 'Of course I'm the only one,' I cried. 'Why would the others say anything, when they're the ones who are *making* the noise?' I dropped the receiver. There was no help from that direction. God knows what the

Russians made of it all. Perhaps they didn't hear it at the top of the house. For their sake, I hoped that was it.

As the weeks passed, I reached the nervous stage where I was scarcely sleeping at all. Even on fairly quiet nights, and there were the odd one or two, I lay tensed, waiting for a row or a party to start up. Finally, four parties within the space of six days destroyed sleep completely. I really did lie awake the whole of one night without so much as an hour of oblivion. And as I lay there, in despair, staring at the ceiling, I made a vow. 'If I am still alive in the morning,' I promised myself, 'I will never spend another night in this house.' And I never did. In my utter exhaustion, I felt that God had shown me what to do.

The next morning, as though following Divine instructions, I walked in a sort of dream and knocked on the door of a lady I knew by sight, who, the boys told me, had complained to the police about the noise from our flats. When she opened the door, she started to say 'Good morning,' but something in my face stopped the polite greeting. 'What is it?' she said. 'Will you help me?' I asked her, 'I am desperate.' And I repeated the words I had rehearsed as I lay awake in the darkness. I asked her to consider whether she might be able to put up a bed for me for the remaining fortnight I would be in Glasgow. 'Think about it,' I whispered, close to tears. 'Don't answer me now. I have to do a broadcast talk, and I'll come in to see you when I get back.'

She looked at me, aghast at my pallor. 'I don't know how you've stuck it as long as you have,' she said. 'We're three doors away, and *we* can't get to sleep for that damnable din. That landlord ought to be locked up.'

I stared at her, silently, praying for deliverance, and a quiet bed.

'You don't have to wait for an answer, my lass,' she said. 'I'll find a corner for you somewhere, even if it's in the middle of the sitting room. It'll juist be to sleep?' 'Yes,' I said, hardly daring to believe salvation was at hand, 'I'll leave everything in the flat and eat there, and just come along to your place to go to bed.' 'Right you are then,' she smiled, 'we'll see you tonight. I'll have your bed ready.' I pressed her hand, unable to speak.

That was the first good thing that happened to me that day.

The second good thing was Archie Lee. Archie and I had arranged this broadcast talk weeks before when I had been in my usual good spirits, and although I now felt strangely light-headed, I thought I would somehow manage to get through it. I could not. I got the length of half a dozen sentences, when my voice disappeared to a mere thread of sound, and Archie thought I was going to faint. He sent for coffee, leaned back in his chair, gazed at me with great concern and said, 'Now what is all this about, Molly? I've never seen you look so exhausted – are you ill? We have plenty of time, so tell me, what is the matter?'

Struggling to hold back my tears, not very successfully under Archie's sympathetic responses, I poured out the whole story of this endless assault on my nerves by nights of incessant noise, culminating in last night's ordeal of not having closed my eyes for an instant.

There was a little silence while we sipped our coffee.

'I'll tell you what we'll do,' he said. 'We won't rehearse at all. We'll go straight for a "take", and we'll do it in short spells. Just a few minutes at a time, not to tax your strength, and you must stop whenever

163

you want. I can easily put it all together in the editing later.' Archie was a senior talks and features producer at the BBC, skilled and experienced, and I was in good and safe hands. 'Now finish your coffee while I make a telephone call.'

While he waited for someone to answer, he put his hand over the mouth-piece, 'I'm ringing my doctor's wife. She's a member of the local baths, and I'm going to ask her to take you down there and sign you in. I'm sure what you need is to lie in their relaxation room, wrapped in warm towels, and then have a gentle soothing massage. Afterwards, she'll take you back to your room and you must promise to sleep for another hour before you leave for the threatre.'

I stared at him in amazement. I could never have thought of such a 'cure' in a month of Sundays. But it sounded so wonderful and so caring that I was in danger of dissolving in tears again.

As the 'phone kept ringing out, Archie said anxiously, 'I just hope she's in.'

She was in.

And she carried out Archie's suggestion to the letter.

She was the third good thing that happened to me that day, and I will never forget any of my three good angels. For I am sure that, between them, they saved me from having a complete breakdown.

Later, when I listened to that talk on the air, I could hardly believe that it had been made under such melodramatic circumstances. Archie had done a good job there, and I sounded as chirpy as a cricket.

When I went to the theatre that night, I felt rested and calm, and I gave the first performance I had enjoyed for weeks. John Grieve said to me, shrewdly, 'Aye, I can see you've had a better sleep. You've got more strength about you tonight.' Your fellow-actor

164

knows the ups and downs of health hazards, and John was aware I'd been peaky for a long time. Not enough to affect my over-all performance as far as the public was concerned – make-up and technique can cover a great deal – but those who share the stage with you sense the subtle difference in attack and 'zing'. It was marvellous to feel again real pleasure in audience laughter and applause.

I knew I was already feeling more balanced when I had been able to respond to the wifie sitting next to me in the bus *en route* for the Metropole. She had uttered a squeak of alarm at the sight of me and said, 'My heavens, hen, you're awfu' late. Should you no' be in the thee-atre the noo?' She had been at the show the previous week and was sure my watch had stopped. She didn't realize that once a show has been running for several weeks, actors know almost to the second the exact time they need leave home, start making up and getting dressed for their first entrance. When I explained all this to her, and that anyway I didn't come on until well into the first act, she said fervently, 'Oh Thank Goad it's a' right, hen. Ah wis feart they wid gie ye the sack if ye werenae there.'

I was amused and touched by her anxiety, and felt once more it could *never* happen in London.

I walked home from the theatre that night, knowing the satisfied feeling that I had given a good perform-ance, and had worked well with John, getting all the laughs our comedy ought to receive if we're in tune with each other. I wanted, too, to feel the cool night air on my cheeks and I wanted, above all, to savour the knowledge that I need not sleep ever again in the hellish background of those flats. After my light supper in the bed-sitter, I went out into the night with my little case containing nightgown and slippers. I closed the door thankfully and quietly behind me, leaving an open-mouthed nurse on the telephone to wonder where on earth I was going with a case after midnight.

The revels were starting up, and I left them to their raucous behaviour.

I timed it just right. The party went on till 6 A.M. and the police had to be called! But I was blissfully unaware of this. I was having the first peaceful sleep in the house of my good angel.

And then, almost before I realized it, it was our last week in Glasgow. Dozens of friends and relatives came to the final performances, realizing it was now or never if they were to see me playing the predatory widow to John Grieve's undertaker, in *The Lums*. We had lovely reunions in my dressing room, for now that I was feeling more rested, I had the enthusiasm for such socializing. It had been sadly absent for weeks. One interesting and unexpected visitor was Bing Crosby's security guard! He had had to visit England at four hours' notice because his dear sister in Corby was dying. When all was over, he came through to Glasgow. He was an avid follower of my weekly page in the *People's Journal* which was sent to him in America, he told me, and so he knew that I was appearing at the Metropole. He had made up his mind he would see the show or 'bust' in the attempt.

A most courteous gentleman, he had asked the manager's permission to send round some chocolates, and with typical American generosity 'some chocolates' turned out to be a 3lb box as big as the top of the chest of drawers. He hadn't even asked to see me, as he didn't know me personally, but the manager guessed I'd want to say 'thank you' in person and he brought him round at the end of the show. Some old friends of my mother were visiting me that night too, and they

166

were thrilled to see the photographs he showed us of Bing's estate, not to mention the security chap himself in the foreground togged up in his uniform of light shirt and trousers, peaked cap, with gun at the ready at his waist! He told us he'd never had to use it in anger! And added 'thank goodness'. He invited me to 'drop in' any time I was out California way, and he told me gallantly that I was far bonnier than my photographs. A nice touch of the blarney which was very welcome after all my sleepless nights and loss of weight.

One person who shared my sensitivity to noise was my old friend and mentor, Ben Lyon. My noisy flat would have driven him crazy. By coincidence, during that last week in Glasgow, a man who came and sat beside me in the bus told me he had been stationed in a big house nearly opposite Ben and Bebe during the war. Ben had come across one night and asked, very nicely, if the billet's radio could be turned down after 11 P.M. as the noise was driving him mad, and he had heavy rehearsals and shows to do which necessitated him getting his rest.

I laughed, because it was so like Ben. He couldn't even stand the jingling of my charm bracelet, much less a non-stop radio blaring out. This man now told me that he had managed to get the rest of the lads to co-operate, and one day when he met Bebe with Ben and was introduced to her, Bebe gave him a dozen tickets for the Palladium for himself and his mates. She also organized hospitality for them in the bar at the interval and gave them a marvellous time, just as a small 'thank you' for letting them have a bit of peace and quiet at nights. When I told Ben about this encounter, he was highly amused, as well as pretty impressed that the man remembered the incident so vividly.

We finished up the short season in the Metropole in glorious style, with two Saturday houses filling our ears and hearts with laughter, and, after two weeks of refreshing sleeps, I felt in great form that night. Strong as a horse and ready for anything. It could also have been the thought that it was for the last time, and that I was going home next day. Although it is sad too when a show breaks up. You live in very close fellowship with fellow-actors, because it is such a personal relationship involving us in imaginary emotional situations, and then like the end of a romance, it is all over and you may never see any of them again. Although we all say 'Oh it's been lovely, let's hope we'll work together again soon,' we know that it is practically a certainty that we'll never work with each other in quite that way ever again. Each goes his own road, hardly ever to unite as a complete company. It's a bit like the friendships made in the army, or the romances of shipboard life, intense while they last but seldom spilling over into everyday life.

We exchanged presents with those with whom we had scenes, cleared our dressing tables, and called out 'Goodnight, goodnight,' and went our ways.

I gave all my bouquets to Mary, who had so willingly provided that welcome bed, and she said she'd never had so many flowers in her house at once, and was only sorry she wasn't having a wedding to show them off.

As for the packing at the flat! Sandy and I thought we would never get it finished. We ended up with six cases we'd to sit on to close them. Added to these were two huge cardboard boxes with all the stuff I'd acquired during my three months in Glasgow.

Irresistible embroidered sheets for our beds at home. Two new dressing gowns. A pair of light-weight quilts. Beautiful double sheets and pillow-cases from Rhona's mother to mark my return to a Glasgow theatre. And even then we crammed things into a shoulder bag and a picnic hold-all!

The fridge and larder had to be emptied, and sorted out into two heaps, one for Lavinia and one for Mary. It was like a wee flitting. Plastic bucket and vase for Lavinia. Coal and lighters for Mary. Sauce for Lavinia. Salad cream for Mary. Frying pan for Lavinia. Kitchen utensils for Mary. And so on, and so on. Later, I had a hilarious note from Lavinia saying it was just like opening a Christmas box, for she was always coming across another unexpected treasure which she pounced upon with joy. We had included a box of Sandy's home-made fudge in her 'treasure chest', and she said she had ham and egg and fudge for breakfast!

I managed to say goodbye to the Russians before I left. The one who spoke German was elected spokeswoman, while the others stood in a circle nodding and smiling. She wished me good luck, good health and much success. We all shook hands and beamed till our jaws ached to make up for our lack of a common language. The spokeswoman informed me I had a 'figure like a young girl' and they all roared with laughter as the fattest lady measured her own wide hips with outstretched hands, and then brought them in to a tiny space and held them against me.

They were delightful neighbours and I only hope they didn't think all Scots behaved as noisily as the other occupants of that house. I learned that when I was asleep in the afternoons, they had told the wee six-year-old Russian child, 'Miss Molly sleeping', and raised a finger to their lips to make him tiptoe through the hall. He was learning English, and loved to say to me any time we met, 'Ow arr yew?' When I would say 'Very well thank you, and how are you?' he would grin with delight and say, 'verree vell, a-thank yew.' He was a rare wee chap, destined to be a footballer, judging from the skill he showed in the park when playing football with his father. I used to see them every night on my way to the theatre, and I wondered what the Glaswegians in the park would have said if they had realized the couple playing so happily nearby were Russians. It was a pity they couldn't have chatted with them. Ordinary people can get on so well together, it's just when politics and ideology interfere that hostility rears its ugly head.

The journey back to London was long and slow, the usual Sunday crawl to allow for engineering works on the line, but I didn't care. I was sitting back relaxing for the first time for weeks, and I had the contented feeling that I had carried out my job to the best of my ability and hadn't faltered by the wayside, sleep or no sleep.

Our neighbours met us at Pinner station and made short work of stowing all that luggage into the boots of their two cars. 'Did you take the kitchen stove?' Stan asked when he saw the array of cases and boxes.

In minutes we were turning into the lane, and there was our house, the house I hadn't dared think about for such a long time or I'd have wanted to run straight home.

Edna had done a lovely flower arrangement in our hall, and it was a perfect picture of broom, roses, antirrhinum, snow-in-summer, daisies, ivy leaves and delicate greenery. But when I opened the kitchen door, her last touch was just too much for my emotional state to take calmly. There, sitting in the centre of the table, was a chocolate cake with a marzipan 'plaque' on top, and written across it were the words 'Welcome Home Molly'. One look and I burst into tears, completely disgracing myself and transfixing everyone with amazement. Edna said afterwards I looked like a wraith, and she was firmly of the opinion that I must never go away again for such a long spell in the theatre. She refused to believe it was lack of sleep which had reduced me to Twiggy-like proportions.

That first cup of tea from our very own china was delicious, and we all enjoyed a slice of the chocolate cake. After a token piece of unpacking, it was nearly midnight before I knew the deep, deep peace of my own bed, my own pillow, with not a sound outside to disturb the silence. It was perfect.

As for Sandy, he wore the smile that won't come off! But he said pensively, 'It's lovely to have you home again, but I'll miss all my wee jaunts north of the border. The week-ends will be pretty tame, after doing my "David Frost" act of commuting between London and Glasgow all those weeks!'

'Well,' I teased, 'will I go away again? Will I look for another play?'

'Just you try,' he said, 'just try, and see what happens. I'm looking forward to having the cook back again.'

Next day, when I went out to look at the garden, it was all so new and so exciting that I felt as if I'd been reborn. I had left Pinner in frost and snow, with hardly a leaf daring to unfold, and now it seemed as though a technicolour fairy had waved a magic wand over the scene for my special delight. I keenly regretted that I had missed the blooming of all the tulips and the hyacinths I had planted. The daffodils too were finished, and most of the wallflowers, but the roses were bursting forth in glorious colour and scent. French marigolds blazed down the side of the path, aubretia spilled everywhere over the stones in the rock garden. Laburnum tassels hung in long golden racemes and showed up brilliantly against the while lilac. Fruit was forming on the bushes, and the double daisies, grannie's favourite, marched thickly down the edge of the front path and round the circular bed where, for the first time, the white broom was in flower. The big yellow broom by the front door looked a picture, and the little seedlings and plants Sandy had put in were healthy and strong looking.

It all looked so lush to me, and represented so much work, that after living in one room for months, I now realized why people always said disbelievingly, 'Do you do all this yourself?' I realized it was going to take me a long time to sort myself out, and return to my regular routine of cooking, cleaning, writing and gardening.

It felt marvellous to be living in a house again, after one apartment, but I found I had actually forgotten where the light switches were in several rooms, and I couldn't remember which keys were for the front door, or the place for the garage keys, or where I kept my tea caddy! I felt like Rip Van Winkle. I had put Pinner and the old homestead more firmly out of mind than I had realized.

Sandy had worked hard in the week before my return and had polished everything to shining perfection. He had done all the white paintwork in the kitchen, and then freshened ceiling and frieze. To complete the job, the window-cleaner had arrived at the psychological moment, so all the windows sparkled to match.

I had forgotten how much colour there was in our place and it was like being presented with a new house all over again. Although the flat in Glasgow looked on to a wild part of the Botanic Gardens, I had felt separated from it, but here when I wakened that first morning, it seemed as though my bed was right in the middle of the garden. Everywhere I looked, my eyes rested on trees in rich summer foliage. I kept rushing to the windows saying, 'It's beautiful, just beautiful,' stopping so often to look that the rest of the unpacking took the whole forenoon.

It wasn't so easy finding places for my things in half-filled drawers and wardrobes as it had been stowing them away in a completely empty flat, but everything eventually found a home and in a surprisingly short time I was fairly tidy.

The linen-basket overflowed twice with clothes which bore make-up marks everywhere. However hard you try to remove greasepaint at the end of each perform-ance, it is well-nigh impossible to keep it off your clothes. The clothes-line presented a remarkable con-trast to the dolly's washing I used to do in Glasgow, where the score was two tea towels, two pillow cases, half-a-dozen hankies, a nightie, and a couple of under-garments at a time. But it had been thanks to my passion for getting my Glasgow washing into the open air that I had got to know the good angel Mary, whose drying green ran parallel to the one for the flats, and with whom I was on nodding and chatting terms before I had occasion to throw myself on her mercy. So I hadn't been a complete stranger to her.

Now, as I surveyed the rows of freshly-washed garments blowing in the sunny breeze, I could allow my thoughts to wander over many happy memories of my stay in Glasgow. I thought of that nice park-keeper in the Botanic Gardens who bought 7lb of peanuts every week from his own wages, to feed the birds. An

173

ordinary Glasgow man you would have said, looking at him, but one with enough care and imagination to place the little heaps of nuts carefully on top of the pole supporting the litter baskets, so that the marauding pigeons wouldn't find a foothold to rob the little finches and the blue tits. He and I had rare long chats about our feathered friends, and he gallantly carried my shopping for me on several occasions when he thought the bags were too heavy for me.

And I thought of the children.

I saw a bigger difference in them than in anything or anyone from my childhood. They looked so healthy and well-cared for, and so well-dressed. No ragged breeks for them, and no hungry-looking faces. I watched them staggering uncertainly towards the swings in the parks, looking so sweet and cuddly and attractive; sturdy toddlers who squealed with excitement when they managed to kick a ball thrown by mammy or daddy. I wonder at what age they turn into the noisy fiends who give us cheek and drive us mad at times?

But above all, I remembered the untranslatable Glasgow humour. The warmth, and the friendliness, which gave me a dozen laughs every time I went into a shop or travelled on a bus.

Somebody said to me recently that this humour and friendliness was bound to lessen as a new generation came along who hadn't shared the involvement or the values we knew in childhood. But I wonder. A Pinner neighbour was up in Glasgow very recently, visiting a relative in hospital. Because it was a day of sleet and mud and she was wearing thin shoes, she had covered them with two plastic bags to shuffle as best she could with dry feet from the hospital door to her car. She hadn't gone two yards, she told me, when she felt a hand firmly placed under her elbow, and a wee Glasgow man was saying reassuringly, 'Ah'll help ye across the road, hen.' She could hardly tell me for laughing, this well-dressed middle-class lady, and she had loved this evidence of what she knew to be true Glasgow friendliness. I rejoiced with her that Glasgow's heart seemed still to be beating warm and strong, even in the hard days of 1983, and there was still a helping hand willingly offered. Long may it be so, I thought, and long may the Glasgow character survive.

And glad as I was to be home, I knew I was going to miss the ease with which I could flee around Glasgow compared with London. Faced with London's sprawling suburbs and enormous distances, I remembered with amazement how in Glasgow I could, in a morning, dash round the Botanic Gardens for my constitutional, whip into town and have my hair done, take a bus out to Milngavie and do my voice exercises as I marched round the reservoir, and *still* be back at the digs in time for lunch around two o'clock. I wouldn't dream of doing more than one of such things in London. In Glasgow, although my friends were scattered all round the city, there wasn't one of them who couldn't be reached within forty minutes of my flat. In strictly boundary terms, Pinner is actually designated a 'village', but I know beyond any shadow of a doubt that it is my native Glasgow which is really the village, with every advantage that this old-fashioned name implies.

CHAPTER EIGHT

When I received an unexpected invitation to attend the big Gala Night in celebration of Scotland at Simpson's beautiful store in Piccadilly, I was spared one worry at least. I would have no problems over what to wear, for I had a wardrobe of TV gowns, most of them worn only once. I decided on the gold tissue outfit. It was a dazzler, but because it had become so horribly creased on the journey to the ball when I wore it the previous year, this time I would carry it over my arm in a plastic cover and change in the cloakroom at Simpsons. There I would rendezvous with my friend Maureen Burnett, and we would go into the reception together.

We were going without our husbands, for we had been invited as Scottish journalists-cum-celebrities, on our own, and we knew it would be easier for us to explore the special displays throughout the store, without the guilty feeling that husbands would be bored hanging about waiting for us. We could wander around, taking notes, free as birds, but we were glad we would have each other's company for that initial appearance at the reception.

I arrived at Simpsons a good half-hour early, to allow me time to change into my glad rags. The first shock came when I asked to be directed to the ladies' cloakroom.

I was informed by two elegant young gentlemen in charge of tickets that there was no ladies' cloakroom as such! Cloaks were to be left in the main hall, where we stood. It was as unexpected as though they had told me there were to be no toilets!

176

'What!' I said, my voice rising to a squeak of dismay. 'Have I to change my dress here? Before your very eyes?'

They recoiled as though I had uttered a terrible oath.

Before they could say a word, another thought struck me. Where on earth was I to meet Maureen now? Simpsons had six floors, every one of which was being used to display the riches, the products and the charms of Scotland. If there was no ladies' cloakroom, where would we find each other?

Even had I chosen to do so I was not going to be allowed to perform a strip-tease in the hall, and after some discussion with everyone in sight, including the lift girls, I was whirled up to the fourth floor. It was exactly like being behind the scenes of a dress rehearsal for a play, nerves and all. The organizers were running about going mad, setting out tombola prizes, placing descriptive cards on everything, arranging dresses for the mannequin parade, answering queries, pushing past with huge boxes, and certainly *not* amenable to having the problem of what to do with me added to their hectic time-table.

I knew how they felt. I hated anyone coming to my dressing room when I was preparing for a show, so I solved the problem for myself by creeping into a changing cubicle. As I shed jersey and skirt, rejoicing that the gold tissue dress sparkled without a single crease, I could hear feet pattering all round me, and voices rising as the organizers checked the time and began to panic. I felt like the small still centre of a whirlpool.

They didn't even notice me when I at last crept out and headed for the lift again, in order to leave my coat and case in the ground floor cloakroom.

177

I placed myself strategically beside the lifts, praying Maureen hadn't arrived while I was changing, and might even now be combing all six floors in search of me. I amused myself studying the fashions of the arriving guests, and was alarmed to see so many mini-skirts. 'Black Tie' had been specified, and I hoped I wasn't going to be the only female to interpret this as meaning long dresses for the ladies. Twiggy appeared in a pink silk mini-dress which I swear couldn't have taken more than a yard of material, if that. Under-neath, she wore long white crocheted stockings, and looked like a pouting pretty-as-a-picture child, out far too late for her own good! Her hair was like pale gold silk, very short and cut in a sort of zig-zag style, and it was a wonderful contrast to meet her years later during rehearsals for a TV play I was in with her fiancé, when she was determined to encourage its silken length. She was quite beautiful by this time, and had a quality of stillness on the screen which spoke 'star' loud and clear. But all that lay ahead.

Meanwhile minis were arriving by the dozen it seemed, displaying underneath silver Lurex, or purple, or pink stockings. And then, at last, Maureen breezed through the door in vivid turquoise sequinned top and, thank goodness, *long* matching velvet skirt.

The mannequin parade was announced, and we managed to squeeze in beside my old friend Hattie Jacques. Hattie was just back from filming in Rome with Peter Sellers, and was absolutely exhausted, but it had been a busy happy time, she whispered, although she hadn't seen as much of the glories of Rome as she would have wished. It's always the way in films, foreign locations sound marvellous, but all the actor does is eat, sleep and work!

The parade started, and mini-skirts were definitely

'in'. There were dozens of them. Just when Hattie, Maureen and I decided they were not for us, one man, emboldened by the sight of a bloomer-suit inches from his hands, pinched the model before our very eyes! That confirmed it. They were decidedly *not* for us.

Afterwards, Hattie said she was too tired to eat and headed for the tombola, but Maureen and I made our way towards the queue waiting for the buffet supper. We found ourselves surrounded by about seven or eight very tall, very good-looking men, two of whom seized us by the hands and sat us down. 'Stay where you are,' they said. 'What would you like? We'll get it for you.' Who on earth could they be, with such dashing good looks and not a partner between them? Before we could start guessing, they were back with plates of lobster tails and salad, sweets and drinks. My curiosity about our dashing Galahads vanished at the sight of the delicious food, and I fell to with a will. Maureen, however, wasn't to be side-tracked and after a few murmured exchanges on my other side, I heard her break into peals of laughter. Our escorts were CID men, who had been sent to organize proceedings if Princess Margaret decided to put in an appearance. They had chosen us to be their 'cover' until she turned up! So Maureen and I were the only people among the guests who knew HRH might be arriving.

I joined in the laughter, delighted at having such a splendid tit-bit for my *Journal* column.

Our merriment attracted quite a bit of attention from the other guests, still patiently queuing for food, and I'm certain all this male attentiveness must have suggested we were Royalty enjoying ourselves incognito, or that our chunky jewellery was real, and worth a king's ransom!

Princess Margaret didn't turn up after all, so we had

179

eight partners between us! And us leaving our husbands at home so we could concentrate on our notes! It needed little encouragement to get us on to the postage-stamp-size dance floor, where a beat group in tartan were cleaving the eardrums with pop music. Round we went, twisting away like a couple of sophisticated Londoners, Maureen and I, while the CID chaps, looking nothing like the conventional idea of policemen, danced opposite us with great expertise.

In one of my more inspired 'twists', I banged back to back with someone, and when I turned round I found myself looking into the eyes of Paul Getty, the richest man in the world, who might have been Barbara Lyon's father-in-law had Barbara not changed her mind and broken the engagement.* I was amused to see him (after mutual apologies) twisting sedately away with his beautiful partner, expression solemn as a judge, with no appearance of enjoyment.

While we were dancing, one of the CID lads decided to try his luck on the tombola, and when he returned he was wearing a deerstalker hat he'd just won. He was also carrying a gorgeous pullover, and holding three little flat packages. The packages held nylons, and he presented me with two pairs, because they fitted my small feet and were no use to Maureen. The third pair he kept for his wife!

Like two Cinderellas, Maureen and I left before midnight. Eightsome reels were being watched and applauded by the English guests and our handsome guardians of the law were keeping a watching brief over everything. We could hardly keep our faces straight as we wished them all a very good night, all eight of them. We decided it wasn't often two respectable

* Walking into the Lyons' Den

180

married Scottish lasses could attend such a grand gala evening and end up practically in the arms of the law!

I don't know what Maureen's Alastair thought about the whole adventure, but Sandy rather reluctantly agreed it was all right that I had accepted nylons from a strange man, because the strange man had been a policeman!

I always seemed to get into hilarious situations when I was out with Maureen. The day we went to a wig shop we had the whole place in an uproar, and the girls said it was the best possible encouragement to trade, for it ended up with everyone buying a wig, even those who had only gone along for company. And that included Maureen. I was the one who wanted a wig. I always had very fine hair, maddeningly fine, and when I grew it long I could seldom if ever go without a hat or a head-scarf. It either flew into witch-like wisps or fell down, and I longed for a short wig of strong Continental hair as a change from this infuriating Anglo-Saxon spider's web fineness.

When I mentioned this tentatively to Sandy, he shuddered with horror. He said he couldn't bear to see me take off a wig before going to bed, so I abandoned the whole idea.

Then one day when I was auditioning for a commercial, the producer said to the short-haired girl who was reading with me, 'What a pity you have such short hair, it looks all wrong beside Molly.'

The girl at once raised a hand to her head, whipped off the 'short hair', saying, 'Oh but this is a wig,' and a curtain of long hair fell to her waist!

I gave a jump. My longing for a wig came back with a fine frenzy, for here, standing beside me was somebody else with exactly my problem. She confirmed that it was a great idea, and thoroughly enjoyed changing her whole appearance and personality, not at the drop of a hat, but at the popping on of a wig.

She gave me the name of the establishment where she'd bought hers. It was one of the few in London which sold reasonably-priced machine-made wigs of real hair which they could tint to match one's own hair exactly. That was *just* what I was after. It wasn't an expensive disguise I wanted, it was a modest transformation to a style which would allow me to go bareheaded in the summer-time, and possibly change my looks for TV. A real cheat-the-public in fact!

Maureen came with me on the day I was to collect it, and that was when the fun began. She was only supposed to be there to act as friend and true critic, and to lend support if it looked awful. The moment I put it on my head, there was instant unreserved approval. 'Oh Molly, it's *lovely*,' she enthused. 'Oh, I want to try one too.' With far greater daring than I had shown in merely choosing to have a wig in my own hair colour, Maureen seized a light honey-blonde curly wig and pulled it over her straight jet-black hair. The transformation was stunning. The honey-blonde tones were beautiful against her fair skin and dark blue eyes. The whole appearance was dramatically altered. Instead of my raven-haired friend of the quiet serious manner, I was confronted by a dizzy blonde who actually started *behaving* like one, giggling and running from one mirror to the next.

Emboldened by this, I seized a red wig and tried it on, and at once looked the double of my niece Maureen. The girl at the next mirror was watching us, and laughingly swapped her blonde wig for a jet-black curly mop, and dissolved in helpless laughter at the effect. Suddenly, everybody at the mirrors was swapping wigs, laughing and rushing about showing the changed

182

appearance to their friends. The shop assistant said we must come back soon! We had been great for trade.

As for Maureen, she not only bought the blonde wig, she wore it to go home. She told me afterwards the effect it had on people was quite startling. Tall dark ladies look capable and independent, and so everyone treats them accordingly. Now she was a blonde, she was both flattered and delighted to be cherished as a helpless little thing. Men heading for the tube actually stood aside to allow her to enter first. She even found a hand under her elbow to assist her through the crush at the ticket barrier! Doors were held open for her in the shops on the way to the flat, and she said she felt herself growing more wide-eyed and feminine and helpless by the minute! Alastair, it seemed, was quite bemused by this impulse buy, but agreed it certainly made a change!

Mine was a great success too. All my friends liked it, and told me it made me look ten years younger. Which made the thought of taking it off quite a problem, especially if Sandy was around. I didn't want to age before his very eyes. Also, he couldn't bear the sight of my own long hair pinned flat to my head when I removed my short curly creation. He said I looked exactly as if I'd been scalped, so I spared him further shocks and never let him see this part of the performance again.

It proved to be a great prop for TV and was absolutely perfect for playing the part of Effie in *High Living*. For this part I brushed it quite straight, and wore a wee kirby-grip in front. I decided Effie would be the type who would stick to the same hair-style from girlhood to the grave. Willie Joss, who has known me from the schoolroom practically, said I looked exactly as I had done when he first met me. 'You mean I've got a right wee ba' face again?' I said, grinning. 'Well,' said Willie with a wink, 'you said it!' That was precisely what he had meant. In the nicest possible way, of course.

I thought I might take it with me when we went on holiday, just for the joy of being able to go about bare-headed, but in the event I forgot to pack it. But it didn't matter. Nothing matters when I am heading for Shangri-la, my paradise on the island of Sark. The peace and tranquillity seep right through the soles of my feet like a miraculous spell, the moment I step ashore. My mind and my heart are calmed, and I am at peace. Sark either says everything to you, or nothing. There seems to be no in-between.

A small incident as we stepped off the boat illustrates exactly what I am trying to describe. A day tripper, a perfect stranger, seized me by the arm quite distractedly, saying, 'Oh I wouldn't have minded a bit if I had missed this boat. How I wish I could stay. I *must* come back again. I prefer this to anything else I have seen.'

He didn't know me at all, but he just had to express his disappointment to someone, because the arrival of this extra boat meant he would have to travel back on it. He had no excuse for staying.

I know how he felt.

I cried the first time I left Sark. And I have met quite a few others who have told me, somewhat shamefacedly, that they did so too. It has that sort of magic. When one leaves, it is like leaving the innocence of childhood behind.

It is no island for those who enjoy noise and bustle, with lots of entertainment laid on. There is only the sea and the sky, day-dreaming and walking, and a single little street of shops which, when the day trippers have left, resembles the setting for *High Noon*. No

184

transistors may be played on beaches or on roads, and the only motor traffic permitted are the farm tractors used in the fields.

The other wheeled vehicles are the magnificent old Victoria carriages drawn by fine horses which stand patiently at the top of Harbour Hill, waiting for the day trippers whom they will take on a tour of the island. The carriages can't be taken down the steep hill to the harbour, or they would be shaken to pieces and they are irreplaceable.

Bicycles can be hired, but aren't a great deal of use, for Sark is a plateau, and one must descend winding precipitous paths or steps cut out of the rock to reach the sea some two hundred to two hundred and fifty feet below. It is not for the very young or the very old, unless they have good strong legs, and an enthusiasm for quiet hidden places. For the island is shy of revealing itself all at once, as all the best places are, and the secret beauty spots have to be searched out using the feet.

I remember one hot summer day walking behind a Victoria carriage filled with elderly American tourists, who were astounded to find us keeping pace with them all the way. 'My word, honey,' called one white-haired matron admiringly, 'you must have strong legs to have walked this far with us in all this heat.' Before I could reply, the driver who was standing by the horse to give the animal a little rest said, 'Oh yes, that pair walk all over the island. They're one of the sights of the place!' We were too. And in later years, we were pointed out as a tourist attraction when I became almost too well known on television.

The first morning after we arrived on the island that year, we had a telephone call from the Dame of Sark, Mrs Sybil Hathaway, inviting us to tea on the Sunday afternoon. She and I had corresponded now and again after my first visit, and she always insisted that I let her know when we were coming over. Sandy had never been in the Seigneurie, the island's official residence, although I had, and he said later that it was quite an experience to meet the Dame and to find in her someone who talked almost as much as I did! She posed charmingly for photographs with me before we went inside, and sent me off into peals of laughter when she threw her walking stick with impressive accuracy at her large white poodles, sending them flying for making a nuisance of themselves. They scooted a split second before the stick reached them!

She was over eighty at that time but you could never use the term 'an old lady' to describe such a vivacious colourful character. She was beautifully dressed in a light jersey dress, face discreetly but charmingly made up, and her silvery hair was very well cut and set, and livened with a gentle blue rinse. She was absolutely full of beans, and we found so much to talk about that we realized with dismay we had overstayed the usual polite hour and had been with her for an hour and a half. She was tremendously interesting on everything relating to the island, and on her travels to the States. When I told her I didn't like flying, she said, 'If you had seen some of the seas I have seen, you would fear the oceans much more.' She was highly entertaining on the subject of the German commanders who had occupied Sark in the war and who returned to the island later as visitors. She of course had had to battle with them during the occupation, guarding the rights of her islanders with zeal and efficiency.

One of the visiting commanders, whom she disliked, arrived on her doorstep one day, and introduced himself. She hadn't recognized him in his civvies after such long years of peace, and although she had no wish to have a tête-à-tête with him, she felt she couldn't leave him standing on the mat. When he had complimented her on how young she now looked compared with her looks when he last saw her, she had said tartly, 'Are you surprised? I had plenty to worry me when you were here.' Although slightly taken aback, he went on to comment on how prosperous the island looked. To which the indomitable Dame had replied, 'Well what did you expect? We're looking after ourselves now without *any* interference.'

I found it very satisfying to hear that little anecdote, and admired her greatly for being so crushingly honest without a trace of vindictiveness. When I said as much to her, she said, 'Oh well, although I didn't like that particular commander, in the end we all starved together, and one had to be sorry for them.'

Daughter Jeanne showed us round the gardens, which saved us going back on Monday with day trippers and holidaymakers (the gardens opened on Mondays), and we saw mesembryanthemum growing in such profusion that we were quite dazzled and determined to grow them in our own garden in Pinner, and we had them there for years afterwards, a happy reminder of a great lady's garden.

Another tremendous excitement on that holiday was when someone dashed into the guest house where we were staying, panting with the drama of it all, to announce that a thief had emptied the till of the nearby hotel. Reports varied that the 'fortune' taken was between £16 and £60, but we later learned that it amounted to exactly £62. No newspaper is published on Sark, but the news went round the island like bush telegraph. We helped to spread the tidings ourselves when we walked over to Little Sark, the scene of many of our bean-feasts, and all work stopped while the 'crime' was discussed. Not a cup was removed from a single table until everyone learned of the affair, down to the smallest detail. There wasn't much to tell, actually, but imagination ran riot, and there was great speculation as to who would cook the criminal's meals when he was caught, for the last occupant of the jail was a girl who had stolen some sweeties nine months previously, and who had spent a few hours in jail at her own request, just to boast she had been inside. They had so little crime on the island (lucky them!) that it wasn't quite certain whether the lady who used to cook the meals on such occasions was still responsible for this duty. Apparently they worked a rota system.

The culprit was caught in a matter of hours, and as he was a Jersey man and not a local, honour was preserved. That is the virtue of a small community and of island life. Everyone knows everyone else, and a dubious character is quickly spotted. The thief could only have been a stranger, for on an island nobody could commit a burglary and expect to get away with it, when the only means of escape is by boat and where everyone is practically counted. So, into the tiny jail he went, but only for a maximum of forty-eight hours, which is the law on Sark, before being transferred to Guernsey.

As the jail had only recently been refurbished and generally freshened up, the general opinion was that he was having a very ritzy supper, bed and breakfast at the ratepayers' expense.

But on an island where everyone left doors and windows open, the Sarkese were shaken to realize a thief had been in their midst. They were even more startled to hear it mentioned on the BBC news. Such a scandal!

We visited Sark every year afterwards, including the year the Dame died. She was rather disapproving of the drinking habits of Denis Price, the actor, who had settled on the island, and at one time I believe 'exiled' him to Guernsey until he behaved himself. The cheap alcohol on all the Channel Islands is a great attraction for those who like to imbibe freely, and the Dame wasn't at all keen to have people settle on Sark mainly for that reason. We saw Denis often, and I had a chat with him while waiting for the boat one year, and he was overjoyed to have been received back into the fold and to be living on what had, for him, become beloved Sark in all ways. But Denis was not a well man, and died within a few months of that meeting.

When we went to visit the Dame's grave in the churchyard the following year, she and Denis Price's last resting places were within yards of each other. All passions spent, all sins forgiven. Both at rest.

On the fly-leaf of her autobiography the Dame wrote the words, 'Very sincerely, for Molly, who loves Sark.'

When visitors leave the island at the end of a holiday, a lovely custom is observed. Or was observed when we were there. Everyone who is able to do so goes down to the harbour, and first-time visitors are given a bunch of the beautiful wild flowers which grow everywhere and which are picked on the way down to the boat. The visitor tosses the flowers into the water as the boat leaves, and if they float back to harbour, that ensures he will return another year. On one occasion there was added spice to this custom when two youths jumped into the harbour *fully clothed* in spectacular farewell to their chums, and were cheered enthusiastically as they made their way back to the harbour steps.

As all activities on Sark tend to be of the simplest, there was enormous excitement one year when a visiting frigate arrived. The crew were immediately adopted and entertained by the whole island. In return, they held 'open ship' for the children, putting on a fancy dress entertainment which was as good as any pantomime. It was like a scene from *The Pirates of Penzance* as holidaymakers perched on every surrounding rock face, while sailors 'walked the plank', turned somersaults, dived into the water, raced round the harbour in small boats with the children, and handed out 'prizes' in the shape of ice creams and jellies. It was a glorious day, and it was well past their bedtime before the youngsters could tear themselves away from such bewitching adults. Later on, the local hostelries echoed with the sounds of revelry by night. Mr Kodak must have made a small fortune that day, as we all recorded the happy scenes for the archives.

There wasn't even a collection taken. Like all the best things on that lovely island; this delightful 'happening' was entirely free.

After our discovery of the magic of Sark, we were urged by my children's hour producer, Josephine Plummer, to visit the Isles of Scilly, or The Fortunate Isles as they are called. 'But you *must* see Scilly,' she cried, after I'd persuaded her to visit Sark. 'If you like Sark, you will love Scilly.'

We weren't able to follow her advice for a long time, because, with my uncertain profession I simply couldn't follow the necessary procedure and book a whole year ahead. And then, one disastrous summer for the resorts, the tanker *Torrey Canyon* grounded on the rocks round Scilly and sent polluting oil all over holiday beaches for mile after mile along the south west coast of England. Holiday bookings were cancelled by

190

the score. An advertisement in the evening paper caught my eye one night. It was from the Town Clerk of St Mary's, Isles of Scilly, assuring all intending holidaymakers that there was *no oil pollution* on their beaches. 'Sandy,' I said in sudden excitement, 'that means there is accommodation this year.' It was the work of a moment to ring up for a brochure with lists of available rooms, and within weeks we were walking up from St Mary's harbour, to begin a love affair with the islands which lasts to this day. Our only annual problem became whether it should be Sark this time, or perhaps we ought to make it Scilly again. We have tried to visit both islands equally, and it is a very unusual year when we fail to recharge the batteries on such peaceful and beloved places. We have friends on both islands, and it is truly like going home to be among them for a brief spell.

One of the most interesting fêtes I have ever opened took place not long after our return from that early Sark holiday.

I had been asked by a colleague to go up to the North Riding of Yorkshire to open the annual fête for a close friend of hers, and to stay the week-end. She painted a glowing picture of the marvellous hospitality I would be given, but I took her description of her friend's house with a large pinch of salt. I realized the week-end offer was kindly meant, but in my experience people will exaggerate unashamedly to find an opener for bazaars or fêtes. Endless telephone calls arranging details for a bazaar which sounds like the Festival of Britain can turn out to be a tiny church hall with a couple of dozen in the audience. Then again, an invitation casually extended to attend an event which sounds limited and parochial in the extreme, proves to be as exciting as a first night. It is impossible to guess what the occasion will reveal. It is all a gamble.

Still, this seemed a worth-while cause. The money raised was to be used to provide holidays for handicapped people who were seldom, if ever, outside their own four walls and who knew little or nothing of green fields or trees. Normally these deprived people saw nobody but their own immediate relatives, and the holidays would be a blessed and unbelievable relief for all of them. Having known the bliss of escape to Sark, how could I refuse to help others to share the joy of a happy holiday.

I wasn't really keen on spending a week-end away from home, but I said yes. Name and address of my hostess and organizer were given, and I set off for the north on the appointed day.

My hostess, a lady in her late seventies, met me at the station. Her warm hand-clasp and vigorous 'Glad to meet you', was accompanied by a humorous lift of the eyebrow and a smile as mischievous as a schoolboy's as she caught sight of the waiting photographers. We posed for pictures, were interviewed at length, and it was very clear from the way porters leaped to see to the luggage, and the presence of a policeman to clear a way for the car, that I was in the presence of a celebrated local character.

A phrase of my mother's stirred in my mind. When I was a wee girl, my mother used to describe those who held exalted positions in the ranks of the wealthy or the privileged as 'the landed gentry'. The words had filled my imagination and I had had a mental picture of ladies and gentlemen impeccably dressed, who never soiled a finger, and who lived mostly in hydropathics. I knew about hydropathics because my mother's best friend was a cook in such an establishment, and our mouths used to water at her descriptions of silver dishes of strawberries buried in layers of cream.

What these rich people did when they weren't taking the waters, I couldn't imagine at all, and as the nearest my mother ever got to them was handling the silver dishes filled with strawberries and cream, and licking the kitchen bowl afterwards, it seemed beyond the dreams of fantasy that I would ever meet such a mysterious breed.

Now, sitting in a chauffeur-driven car, behind this lady, I wondered. During the drive she excused herself from taking part in the conversation because she simply had to finish a hot water bottle cover for the fête. All I saw of her for the next fifteen miles was the back of her neck as she bent industriously over her stitching.

We were to go first to the Holiday Home which, I discovered, she had given to the Council many years before for this specific purpose. Mentally I decided it had been too large for her at her advanced age, and after giving it away, she had moved to a tiny bungalow which she could maintain more easily. Yes, that was surely it.

At the Home, where she was given a rapturous greeting from the handicapped holidaymakers and the staff, we drank tea in the kitchen using tablespoons for stirring because all the teaspoons were in use. There was no standing on ceremony! We poured milk from a metal gallon can without excuse or apology offered. My mother would have been 'black affrontit' if we had been her visitors! While the rest of us ate scones, this splendid old lady lifted the lid of a pan, sniffed appreciatively, and ladled out a large helping of baked beans which she had with toast. 'Aha,' I thought, 'Toffs can get away with murder!' This was definitely toffs' behaviour. The moment she had swallowed the last crumb, she leaped to her feet and began shellng hard-boiled eggs for the evening salad meal.

I was free to wander around, seeing things for myself while she issued instructions non-stop in connection with the fête. I was absolutely astounded by her energy, and impressed with her authority which was quite unforced and obviously as completely natural to her as breathing.

She took a final look round, then called out 'Grant!' The tall white-haired chauffeur appeared and waited, smiling, while she made up her mind as to whether he or she would be driving. 'You'd better do it,' she decided. 'I haven't time. I must finish the hot-bottle cover.' Not a word of conversation did she utter as we bowled along busy roads, but she lifted her head occasionally to bellow, 'Speed fiends! I hope you get caught!' to overtaking cars which were exceeding the speed limit. I was irresistibly reminded of Miss Chree, and my heart warmed to this eccentric lady.

We approached lodge gates and I had just concluded that this must be her own little house, when we swept through, and with the briefest look up from her sewing she told me we were now entering her property. Ten minutes later we drew up at a house which was little short of a stately home, surrounded by 700 acres of farmland! It was at least *four times* the size of the Holiday Home she had given away, and could have housed a small army. The door opened, and for the first time I walked on a stone flagged passage inside a private house. We were immediately enveloped by dogs. I would have sworn there were at least a dozen, but a calmer look reduced the real number to six. A large collie rejoiced in the name of Rosebud. Two pekes answered to Chou and Chinko. A little blind terrier was called Jane, and the two whippets, Crumpet and Silver, were the parents of seven puppies which frisked in a sort of play-pen near the vegetable garden. I learned that the play-pen, complete with puppies, was transferred to my hostess's bedroom at night, where she fed and tended them with loving care, for they needed nourishment every few hours.

I was quite dazed as I mounted a staircase lined with stuffed heads of foxes, rabbits and hares. A pair of budgies twittered from a perch, and a magnificent parrot called Horace sat in an enormous cage. He had been given to my hostess forty years before by a Norwegian sailor, and as nobody spoke Norwegian to him, his conversation consisted of two words 'Hullo Horace'. When we went in to dinner later, Horace was carried in state to the dining table by the butler, and transferred to a smaller cage, where he consumed with enormous gusto pieces of toast thickly spread with marmalade. 'The toast is only a raft, you understand,' explained my hostess kindly. 'It's the marmalade he really wants.' I knew how he felt. I eat jam and lemon curd that way! He ate kedgeree in the same way, but his party piece, I was told, was walking upstairs to bed at the end of the day, and this I determined to see.

In the meantime, we all settled down to our meal, which was brought in by the butler and laid out on silver dishes on the sideboard, as described in the best novels. And exactly as described by my mother's friend, the cook from the hydropathic. My mother should have lived to see this hour. I was actually living with one of the landed gentry, with butler, silver, animals, eccentricity, the lot! There were even silver dishes of strawberries and cream. I wondered if the girl in the kitchen licked the cream bowl, as my mother had done.

Afterwards, we arranged ourselves in the drawing

room to watch TV and in five minutes the door opened and all the dogs rushed in. They leaped over shoulders, cantered over bosoms and knees to find their favourite corners, and promptly went to sleep. We dared not move in case we disturbed them. In suburbia, apologies would have been offered and assurance sought that the animals weren't being a nuisance. Not here. In this moated grange, it was simply not done not to like dogs. I was thankful that in this respect at least, I fitted in to the manner born.

After we had said our goodnights, I softly opened my bedroom door to look for Horace. There, sitting on the landing as though on guard, were the collie, one of the pekes and Horace. I shook with laughter at the thought of this menagerie strolling around during the night. In the distance, I could hear the seven puppies yelping in my hostess's bedroom.

My early morning tea was brought on a solid silver tray, poured from a silver teapot, and cream added from a tiny silver jug. The curtains were opened to reveal miles of open landscape. Not a house in sight. Just little lambs gently grazing with their mothers close by. I felt I must be dreaming, or taking part in a play.

When I went down for breakfast, there wasn't a soul about. I strolled round the large garden, and then arrived at what was clearly the outside of a private chapel, attached to the house. One of the house guests found me staring up at it and escorted me inside. It had seating for fifty-two people, an altar made from a single piece of exquisitely carved wood, a pipe organ, and little footstools worked in fine tapestry by my hostess. I was past being surprised at anything by this time, and took in my stride the news that the old lady took many of the services, particularly those held for the handicapped holidaymakers. When I paused to admire a tiny carved bowl set in the wall by the door, my fellow-guest said that during the war the soldiers who had been invited to attend the service mistook this fitment, intended to hold holy oils, for an ashtray and stubbed their cigarettes out before taking their seats! I can only trust the good Lord forgave their ignorance, since no insult had been intended. For they had all greatly respected the old lady.

Chapel or no chapel though, I was getting pretty hungry, so I overcame my awe of the butler and searched him out in his pantry and enquired when we were likely to eat. My fellow guest had gone to look for his children. I reminded the butler that it was well after half-past-nine. Clearly the gentry were no early risers. 'It is all ready, madam,' he informed me gravely, 'I can bring yours if you wish.' I did wish. In a moment, the hot silver dishes were ranged along the sideboard, and I helped myself to eggs, sausages and bacon, and made tea from water heated in a silver spirit kettle. I was just infusing the brew when six more house guests appeared, delighted to find breakfast organized. How different from tenement life, I thought, concealing my laughter, as we all found our places round the vast mahogany table. At any moment I expected Noel Coward or Rex Harrison to put in an appearance!

We were tucking into our various dishes when our hostess arrived, not a bit put out by the sight of all her guests already breakfasting. A lifetime of attention had given her complete detachment from the humdrum business of catering for guests. How easy it must be to entertain when other hands do the work! And how marvellous to be able to delegate with such confidence. That was a great strength. With complete concentration she attacked her kedgeree, then turned to the pile of correspondence by her plate. She whooped with delight on catching sight of the note on top of her mail. It was from the farm manager, to inform her that ten piglets had been safely delivered of the sow the night before, also two calves from expectant cows!

It was an old Ealing film to the life. Michael Shepley would have felt quite at home.

'Now you mustn't go near the piglets,' our hostess warned the children at the table. 'Pigs eat their young if they're disturbed.' '*Ooooh,*' the children breathed, fascinated and horrified. 'Go up to the long field, see Grieve and he'll fit you up with some horses and you can ride back here for lunch.'

It was a world away from our mothers' instructions, 'Away an' play oot in the back court. Don't go faur, it'll no' be lang tae dinnertime.'

These children of the gentry clearly adored the morning's activities arranged for them, and vanished, leaving us to our crispbreads and honey from the comb.

I gazed dreamily at the ceiling so high above me. Having lived in small modern houses or tenements all my life, the sense of space in this magnificent old place was more restful than I could have dreamed. 'I love it,' I told my hostess enthusiastically, 'but I could never keep a place of this size clean.' 'Nor can I', she laughed cheerfully, and pointed to a fine layer of dust on the mantelpiece. (My mother would never have drawn anybody's attention to such a thing!) 'I wouldn't mind a little house,' she said thoughtfully, 'if it weren't for the dogs.'

The others round the table smiled and shook their heads as I did. We who were enjoying, for a brief moment, the space and graciousness of an earlier age which took for granted lofty ceilings, endless corridors, vast windows and miles of rolling landscape, and

198

devoted staff, knew beyond a shadow of a doubt that our hostess, who had lived in this setting for over fifty years, could only survive in her own splendid environment. We could adapt to her style much more easily than she could to ours. There wasn't an ounce of snobbery in her, but space and a rich setting was her natural place in the scheme of things.

A fleet of cars left with the rest of our house party, heading towards the fête. I was collected by limousine and taken to another magnificent house to join their party. For the first time I learned that I was to be introduced at the fête to the Duchess of Kent's mother, Lady Worsley, and the lunch had been arranged so that she could make my acquaintance before she did the actual introduction at the fête itself! The house had a beautiful swimming pool, a fountain and magnificent gardens, and I found myself strolling with all those landed gentry as though mixing with near Royalty was an everyday occurrence to me. I tried to copy their casual attitude, but inside the butterflies had robbed me of appetite. I could hardly eat a bite of the splendid cold buffet, although I admired the efficient way His Lordship dealt with the turkey, ham, tongue and duck with a newly acquired electric slicer. It was the first time I had seen one in use in a private house, and I never see one now but I am transported to that fine Yorkshire estate.

Faced with all this aristocratic grandeur, I was growing distinctly nervous over my opening speech. My usual 'church bazaar' speech with its modest hopes would never do for this occasion, so I changed my prepared piece and told them instead of my hostess's feverish finishing of the hot-bottle cover, of her yelling at the speed fiends, and of our 'dainty tea' with tablespoons for the sugar, and a milk churn for a milk jug. The holiday-makers were ecstatic with this description of their benefactor, whom they all recognized as a true eccentric, and my hostess dissolved in laughter at finding herself the heroine of my opening speech.

The local papers were very impressed that I didn't charge a fee for opening charity affairs such as this. I could assure them, hand on heart, that they gave me much more entertainment at that house and fête than I could possibly have given them.

I bought *four* hats, chic reminders of one of the most colourful week-ends I had ever spent. They had *all* come from Fortnum and Mason, the Queen's store in Piccadilly, and had been donated by my hostess of the luncheon party. They were far better than any fee, and I carried them back to Pinner in triumph.

Lady Worsley bought one of my cookery books for her daughter, the Duchess, and I treasured the thought of one of my very own recipes providing a dish to set before the Duke and the children.

I wouldn't have missed any of it for a thousand pounds, which was, incidentally, just what the sale made. I knew for certain that not one penny of it would be wasted.

CHAPTER NINE

That was a very happy, busy varied winter following my taste of high living. Work gradually picked up, month by month, and the bank manager was no longer a figure to be avoided. The overdraft was melting like snow in the sun. I had a nice little part in one of the first plays for BBC 2, with the odd title *The Elephant*

You Gave Me, which starred Kenneth Haigh, and also featured that grand actress Dandy Nichols, who was later to rejoice all hearts with her fine characterization of the dreaded Alf Garnett's wife in *Till Death Us Do Part*. I'm always amazed at how quiet some of the finest performers are, when I am such a chatterbox. Dandy scarcely opened her mouth. Maybe that is the answer, of course! They keep all their vitality for the audience or the camera, whereas I am so excited just working alongside them that I erupt into compulsive conversation. The public and the private faces are, in most cases, very different.

For some reason I had thought BBC 2, because it was a very top-class new channel, would demand a different style of acting. To my amazement, I discovered it was not one whit different from working for BBC 1, apart from the prestige of being in at the very beginning. So, all fears at rest, we settled down to enjoy ourselves.

Dixon of Dock Green was a special pleasure, for it brought me into the same studio as Jack Warner, an actor I had admired for years and had met many times socially, but had never worked with until then. The location for the outside scenes was only ten minutes from Pinner, and when I saw the house they had chosen I rather regretted not suggesting using our house. Not only would we have had a welcome 'rent' for this, I needn't have had to be up so early in the morning, and I could have fallen straight into bed at the end of the day's filming! However, when I saw the clutter of cameras and sound booms, I realized I would have had a small heart attack at the sight of all this machinery being dragged through our practically new abode. I had chosen everything with such care, I'd never have been able to concentrate on my acting for guarding my precious wallpaper and floor coverings from marks and scratches. So it was just as well somebody else had that headache! There are times when money is not the most important consideration. Or even getting to bed early, come to that.

In *Dixon*, my main scenes were with Ian Trigger, a Scots lad who could have been my twin for height and build. In fact, when he later visited us in Pinner, the local shopkeepers who saw us marching up the High Street side by side were sure we were brother and sister, and were highly amused by our lightness and fleetness of foot. They said they were sure we would take wing and fly away at any moment!

Ian is an excellent actor, who later made a great impression at the Edinburgh Festival in Brecht. The last time I saw him was in *Outside Edge* at the Queen's Theatre with Julia McKenzie and Maureen Lipman. It was absolutely hilarious, with Maureen and Ian using Ian's tiny build to wildly comic effect. Every time she caught sight of him, she opened wide her arms, and he dived inside her huge hairy fur coat and disappeared from sight for what seemed like half-an-hour. When I saw him after the show, wiping tears of laughter from my eyes, I marvelled that he hadn't suffocated, but while he agreed it was pretty stifling, the sound of the audience laughter had kept him breathing effortlessly throughout! That show deserved to run and run, but in the unpredictable way of show business, it came off far too soon, in spite of brilliant performances from the entire cast. I consider Julia McKenzie as fine a straight actress as she is a singer, and that's saying something, and my assessment has proved dead right as the years have passed. It was no surprise to me when she took the top award for her performance as Miss Adelaide in *Guys and Dolls* in 1982, and I am certain she will go on from strength to strength. Her mother is an enthusiastic fan of her bonnie and talented daughter, much to Julia's embarrassment, and any time Mrs Mac and I have chatted on the 'phone we've had a great time enthusing over this clever red-head. There is also a loving supportive husband in the background, which I know from personal experience is a great strength.

Market in Honey Lane brought me into the cast because they couldn't find two enormously fat ladies for a scene in the market, and decided one huge fat lady with a wee thin creature like me would provide an even funnier contrast. I hadn't the least idea who else would be featured, apart from John Bennett who was so moving as Bosinney, the lover of the beautiful Irene in *The Forsyte Saga*, and who played a barrow-boy in this production. When I got to the studios, I found to my delight that my old friend and colleague Alfie Bass was 'guesting', and was sporting a huge bushy beard, in preparation for his part in *Fiddler on the Roof*. He was due to take over from the great Topol, who was giving a performance of towering brilliance. I didn't envy Alfie having to follow such a star, but I learned later that he more than held his own, and the cast loved him just as they had Topol.

Majorie Mason was in this *Market in Honey Lane* episode too. I'd only ever seen her on the screen, always playing character parts, and was very impressed to find a stunning looking, beautifully dressed lady, very glamorous away from her kitchen pinny! I noted with approval her warm orange sweater exactly matched long suede boots, and even her wrist-watch had a matching orange suede strap. She was very friendly, and I liked her very much. She, I may say, talked nearly as much as I did!

I almost had to cancel this show, because just when

203

I hadn't a minute to think of dental appointments, I bit unwisely on a chop bone and split the root of a tooth as clean as a whistle!

This meant several appointments for emergency treatment, and ended with the roots having to be whipped out and another tooth pushed at once into the vacant space! I was reminded of my dear Bebe and her wisdom teeth extractions before going on to do a wild adagio dance in Blackpool* and with that example to sustain me, went to my first rehearsal for the TV show with my mouth stiff and frozen from the last injection, and the bleeding gums throbbing. There is truly nothing more effective for forgetting your miseries than having something else to think about. I was plunged instantly into the business of following the script and absorbing the complicated designs for the market sets, and as nobody knew about my tooth traumas, I almost entirely ignored them myself. If I had been at home, I would have been rinsing out my mouth, taking aspirins and feeling very fragile. As our old company Manager used to say when I was working in the theatre, 'Old Doctor Greasepaint' is utterly reliable for miracle cures!

When it came to recording day, the glamour of show business was non-existent. They had built a market outside in the perishing wind and rain. I had never dreamed we would be copying the real thing to this extent. There was a long street, with shop-fronts, pillarbox, milk cart, postman, bus driver and all sorts of vendors. And all of my scenes were outside in the market!

We were up and down that windy wet thoroughfare from ten o'clock in the morning until almost five

* Walking into the Lyons' Den

o'clock, and indeed we only stopped because the light was going. Fortunately for us, it was shot in black and white, or our red noses would have caused a few raised eyebrows from any good temperance society. It was sheer bliss to get back to the canteen for a hot meal. It's a wonder we didn't catch pneumonia. In the canteen I found myself beside Kathleen Harrison, looking very dressy in a pink outfit and lots of sparkling jewellery. This seemed a bit unusual for her character as Mrs Thursday in the series of that name, but she told me that it was to be the last recording of the series and she was going out in a glorious burst of fashion.

I was amazed when she told me she had never forgotten my speech at The Woman of the Year Lunch, it had made her laugh so much. I was very touched that in the midst of her busy recording day she had found time to recall what I had said, especially when it had all happened years ago.

My resistance to germs must have been lowered with all those hours in the wind and rain, for when I had to go into town to see someone who wished to put my voice on tape for possible future advertising, I was perfect 'host' for the battalions of germs his secretary sprayed all over her typewriter and me. She positively *pulsed* with bacteria, sneezed non-stop, and the hot-house atmosphere did the rest.

It was maddening, for I had just received a booking to play a small part on radio for the first time for ages, and it was for a Third Programme play. All actors are neurotic about their voices, in whatever medium they are working, but on radio the voice is of paramount importance instead of being just one thing among many you have to worry about. So I went into the attack without delay, Weir versus the bugs! Sandy always says I try so many things, I'll never know what cured me. He leaves it to nature, but actors can't afford such a leisurely process. I swallowed hot drinks, rubbed on potions, remembering to follow Bebe's advice and anoint my feet too. I swallowed pills by the dozen, gargled, and followed the early-to-bed routine. I inhaled heads of choking steam from boiling water laced with Friar's Balsam, and thanks to this regime, recovered my voice just in time to play my little part in *Joan of Arc*.

Performing in plays is a wonderful way of adding to one's store of knowledge. Until I read the script, I had no idea that Joan of Arc had a soul-mate from the North of Scotland who was a 'daughter of the devil', a witch in fact, and I was to play this strange creature. Apart from Joan, I was the only woman in the script, if indeed a witch can be called a woman, and the director was delighted with the eerie quality of my voice which still held traces of hoarseness. So my cold turned out to be a blessing in disguise, and although I didn't realize it at the time, that witch was a portent of things to come!

Mary Morris was a brilliant Joan, and was most intrigued to discover how I fell heir to her water-colour of the Lion and the Unicorn which she had given to my understudy in *The Happiest Days of Your Life*.

My understudy, fed up with sitting in the dressing room doing nothing, and having recently met the playwright Tennessee Williams, set off for America to pay him a visit, and when she was clearing out her things, came across the water-colour which had been given to her years before as a first-night gift from Mary Morris. She didn't want it to be thrown out, and yet didn't see how it was to go in her case, so she tossed it over to me with the words, 'Here Scotch, I think you'll like this and I know you'll take care of it, for you love everything connected with our profession.' I still have it, and it hangs in the bedroom, even as I write.

When this snippet in a Third Programme play was followed by a lovely TV booking for an episode in the Eric Sykes series, I began, cautiously, to believe I was back in the show-biz swim again. We were almost solvent, and this might be the moment to indulge my dream of having a little gazebo built in the garden.

I love the outdoors, and ever since I had seen Bernard Shaw's little writing house at Ayot St Lawrence, I had longed for just such a building where I could write my scripts for *Woman's Hour*, plan my pieces for the *Journal*, and at the same time enjoy the sensation of working in the garden.

I talked Sandy into it by telling him it would become a tiny summer-house for both of us in winter, when I would be writing indoors again. We would keep the deck-chairs there, and when the sun shone on cold wintry days, we would sit basking in our deck-chairs reading, safely out of the wind. It would extend the feeling of summer for us, and be far more enjoyable than sitting in the house.

I think it was the thought of gaining more space in the lean-to, by losing the deck-chairs to the gazebo, which sold the idea, and he agreed we would buy it between us. There wasn't enough spare cash for either of us to do it separately!

Franklin Engelmann had had a good craftsman working for him in his new vast mansion over at Harrow Weald, and although he was a 'fitted wardrobe' man, and had never tackled a garden house before, he was most enthusiastic to try. 'I'll be the guinea pig,' I said, 'and if it's any good, you'll be able to say on your brochure that you build and supply garden gazebos.'

So because it was in every sense a 'model', with this excellent carpenter following my drawings and ideas, nothing was skimped in the way of time or quality.

We chose a site within sprinting distance of the kitchen so that I could reach the telephone with minimum delay, and as a small hut once stood on that spot, the concrete base was already there.

The carpenter was as excited and interested in the whole project as I was. All through the snowy spell he worked, delighted to have a worth-while job when things would otherwise have been quiet. And when it was finished, and my typewriter sat on the long formica bench under the window which faced the kitchen, my cup truly ran over with joy. I loved it from the word go. The small distancing of myself from the domestic atmosphere of the house made an enormous difference to me as a writer. But, alas for our plans for wintry deck-chairs basking together, I behaved like the camel in the legend. I had no sooner got my nose in, than my head followed, then my body, and soon the files came and with them the reference books. There was no room now for the deck-chairs, and they were moved back to the lean-to. I had a light installed, then a fan heater, and when the time came that I ought to have moved back indoors, I refused to budge!

'Here,' said Sandy one day, 'what happened to the idea that I was to enjoy that gazebo in winter time? There's hardly room for a mouse, much less me. You should be working inside anyway, in this cold weather.'

I gazed at him, conscience-stricken. He was quite right. Half of it was his. But I knew in my bones I would never move back indoors to work again.

'Sandy,' I said, doing a swift piece of mental arithmetic with my bank balance, and adding the Sykes' cheque which was still to come to swell the total, 'if I give you your money back, can the gazebo be all mine?'

'But you'll freeze out there when it gets really bitter,' he protested.

'No I won't,' I assured him, 'the fan heater is warm as toast in such a wee building.'

He saw I couldn't be prised out of my beloved shell. 'All right,' he said, 'I like my big easy chair in the house anyway.'

With the state of our finances just then, I think he felt he had come into a small fortune when he got his money back!

And I knew the bliss of the writer who doesn't have to tidy a thing away, because there would be nobody to disturb so much as an envelope, nor would my apparent untidiness give offence, for it wasn't a part of the house. It was my den. My writing den. It was almost as wonderful as the night when I had fallen asleep in the very first room of my own.*

But on that first winter in my gazebo in the garden, the saddest piece I was to compose was to be my impression of the death and funeral of our beloved war-time Prime Minister and saviour of us all, Winston Churchill.

With January had come harsh winds which cut to the bone, and flurries of snow fell week in week out. Sir Winston was over ninety when he was stricken with cerebral thrombosis, and in spite of a formidable constitution which had enabled him to survive several severe illnesses and mishaps through his seventies, we sensed from the medical bulletins that at his great age, he was fighting his last battle.

The traffic moved quietly past the house where he

* Best Foot Forward

lay sinking into a deep, deep sleep. People delivered flowers and telegrams, and there was a moving mention of a bearded man who knelt in a nearby doorway, reading from a pocket bible. A small boy delivered a plant he had bought with three shillings borrowed from his mother, money which he would faithfully repay from his pocket money in the weeks to come. To a reporter he said, 'I thought Sir Winston would like something. I have read about him in history books. I think he is a very great man.'

Men in the crowd at Hyde Park Gate took off their hats as Lady Churchill's car went by.

For ten days the bulletins brought us news. 'There is no material change'. The anxious crowds fell silent as Lord Moran read the words from the doorway. Later, we were told, 'He is slipping into deeper sleep and not conscious of pain or discomfort.'

And then that final bulletin which told us the tempestuous years were over. All whose lives had been touched by this great man knew the time had come for heart-felt tribute, and there were millions of us.

We who were privileged to live in London at such a historic moment, walked about with preoccupied faces, wrapped in our own thoughts.

We stood silently before store windows which displayed huge portraits of the man in our thoughts – Sir Winston, caught in various poses.

Here the strong glance captured by Karsh, there the softer expression by Vivienne, and always at the foot of the portraits there were huge bowls of arum lilies, sometimes mixed with branching sprays of white lilac.

Children gazed with wonderment at the huge flags fluttering at half-mast – a sight somehow as touching as anything else in the mourning capital.

It was like a bereavement in the family.

I knew it would be impossible to see all of the funeral procession except on TV, but there was one personal contact I could make and that was to take part in the pilgrimage to Westminster Hall where the great statesman was to lie in state for three days. There I could say my 'thank you' with the rest.

My neighbour and I set off from Pinner at nine o'clock in the morning, and after a heating cup of coffee in town walked slowly along the long queue through the gardens along Millbank to Lambeth Bridge. We knew it must be a long wait, for there were thousands ahead of us but it didn't matter. For we knew also that we wouldn't have lived to suffer even this small discomfort if it hadn't been for the courage of this man to whom the whole of London seemed to be moving to pay their last respects.

The wind from the river blew chill and penetrating, and the snow froze the feet, but everyone seemed indifferent to it.

It took one and a quarter hours to reach the doors of Westminster Hall, but somehow it didn't seem long, and almost before we were mentally prepared for it, the silent tableau was before us.

The silence was absolute. Not a cough or a sniff broke it.

The tall, deeply yellow candles flamed steady in the stillness, and the Union Jack, with the Insignia of the Garter on its cushion on top, completely hid the coffin. Somehow it seemed impossible to take in, that under that flag our beloved Churchill himself lay.

I could more easily imagine he might be standing somewhere in the shadows, his own eyes full of tears as he watched the great tide of love for him flow ceaselessly through that hall he loved so much.

There was only a dim wintry light. It was, in fact, almost dark in that great hall.

But suddenly, just as we reached the far end and turned for a last instinctive look, the floodlights gradually came up to let the TV cameras photograph the changing of the guard round the catafalque. The whole scene was suddenly transformed to a magnificent tapestry in glowing silks.

The moving feet of the hundreds paying homage stopped – everybody froze in his position, and four officers of the Household Cavalry appeared.

The lights struck flashes from glittering breastplates and lit up their brilliant snowy plumes and scarlet jackets. They moved slowly, as in a dream, and when at last they reached their positions they each raised a hand dramatically before letting it fall on the sword hilt, then with a single sharp movement clicked their heads forwards in bowed reverence.

The naval officers whom they had relieved moved away with the same unreal slow motion, reached the little side door, saluted and vanished.

A sigh as the beauty of the moment whispered round the hall, feet started moving automatically and we were outside in the cold air.

I have only to close my eyes to see it all again.

I was among the first four thousand who passed by, but by the end of those three days there were to be close to half a million. I was saying my own 'thank you' for the courage he gave me during the war. And for the comfort he brought to my mother, a frightened widow who was terrified of the blackout and air raids and sheltering from bombs, and yet could still thrill to his speeches.

She loved his fierce determination, his 'British bulldog' expression as she described it, and his uncompromising defiance. After each broadcast, she would say, 'My, he puts new life into you.'

I'm sure she spoke for millions of other frightened women when she used those words. And isn't it marvellous that through the magic of radio and TV we can hear those throbbing tones still, when extracts from war-time speeches are played?

The electronic age conveys a sort of immortality, preserving as it does the speeches and actions of people long dead so that, in a sense, part of them is always with us, to enjoy, to admire and to cherish.

On the morning of the funeral I was, like everyone else, on my way very early, and the trains were filled with silent travellers, many in their best dark clothes. I was going to watch the procession from the offices of the *People's Journal* in Fleet Street, and the caretaker had kindly lent his TV set so that we could watch what was happening at other points along the route.

It was barely 7.30 A.M. and the crowds were already lining the streets, quite silent, seemingly careless of the biting cold.

As we watched the scene on television, with the procession drawing steadily towards us, Fleet Street gradually became lined with soldiers. Sand was laid down to stop the horses slipping, sand which looked amazingly colourful against the grey streets, in contrast to the black and white picture on the TV screen.

A command rang out to the soldiers, 'Reverse Arms', and we knew the procession was with us. The mass of soldiers, sailors and airmen seen on the screen became marching feet below our window.

Then the gun carriage with its precious burden was below us, and we gazed down at the glittering Garter Order and other decorations on their vivid cushions. The banners of the Spencer-Churchills and the Cinque

213

Ports, so ordinary on the television screen, sprang to vivid, sumptuous life, brilliant in scarlets and gold, greens and blacks, as though woven out of shining metal.

They lit up Fleet Street all the way till the cortège disappeared round Ludgate Hill.

Mountbatten looked handsome and strong as he stepped out quite alone in a gap between himself and the preceding and following officers.

But Sir Winston's son, Randolph, looked grey and exhausted, as if he had had quite enough by the time he reached us on that long, long walk to St Paul's.

Ben Gurion, too, walked alone, a tiny figure with his black silk top hat, determined to make his pilgrimage on foot despite his age and his frailty.

It was moving to see the maces hooded in black, and the drums with their mourning black covers.

But the lovely coaches carrying the ladies of the Churchill family somehow seemed romantic, in spite of the sombreness of the occasion, a reminder of a more graceful age, with the crimson-coated coachmen standing at the back.

Sarah and Mary Churchill looked pale through the glass of the coach window, but of Lady Churchill, to whom every heart went out in sympathy, all we could see from above was one dark-gloved hand.

We followed the service on television, and, like millions of others no doubt, joined in the well-known tunes, favourites of Sir Winston. *To be a Pilgrim*, with its stirring opening lines, 'Who would true valour see, let him come hither'. Then came the *Battle Hymn of the Republic*, 'Mine eyes have seen the glory of the coming of the Lord', sung with a vibrancy and strength which made the spine tingle. *Fight the good fight* seemed almost a command from that figure in the coffin, before it was carried out of the Cathedral to the old hymn *O God our help in ages past*.

We put our heads out of the window, to catch the sound of the bells of St Paul's as Kings, Queens, rulers, and princes left, and later we turned our eyes to the skies to watch and listen to the roar as the sixteen Lightnings of Fighter Command flew overhead.

The Flowers of the Forest, that most poignant of tunes turned the heart, and then came the nineteen guns firing in salute, the first time that more than seventeen guns had been given to a commoner.

But that great heart which was being laid to rest beat in the most uncommon 'commoner' any of us living would ever know.

We later visited his grave, Sandy and I, and stood in silence before that plain stone with its simple inscription, WINSTON LEONARD SPENCER CHURCHILL, 1874–1965.

But between the funeral and our visit to Bladon Churchyard, we had our own health problems. As the song has it, 'In every life, a little rain must fall', and we had a veritable cloudburst in the space of twelve months. It started with Sandy. He had been having trouble with 'indigestion' as we thought, which I could generally put right with judicious feeding of bland foods like tripe and porridge, steamed fish and scrambled eggs. However, a frightening haemorrhage during a holiday in Scotland was a danger signal impossible to ignore, and I marched him straight to the doctor as soon as we returned to Pinner. It was a duodenal ulcer, and surgery was advised. Sandy had never been in a hospital in his life, and as a very shy, private person, he hated the very idea of bed-pans and other indignities! They were the least of his worries

215

though, when he floated to the surface after the operation, and found he had twenty-four clips holding a long wound together from chest to waist, and burning thirst which his surgeon forbade him to quench. When I went in to see him, his eyes were quite wild-looking. 'I'm parched,' he whispered. 'Can you get me even a drop of water.' The nurse told me that Sandy's surgeon found there was far less afterpain in the area of the wound if nothing was eaten or drunk for at least twenty-four hours, and later Sandy said he knew it was a good regime to follow, for the patients of other surgeons who were allowed to eat and drink suffered agonies afterwards. However, just then, all he knew was that he felt he would die if some liquid didn't reach his throat. So I squeezed the juice from one of the grapes I'd brought into a teaspoon, and trickled it slowly into his mouth. The look of bliss on his face was unforgettable. Looking stealthily round, as if I was giving him poison, I squeezed another grape, and trickled it even more slowly, to make it last longer. 'Now that's all I can give you,' I said. But when my cup of tea came, I relented and gave him drop by drop, two teaspoonsful of the liquid. The small indulgences did him no harm, as it turned out, and he was able to eat and drink in small quantities next day, without discomfort.

He adapted amazingly well to the hospital life, and it was all made infinitely more bearable because he happened to be there during the World Cup football matches. I may say that that men's ward cared not a jot if they had any visitors the day England played Germany at Wembley. Rhona had come to stay with me for the week-end, *en route* for Nice where she was to join up with brother Tommy, and we two were left to talk to one another by Sandy's bed, while the men

216

practically burst their stitches with excitement when England beat Germany. I couldn't have arranged a more interesting diversion for Sandy if I'd timed the whole thing myself.

When he was allowed to come home, I was warned that he would have to take it easy for quite some time, as this had been major surgery, so I gave him the full treatment. Special diet, with lots of easily digested tasty foods, plenty of rest, and a lovely recuperative holiday on the Isle of Wight, where he found to his delight that his strength improved daily. The surgeon had said it would be about two years before he would really be back to normal health and strength.

In the meantime, I had light-heartedly gone into one of those X-ray scanning caravans, fully expecting to be given a clean bill of health. To my horror, I had a card inviting me to go along for a fuller X-ray at the chest clinic! They weren't quite satisfied with a shadow on the small X-ray, so would I please ring and make an appointment. How could I tell Sandy? I was already seeing myself lying in a sanatorium, doing my Elizabeth Barrett Browning act, not able to do a stroke of work for months, and not able to look after Sandy.

I didn't tell Sandy. I simply couldn't worry him at this stage of his own convalescence so I went alone, while he was resting. I was ostensibly shopping in Harrow. By the oddest coincidence the specialist who saw me was the self-same surgeon who had operated on Sandy, so we were no strangers to one another. After the X-ray, I was told that the 'shadow' was a recent scar indicating that I had had pleurisy only months earlier. No wonder I had felt so wretched after *Market In Honey Lane*. I hadn't taken pneumonia as I flippantly pretended we might, but I *had* had pleurisy. Followed by that heavy cold.

Now it appeared that my salivary gland had been affected, and so I was harbouring a constant low infection which would make me susceptible to all cold bacteria which came my way. The surgeon advised me to have it out. 'You have plenty of glands,' he said cheerfully. 'I'll just winkle it out and you'll be much fitter for your work afterwards.'

The way he described it, it sounded as simple as removing the eye of a potato. No trouble at all. I could arrange my own time and they would fit me in.

I was very attracted to the idea of getting rid of a possible source of colds, for I took 'flu and colds with monotonous regularity each winter, and it was a constant worry when the voice and vitality were affected, for both were my stock-in-trade.

I was so responsive to the whole idea, that Sandy too was lulled into believing it was almost as simple as having a tooth removed. Possibly even simpler.

Which is why neither of us was prepared for the grisly reality. When I came out of the anaesthetic, with a convulsive heaving which indicated urgent need of a basin, a nurse's voice said sharply, 'Don't be sick now. You'll just burst your stitches!' 'I can't help it,' I muttered thickly, 'I must have a basin.' She held my head. I groaned and heaved. 'That's enough,' she commanded. 'I'm taking the basin away. I'll get into trouble if you burst your stitches.'

It was only then I caught sight of Sandy sitting at the other end of the private cubicle, pressed as far back in his chair as he could go, a look of fear on his face. 'I must look positively ghastly,' I thought, 'or he wouldn't look like that.'

I tried to speak, and found my mouth wouldn't form the words properly. What was the matter? I put a hand to my neck feeling for a plaster or bandage, but

218

there was none. Apparently this surgeon had a theory that spraying the stitches with a sort of clear plastic would be better than any sort of solid covering. 'Give me a mirror,' I said sluggishly to Sandy. 'I wouldn't bother just now,' he said. 'Wait till you feel better.'

I feared the worst. 'Give me a mirror, please Sandy,' I said. Silently he handed it to me.

I looked at myself and recoiled in horror. No wonder poor Sandy looked terrified. I had a gash across my neck as though I'd been slashed by a razor. Twelve stitches were clearly visible through the plastic. But, worst of all, my mouth was slewed right round to one side, and I couldn't speak properly!

Would I ever act again? Had this mad surgeon ruined my career for good? What was I going to do? He had told me he was just going to 'winkle it out', and never even gave a hint of danger. Had he bungled it?

Well, it turned out with any gland operation there was a 'slight danger' that nerves would be affected, or even cut, for the area of the salivary gland is a network of face nerves. If the brute had told me that, I'd never have let him near me with his scalpel.

However, he now told me soothingly, that if I massaged the side of my mouth daily, as often as I thought about it, with a good cream, all would be well, and in about three months I would be as good as new! My confidence in him completely destroyed, how could I believe a word he said?

When my neighbours visited me, they took one look at my face, and then began talking animatedly to one another! They clearly couldn't think of a word of comfort, and thought it best to ignore the whole disaster area!

When I went back to the hospital to have the stitches

out, the nurse, the sister and I were nervous wrecks by the time they had managed to pry away the almost immovable plastic covering. They had never had to deal with this till now. 'The next time that surgeon uses plastic,' the sister fumed, 'he'll come and take it off himself.' It was such a mess, they couldn't even be sure that they had taken out all the stitches. If any had been left in I was to come back immediately, in case it set up an infection.

This whole performance took more than half-an-hour, and so shattered me that they actually provided me with a tot of brandy before they would allow me to go home. And I didn't even ask for it either!

I followed the surgeon's advice though, and persevered with daily massage, and it took all of three months before my mouth was back to normal and I was able to say every letter of the alphabet with ease. Even today, in cold weather, that side of my mouth still feels stiff. 'Winkle it out' indeed! The man was a sadist!

But he was right on one score. Never in the future was I to be so susceptible to colds or sore throats, and that was a very desirable bonus in my profession.

While I was convalescing, I had a 'phone call from Jimmy Logan, who wondered if I would like to come back to Glasgow's Metropole and work for him again. He was putting on a play with a part which was exactly right for me. It would have been lovely to have celebrated what we thought of as the end of our hospital cantrips by another season in Glasgow, although *not* at the same digs, but when I read the play I realized it would be impossible. It was far too 'physical' a part, involving hanging upside down from bunk beds, and being used like a rope in a tug-of-war, and I simply couldn't risk opening my neck wound so soon after the operation. So, regretfully, I had to say no. But it was nice to be asked. Actors always believe that where one job is on offer, others will follow. One has not been forgotten or overlooked. That's the main thing. It's a very insecure profession, and we need constant reassurance.

Sandy approved my commonsense decision, and gave me full marks for thinking of my health first. He was now back at the office, and that dreadful ulcer scar was gradually growing less livid. I used to urge him to take off his shirt in the garden, to let the sun do its healing work, and he was getting back his nice tanned look again.

And then one morning when I heard the alarm go off, I discovered Sandy wasn't in bed in our room. He was next door. 'What's the matter?' I said, in slight alarm. His face was very red, and his eyes looked feverish. It transpired he had felt out of sorts during the night, and had tossed and turned so much he had decided to creep through to the back bedroom in case he'd waken me. He knew I had a date to go to a matinée with a neighbour in the afternoon, and he didn't want me hopping around half the night when I was still convalescing myself.

I looked at him, and I felt slightly uneasy. 'Sandy,' I said, 'I don't think you ought to go to the office today.' My heart turned over when he said meekly, 'No, I don't think I will.' There was definitely something wrong for normally I would have had to stamp my foot and shout to the heavens that I knew best before he would have agreed not to go to work, especially when he had been away from the office for weeks following the ulcer operation.

'I'm going to ring the doctor,' I said.

When I described the symptoms, our doctor said

there was a lot of gastric 'flu going around the village, and it sounded very like an attack of that. I was to give him something nourishing like Bovril, with dry crackers, and maybe a little bit of scrambled egg. He was to stay in bed, and I was to collect a prescription, and administer the medicine three times daily. There was nothing to worry about, so he wouldn't come to see him.

I did all those things, and Sandy, now sponged and refreshed, refused to hear of my cancelling the matinée. 'I'll be perfectly all right,' he assured me. 'You know how I can throw off things easily when I get a good sleep.'

We had both felt that, having spoken to the doctor, there was no cause for real alarm. The doctor, after all, knew of the recent operation, and if he didn't think it necessary to call, then there could be no reason to worry.

So I went to the matinée with my neighbour, and enjoyed a play which held us enthralled from first to last. We had intended finishing our afternoon out by having tea in town, but because of Sandy's unexpected gastric attack, I decided I must go straight home.

When I got upstairs, Sandy's face was scarlet, his eyes glazed, and he had been sick five times. I rang the doctor immediately. Lo and behold, the doctor who had spoken to me in the morning had gone on holiday! Without a hint of his plans! Otherwise I would have insisted on a visit then, for he knew all about Sandy's health.

The young doctor I spoke to listened patiently to my description of the symptoms, and of the recent ulcer operation, and said he would be along as soon as he had finished surgery. When he did come, he examined Sandy very thoroughly, asked a few questions and then turned to me. 'This is not like any gastric 'flu I've seen,' he said. 'In view of the recent operation, I am going to send for an ambulance. He must go back to hospital.'

He picked up the 'phone. 'Get his things ready – pyjamas, shaving stuff, you know what is needed.'

The hospital were not at all keen to accept him, and only the doctor's insistence that he would take no responsibility for a patient they had themselves recently operated on and now refused to examine, made them change their minds.

'The ambulance should be here within the hour,' he said. It was now about seven o'clock, and it had turned to an evening of wind and rain.

We waited, and we waited. Sandy tossed feverishly. I checked and re-checked the contents of the little case. I tried to drink a cup of tea, and my mind raced to all sorts of possibilities. Could the ulcer have burst inside? Could it be an internal haemorrhage? I could think of nothing except ulcer complications, because the surgeon had told me after that operation that he had hád 'a good look around while he was inside' and that Sandy was in very good shape in every other respect.

I kept running downstairs and wiping the condensation from the windows, gazing out into the storm-lashed lane for any sign of an ambulance. At nine o'clock I rang the doctor, who had left his home number, and who now answered in some irritation. However, when he discovered that Sandy was still with me, his tone changed and he said he would check and ring me back. Within ten minutes he rang to say there had been a train disaster at Harrow, and every ambulance in the county had been called to assist. I was to wait for another hour and if there was still no ambulance, I was to ring him again.

At half-past ten I rang him. I was utterly distraught by this time and Sandy was almost beyond speech. The ambulance came at eleven o'clock, and Stan, my good neighbour across the lane followed in his car so that he could drive me home. I could never have trusted myself to drive our own car, I was so overwrought.

When we reached the hospital the first little fracas which stirred me out of my fearful state was when a little Asian nurse with a black pigtail down her back told me off for arriving so late! 'Why are you here at this time of night?' she demanded. 'Why do you not arrive earlier?'

I couldn't believe my ears.

'Because,' I said slowly and clearly, 'I have been sitting waiting for an ambulance since seven o'clock and it only arrived within the past half-hour.'

The ward-sister arrived before we could come to blows!

Stan and I sat waiting together, while Sandy was taken away for examination, and I filled in all the necessary forms and gave the essential details they required.

A Chinese doctor appeared, or at least one who looked Chinese, with slanting dark eyes, long narrow build, and yellow complexion. At first I couldn't take in what he was trying to tell me. And then the words sank in. He wanted to operate immediately. It was an emergency and there could be no delay. 'But what is it?' I cried. 'He had major surgery only ten weeks ago. What is it?' It was, in his opinion, a perforated appendix. If he had said smallpox it couldn't have given me a greater shock.

CHAPTER TEN

I will draw a veil over the subsequent shocks and alarms, but suffice it to say that Sandy's body took real punishment, and the second operation took a lot of getting over. On the worst days, I sought the therapy of the hands for comfort, and unpicked and let down the hems of all my kilts, a formidable task which I had contemplated tackling 'some day'. Now was the day, and the work kept me sane, and enabled me to be cheerful and encouraging during the weeks I drove back and forward to that hospital. I never see the pale blue bias binding round the hems of those kilts, but I am reminded of that traumatic period in our lives. I ought to have used brown or black to match the tartans, but it was no time to be finicky when the shops were shut, and my need was urgent. So I used what I had in the house.

There was one strange result of those operations. Sandy's metabolism changed completely and became exactly like mine. Before those illnesses, he tended to put on weight very easily, for he had always been what would be politely described as 'well built'. Now he shed all his surplus fat, and he never again put it back. Like me, forever afterwards he could eat all the chocolate, sweets, pies and cream he fancied without adding an ounce to his frame. When I said as much to some actor friends, they groaned with envy and said, 'My God, I'd gladly undergo two operations if I could eat anything I liked without having to worry about my weight.'

Any time Sandy was feeling a bit low, I would

remind him of the actors' reaction and it would make him laugh. Now it was all over, he had to admit it was a great bonus. Not only good health, but lean good health.

We were cautiously beginning to feel we had finished with hospitals when, believe it or not, I stretched my arms luxuriously in bed one Saturday morning, gave an almighty yawn – and found I couldn't close my mouth! Sandy came rushing upstairs when he heard my muffled yelps of alarm, and nearly burst his wound laughing when he saw me sitting up in bed with wide-open mouth like a face at a fun-fair, waiting for a ping-pong ball to be thrown.

It was no laughing matter for me. At the out-patients' department the little Asian assistant clasped expressive hands in dismay, held my hair aside to allow a picture to be taken, and with great delicacy pinned it all up again, showing great pleasure in its blonde colouring. I think he must have been a hairdresser before he took up medicine! That was the only comedy touch I could enjoy, for the X-rays showed I had dislocated my jaw! With yawning! It was almost beyond belief. I never realized such a thing was possible.

Eating was a problem for a week or so, and I became quite terrified to yawn or sneeze. I was told that in future I must never yawn with arms stretched above my head. If I must stretch, then I must hold my arms out in front of me, parallel with my shoulders and never higher. No wonder I became an authority on yawning. Now that I was aware of the bones and muscles we use in producing a yawn, I realized that very few people could yawn convincingly on film or TV. Even Sandy recognizes phoney yawns now, and chimes in with me, ''Mmm, not a good yawn – more like a sigh,' when a character depicts this weary mime unsuccessfully on the screen.

When at long last my jaw was behaving itself properly, and I could safely appear in public, my first invitation was to preside at a Salvation Army Rally in Harrow. This was an excellent opportunity for me to display some gratitude for safe deliverance from all the slings and arrows against our poor vulnerable physiques, and render assistance to a very good cause. Thus it was I found myself behind a pulpit, with the Mayor of Harrow himself sharing the platform with me, and Brigadiers and Commissioners in attendance.

My grannie would have been proud of me, had she seen me leading the prayers and the hymns. As for Auntie Tassie, the one salvationist in our family to wear 'the bonnet', and who had taught me to sing in harmony with her, she would have been starry-eyed to have heard her 'pupil' up there with the top brass, harmonizing with the best of them.

I had to give a little address and, seeing the hall filled to capacity with uniformed Salvationists, I thought I would amuse them by telling them of my childhood passion for the Salvation Army, of how I had marched up Springburn Road on Saturday nights behind the band, and had been converted not once, but twice. To my astonishment, instead of laughing as I had hoped, they shouted with one voice, 'Hallelujah!', and raised their hats in the air! The Mayor and I dissolved in disgraceful laughter at this unexpected reaction, and had to turn away and pretend to consult the running order before announcing the next item.

A week or so later when a leaflet arrived telling me of the next RADA classes, I thought it would be a good idea to do another course, just to make sure those mouth muscles were working properly. I hadn't really been tested since the gland operation, and I knew it would be great fun to be back with my fellow-professionals again. I wondered if those classes would bring me some good luck again in the way of work, for I was beginning to regard them with some superstitious anticipation, since previous classes had coincided with most welcome offers. I couldn't have dreamed what *this* course of study would bring though.

The first sign came when I was sitting peacefully in the gazebo writing, with my hair pinned up under a scarf, and wearing gardening trousers because I intended working outside later. There was nothing in the diary except a visit to Harrow Council to try to buy a lamp-post. The 'phone rang, and when I answered it I discovered it was an advertising firm and they wanted me to go immediately to an address in London to discuss a possible commercial.

'What, now?' I said. 'But I'm in my working clothes and my hair's a mess.'

'All the better,' came the reassuring voice. 'We don't want you too chic!'

Too chic indeed, there wasn't a hope of that.

Nor was there any hope of my dashing in the moment they crooked a little finger. 'If they know they want me at half-past-eleven,' I thought, 'then they knew it at ten o'clock this morning, so they can wait.' The nerve of me. When I think how it all turned out, I am amazed to recall my own coolness.

I informed them I was in the middle of a piece of writing which had to meet a deadline (which was true), and that I must have a cup of tea and an egg before heading for London, for it involved four trains. I've seen the day when I would have leaped to do their bidding, only to have to swallow disappointment in the end when they decided I wasn't 'right'. Now I would go when it suited me, when I had finished the job in hand.

There was a little silence at the other end. Then, 'When can you be with us?' I think I had really stunned them, for at that time everyone wanted to be in adverts on television. I calculated my timetable. 'I'll be with you as near three o'clock as I can manage,' I said. 'It will all depend on the trains.'

'Don't look too smart,' the voice said.

I finished my article, I had my welcome tea with a boiled egg, changed into one of my lengthened kilts and a jersey, with my short fur jacket on top, and went for my train. At the reception desk, I found there were several other females to be seen besides me, but the casting lady seized me and whisked me off to the ladies' room, whipped off my jersey cap, approved my hair-style with the bun on top of my head, ruffled it a bit, and said 'Good luck'. I was glad I hadn't rushed into town without lunch, for it was obvious the testing was going to go on all day.

I had my test in a large room with a small video-camera to record my 'audition', with one of the male members of the staff reading the part of my 'niece'. I was sure I was a flop, for he stood behind me, and I kept turning my head to say my line to him, so that my face was away from the camera practically throughout. However, they appeared to like the look of me, and they certainly found my hairstyle exactly to their taste, and I was told I would be asked back again for proper camera tests.

Four hours later I was back in the gazebo and getting on with a piece of writing for *Woman's Hour*, having pushed the audition to the back of my mind.

There is no doubt enormous trouble is taken in the advertising world to get the right person from every point of view, and I had four more tests for voice, face, and characterization before I was told I had got the part. And for each of those auditions I travelled in four trains to get there, and four trains back, without knowing whether or not all this rushing about would result in my being chosen.

And that was how I became Mrs M. in the Flash commercial.

The first shock was to learn that the filming would involve a 6 A.M. rise for me! I never dreamed a thirty second commercial would take such a long time. It was summer time though, and it didn't seem so agonizing when the sun was shining and the birds at least were up. I laughed sympathetically when I read of an interview with Peter O'Toole, who also hates early rising. He said that when he gets up at the crack of dawn for filming, he always feels he and the man about to be guillotined are the only two creatures in the world awake at such an hour! I agree wholeheartedly with this sentiment!

However, apart from the early start, life was made very easy. A car fetched me and brought me home. Tea and coffee were brought to my room. A car took me to lunch and returned me to the studio. I even had my name on my dressing room door in gold letters on a midnight blue background. Who would have believed there would be all this star-treatment for a commercial! I was to learn that more detailed care was given to this work than to the biggest films for the cinema.

Luckily I didn't find the domestic part too arduous, but there were *hours* of standing for lighting and camera work, and I found myself subsiding on to the doormat or a stool whenever I wasn't wanted, simply to rest my legs. I can walk for miles, but standing around was murder! On the subject of legs, I made an amusing discovery one day, when the camera had to 'pan' up from my feet to my face. I had no idea that feet could denote anything when standing completely still, but when they examined mine through the viewer, they decided I had feet which were far too young, and that even the way I stood was too youthful! So we had to make a few adjustments to get that right. I wonder if it was in commercials that Beryl Reid learned to get the shoes and the feet right first, and the rest of the character would follow?

We had a visit one day from a German director who was in England to see how we worked over here, and he was flatteringly complimentary. He said he had never seen work done so quietly and with such discipline, and that this could never happen in Germany. I was amazed. I thought Germans were noted for their hard work.

He was most impressed that when an electrician was wanted, he was on the spot. Likewise with a property man, carpenter or painter, indeed anyone at all who was working on our shows. As for me, he informed me it was obvious that I thoroughly enjoyed my work, and he was very intrigued to find an actress with such enthusiasm. Was it perhaps that they didn't like working on commercials, I wondered?

'In Germany,' he told me earnestly, 'the pay packet is all, and we would be very lucky indeed to find such interest and pleasure from our people.'

Who would have believed it? We all felt six inches taller after that!

At lunch-time each day, it was like the penny matinée when we dashed along to the small cinema to watch the previous day's 'rushes', i.e. the running of the film scenes we had shot the day before. I found it very amusing to observe how everyone reacted to his

231

or her own contribution, and ignored the work of others. I, of course, was most interested in my performance and in what the camera lighting had done for my face!

The lighting chap was riveted to the effect his lamps made, while the make-up man audibly checked that his skills were flatteringly evident.

The sound engineers listened intently to make sure the quality of their work was all they had hoped, and the advertisers and clients were concentrated on ensuring that the product was shown correctly.

There was exactly the same reaction from a wardrobe lady on a film I was in some time later.

When I discovered she had been on *Othello* with Sir Laurence Olivier, I flew along to ask her how they had rehearsed the big dramatic scenes. I was longing to know what it had been like to watch my idol at work. I had been in floods of tears when I had seen the film, it was so moving.

'What was Olivier like, Margaret?' I asked her eagerly, as her eye checked that my costume was correct in every detail.

'Well, dear,' she said, 'you know that shantung robe he wore? He only 'ad the one, and I 'ad to make him another three so we could always have a couple in the wash.'

I stared at her, baffled. Then I tried again.

'What about that agonizing scene when he strangles Desdemona? Did you find that very moving to watch on the set?'

'I should just think it did,' she said. 'Desdemona only 'ad the one nightgown and I was terrified he'd tear it at rehearsals. I hadn't another thing she could wear.'

232

I gave up, laughing. Truly the agony had passed her by.

She had had her own private anguish.

They had no trouble with my wardrobe for Flash, for I supplied my own. I'm always held back from parting with too many clothes to jumble sales and the like, for with my small build it is easier to provide my own things than to spend hours chasing round the shops and for the part of the helpful 'daily' I knew I would just be required to be neat but not too dressy.

As I am a natural hoarder, it is a good excuse to hang on to my 'old duds' as my mother would have called them. Spike Milligan says when he is extravagant, he senses the shadow of his economical mother breathing down his neck. I told him he was lucky in having only one shadow. I had two. My mother and my grannie!

All social life came to a complete halt during the filming for this commercial. Up at six, home at eight, sometimes nine, bed at ten, and no television. I was much too wearied to do more than have a saunter round the garden to check that all the plants were behaving themselves, before falling into bed.

When the advert was shown on the screen, I was amazed at how quickly I became the focus of all eyes wherever I went. I could normally walk about our village without causing too much comment, for they were used to me by this time, but one day when I needed a new sponge for my floor mop I had to carry the whole mop with me so that the man could fit the sponge in the shop.

It didn't dawn on me that I looked as if I'd stepped straight out of the TV screen from my floor-cleaning act, until I noticed everyone grinning as they caught sight of me. At last a woman in the supermarket couldn't resist speaking. She tapped my arm and said, 'Hullo Mrs M. Looking for some floors to clean?' At that the entire shop was convulsed with giggles, and only then did I appreciate I must look like a walking advert. It was a bit unnerving to be followed by peals of laughter as I left the shop, particularly when the English are normally so douce when faced with even the strangest sights. So I decided to enter into the spirit of the thing, and pretended to clean up the pavement in front of the next lot of neighbours!

And when we had a Pinner week to raise funds for charity, by common consent I and a group of enthusiastic youngsters were roped in and sponsored at a penny to sixpence a flag-stone, and scrubbed the High Street from top to bottom with Flash. It was like a scene from an Italian film – the young ones wore a wild assortment of clothing, bowler hats, huge straw garden-party cartwheels garlanded with flowers, sea-going gear, and ponchos, and *all* carried cushions or bed-rolls or pads to kneel on.

The art shop owner provided trays of hot steaming tea and biscuits to keep us all from catching pneumonia, and the entire village turned out to film the spectacle. A lady who had moved to Pinner only five weeks before, was enthralled with all this community activity. She obviously thought it went on all the time, and nobody had the heart to disillusion her. I had the distinct impression she imagined Pinner revolved round the Flash commercial!

In spite of having been in show business for years, it was with my appearance as Mrs M. that anonymity vanished forever. It was quite staggering, for long before I was aware of the nationwide appeal of 'commercials' I had grown used to being recognized by the

234

public, but for a variety of reasons, and not all at the same time.

To some I would always be 'Tattie' of *ITMA*. To others I would forever be identified as 'Aggie' of *Life With the Lyons*, while to aficionados north of the border, the mere mention of *The McFlannels* broadened their smiles and caused them to remember with affection 'Ivy McTweed', that gallus Glaswegian written for me by Helen Pryde.

I could never have dreamed that all those long-established characters would fade into insignificance when compared with the riveting appeal of Mrs M. armed with her Flash packet, ready to do battle with floors, baths, working surfaces and scuff marks. There must surely be a universal appeal in watching dirt being removed from our work-a-day world, while every variety of smut is allowed to linger permissively in our mental areas!

I found I had only to walk into a strange shop for every head to swivel in my direction, like pointer dogs in search of their quarry. 'Do you use it yourself?' was the greeting, with a nudge in the ribs of the nearest assistant. 'Of course,' I replied for the hundredth time, 'what do you think?'

'Come round the back then, Mrs M.', they chirruped encouragingly. 'We could do with you here. Look at the state of them floors.'

The entire shop would come to a standstill. Nobody was served. I could only hope nobody who was in a hurry would wish to lynch me, or worse, stop using Flash as their revenge!

In an endeavour to bring the floor show to a conclusion, I usually smiled and said, 'I'm a *very* expensive charlady, you couldn't afford me,' which little bit of patter brought exaggerated laughter, and then I'd repeat my request for whatever it was I had actually wanted to buy. Shopping took *hours,* and Sandy refused to go into any store with me thereafter.

It had its advantages of course. When I found a pair of boots in a top shop and had neither cash nor cheque book with me, because *everyone* in the shop vouched for the fact that I was indeed Molly Weir, who was also Mrs M. in that Flash advert, I was permitted to walk out of that exclusive establishment clutching my precious boots on the promise that they would get their cheque when I returned to my hotel. I couldn't quite decide whether it was faith in Flash, or in Flash's credit rating, which gave them such confidence that I was to be trusted out of their sight with the most expensive boots in the shop.

On a visit to Glasgow, I was photographed in George Square by the newspapers, and it happened to be the day that the Scottish football team which was about to set off for their European game in the World Cup were assembling at my hotel. The fans were out in full force and the moment footballers and fans caught sight of me, there was a roar of recognition, 'Heh Molly, how's it gaun?' and then they informed one another with delight, 'It's the wee tart that dis the Vim!' The friend who was with me collapsed with laughter, 'It's a good job that Flash doesn't hear them,' she giggled. Glasgow never changes.

I was soon receiving painful back-slapping approval from hefty male fists, with demands all round for my autograph. If I'd scored the winning goal myself, I couldn't have met more popular approval.

I've been 'taken off' by Benny Hill, Stanley Baxter and the Goodies.

On a Thames TV show *Looks Familiar*, when a comedian identified Tex Ritter, Denis Norden asked

236

him if he could remember the name of the horse. 'Yes, I think I can,' came the reply. 'It was called White Flash.' With characteristic wit, Denis interposed, 'As now ridden by Molly Weir.'

I sometimes tried to hurry the shopping by denying my identity. Once in an enormous queue at a green-grocery stall at Christmas, the moment I asked for a pound of sprouts the youngest lad jumped as if he'd been stung. ''Ere,' he said after an urgently whispered word with the lad beside him, ''e sez you're the lady wot does them baths.' I stared at him and repeated, 'A pound of sprouts please.' He ignored my request. 'Go on, tell us,' he said, '*are* you the lady wot does them baths wivout scratching?' 'I'm very flattered,' I said evasively, 'I'm always being told I look like her.'

He weighed the sprouts reflectively, then pushed an empty paper bag over, 'Go on love,' he said with a grin, 'sign 'ere. I think you're smashing.' What could I do?

But the accolade came at a party given in honour of Morecambe and Wise. I'd never met the lads before, and when I was thanking them at the evening, I said to Eric, 'How lovely it has been, Eric, to meet you both in the flesh.' Like lightning came his response. 'How lovely it has been, Molly, to meet you in the *Flash*!' Boom – boom!

It was a long, happy, and enjoyable association with a company which was always considerate, and we had a great relationship from first to last. But oh the jokes! Coming from the more modest north, I didn't realize for a long time that Flash had any other meaning than that of a fast-cleaning floor powder or a bright light. I know better now!

It only came to an end as a result of the ITV technicians' strike in 1979 when advertisers had time to take a long look at their account books, and realized they had lost less through being off the screen, than they would have spent had they continued with regular advertising. Confirming, if proof were needed, my long-held belief that nobody benefits from a strike, and the innocent come off worst of all.

The gravy train maybe stopped for me, but I am still asked to clean pub floors, Post Office floors, other people's kitchens, railway compartments and super-market floors. As far as the public is concerned, Mrs M. is still going strong!

I was destined to miss the last few classes from that particular RADA course, for the superstitious belief of mine that 'a gaun fit's aye gettin'' brought another offer for me. This time it was from Scotland, to appear in a new BBC TV series with the immensely popular Scots comedian, Lex McLean. I had never met him, but I knew he could fill the Glasgow Pavilion for as long a season as he chose, and that he seemed to be in the tradition of the great Glasgow comics.

So before the classes came to an end, I was heading for Glasgow, to my new digs, very curious to meet this man McLean, whom everyone else but me seemed to have seen. People were astounded to find that I had never met him. 'What! You've never seen him in the Pavilion? A bit near the knuckle, mind you, but terrific, brings the house doon. Aye, he'll have to tone doon his patter a bit fur the BBC.'

I didn't know what to expect when I went along to the first rehearsal. Would he be a quick-fire joker like the late Max Miller? A cheerful chappie like Charlie Chester? A shrewd humorist like Ted Ray? An expansive charmer like Jimmy Logan? I didn't even know what he looked like.

I was early, but the room was unlocked so I began

studying my script. A few minutes later a dark quiet man strolled in. He was sprucely dressed in a neat navy suit, and his thick dark hair was smoothly brushed back. With a nod to me, he moved to the piano, sat down and set my toes tapping with some excellent swinging music. The band arranger, I wondered? I looked at him more closely. There was an air of self-confidence and power about him, and a suspicion dawned that this might just be Lex McLean himself. It was! Looking utterly unlike my mental picture of the comedian everybody had been trying to describe to me.

The most striking quality about him was his quietness. I had expected punchy delivery and a fire-cracker style, but I found his rehearsal tone was extremely muted. In fact I had to keep my ears pinned back to catch my cues, and I have exceptionally good hearing. But one thing stood out a mile. He had a fantastic memory. In my experience this was really exceptional, for music-hall comics seldom work from scripts, and are consequently poor memorizers when working from the written page. Not Lex. I never saw him with a script in his hand, and he shook me rigid by knowing the entire thing from A to Z at our first rehearsal. Because I find it difficult to un-learn, I never memorize anything untfl I'm assured there will be no changes. So there was I, with my few tiny scenes, working from a script, and McLean, with pages and pages of dialogue, saying it all off by heart.

Because he was a master of the ad lib, with a lightning brain always ready to deliver the fast gag, television was an appalling discipline for him. Camera crews work from a camera script, with every single shot worked out like a jig-saw puzzle. If the shooting script indicates, 'Shot 29. Close up of Lex on the line

239

"That's whit we're here to find oot",' and Lex delivers a different line, then he doesn't get a close up, the TV gremlins take over, and the show grinds to a halt. When you work with cameras you work as rehearsed, or it's chaos.

It was a new world for Lex McLean, but it was interesting to see how fast he learned. He soon adjusted to the sickening fact that if a show over-ran because he couldn't resist the temptation to stick in a few gags, then they just had to come out on the cutting room floor later. There's no magic which will stretch an allotted time of twenty-eight minutes to thirty-five. And if editing is to make sense, a lack of discipline means a lot of good material must be sacrificed.

Off stage, I enjoyed his dry, laconic sense of humour. One day I thought I'd better let the director see the outfit the wardrobe had for me as Walter Carr's wife, and I put it on after lunch. I thought it might be a bit elegant for the character, and wondered if I'd toned it down enough by adding a chain-store pull-on hat and cheap fabric gloves. Lex took one look at me and said, without even the hint of a smile, 'Cheap hat and gloves? I don't know what you're talking about. It's the best dressed you've been since I met you!'

I roared with laughter, for I had been rehearsing in my best clothes, and because of the iciness of the rehearsal room, had even been wearing my mink coat! Cheeky monkey that he was, he knew I'd enjoy the joke. It was so pleasant to be on such matey terms so quickly.

When any of us would dry up at rehearsals, he would gaze at the ceiling and sigh with long-suffering patience, 'Aye, and the BBC told me I'd be better off surrounded with actors. Actors did they say! H'm!'

He had us all eating out of his hand in no time with

ABOVE: Molly entertaining neighbours to tea in their present home in Pinner, 1962 (*Photo: D C Thomson & Co Ltd, People's Journal*)

LEFT: On the top of Duncryne, near Loch Lomond 1962. L. to R. Sandy, Molly and brother Tom (*Photo: A D S McPherson*)

ABOVE: Miss Mackenzie's class –
Molly in gym tunic (made from
mother's costume jacket) second
left of second back row

RIGHT: Grannie

RIGHT: The Dame of Sark welcomes Molly to the Seigneurie, 1972
(Photo: A Hamilton)

BELOW: BBC celebrations – 50 years of Broadcasting. L. to R. Kathleen Garscadden (Auntie Kathleen of BBC Radio *Children's Hour*), Wendy Wood, Baillie Jean Roberts and Molly, 1973
(Photo: R. L. Nicholson)

Still from the film *Scrooge*, 1971. Molly on L. with Albert Finney as Scrooge

Finlay's Casebook, 1972. Molly as hotel proprietrix (very genteel!)
th Esmond Knight *(Photo: BBC Radio Times)*

Auntie Kathleen's tribute from BBC TV in 1973. Top: Magnus Magnusson, Back Row: Peggy O'Keefe, Ian Whyte, Howard Lockhart, Gordon Jackson, Moly, Father Sydney McEwan. Front Row: Moultrie Kelsall, Ruby Duncan, Grace McCherie, Archie Lee, Auntie Kathleen, W H D Joss, Moira Anderson and Rikki Fulton *(Photo: Whyler Photos, Stirling)*

Oh Father! BBC TV 1973. L. to R. Molly as Sister Cecilia, Derek Nimmo as Father Dominic and Gaye Brown as Sister Anastasia *(Photo: BBC)*

ABOVE: Molly as Hazel the McWitch in *Rentaghost*, BBC TV 1978-83
(Photo: BBC TV)

LEFT: Molly as she appears in *Tea-time Tales* STV.
(Photo: Mark Gudgeon)

LEFT: Molly aged fourteen with mother during Perth holiday. Both wearing dresses made by mother, Molly's sewn, mother's knitted in silk.

BELOW: Tandem halt with Sandy by the shores of Lock Earn, Perthshire. Courting days 1937 *(Photo: A Hamilton)*

other and father – courting days

Worker's Playtime, BBC Radio 1950. L. to R. Denis Lotis, Cyril Fletcher, Tommy Reilly and Molly. Extreme R. producer Bill Gates *(Photo: Chaplin Jones)*

Life With the Lyons cast, BBC Radio 1950. L. to R. Richard Lyon, Molly, Doris Rogers, Ian Sadler, Bebe Daniels, Ben Lyon, Barbara Lyon, David Enders and Horace Percival *(Photo: Press and General)*

Keep Smiling cast, BBC Radio 1951. L. to R. Charlie Chester, Edna Fryer, Molly, Deryck Guyter, Len Martin, Frederick Ferrari *(Photo: BBC)*

ABOVE: ITMA cast at
Olympia, 1947, (BBC
Radio) L. to R. Jack Train,
Tommy Handley, Molly and
Lind Joyce *(Photo: London
News Agency Photos Ltd)*

RIGHT: Theatrical Garden
Party, London, 1947. Molly
(from *The Happiest Days of
Your Life*) still star-struck
gazing at Noel Coward and
Margaret Lockwood *(Photo:
International News Photos)*

Molly aged thirteen, wearing the dress she made at school

LEFT: Molly tries out a new idea for a Flash advert. Newcastle, 1978

BELOW: *This is Your Life, Molly Weir!* Thames TV 1977. L. to R. Eamonn Andrews, Molly and Sandy *(Photo: Thames TV)*

Molly and Sandy outside their first Pinner home, 1949 *(Photo: V R Devan)*

Molly

this gentle leg-pulling, and we were all rooting for him, and praying he would make a real success at this new branch of the trade for him. He had absolutely no side, and he was after all an established star of the music hall.

As soon as people knew I was working with him, I was bombarded with questions. 'Whit's he like to meet in real life Molly?' 'How dis he like workin' on the TV?' 'Is he gonnae be good?' I began to appreciate the courage he was showing in tackling this new branch of the profession, with all the fans judging him from his Pavilion appearances.

After I'd worked with him for a week or two, I tried honestly to assess what I saw in him, so that I could give a true answer to all those questions. Glasgow folk are great listeners. I was well aware that nothing arouses such a strong response as comedy. People can be lukewarm about tragedy or drama, but there are no half measures where humour is involved. They either love the comic or they can't stand him, and the more individual he is, the stronger are the reactions he arouses.

In Lex McLean I found a great potential TV comic.

The man was an original. That to me was his great appeal. He copied nobody. Yet, at the same time I saw in him a lot of the qualities of the more durable comics. He had something of the bumbling eccentricity of W. C. Fields. He had a bit of the sadistic humour of the late Arthur Haynes. And a little of the outraged confidence of Hancock. But above all he was himself. That was his great strength.

One of the things he had to combat was the in-built resistance to his quieter TV style from those who admired him most in the theatre. They seemed somehow to fail to realize he could be equally funny in situation comedy and appeal to a much wider public, but it had to be a different approach when it was going into everybody's front room.

On the positive side, there was a great deal of goodwill for him, in Glasgow at least.

I liked the chap who said to me, 'I'd *like* him to succeed on TV, Molly. And yet, in another way, I hope he doesn't succeed *too* well. I don't want him to turn his back on the music hall altogether – for this man belongs to the theatre.'

Had he lived long enough, I think he would just as surely have belonged to the world of television.

My friends who came to the show were highly delighted to meet Lex and very surprised to find him such a nice-looking man and so quiet compared with his rumbustious professional personality.

They were amazed at the number of cameras and the endless technicalities involved in a TV recording. They told me, with great perceptiveness, that watching me having to stand for a full five minutes with the telephone receiver held to my ear, waiting for the 'count-down' gave them palpitations of terror. Young Claire said if she'd had to do that, her hand would have shaken so much she'd never have been able to utter a word. It is all so much more nerve-racking than it seems when it comes out of the small screen, but of course that is partly what we are paid for, to make it look dead easy!

Indeed I could have told them that the recording had been graced by a complete lack of temperament. Producer and director were paragons of encouragement and quiet enthusiasm. Oh it does make life so easy when people go about their work in such a relaxed frame of mind, for there's nothing more tiring than tantrums. That's why I could never believe in the story

242

of that Bette Davis film *All About Eve* where she played the fiery temperamental jealous actress. If they had had all those fights before a show, they would have been so exhausted and drained they could never have had the strength to give a performance.

The most temperamental thing in our show was the wee budgie who was one of the 'stars'. It was a trained bird, and should have nipped smartly out of the cage when the door was opened, so that Walter Carr as 'my man' could chase it. After the first rehearsal on recording day, it went into a huff with all the shouting and chasing, and when it came to the 'take' it sat tight and firmly refused to stir so much as a claw! But actors are used to emergencies, and Walter Carr did a pretty nifty piece of faking and all went well.

By an oversight, the producer forgot to introduce me to the audience when the rest of the cast were introduced before the show, and they were quite stunned by my raging entrance when I stormed in and berated my hen-pecked husband. A friend in the audience told me they all fell to whispering 'Who's that?' and, by the time they had decided it was Molly Weir, I had stormed out again! Out, out, brief candle!

Needless to say, Lex McLean was a riot and the audience adored him.

There was a terrific clamour for tickets for those recordings. Everyone in Glasgow, it seemed, wanted to be in at Lex's TV début. Even dear Auntie Kathleen of Children's Hour came, although I fancy Lex's Pavilion patter would have made her hair curl! I hadn't seen her for years and it was a real treat to spy her sitting out front. We had a swift and friendly reunion at the end, and in spite of my severe hair-do for the character of Walter Carr's battle-axe of a wife, she found me hardly changed at all. That was Kathleen to the life. Always the encouraging word.

That was the final recording of the series and it was time to say my good-byes. My digs had been marvellous, a real home from home, but once more when living the tenement life, I met that scourge and terror, the noisy upstairs neighbour! The house where I stayed was beautifully quiet, with its own front door, but that human poltergeist above turned night into day when she couldn't sleep, with never a thought that somebody underneath might be trying to get a night's rest.

She cleaned out her kitchen, trailing furniture from one side of the room to the other. She ran a bath, used gallons of water for hours during her cleaning frenzies, and sent gurglings down the pipes non-stop. Added to this Niagara of sound, she had apparently never heard of bedroom slippers and stamped about in what sounded like tackety boots! All this in the wee sma' hours of the morning. I never even clapped eyes on her. No doubt, having effectively massacred my sleep on many a vital night, she was deep in slumber during the hours of daylight.

My landlady was such a gem that I couldn't worry about the insomniac above my head. I was greatly touched when this gentle provider of a home from home said to me, in parting, 'Now I know what a mother feels like when the last bairn goes to school. I'll just not know what to do with myself next week when you've gone. It'll be so *quiet*.' I was certain I would have driven her mad with my constant invasion of her kitchen for my endless tea-making, but not a bit of it. She stoutly maintained that I was no trouble at all, and as far as noise was concerned, she hardly knew I was in the house. She had loved our little tête-à-têtes and would miss me more than she could say. That was a happy thought to take back to London.

The taxi-driver who came to take me to the station was a turn in himself. He mistook me for the landlady's wee sister, and gaily invited her to join us in the taxi for a wee hurl, there and back! He was amazed to discover we weren't in fact related, and kept saying to me, 'My, she's awfu' nice, awfu' nice.' As though he had never expected anyone who let rooms could be so charming. Then, as I chatted to him from the back seat where I kept a foot on the cases to stop them tumbling all over the taxi as he whirled us fiercely round corners, he said, 'My, I wish I could keep you in the back there a' day – you're such a nice wee thing!' I was fairly swept off my feet with such unexpected gallantry!

It was a hilarious farewell to my native city and a fitting end to a most enjoyable episode.

The train journey back was sheer bliss. I have never felt the hours pass so smoothly. I was so wearied with all the non-stop chatter and visiting and chasing around I had done while I was in Glasgow, that I was more than ready for complete quiet. I established myself in a non-smoker, exchanged my boots for slippers, blew up my little cushion and tucked it into the small of my back, and settled down comfortably in a compartment I had entirely to myself all the way.

I only stirred once to drift along to the buffct car, where I enjoyed a delicious afternoon tea. Nothing could go wrong that day, it seemed. Sandwiches were fresh, toast piping hot and dripping with butter, Swiss roll fat with apricot jam and soft and spongy. The Ritz couldn't have done better. The car attendant, braced to receive complaints, hardly recognized the compliment when I told him it was one of the nicest teas I'd had on

British Railways. When he did take it in, he obviously wanted to continue to bask in this rare approval, and turned to the man opposite and said, 'Was yours all right sir?' 'Very nice!' came the short and crisp reply. *Nothing* like my enthusiasm, his lifted eyebrow seemed to say, but it would do.

We drew in to Watford dead on time and there was Sandy flying up the platform to meet me, and we were home in Pinner before the train reached Euston.

My predictions of a great television future for Lex were never to be realized. There were only two more short series before a stroke stopped him in mid-tracks, and slowed down that quicksilver brain and removed hope of a full working life. Seven years after I met him, he was dead, and with him went the last of the old-style music hall giants who, by sheer force of personality and character, could hold an entire theatre in the palm of their hands.

Speaking at a Burns' dinner on one occasion, I ventured to tell one of Lex's less colourful jokes, and I had only to say, 'I heard this story from Lex McLean,' to bring the house down. As always, as soon as the speeches were over, I was assailed on all sides by the revellers, wanting to know what he was like 'in real life'.

It is a happy memory for me that I was in at his television début, and a tragedy for Scottish theatre that he was taken far too soon.

His name will never be forgotten though, for in the legends of the great Scots comics, Lex McLean has an honoured place.

CHAPTER ELEVEN

One of the dreams I have hugged to my bosom ever since I had the luck to become an actress was to play in *Macbeth*. Not Lady Macbeth, not even Lady Macduff. No, the part which intrigued me beyond all others was that of the first witch. It's hard to say just why this part has so fascinated me, unless perhaps it's because while for so many years I have tried to amuse people and make them laugh, something in me longed to strike terror in the hearts of an audience for a change.

When I grew my hair long, I found myself thinking it would be perfect for the witch, because I wouldn't have to wear a wig. When brushing it at bed-time, I used to shake my unkempt locks over my face and hiss at Sandy, 'A sailor's wife had chestnuts on her lap.'

'Yes, yes,' Sandy would say, catching the spirit of the thing, 'don't call us, we'll call you.' The whole thing became a long-running joke.

The first thing I did, as soon as I got to know our voice coach well enough during the RADA courses, was to coax her to listen to my interpretation of the witch. It seemed to please her well enough, but my attempts to get into a company which was putting on the play met with no success. They'd taken on all their actors for the season and had no need of an extra witch. Foiled again!

I even had the temerity to approach the great Peter Hall who held the reins at the Royal Shakespeare Company, with a request that I might be included when he was next auditioning for the new season of plays. When he did summon me, it was almost like the bedroom performance for Sandy, only instead of my nightgown I wore my short modern skirt, which wasn't nearly so effective I felt. There was a long unbroken silence while I took out my hairpins and let my hair down, and I was irresistibly reminded of the time when I had climbed up on to the Rechabite hall stage and kept an entire audience waiting while I removed my long amber beads, and then my cardigan, until the hall rippled with laughter at the sight of me preparing for a wild Highland Fling. This memory was almost my undoing, and I felt I would simply die if Peter Hall burst out laughing.

He didn't. He gave me all the time in the world to impress him, and in the end was gracious enough to say that he liked my witch, but added, reasonably enough, that he couldn't take me on for a Royal Shakespeare season on the strength of one part. I swallowed my disappointment and picked up my hairpins. I didn't *want* to be taken on for the season. I would have died of fright if I'd been asked to tackle anything else in Shakespeare. I wanted to tell him that Macbeth, after all, was the only Shakespearean play set in Scotland and that at least one of the witches on that blasted heath ought to be a Scot, preferably me. But of course I couldn't argue along those lines. The next budding star was waiting in the wings, so I smiled and thanked him and went home.

That night, as on other sleepless nights, instead of counting sheep I went over the first witch's longer speeches. I hadn't entirely given up, but as the years rolled by, I wondered if only my pillow would ever really appreciate my performance.

And then one afternoon, out of the blue, when I got

back from one of my latest RADA classes, the telephone rang. I turned the gas down under the kettle and reached for the 'phone. 'Derby Playhouse on the line,' a voice said. Derby Playhouse? What could they want? I didn't know anybody there, and I was sure nobody in Derby knew me. Next moment the manager's voice was uttering the unbelievable words, 'We are putting on *Macbeth* shortly, Miss Weir, and we wondered whether you would like to play first witch?'

I nearly dropped the telephone into the sink in sheer excitement. Instead of playing it cool and pretending to be hard to get I gasped out, 'Would I like to play the first witch? Yes, oh! yes I would! I've wanted to play this part all my life.'

'Well,' he sounded slightly taken aback at my enthusiasm, then gave a little chuckle, 'now's your chance.' He gave me the dates. Two weeks' rehearsal in Derby and two weeks' playing. I was feverishly turning over the pages of my diary. There was nothing that couldn't be re-arranged. The biggest sacrifice would be our week's holiday which we'd planned three weeks from now, and which would clash with the *Macbeth* production. Impossible to take it earlier, due to Sandy's office rota. I said I'd give a definite decision next day, but it was almost certain I would be able to do it.

As soon as Sandy came up the path, I had the door open and was tumbling out my news. He was fairly staggered. Like me, he was slightly bemused that the private joke was going to be turned into reality. He didn't mind a bit about the holiday, which he could equally enjoy a little later. 'Of course you must do it,' he said. 'Now's your chance to see if you really *can* do it. It's high time you did that witch performance to an audience of more than one. And maybe when you've

249

got it out of your system, we'll get some peace from all that muttering into your pillow.'

Next day at the RADA class, everyone was agog at the thought of my going to play one of the Weird Sisters, complete with beard. It was maybe a laugh for them, but I was into serious training immediately, concentrating on movement, mime and voice, so that I would be in great shape for Derby. The class were also impressed that once more my belief that the RADA courses were a magic talisman which brought work to me, had done it again. It was quite uncanny.

When I set off for Derby, it was with the happy certainty that I was well prepared, and that I would be home each week-end for, unlike Glasgow, it was reasonably close to London and travel was easy, with a good service of trains.

The director was astounded to find me word perfect at the first rehearsal. How could he know I'd learned this part over half a lifetime? We rehearsed on stage, which was already set for the evening's performance of *The Winslow Boy*, with furniture and moveable scenery pushed aside to allow us freedom of movement. We leaped on and off rostrums, disappeared into fireplaces, and circled menacingly round a tea-chest pretending it was a cauldron.

I had to change my interpretation here and there, because our ideas didn't always coincide, but the director was generous enough to say that most of the good notions were supplied by me. I think he was a bit bowled over by my keenness, and the zest with which I rushed into discussion over every tiny nuance of expression. Bebe would have loved such intense involvement – this chap, I think, began to feel he really had been lumbered with a weird sister!

As for the other two witches, I never gave the poor

things a minute's peace. As soon as the director had finished with our scenes, I found a quiet rehearsal room backstage and insisted on going through every gesture until we moved smoothly and confidently as a team. They humoured me, for they had realized by this time it was more than just a part of me. It was an obsession.

The clothes were splendid. Long canvas dresses, sprayed with green paint to give a mildewed effect, and fringed raggedly at wrists and hem. We found later, to our cost, that the dye came off on our undies and on our skin, and we presented a most macabre sight when we took them off. Dirty green skin isn't exactly an enticing sight during social activities! Especially when finger-nails and toe-nails assumed a green bloom to match!

Over the dresses went flowing black net capes, with wide panels floating down from the arms, and when we raised our hands we resembled birds of prey, rather like vultures. Not exactly my favourite bird, but great for the sisters. But my plans for wearing my own long hair hanging down in lank locks came to naught, for the director had the eerie and effective idea of making us resemble fallen nuns, and so all hair was concealed under black hoods like balaclavas, with black net triangles floating down like wimples. However, I was determined I wasn't going to resort to crêpe hair and glue for the whiskers for an aged witch, so I pulled my long back and side hair through the chin part of the balaclava, and provided a highly satisfactory home-grown beard. The supreme compliment for this piece of realism came when brother Tommy saw the photographs and said in some amazement, 'How did you manage to grow a beard? I'd never have believed it!' I was elated.

Between rehearsals I went for long bus runs and kept searching for decent digs. We'd booked into a hotel for the first week, till we could look around for private rooms. Hotels aren't a bit of good for actors, especially where they only provide bed and breakfast. It's awful having to eat out for every meal, without even being able to boil a kettle or poach an egg when the mood seizes you.

The Winslow Boy company and our cast were all at the same hotel, whose proprietrix had the sketchiest idea of the duties of a hotelier. She knew she'd promised to provide tea for actors who had to work in the theatre at specified times, but she disappeared for hours on end and nobody could be sure if she'd return this side of bed-time. Husband's attire was semmit and slacks. He regarded the hotel like the Forth Bridge, and never had a paint brush out of his hands, so while everything sparkled with clean paint, kettles and kitchens were beyond his interest or understanding.

As the kitchen was kept locked when madam was out, actors' fingers were gnawed almost to the bone by the time she appeared, to enquire dreamily if anybody wanted tea! So, having seen *The Winslow Boy* actors becoming quite neurotic with this unreliable hotel service, we in the *Macbeth* cast were rushing about trying to find bedsitters where we could have cooking facilities, and would be able to eat and drink to our own timetable once the play opened.

Derby at that time was a hive of heavy industry. Factories employed thousands, and apprentices booked in for a whole year at the start of each season. Naturally people with rooms to let preferred such long lets, and weren't at all interested in actors who came for only a few weeks. Consequently, rooms for casuals like us were as scarce as hen's teeth. However, I discovered through another actress who was leaving the town, that there was an excellent room just across the road from the hotel. The landlady's son was going on a course to another town and his room would be free from that weekend. It was like being in MI5, chasing clues of disappearing tenants and possible addresses! I rang the doorbell, made the acquaintance of Madame K. who, at two o'clock in the day was still in pale satin dressing gown, and it took only five minutes to find we liked each other. A deal was struck, and I was accepted. It was a grand wee flitting. I just packed my case, crossed the road with it, and took off for London and Pinner to give Sandy all my news. It was lovely knowing that when I returned for Monday's rehearsals, I would know where I would rest my head and best of all, would have use of a kitchen practically to myself. Madame K. turned night into day, hence the satin dressing gown in the afternoon. She rose late and didn't retire to bed until the middle of the night, so our domestic arrangements were smoothness itself. I was well out of the way by the time she rose in the late forenoon or early afternoon, and however late I returned from the theatre it wouldn't disturb her, for she was merely starting her evening's activities then.

We became great friends, and she loved to hear all about the house at Pinner, and the garden, and what happened at rehearsals when I worked with Renee Houston. She adored Renee and couldn't have enough backstage chatter about her.

I found the Derby people very friendly, and everyone kept asking me about Bebe and Ben, until I began to feel I was as well-known there as in my native Glasgow.

But my favourite encounter was with a perfect coughdrop of a lady who sat beside me in the bus one day when I had a few hours off rehearsals, and decided to go for a walk round the moors on the outskirts of the city.

She was beautifully dressed, middle-aged, and she told me she was off to visit a friend who worked in one of the nearby stately mansions. Patting her ungirded tummy, she said with a laugh that it was a pity she couldn't wear her new two-way stretch so that I could have appreciated the cut of her best skirt. But it gripped her like a vice, and the thought of it pinching her for two solid hours was more than flesh and blood could bear, well her flesh anyway!

'So my friend will find a fat woman when she meets the bus,' she sighed. Then she laughed infectiously, 'So what? I *am* a fat woman!'

I was charmed by her spontaneity. I learned that her first husband had been about twenty years her senior, and in his eyes she could do nothing wrong. Her present husband was ten years her junior, and in *his* eyes she could do nothing right!

'Always marry an old man, pet,' she said. 'They treat you like a toy, and it's lovely.'

She had a terrific sense of humour, and when she told me her present husband, a foreigner, had been a lodger in her house, I risked saying, 'Ah, the classic situation, the lodger marrying the landlady!'

'Exactly,' she said. 'Do you know I never even knew his proper first name until I saw it in the Registry Office. I can tell you, the Registrar gave us a funny look when we both gave the same address!'

She roared with laughter when she told me how he had proposed.

Not a word of love. He had merely suggested it would save him a lot of income tax, and she wouldn't have to take in lodgers any more.

'Now,' she said, 'I've got a queer old name that nobody in Derby can pronounce, and a husband who never moves outside the house.'

What a character. If I hadn't already settled with Madame K., and my fat friend hadn't had three cats, I'd have been her lodger for my stay in Derby, for she invited me cordially to come and lodge with her the moment she knew I worked in the theatre.

All this took place in the course of a bus journey. No wonder I love touring. There's an adventure round every corner, and it's the best possible way of getting to know people.

I was glad I had all this fresh air on the moors, for rehearsals were hotting up, and on the following Monday we rehearsed from ten in the morning till ten at night. Then there was a dress rehearsal on the Tuesday, when we saw ourselves in our clothes and worked on the real sets for the first time.

Suddenly the whole thing sprang to life, and the stage setting was gorgeous. A basic set with rostrums and back hangings was transformed from blasted heath to castle by the skilful use of magnificent lighting.

On opening night I discovered to my astonishment that I, who am normally palsied with fear, felt only exultation and excitement. There was possibly just the smallest feeling of nervous anxiety. But uppermost was the tingling thought, 'The moment has come at last. I'm going to do it. I am actually going to play first witch in *Macbeth*.'

The curtains parted under a menacing drum-beat. The audience broke into spontaneous applause in appreciation of the set. Then there was a gasp as the single spotlight revealed the three witches staring out at them like vultures. The applause continued. I was to speak on a soft cymbal roll, and the rest of the

255

music was timed to finish on an exact word. I was terrified I wouldn't hear my music cue because of the clapping. I hadn't expected this. I was unprepared. My mouth went dry. Was I going to mistime my very first line? I couldn't bear it. And then, just in time, the applause died away and at last I heard myself intoning those famous opening words, 'When shall we three meet again?'

It was a splendid moment. I'd waited a lifetime for this.

That murmur of horror at our appearance was the very stuff of theatre, and it was marvellous to be accepted as Shakespeare's witch.

They liked us, and so did the critics, and the BBC TV people actually sent over cameras to film me rehearsing on stage. They had known me so long as a comedienne, they were greatly interested and intrigued to find me playing such a part.

Next I was interviewed for the Midlands viewers and then on radio. It was all the greatest fun.

My landlady was very impressed by all this attention from the media, and her mother, who came to the opening night, decided I didn't say a wrong word.

I have to confess I hadn't a clue about a witch's make-up and the third witch was a tower of strength in this respect. She had a great knowledge of the human face and what could be done with it, and she painted in lines and hollows and shadows until I hardly knew myself. When she'd finished, and I pulled on the balaclava and arranged my 'beard', I don't think even Sandy would have recognized me.

Macbeth had a hard job keeping his face straight when he looked at me, but I stared at him with such fierce intent that he recoiled slightly, as rehearsed, but raised his sword with such sudden alarm that he nearly caught the side of my face with it. It was a dangerous moment. We almost laughed.

But I made some wonderful discoveries. I learned that it is almost restful to hide behind weird clothes and the verse of Shakespeare, compared with the poised desperation of modern comedy. Nobody is going to criticize his dialogue! I also found to my surprise what a relief it was not to have to smile to captivate an audience.

There was something of the air of a séance in the witches' cauldron scene, and it was deeply satisfying to sense the complete stillness and rapt attention of the packed theatre. Not a cough, not a rustle broke the tension. I was amazed to be told by one lady, though, that my hands in this scene looked far too young! Just like my feet for Flash apparently! I had pencilled in veins, and I had darkened them with grease-paint to simulate thin twisted fingers, but the fierce spotlight had blotted out all my best endeavours, and left only the strong typing fingers for all to see! Well to be noted by one lady at any rate! I hoped nobody else was so minutely observant.

But the greatest reward was with the school matinées. I had been warned that the kids could be terrible, and might even disrupt the performance, so I was ready for them. It sounded like a monkey-house of chatter as they all took their seats, and when the curtain rose there was a crescendo of giggles and some squealing as the spotlight revealed the three witches. I remained utterly still, glaring out malevolently, and by my own silence imposed utter silence throughout the auditorium. Only then did I rasp out the opening line to a now attentive, stilled audience.

From those first words they were rapt and with us every step of the way, totally involved. They hadn't much time for the love chat, but the blood and witch-craft were applauded till the rafters rang. Lady Mac-duff's death and piercing screams brought the house down! And at the end they cheered and whistled and stamped. All this for 'Wullie' Shakespeare and *Macbeth*.

I was most flattered when several of the actors told me I had a 'fantastic control' of an audience. Now *that* was worth the trip to Derby alone, to find that I could do this. And it wasn't so fantastic really. I had simply tested out my theory that the way to silence a noisy audience was not to try to out-shout them, but to stand quite still and wait for silence. And it had worked. I do the same whenever I speak in public and it never fails.

There was a marvellous bonus after every perform-ance when I removed all that make-up which had transformed my normal pale-skinned self to a hook-nosed, lined and withered crone. The contrast was so startling as the layers of age were removed, that for the first time in my life I felt almost a beauty. It was a complete delusion, and I'd see my usual work-a-day self in the morning, but it was pleasant to bask in it for a few minutes each evening, as in the fairytale mirror which only revealed 'the fairest of them all'.

Incidentally, by the end of the two weeks, I had proved such an apt pupil under the teaching of the talented third witch, that I could achieve the full horrifying effect with my make-up pencils without having to trouble her. That is the wonderful thing about the theatre, one is always learning something.

We witches had a lovely lot of free time in the dressing room, for when the cauldron scene was over that finished us for the play. It was a satisfying feeling to know that we had made our contribution to the play, and could now relax and do whatever we liked until the final curtain calls. We couldn't take off our make-up, but we changed into our dressing gowns, put our feet up, and got out our knitting or sewing or a book. I dispensed coffee and chocolate biscuits, and while we chatted we listened to the rest of the play coming over on the Tannoy so that we would know when we must start to get ready to put on our witches' garments again for the curtain calls. I used to wonder what the audience would have thought if they could have peeped in and seen such domesticity from such a fearsome trio.

Meantime Lady Macbeth flew through our room for her various costume changes, always anxious to know how this or that scene went. It was quite a sight to observe her in her nightgown walking about backstage waiting for the sleep-walking scene, smoking a long, thin cigar. I was sure she'd forget some night, and go on stage with it, and turn the whole thing into farce!

On the night when one of the witches had a birthday, we celebrated in great style after our cauldron scene. With one ear on the Tannoy, we had a real party, with everybody rushing in to join us when they had a free moment. Nobody watching the tragedy being enacted in the theatre could have imagined what was going on in our dressing room. The room was a-buzz with excitement and activity. Gaily-wrapped gifts were everywhere. I gave silk tights, somebody else gave perfume, another handed in wine, Lady Macbeth provided a cake, and young Macduff supplied champagne, if you please! He caused a small panic when the cork flew off with a loud explosion and hit the stair-light fairly and squarely, plunging the staircase into darkness. Everybody had to creep up and down in the dark afterwards, till the end of the play.

Our young champagne Charlie could hardly pour the bubbly for laughing, but at last we all stood with our glasses raised and sang 'Happy Birthday to You', while Lady Macbeth and I danced round the dressing room singing, *The Night They Invented Champagne*.

Meanwhile the Tannoy told us that poor Macbeth was working out his destiny on the stage downstairs. We kept a bottle back for him for the end of the show. I only hoped no sound of our hilarity was reaching him. Or the audience. Or the manager!

Lady Macbeth and I were twin souls when it came to complete dedication to our work in the theatre and to this play in particular. We had earlier almost come to blows during rehearsals when she wanted to cut short the time allotted to the witches' scenes. When I saw that the director was going to succumb to this fiery red-head, and dismiss us after a mere fifteen minutes, I blazed out in righteous wrath, 'Everyone is important in this play,' I said. 'This is *our* time for polishing *our* performances, and it won't do you a bit of good, however brilliant you are, if we are the weak links in the chain.' For good measure I added, 'I'm surprised at you. Considering I have "heard" you do your big speeches every night after rehearsal, I can hardly believe that this is how you repay me!' Oh I was on my high horse and no mistake. I can't bear injustice. Meekly she bowed that gorgeous flaming head, 'You're quite right Molly,' she said, 'I was being selfish.' After that, we were bosom buddies, for she realized I was just as keen on perfection as she was. When anything went even slightly wrong, she would moan to me as we anguished together, 'Oh Molly, we care too much.'

I often think that play-acting is about the only job left nowadays where everything is taken so much to heart. With television and radio, pre-recording has meant that mistakes don't involve the same heart-stopping terror. With a stage performance, it's all happening there and then, and there is agony over every single thing which is less than perfect.

There was one ghastly night for me when the dry ice was missing which should have sent its weird and concealing smoke round my hands as I uttered wild incantations and brought forth the ghosts of dead kings. I found myself staring into a stoury cauldron containing only empty match-boxes and assorted litter, over which I raised my now despairing arms. The squeaks of the third witch as she tried to control her giggles, did nothing for my own composure. Goodness knows what the audience thought, for as there wasn't so much as a wisp of smoke to conceal the mechanics of the business, the parade of ghosts that I was supposed to be conjuring up had to be cut. With my back to the audience, I hadn't a hope that my descriptive powers would be an adequate substitute for the missing wax-works! It was a nightmare, and my speech seemed endless, and the memory of it sent me leaping up in a sweat during the sleepless night which followed.

Lady Macbeth's own trauma came when the candle wasn't ready for her big dramatic scene. Always a worrier, the shock of that missing candle played havoc with her throat muscles, and her vocal power deserted her when she needed it most. She was quite distraught as she tottered through our room at the end of the scene. 'How was it, honey?' she moaned, desperate for reassurance. 'I know it was awful. But how was it?' It took a good ten minutes walking her back and forth before she would be convinced that only we, who knew and were sensitive to her every nuance, would have noticed anything. Without a glance at one another, we lied in ringing tones that the faint echoes of her voice had somehow added an extra terror to the scene. We knew her need! Even then, we had to give her a switched egg with milk and sugar to strengthen her for her next entrance.

A faulty curtain one night almost destroyed Macbeth's performance, and he was practically suicidal.

We all sympathized with him over that curtain, for although nobody out front would even know anything had gone wrong, *he* knew his timing had been ruined and nothing would comfort him. Early in the rehearsals he had impressed upon all of us the necessity of being fit for our performances in Shakespeare, and had persuaded everyone he could cajole to enrol at the local baths, to swim, to enjoy the saunas, and to try our hand at weight-lifting. Needless to say I was a most willing acolyte, and I suffered with him when anything went wrong. Nothing less than perfection could satisfy us. He himself prepared like an athlete about to compete in the International games, and all this training was nullified on that dreadful night by a carelessly manoeuvred curtain. Poor Macbeth!

Lady Macbeth existed on vitamin pills, and had an ambition to be the thinnest actress in London. She was staggered by the amount of food I bought. When we would be strolling through the town on small shopping sprees, I would say, 'Oh I think I'd better just get another wee pie in case I need it.' I couldn't pass a food shop without buying something. Apparently she told one of the actors, quite seriously, 'I think Molly must have had a very deprived childhood. She is just like my Russian grandmother, she has a food compulsion.' She could have been right. For I was brought up by a mother and grannie who always advised a wee 'roughness' in the tins, in case there would be an unexpected mouth to feed. Scottish hospitality is a prized virtue, and the lessons learned in childhood remain with me always.

I went to see our Lady Macbeth in a lunch-time performance of a play when we were all back in London. Afterwards we went to a French restaurant for afternoon tea, where we were joined by Fenella Fielding, our old RADA chum and a trio of other friends who had also been to the show. They were *all* on a diet, and when I stretched out my hand for a vanilla slice, five pairs of eyes fastened on the enormous pastry. There was a swift intake of breath and whistle of disbelief that I actually intended to *eat* such a fattening thing in the middle of the afternoon. 'Darling,' shuddered Fenella, 'I could put on two pounds just *looking* at all those calories.' Our Lady Macbeth, now satisfyingly gaunt from semi-starvation, looked at her friends and said, 'Didn't I tell you she had a food compulsion, just like my Russian grandmother?' Her grannie had obviously had the same strong effect on her as mine on me! There was a moody silence as they sipped China tea and watched me with hungry eyes as I devoured that delicious forbidden sweet. I ought to have felt guilty, but I didn't, just a bit self-conscious at such an accusing audience!

The third witch, who had helped me with my make-up was another coughdrop, but of a different flavour. She was fairly small, with tiny feet and curvy Betty Boop legs, a beautiful skin and thick fair hair, but with the plumpest figure and largest bust I had ever seen in my life. The men working on the ladders around Derby used almost to fall off in shock when she passed by underneath them. You will know I do not exaggerate when I tell you that once, in London, when she was appearing in a play a few months later, the drama critic of the *Standard* wrote in his review, 'I do not understand the reason for the wearing of an enormous false bosom by the wife in this play.' When I read it, I laughed and said to Sandy, 'I've got news for him. Every inch of that bosom is real. I ought to know, I shared a dressing room with her for a fortnight in Derby.'

Next night a letter was published in the *Standard* from the leading man in the play, which read, 'With regard to your critic's reference to Miss X's false bosom, I have every reason to know that it is real, for I am seduced by the lady twice nightly!'

Well, when we heard that there was to be a film made of *Macbeth,* the third witch and I decided we'd love to appear in it and we asked if we could be auditioned. I then discovered, to my horror and some amusement, that it was to be performed in the nude, and withdrew my request. Anybody who knows anything about Scottish weather and the draughtiness of Scottish castles would know nobody in their right mind would shed so much as a sock of their own free will. Third witch, giggling, said she was going to go ahead with the audition just to see what happened. Roman Polanski was to direct, and she was summoned to see him. She told me afterwards that after he had explained how he wanted the play presented on film, he had eyed her a bit apprehensively. Then he had said, 'You do understand that it is to be performed in the nude. Have you any objection to this?' Whereupon she had flung herself upon him exclaiming with a glad cry, 'I thought you'd never ask!'

End of interview.

She had thoroughly enjoyed the joke, but I don't know how long he took to get over it.

She is a first-class actress, and has excelled in everything she has done, and I'll always be grateful to her for all those lessons in make-up and for her realistic approach to the profession. I learned a lot from her.

I had intended embracing the domestic life when I returned from Derby, for it was getting very close to Christmas and there wasn't a thing started in preparation for the Festive Season. Before I could even assemble the fruit for the cake, I had a call to go to Glasgow to take part in a series on the life of Robert Burns, starring John Cairney. I had thought I had lost the opportunity to appear in this, because the part originally intended for me had vanished under a bit of re-writing. However, John Cairney wrote a new scene specially for me as Mary Campbell's landlady at Greenock, and as so many friends were in the series, I found this invitation irresistible.

John Cairney had a fantastic resemblance to Burns, and when he put on his 'Edinburgh gear' as the girls called it, he was the Raeburn portrait come to life. He so steeped himself in the history of Burns, that he could tell us every incident from the poet's life as though he'd been there sharing it all.

There was a huge cast, and I met more old friends in this episode than I'd worked with for years. Jimmy Gibson, a lovely old actor who was also in *The Lums* played Holy Willie. It was a wonderfully sly piece of acting, santimoniousness oozing from every pore, and for me Jimmy was the definitive Holy Willie. It was also interesting to see John Morton playing an official body, something in the Council I think, looking hilarious in his black breeches and curly wig. I'd only ever known John as Willie McFlannel, my friend and ally in *The McFlannels*, and it was quite an experience hearing him deliver an entirely different type of dialogue. There was Ewan Roberts with whom I'd worked in London in films, big Archie Duncan and Effie Morrison as Mr and Mrs Armour, and my old friend Jean Faulds was Mrs Burns. John Laurie (my husband in *The Clitheroe Kid*), played the hell-fire minister, preaching damnation against the wild excesses of Rabbie, and he sent the congregation and all of us into hysterics in rehearsal when he thumped the pulpit so passionately that he smashed it and sent the wood splintering in all directions. He was the fiery minister to the life.

At lunch-times the canteen rang with the sound of chatter and laughter. Whatever the English view of the taciturn Scot, the Glaswegian talks and laughs so much it is like a continual cocktail party. I was very impressed in this production at how patient the directors were, and how tolerant of our need to catch up on all our news during those long, lively lunch-hours. It could never have happened in London, as Ewan Roberts, John Laurie and I were the first to testify.

It was a special treat for me to be working with Effie Morrison again. She and I played Bella and Ivy in *The McFlannels* together for years, as well as in many a Children's Hour and drama production. One of Scotland's finest radio actresses, she was entirely without affectation, and we enjoyed a strong true friendship from first to last. The entire country came to know and to love her as the redoubtable Mistress Niven in *Dr Finlay's Casebook*, but in Scotland she had a whole gallery of characters at her command. Effie was never one to dress ostentatiously, nor was she flashy in any way, so I was all the more moved to express undisguised admiration of the beautiful pearl necklace she was wearing to rehearsal one day. She was delighted I had recognized they were 'good ones', and told me cultured pearls were the only baubles she coveted. Now that she was doing quite well, she had treated herself to this lovely long rope. A friendly jeweller in Sauchiehall Street guaranteed she wouldn't be 'done', and as soon as she knew that I too loved pearls, she insisted that I must go and introduce myself to him. 'Just tell him Effie sent you,' she said, 'and he'll make sure you get the real McKay at a fair price.' This seemed to me a marvellous idea. A true-blue Scottish jeweller with impeccable credentials! There and then I made up my mind to throw caution to the winds, and acquire a cultured pearl necklace which would be a souvenir of this happiest of Scottish engagements, and of my friendship with Effie.

I happened to go to the shop on a day when the charming gentleman owner had attended an auction, so not only did I order a double necklace of cultured pearls, but I bought a small selection of Scottish brooches which he warmly recommended as 'great buys' and which have given me pleasure over the years. It must have been the fastest sale he'd ever made of items he'd bought at auction. The auction tickets were still on the boxes. But I have always found it wise to trust the expert, and I knew Effie's friend would give me only good advice. When I went back later to collect my specially strung double necklace, he decided my rings wanted cleaning, and while we talked a young girl took them away, and returned them bright and sparkling like raindrops in the morning sun.

When Effie and I appeared together some time later on Bill Tennent's *Dateline* for Scottish Television, we both wore our cultured pearls, and felt we were giving a rich and lively imitation of the Dolly Sisters! Bill told me that he had been trying to get Effie on to this programme for some years, but she hated appearing as 'herself', and always refused. Then someone who had seen us together in the canteen, giggling and chatting non-stop as usual, had advised Bill to use me as bait! It worked! I was immensely flattered to know Effie felt we would have some fun together and make an enjoyable programme, for she was not only a friend, she was an actress for whom I had the greatest respect and admiration.

Bill was delighted with the programme, which was done from Glasgow. When we were speaking of the things which made us cry, I confessed that I had only to think of a marvellous scene in a film called *La Strada*, where Anthony Quinn violently assaulted a young circus hand, whose watch is broken in the fight. He is dying, but is unaware of this, and his look of despairing shock when he sees his precious watch has been smashed, combined with his ignorance of the fact that the blow to his body has been fatal, broke my heart. I had only to think of it for any sad scene I had to perform in a play, to send the ready tears rolling down my cheeks.

To my surprise, Effie said that what she found heartbreaking was the *Jeely Piece Song*. I had never thought of it like this. Coming from Glasgow, I found it quite hilarious, but Effie found great poignancy in the words which told that whole generations of Scottish children would never know the special bliss of the sound of a piece spread with jam landing from a kitchen window on to the back court. Coming from the islands as she did, she had a great love of the folklore of the tenements, and in Adam McNaughtan's cleverly expressed song of the jeely piece, Effie found infinite sadness. When I thought of the opening lines, I began to see what she meant:

Oh ye canny fling pieces oot a twinty storey flat,
Seven hundred hungry weans will testify tae that,
It it's butter, cheese or jeely,
If the breid is plain or pan,
The odds against it reachin' earth are ninety-nine tae wan.

When we'd finished our stint with Bill Tennent, I wondered whether Effie had yet seen the Pavilion pantomime. I always tried to see Rikki Fulton and Jack Milroy when I visited Glasgow during the pantomime season, for I loved their Francie and Josie characters and their Glasgow humour. To my joy, Effie hadn't seen the show, so we flew along and just managed to get two circle seats for the first house. That's the beauty of Glasgow, almost everything is within sprinting distance.

The audience, all of whom appeared to have watched us in *Dateline* were amazed to find us sitting among them when the lights went up for the first interval. They came over in droves to make sure it really was us. 'Hiv ye been here a' the time?' they asked us incredulously. Or, 'My, you ferrly goat here quick efter the show.'

At the final curtain, Rikki had the spotlight turned on us, and we had to stand up and take a bow. Our pearls looked gorgeous in the limelight!

We went round to see Rikki and Jack afterwards, and what with the laughter during the show and the capers in the dressing room afterwards, we were quite hoarse when we tottered down the stairs, exhausted, and left the theatre.

Rikki was amused by my observation that although their cocky little walk looked easy, it was not, because in a scene where all the chorus girls came on dressed in Francie and Josie suits and strutted round the stage in imitation of Rikki and Jack, there wasn't one of them who quite managed it. 'Aye,' said Rikki sagely, 'you're quite right. It's no' as easy as it looks.'

Incidentally, long long after this when Rikki had graduated to straight acting, and had given a great performance in Molière's *The Miser*, which was done in the Scottish vernacular, I had a very amusing letter from a lady in Barra, in the Western Isles. She and a friend had been speaking about books, and she told him how much she enjoyed my writings. The friend had said, 'She wrote that play that was on television the other night.' 'Which one?' she asked. He replied, 'That one that was called *The Miser*.' Trying to be as tactful as possible and not wishing him to give credit where none was due, and perhaps display his lack of knowledge of the French classics in less friendly company, she had said, 'Actually it was by Molière.' 'Molière,' he echoed, 'well then she must have translated it into the Scots language.'

She finished her letter to me with the words,

'So take a bow Molly Weir. Or is it Moli-Ere?'

I treasured this letter from such a witty lovely lady.

And I treasured the splendid loyalty of the man who refused to believe I had nothing to do with such a fine play.

Such gems are pearls of great price – even richer than the cultured pearls from Sauchiehall Street.

I only saw Effie twice after that. Once when I was through in Edinburgh recording a piece for *Story-time*. She introduced me to Eileen MacCallum, another fine actress, and we had a lovely long talk over the teacups. Eileen had just acquired a nice wee hideaway in a northern part of Scotland, and I was astonished to learn that even in remote parts of my own country, vandalism had to be guarded against. I felt saddened, and could echo the words of Macduff, 'Stands Scotland where she did? Alas my poor country.'

The second time was from a bus in Glasgow. I said to my travelling companion, 'You wouldn't believe to see that wee body with her shopping basket that you were looking at one of Scotland's finest artistes, would you?' 'You would not,' she said. Then, taking a closer look, 'Is that Effie Morrison?' 'It is,' I said, and we both hoped she would look in our direction so that we could wave to her.

Did some sixth sense tell me that this would be the last time I would ever see that sturdy figure I had known so long? For whatever reason, I watched her out of sight, craning my neck to catch the final glimpse of her as she reached the far pavement and our bus got the green signal to move.

I never saw her again.

She died alone in the night, and as it was at that season of the year when there were no newspapers for several days, her death passed almost unremarked. Unremarked that is, except by those of us who were privileged to be called her friends.

Four or five years ago the BBC repeated a marvellous radio play which starred Effie and another superb radio actor, Bryden Murdoch. I was so moved by the superb performances and the voices of my old colleagues, both long since dead, that I wrote to the producer expressing my appreciation and my admiration.

In his reply he wrote,

'Interestingly the "read-through" for this particular play is the only one I have known where the cast applauded at the end. It was a lovely and enriching moment – all the more so through Effie's own genuine modesty and confusion.'

That was Effie through and through.

I never wear my cultured pearls but I think of her. I love to remember that one little touch of ostentation she allowed herself, and of the pleasure her necklace gave her. I hope she was wearing it on the night she died. I think she might well have described that as 'going out in style'.

CHAPTER TWELVE

My superstitious belief in the power of those RADA classes to attract work to me like a magnet, was confirmed yet again when, having decided that I wasn't going to get a part in the film *The Prime of Miss Jean Brodie*, I enrolled for another voice and movement course. The ink was scarcely dry on the cheque when I had a summons to attend the *Brodie* studios on the following Monday morning. 'What part am I being considered for?' I asked. 'One of a pair of oldish twin sisters,' they said. 'Your size seems about right and we've found someone who looks a fair match.'

I don't know how I arrived at the studios without having a heart attack, for I was held up in commuter traffic for a full half-hour at a roundabout, and the clock had ticked round to nine o'clock, the precise hour at which I was due at the studio, before I could crawl forward.

Once clear, I who normally proceed at a dignified thirty miles an hour, put my foot down and went like a greyhound from the traps down the long clear road beyond, and tumbled out at the studio doors at 9.10 A.M. I had done the last six miles in ten minutes, which is pretty well in the Stirling Moss category for me!

There, sitting patiently drinking coffee, was my 'other half', the wee Scots lady who would play my sister if the director liked us. There was scarcely an inch between us for size. 'Well,' I said, 'if they want two wee pixielated sisters, I'd say they'd got them, wouldn't you?' 'I would indeed,' said Helena Gloag, whom I was meeting for the first time. She had come all the way from Oban, from another film, and had arrived an hour early off the night train. I who came from Pinner was late! 'Twas ever thus where car travel is involved.

We were taken to the director's caravan, to await his arrival from the set, where he was busy directing Maggie Smith in one of the schoolroom scenes. I was wearing my headscarf, as usual, to keep my hair looking reasonably tidy. He measured the two of us with his eyes. 'Mmmm,' he said. Then, to me, 'Take off your headscarf, please.' The moment he saw my bun and my little side tendrils, his eyes lit up. Without taking his eyes off my face, he said, 'You're a bit young for what I had in mind, but you can just be sisters instead of twins. The hair is perfect.' Before he even told us we'd got the parts, he said to the girl beside him who was taking notes, 'Order another wig for Miss Gloag exactly to match Miss Weir's. Miss Gloag will play the older sister, but the hair must match.'

Helena and I grinned from ear to ear as our eyes met. 'We've got the parts,' we mouthed, as the director completed his notes about clothes and dates.

The girl told me afterwards that the director hadn't known quite what he wanted for the two little sewing mistresses, apart from the fact that he'd have liked them to look like twins, but the moment he saw my hair he knew it was dead right for the odd little pair of sisters he had in mind. What a piece of luck.

Next day I had to go through Covent Garden to reach the famous firm of theatrical costumiers for dress fittings. It was a fascinating place in those days. Outside one tiny shop front a veritable army was unloading the most exotic looking 'hands' of green bananas. The whole thing was like a ballet, performed by a dozen men with rippling muscles and flexible bodies, bending, dipping, throwing, all in spell-binding rhythmic sequence. Looking at them, one could imagine they had rehearsed it for public performance. And not a soul in that narrow street to appreciate their efforts but me. Nowadays the market is far from the bustle of theatrical London, and the modern Covent Garden resembles an Italian piazza, but I still miss the movement and the scents of fruits and flowers and vegetables from all corners of the kingdom.

The costumiers was almost as busy as the market outside. TV designers, film designers, actors, wardrobe masters and mistresses all milled around choosing, trying on, measuring and being measured. That day I was merely having measurements taken, but in such detail that I was astonished. Even the muscles of my upper arm were measured! What for, I wondered? Surely I wouldn't be wearing such skin-tight clothes that such meticulous measurements would be necessary? The period of the film covered the thirties, so I couldn't imagine it was going to be a very exciting time for fashion.

When we finally saw the clothes, they were very prim but of excellent quality. Silk blouses, tucked into long fitted skirts for everyday wear, and we had attractive printed silk dresses for the end of term party.

And Helena's wig was so good, it made me wonder if it was worth all the trouble of growing my own hair. They had copied my style so exactly that it was like looking at a reflection of my own head. It was quite uncanny. The director eventually didn't know which of us had the real hair! It was like that old advertisement, 'Which Twin has the Toni?' The only advantage I had was that under the intense heat of the studio lights a wig becomes heavy as lead, whereas one's own hair accepts it quite normally.

I was thankful it was high summer, and soon fell into the routine of a 6.30 A.M. breakfast, then into the car by 7.25 A.M. and a twelve miles' drive to the studios. It was quite challenging for me, as a fairly inexperienced driver, to find myself the only female on roads packed with lorries, delivery vans, and long-distance speeding travellers. I used to see the same people every morning, and learned to look out for the solitary chap on a motor bike at the same spot at a given time, to check that I wasn't running late. Then there was the elderly hero on a push-bike. I always met him on the steepest part of the hill, where it was only too easy for him to start wobbling. It was such a busy narrow road that I always slowed down to a crawl to make sure I didn't skite him off his bike!

One morning the entire cast who used that hill arrived late, because a heavy lorry had overturned and shed its load and nothing could move. The chaser-up was in a panic, because filming is such a costly business with so many people involved, that even one person holding up the action can cause such an expensive delay that tempers explode in a flash. A scout on a motor-bike was sent out to see what had happened, and once he had reported back they re-arranged the schedule and shot another short scene until we late arrivals had been dressed and made-up. We had two assistants whose sole job it was to round us up like sheep, chivvy us, deliver us to make-up or hairdressers, and finally hand us to the director brushed, groomed and ready for the 'shooting'. Their jobs depended on taking this responsibility seriously, so they stood no nonsense. So it seemed quite natural to me that on that traumatic morning I should apologize profusely to the chaser-up and not to the director!

The Prime of Miss Jean Brodie got off to a very unusual start. There was no hanging about waiting to be called for a particular scene. We were handed hymn sheets, and music, and we were off! For four solid days the teaching staff and 240 girls sang hymns, non-stop, from morning till night.

When we weren't actually rehearsing with full voice, we were rushing to the piano where Gordon Jackson sat, urging him to play over the notes just once more, for each one had to be perfect. I'd forgotten Gordon was such an able pianist, a talent which was given full rein in the Brodie film where he played the part of the music teacher. It was marvellous to have him to keep us right, for he was so good natured and didn't mind how often he had to repeat a particularly difficult phrase until we were note perfect. It was a very difficult hymn musically, and even Maggie Smith actually came to me one day to check a tricky phrase to make sure she'd got it correctly! Gordon had recommended me to her!

In the end, that first hymn was written on our hearts, and for years afterwards when Gordon and I sent cards to each other, we finished up with *Lord behold us with Thy blessing*, Love Molly. Or, Love Gordon. I don't know what the postman thought!

276

A professional choirmaster had trained the school-girls, and I found it most moving to gaze down on an assembly hall filled to the far corners with fresh-faced pupils, hymn books held demurely in front of them. Gordon struck a chord, and the lovely sound of sweet young voices rose to the rafters. Somehow in the early morning, in the setting of a film studio, it seemed unbearably touching. I was only kept from shedding a sentimental tear by the antics of Celia Johnson. I had thought she would be very grand, and completely serious. Apart from the classic *Brief Encounter*, I had only ever seen her in the theatre in strong meaty plays, like *Ghosts*, and *The Master Builder*, and was a little in awe of her. But during those hymn-singing sessions she was hilariously funny. She kept thinking she was singing flat, and during her little solo section she would turn those huge anguished eyes on Helena and me and implore us, 'Sing out now, as loudly as you can, I need all the help I can get.' The director, meantime, was calling out to me, 'Stand back, Molly, I'm picking up your voice with Celia's.' The moment I took a pace back, Celia would hiss out of the side of her mouth, 'Move closer, I can't hear you, I'm going flat again.' It was a nightmare. I wanted to please her, I so admired her, but I didn't want the director's wrath to fall upon my head for hogging the microphone. In the end, I craftily compromised and kept my feet where Celia could see them from the corner of her eye, but tilted my head to one side, away from the mike. It worked, and after one of the recording sessions she turned to me and said, with mock self-congratulation, 'Oh that's the best I've *ever* sung it. I was truly *splendid* that time!'

When I suggested she might have to do it all again if it wasn't quite to the director's liking, she clutched her bosom and with pretended horror exclaimed, 'Oh but I *couldn't*. I'll *never* be as good as that again.'

She was such fun, and so childishly delighted with herself for being able to keep in tune, that she completely de-fused the terrors all of us endured in case we would ruin a 'take' by singing a wrong note, or coming in at the wrong time. There was no side about this great lady of the theatre. And she was truly a lady. Natural and unspoilt, she was unexpectedly a comic in real life, and I treasured the friendship we started on this film.

Lunch-times at Pinewood were almost as animated as in the STV canteen in Glasgow. We had our own all-Scots table, which I may say was the noisiest in the restaurant, especially when Gordon Jackson and I started recalling our scenes in the film *Floodtide* with Jimmy Logan, when we ruined 'take' after 'take' because we couldn't stop laughing. How we didn't get the sack, I'll never know, for J. Arthur Rank himself was standing at the back of the set watching us. I hadn't known he was there until Gordon said, 'Oh there's Uncle Arthur turned up to see how we're getting on.' When I realized he meant the great J. Arthur Rank I practically fainted. It was my first big film and I was certain it would be my last. It was on *Floodtide* that Gordon met Rona Anderson, who later became his wife, and now here we were again, all three of us, working together on a film for the first time since those early days. It was great fun, and every meal became a party.

By coincidence, our final piece of filming was to be the end-of-term school dance, and it seemed almost like a farewell party for those of us who wouldn't be required any more, our little moment of importance and glory over. You can never believe a film can

278

actually still go on when you're back at the kitchen sink at home, but the plain truth is the only people who go right through a film from start to finish are the stars. We supporting players are very tiny cogs in a very big wheel.

For the end-of-term dance we wore our silk party dresses, and we teachers manned the long table which ran across the top end of the room, and which was laden with plates of sandwiches, mounds of cakes, and fruit, and bowls of fruit punch. We were under strict instructions that not a morsel of food must be consumed during rehearsals, for there would be no more available until the afternoon, and the full table of food was required intact for the background shots. Nothing must be eaten until the final 'take', which would probably not be until after the lunch-break.

It was like trying to protect food from the starving hordes!

Those schoolgirls, so demure and virginal in their long white dresses, had been plunging into the vigour of the waltz from around half-past nine that morning, and the exercise had made them ravenous. At each break in the filming, they flew at the table like vultures, seizing sandwiches and cakes, and gulping down pints of fruit punch.

The man in charge of food supplies kept begging us piteously, 'Don't let them eat the *cakes*. I'll have to carry the can if they eat the cakes.'

I felt like a goalie under attack from Kenny Dalglish!

All I could do was to thrust paper napkins at the girls and implore them not to mess up their dresses with the debris of their illicit feasting. I remembered the wardrobe mistress's anguish over Olivier's robes, and could imagine the hysterics in wardrobe if 240 dresses had to be laundered in the lunch-hour!

279

My biggest excitement in this film, though, was to find myself sitting in the studio restaurant, with Sir Laurence Olivier sitting only two tables away. The others at the table were tolerant and amused when I whispered, starry-eyed, 'I'm actually sitting in the same room as my hero! Isn't it marvellous? Oh I wish I could turn round and gaze at him.' 'Don't you dare!' said Margaret, who worked with him in the theatre. 'He's very shy. Let him enjoy his lunch in peace. You're not supposed to stare in a film restaurant. You're an actress, not a gawping member of the public.' That brought me up with a jolt. So I was! I was an actress! Sitting among actors. It was a pity all the same that I couldn't look. Just for once I wished I was a gawping member of the public. My food stuck in my throat at the proximity of my idol. Sir Laurence sat there quite unaware of my adoration as he ate his lunch. But I did get a good look at him as he walked out of the restaurant later, and my yearning sigh nearly wafted him out of the door. So near and yet so far. Actors, above all people, have to respect the privacy of the great.

Quite the most unexpected tit-bit came my way because of the Brodie film. One day as I was crossing to the set, I happened to bump into the casting director, Budge Drury, whom I had known for many years. 'Oh Molly,' he said, 'I wonder if you could pop into my office sometime during the lunch-break. I have somebody coming who'd like to have a look at you.'

At one o'clock I put my head round the office door and found Budge sitting opposite a large important-looking man who was the American movie tycoon to the life. I had visions of being whisked off to Hollywood, all my childish dreams of being a movie star about to be fulfilled! Not a bit of it. It seemed they were filming *The Beverly Hill-Billies in London*, and had over-run their schedule. There would now only be enough time to film the original American actors in close-up as they drove around London in their old car, before catching their 'plane to return to the States. So they were looking for 'doubles' for the long-shots they needed to complete the film. As there would be no time to make new clothes, and anyway the distant shots had to match the close-ups in every detail, what they needed were reasonable copies of the Hollywood cast. Size was all-important. The actors had to fit the clothes. The American director, it seemed, had seen me in the restaurant and thought I looked a dead ring for granny's clothes, for in my thirties silk dress I was as thin as a whippet. Would I be interested in playing granny's double for a day?

Brodie would be finished that day, so I was free to accept if I wished. I would be paid £100 for my trouble. A whole hundred pounds for a single day! That fairly took my breath away. I had to work for a week for that sort of money in Pinewood, but it wasn't the money which excited me, it was the fun which such an unusual job promised.

Fate gave us a gorgeous day for our 'doubling' act, the one sunny day of that week, and it was an unforgettable experience from start to finish. We 'doubles' reported to the Dorchester Hotel, the favourite 'howff' of American show-biz people, at 9.00 A.M. sharp, and found make-up, hairdresser and wardrobe already assembled, waiting to transform us into carbon copies of the famous American characters.

The hairdresser was delighted I had my own long hair and needn't wear a wig, and she soon had it slicked down into granny's screen style, complete with neat little bun at the nape of my neck. It was so tightly combed into the bun that my scalp ached for days afterwards, as if I'd changed my parting. Which I hadn't.

Granny's cotton two-piece fitted me very well, and when I clapped on her wee flat purple hat I hardly knew myself from the real thing. One of the American company came into the suite just then, and the sight of me rocked him on his heels. 'My gosh,' he said, 'I thought I was seeing things. I've just left granny on the other side of the park.'

Meantime the actress doubling for Ellie May became that character's spitting image as soon as she was dressed in the pink tight-waisted frilly dress and had the necessary hair-piece added.

We were both quite dazed by the success of our impersonations of characters we'd watched on the screens for years.

The two male doubles hadn't such a close facial resemblance to the American actors, but their build was dead right, and of course the clothes did the rest. It was most impressive to see the transformation. The chap who was playing Max Baer's part arrived in very trendy tight black slacks, with matching skin-tight top, looking every inch a man-about-town. In five minutes he re-appeared, the complete country hick with wide tie, sloppy jacket, and a thick piece of string holding up baggy trousers. He had been specially picked because he was a stunt driver, and it was his job to drive us round London in the famous old car with the rope round the bonnet.

While we sat enjoying the luxury of the hotel, sipping coffee and nibbling nuts and crisps, the real principals were being shot in close-up in various parts of London.

No expense was spared to keep us happy and comfortable. They brought us a menu, and we ordered lobster and salad, without even having to look at the price! Anything we wanted was ours for the asking. It was served in the sitting room of the suite, for we couldn't appear in the dining room dressed as we were. I'd never experienced such attention or savoured such luxury. A whole suite in a top class hotel, no less. When the real granny came in, she took one look at me and gurgled with laughter. 'I thought I was looking at myself,' she said, as she handed me her purple velvet shoulder cape and her spectacles. When I put them on, I was a completely acceptable copy, and felt sure nobody would know the difference. They didn't. The real Hill-Billies had come into the hotel about ten minutes before we descended the stairs, and the hotel staff didn't spot the change. They waved to us from doors and windows as we stepped into a *white Rolls Royce*. This was our transport to the location! American movie luxury with a capital L.

At the other side of the park we transferred to the old jalopy with its roped bonnet, old-fashioned luggage, and patchwork quilt for our knees. Then began the most comical ride through London I could ever have imagined in my wildest dreams.

The camera truck went ahead of us with camera, crew and directors positioned both inside and on top. They filmed us following them, passing them and ahead of them. All hell broke loose as soon as we were spotted. Buses, cars and lorries hooted in ear-splitting salute. Bikes rang their bells. Passengers and drivers and pedestrians waved and cheered and applauded. We drove round and round Trafalgar Square, to the excitement of bus-loads of tourists who hammered on their windows and waved furiously, faces wreathed in smiles of pure delight. I'm sure they thought it had all been arranged for them as an added attraction.

Every amateur camera was trained on us by Londoners and holiday-makers amid yells of 'Hullo Granny'. I swear the very pigeons came to a standstill, their coo-ing checked by the sight of us.

At Piccadilly Circus the hippies, for once, took a back seat. They forgot their sophisticated boredom, and waved their bush hats in the air, glad of the diversion. They shouted, 'Look this way,' and bade us gaze into their cameras, and invited the curvy Ellie May to join them by the fountain. When we had to stop for the traffic lights, people rushed from all directions and begged for autographs. Nobody doubted for a minute that we were other than the people we appeared to be. Truly, clothes maketh man.

Even a detachment of police coming out of their headquarters called, 'Hullo Granny'.

Next we speeded along the Mall to Buckingham Palace. By this time it was the rush hour, and bus queues shed their irritation in amazed laughter the moment they saw us.

On we sped to Covent Garden, whizzed through the market, then round by Drury Lane. When we reached the Strand, it was seething with traffic and jammed with people trying to get home from work. One sight of us, and nobody cared where they were supposed to be going. Drivers leaned from windows, bus conductors forgot to ring their bells, and car enthusiasts gazed longingly at our old banger.

During all this, our splendid stunt driver somehow managed to keep us within sight of the camera truck. I disgraced myself by waving back at people when I wasn't supposed to, because I couldn't bear them to think I was too high and mighty to respond to their friendly waves. 'Don't wave,' the director kept hissing at me when he was within shouting distance. This was followed by, 'Don't smile,' and we had to do another full round of the circuit without a wave or a smile from me! How awful I felt at having spoilt the shot, and me being paid a whole hundred pounds for this.

It was non-stop motion, and the whole thing became like one of those endless dreams where you're rushing about in strange clothes with everyone gazing at you. But somehow it wasn't embarrassing because there were four of us and we were disguised as other characters.

When we got back to the Dorchester, I was exhausted, not from work this time but from laughing. I could say, with my hand on my heart, that it was the daftest job I had ever done. Not to mention the highest paid!

But there was a strange sort of anti-climax which I never forgot. When we came out of the bedroom, after having changed into our own clothes again we found the sitting room of the suite occupied by the full American production team. They sat talking and sipping drinks, relaxing after the day's work. We stood expectantly, waiting for the usual thanks, and possibly the offer of a drink. At the very least we imagined we would be wished good-night. Nothing of the sort happened. They entirely ignored us. Suddenly I remembered Ben referring to domestic staff as 'hired help', and I understood. It was obvious that they saw us 'doubles' merely as hired help, with whom they had finished. Their attitude clearly told us we'd been paid, hadn't we? What more did we want?

We looked at one another, baffled, wondering how to get out of the room with dignity. At least that was what I was wondering, but I had my understanding of American ways to help me. So I smiled and said, loudly and clearly, 'Goodnight, gentlemen. Thank you for such a pleasant job. I hope the film will be a great success.'

They glanced up with a start, surprised. 'Oh,' one of them said. 'Oh! that's all right. Goodnight.'

We were swept from the room, our pride intact, but laughed all the way down to the ground floor. 'They may have the cash,' the trendy male with us said with satisfaction, 'but when it comes to good manners, we can show them a thing or two.'

I suppose that such an impersonal style reflected the real American movie business. I always forget this is just what it is to tycoons, and to some actors too come to that – a business. For me it is always a labour of love for which I happen to get paid.

One of the challenges I kept refusing was to go on the list of public speakers of a well-known agency. Luncheon clubs were springing up all over the country, and there was an insatiable demand for people who could entertain the ladies (they were mostly ladies' clubs) for half-an-hour or so after the meal, and give them a peep into the working life of whatever profession the speaker followed. Public speaking and acting are two entirely separate talents, and I felt it would be an insupportable ordeal to have to spout forth, non-stop, for anything from half-an-hour to forty-five minutes without interruption. Talkative as I am, I knew it was one thing chatting with friends who would all chip in with their own comments, but it would be quite another cup of tea standing up like a one-woman show, without a cue to break the flow. 'My goodness,' I thought, 'if I stop to blow my nose or clear my throat, there will be complete silence.'

So I kept saying, 'No, no, I might not be good at it. I couldn't charge a fee for something I don't even know I can do.'

After becoming a national face and name with the coming of the Flash commercials, the approaches from the agency came with increasing frequency. At last I said, 'Put me on your stand-by list, and if anybody breaks a leg I'll be available as a substitute speaker, and then not too much will be expected of me.'

The voice at the other end of the telephone chuckled. 'You and Sheridan Morley have exactly the same attitude,' she said, 'and we're asked for you two more than for anyone else.'

It was Preston Lockwood, an actor friend, who finally persuaded me to go on the list of speakers. 'You'll be a natural,' he said encouragingly. 'Mind you, you'll probably hate the first twenty, and then you will actually find yourself enjoying them.' 'The first twenty,' I exclaimed in horror. 'Do you mean I have to go through *twenty* engagements before I can enjoy them!' 'Yes,' he said, 'But after that you'll love them. And it will be very good for you to be in close touch with a real live audience again, and to know you can entertain them by sheer force of story-telling ability.'

That was the bait. The lure of the live audience, and the challenge to prove to myself I could stand up alone and engage their interest for half-an-hour.

So began a sideline which, as Preston truly predicted, would become more and more fulfilling and rewarding as time went on. A sideline which has enabled me to see more of England than I could have dreamed possible, and which has indulged to the utmost my love affair with trains. Indeed I've become as well-known as a bad penny to railway guards from Penzance to Aberdeen, and have roped in area managers, station managers and signal box attendants to relay messages to anxious secretaries when trains have been delayed or cancelled. I'm as possessive about trains as the redoubtable Jimmy Savile, and because I like them so much, I can be honestly critical of their shortcomings when they let me down.

That first lunch was an ordeal, though. I chose Southport for my début, not only because I love seeing holiday places out of season when everything looks clean-washed and free from crowds, but I felt it was far enough from home to be a novelty. I had imagined a sort of candy-floss and iced-lolly sort of holiday town, but it bade fair to rival Princes Street in Edinburgh with its beautiful shops, lovely buildings and fine trees in full autumn foliage. I was most impressed, and as soon as I'd booked in at the hotel where the ladies had reserved a room for me, I went striding over the sands, drinking in great gulps of fresh sea air. I hoped the ozone would hold a threatening 'flu-cum-cold at bay. I could feel my chest tightening, my nose blocking, and my voice displaying terrifying signs of disappearing. It was the very worst moment for such a thing to happen. I'm almost a hypochondriac about colds at any time, but when I was about to fulfil my very first speaking engagement a heavy cold was enough to send me into a neurotic frenzy! Sandy had wanted me to cancel the date, for he too knew all the signs, but I felt I'd worry the organizers more by *not* turning up than by turning up and breathing thickly and wheezily.

The hotel people were marvellous and provided an extra blanket, a hot water bottle, and a hot drink laced with rum and lemon when I went to bed.

During the night I wakened soaked with perspiration, which brought down my temperature, but left me as weak as a kitten. My legs felt quite wobbly when I ventured out for another healthy intake of sea air and a stride along the front, before changing into my 'speechifying' clothes and meeting the chairman.

The Masonic Hall, where I had to speak, was a fine building and the place was abuzz with ladies in beautiful suits, plus an impressive scattering of mink hats, and a terrifying air of expecting me to deliver a clever, polished speech.

The lunch might have been grannie's oft-quoted horror, 'Stewed donkey's ears' for all I tasted of it, but I certainly proved that one fear drives out another, for I was concentrating so much on keeping my voice free of 'frogs' and my nose clear for breathing that I just didn't have the time to worry about another thing.

I was using a hand-mike for the first time, the sort clutched by pop singers, and I found this a great help. It let me move my head around to take in all the company, and it allowed them to gaze in my direction from all corners of the room, if they had a mind to do so. It also enabled me to turn away very easily when I had to clear my throat or cough, without making a big production of it.

They didn't laugh without reason, those Southport ladies, but when I did get laughter then I felt I'd deserved it, and it was all the sweeter.

Suddenly before I realized it, it was all over and I was sitting down to warm applause. My legs were shaking, my voice was almost gone, but I'd done it! I was a public speaker. I hadn't enjoyed it much, but at least I had survived. Only nineteen to go to prove whether Preston was right or wrong!

The best laugh I had was when somebody at the top table said to me approvingly afterwards, 'It's the first time I've noticed not one single old lady falling asleep!'

I learned later that this is the accolade. If you can keep the regular elderly sleepers from dropping off, you're a success! In fact, I adopted a new slogan to make them laugh, 'Where Weir speaks, nobody sleeps!' The microphone is an indispensable ally to reach the sleepiest or the dullest ears, and I always insist on one. I remember speaking at a fête in the open air once, and when the man who was introducing me waved the mike away with the words, 'I don't need this', I rescued it, and said, 'Well I do.' A voice from the crowd said, 'He *thinks* he doesn't but those who can't hear him know better!'

The next year following my Southport début, when I was asked to speak at the Dorchester at the Agency lunch, where all the speakers and the secretaries of the clubs were gathered together for the annual shindig, I emphasized this point that a microphone, properly used, was a tremendous asset, especially in an age where everyone has a hand on the volume control of radio and television at home, and has grown used to a certain level of sound. The human larynx can't compete with this expectation, especially for a full half-hour or so. Somebody yelled out, like my fête introducer, 'I don't require it.' The Duke of Bedford, to my satisfaction, rose to endorse my plea for the use of microphones, which enabled a speaker to use a normal conversational tone, and not have to declaim as though a lecture were being delivered. 'Weel done, you pawky Duke,' I thought. I always felt a warm spot for him afterwards.

This experience in public speaking was to stand me in good stead when the militant Trotsky element raised its ugly head at the meetings of Equity, the Actors' Trade Union. Like all other Unions, ours began to be bedevilled by various militant groups. There were the Trots, as they became known, the Maoists, the Workers' Revolutionary Party, and other politically motivated pests. We are supposed to be a non-political Union, just as we are non-racial and non-sectarian, but this didn't stop the mad Motions being argued at furious meetings, Motions which had nothing whatsoever to do with us as actors or our work or rewards. We found ourselves being asked to support some IRA activities, of all things! To discuss the steel industry. Apartheid. Chile. Abortion. In other words, all the popular platform pieces spouted forth by extremists at most Union meetings.

Vanessa Redgrave and her brother Corin were the lynch-pins of the Workers' Revolutionary Party, and nearly drove the real acting fraternity among us mad with their constant 'Motions', their 'Points of Order', 'Points of Information', 'Reference Back', etc, etc – all the usual jargon guaranteed to make the knees ache with boredom, when the blood pressure wasn't mounting at their effrontery.

There was one hilarious moment at an endless meeting when Vanessa Redgrave got up so often to preach the WRP doctrine that even a dog at the back of the theatre yawned noisily and gave a long howl of protest. The beast was in the arms of a militant sympathizer, and in the ensuing roar of laughter at its canine sagacity, I feared for its safety at this lack of respect for the high priestess of protest.

Among the moderates, I was the lone female voice which dared to sound off against this left-wing policy. I hated doing it. My legs shook like jelly as I made my way forward to the stage, but somebody *had* to speak up for moderation and commonsense and it seemed I was the only one who could nerve herself to do it. Actors need scripts, as a rule. They are not good at ad lib speaking, but although I was a nervous wreck each time I faced the mob of disciples which the militant

291

groups had commanded to follow them, at least I could do it. In fact, I found myself being praised more for my Equity speeches than for my show-biz performances! As Sandy was wont to say, 'You're the most militant moderate I've ever come across.' Nigel Davenport gave it as his considered opinion that I was as brave as a lion, so you will know what courage was required to get up to speak at those meetings. Even Robert Morley could hardly disguise his amazement at the length of time I gave to shooting down those wreckers. 'Don't tell me you're still going to those ghastly meetings,' he said. And he launched into a superb imitation of the left-wingers leaping up, parroting 'Point of Information', 'Point of Order, Mr Chairman', 'The question be now put', until he had the assembled company falling about in laughter.

It was no laughing matter really. The meetings became such a shambles, such shouting matches of waving fists and tasteless barracking that moderates stayed away in droves to preserve their sanity. And in the end, as I write, 'Motions' which were quoted in the press as having been 'overwhelmingly passed by a two to one majority', meant only that of the 100 or so people who could still brave the meetings out of a membership of 30,000, the hard core who did turn up were still those politically dedicated to using the Union for their own purposes. They never give up. Their capacity for destruction is inexhaustible, as is their lust for power.

One of my great supporters was the late lamented Barbara Mullen, Janet of *Dr Finlay's Casebook*. I was always wistful that I wasn't playing the splendid Janet myself, but how could I grudge it to somebody who played the part so winsomely as Barbara did? I was in quite a few episodes, playing various characters, both

292

on radio and on TV and she and I became firm friends. She used to ring me up and in that wee twee voice would say, 'Hullo Molly. It's Barbara,' as though I didn't know another Barbara in the whole wide world.

At the Equity meetings, she detested the Trotsky and the WRP elements as much as I did, and although she hadn't the nerve to get up and speak, she used to paralyse me with suppressed laughter by taking fits of coughing at strategic moments, just when the subversive speakers were reaching the climax of Communist propaganda. The followers of the militant Trots and WRP were furious with her, but they hadn't quite the courage to tell an obviously distressed little lady to shut up! What a splendid act that was!

That coughing wasn't as much of an artifice as I supposed, although she could produce it at those meetings to excellent effect. In fact when I did some new radio *Finlays* with her, I was dismayed at how delicate she seemed, and how exhausted at the end of the recordings. I remember one particular *Finlay*, when I had the main part as a much put-upon wife who turns the tables on a bullying husband, and Barbara had hardly a thing to say beyond, 'Arden House. I'm afraid Dr Cameron isn't here.' She sank into a chair at every opportunity, and at the end of the afternoon, needed my hand at her elbow to get upstairs. 'A taxi, a taxi', she murmured, as though at the end of her strength.

She rang me later to say that her daughters were sending her and her husband off on a holiday to Rome. 'Like yourself Molly,' she said, 'I never take a holiday. I can't remember when I last had one.' 'Oh but Barbara,' I said, 'you're quite wrong. I *always* take holidays. I can't afford not to. I regard holidays as an investment in good health. I'm so pleased to hear

293

you're going away. Make the most of it, and have a lovely time.'

She wasn't long home when I switched on the television one night to watch the news, and Barbara's gentle face, with the wide forehead and clear light eyes, flashed on the screen and my heart turned over. I didn't have to hear the reader telling us she was dead. I knew. That terrible weakness which had worried me at our last radio recording was the unrecognized sign that strength and health were ebbing away from her. She was greatly loved by her public, and has her own place in show business history.

I'll tell you a strange thing though. To this day I am constantly mistaken for her! That would make her laugh. When we emerged from the Equity meetings, walking side by side, the public used to do a double-take, wondering which one was Janet and which Aggie, and yet we weren't really alike taking us feature for feature. It was just a similarity of build, colouring, and our un-English voices. She told me that she even signed autographs in my name, not to hurt folks' feelings.

That was Barbara all over.

CHAPTER THIRTEEN

With years of experience of my mother's flittings in Glasgow to back my advice, I was more than ready to lend a hand when Sandy's sister Rose and husband and family moved right across London to Windsor. Strictly speaking, it couldn't really be called a 'flitting', for they were moving to the lush pastures of Windsor Castle. And not only Windsor Castle, but were to dwell in one of the actual Towers! This glamorous new address came about because Rose's husband, Tom, had been promoted to district officer and would be in charge of the castle maintenance for the foreseeable future. And the new job meant 'living above the shop'. And what a shop!

With Springburn flittings in mind, I advised Rose to keep a few items of food aside so that we could eat when we reached our tower, and I prudently packed a few flasks of coffee and boxes of sandwiches to keep hunger at bay. Castle or no castle, a good many things can go wrong between packing and unpacking, and a contented stomach is a great help in coping with all difficulties.

The whole affair was such a far cry from the old horse and cart days of childhood removals that I felt it was almost as exciting as a first night at the theatre. I think it was equally so for the removal men, for I don't believe they had the slightest idea that they would be moving simple household goods from suburbia to a Royal Tower, and their faces when at last they stood in a magnificent drawing room had to be seen to be appreciated. Jaws fell open, eyes widened, and Adam's apples shot up and down as the glory was registered.

It turned out to be unexpectedly hilarious, in spite of all plans, for there was an official ceremony going on at St George's chapel that day, which meant that our timing had to have the precision of a military operation. In fact it had to be flawless if we weren't to have the Queen's car and our removal van arriving simultaneously.

When Sandy and I took Rose over to Windsor to await Tom's arrival and that of the removal van, the policeman on duty had to be telephoned with the number of our car, so that he'd let us into the place.

All unofficial traffic had been suspended, apart from the cars attending the chapel ceremony, and even if our flitting was important to us, it was hardly part of the ceremonial occasion!

In the past when we had wandered about Windsor Castle with our tourist friends, I had often wondered who were those privileged people who drove past us in lordly fashion, and never dreamed the day would dawn when we ourselves would pause at the gate, braking strongly to make sure we didn't disgrace ourselves by sliding back into an official vehicle, announce our destination, and be waved in with a salute by a policeman. I was glad Sandy was driving, for that slope into the castle is like a hill start, and I'd have been terrified I'd stall at such a moment.

As soon as we reached the door leading to the tower, we had to race with the speed of scene-shifters to empty the boot of our flasks and food, and get the car out of the way to its allotted parking place. This was instantly followed by the same hectic performance by Tom, who had now raced up in his car. It was getting dangerously near the Queen's arrival, and it would be a dreadful start to the new job to have Her Majesty squeezing past our old jalopies to get to her own part of the castle.

We had just sat down to draw breath and eat a sandwich, when the removal van swung round the corner and drew up at the door. We leaped into action again, and directed it elsewhere until the Royal car was safely past. When we returned to our sandwiches, I laughed and said, 'By Jove we never had such traumas with our old Springburn fittings. The only worry then was to make sure the horse and cart didn't get in front of a tram-car!'

Who would have thought the day would dawn when

a major concern would be to have to keep an eye on the clock so that the Queen and her entourage wouldn't clash in the middle of our flitting? The very idea would have seemed too fantastic to envisage. But it was all happening!

It was at that point in the proceedings that Rose decided we simply couldn't pass up a chance of seeing Royalty virtually outside the new front door, 'Come on,' she said. 'Finish your coffee, we're going out.' We pulled the door behind us, so that the removal men could get in, and we took up our places among the sight-seers opposite the side entrance to St George's Chapel. 'Rose,' I said, laughing and scandalized at the same time, 'how can we dare to do this when the men will be emptying their van and the packing cases without a clue from you where the things are to go!' 'Och,' said Rose nonchalantly, 'we'll sort it out when we get back. Don't worry,' and she gazed around her, apparently without a care in the world. My mother would have been aghast at such an irresponsible attitude, with a whole van full of furniture and packing cases of china to be unloaded, but actually it is marvellous to have such a temperament as Rose's. To be able to seize the moment and leave dull chores to a time when nothing exciting is happening. So as it wasn't my furniture, I copied her example, relaxed and gave my whole attention to drinking in the scene.

The crowds lined the emerald grassy banks, the beautiful cars and carriages rolled past, and we had a front-row view of the Queen, Princess Margaret and the Queen Mother, all dressed in their summery 'braws', smiling and waving to us as they passed. The polite English and foreign crowds applauded enthusiastically. It always seems strange to me to applaud a Royal appearance, instead of shouting a lusty 'Hurrah'.

Maybe we Scots are more extrovert, but a cheer seems to convey so much more than hands genteelly clapping. Rose, suddenly conscious of her position and the new address, and guessing what was in my mind, hissed in my ear that I wasn't to open my mouth. Afterwards, in complete contrast to our previous visits to Windsor, instead of strolling around to admire the park and the gardens, we flew back to the tower, and spent *hours* unpacking an endless succession of tea-chests, arranging the contents in cupboards, in kitchen fitments, on shelves, on the floor, anywhere to get the chests emptied. I don't know why we rushed about like this. The men were fair bemused, for they could have done it perfectly well themselves, but because we've always been so used to doing everything for ourselves at past flittings, we simply could not stand around doing nothing. It takes years of training to be a lady!

The men drank brewing after brewing of tea with lip-smacking enjoyment, and tourists took snaps of Rose and me as we leaned from tall narrow casements to take in the view. I hoped they might mistake us for visiting Royalty, but I very much doubted it, in our slacks and headscarves.

I thought of my mother and her sigh of tired satisfaction after one of her frequent flittings, as she surveyed a good range, and a nice capacious bunker, plans already forming in her thrifty mind for papering the walls and whitewashing the ceilings off her next few weeks' wages. How she would have revelled in the beauty of this house, with its magnificent wallpapers, golden parquetry flooring, long fitted kitchen with its hatch for easy serving of food into the well-proportioned dining room beyond. A pink glass window gave a mysterious glow in one corner, and a door led to a butler's pantry! A butler's pantry! It was the very stuff of story books. From close to castle in one mighty bound!

The views were as breathtaking as the house itself. Just imagine looking out of your kitchen window over the Windsor moat, with the tower in front of you. By Jove, that fairly takes the sting out of the washing of the pots and pans! The view from the lounge windows took the eye over green lawns, past Queen Victoria's statue, over the lights of Windsor to the hills beyond.

Best of all, in this crime-ridden age in which we live, was the awareness that everything was guarded by the Queen's soldiers and police. I always tell Rose that she has much to be thankful for in this respect. Not for her the last-minute checking of all the doors and windows before she goes on holiday. Not for her the hiding away of precious possessions. She can simply pull the front door behind her, and have perfect confidence that all is well. Only the rest of us, whose sense of safety diminishes with every lawless year that passes, can appreciate what ease to the mind such security gives.

But the one treasured advantage I have in my wee house in Pinner is, that I can hang out a washing, dry it in the wind and sun, and savour the irreplaceable perfume of sun-dried linen under my nostrils when I tuck the sheets round me. You can't put out a clothes-rope in a Castle! As the old Aberdeen poem has it, 'Dam't there's aye something.'

I wondered what Royal occasions we'd share in later on, for I had had a most wonderful privilege when Tom was district officer at the Palace of Westminster, before the move to Windsor, when I was invited to be a spectator in the Royal Gallery at the State Opening of Parliament.

It was a bit like filming, for I had to be up at six

o'clock in the morning, nibble a bite of breakfast, get dressed in best bib and tucker (the card said, Ladies: Day dress with hat), then drive across to Rose and Tom's where I left the car, before the three of us headed for the crowded uncertainty of the London Underground.

I can tell you we got a few stares in the train surrounded by folk in their work-a-day clothes while we sat self-consciously in palace gear. In my case I'd decided nothing less than my black coat with white mink collar and matching hat would do, which isn't exactly my usual underground style of dress. A big cape would have been a useful cover-up at that hour in the morning!

With Tom in charge of us, once we reached Westminster we had no need to queue anywhere or even to ask the way, for he had an important rôle in the proceedings and an official position. A policeman waved us through just as Geoffrey Howe hurried past with a stiff enquiring look, no doubt checking whether we were MPs momentarily unrecognizable in the disguise of unaccustomed finery! Next moment we were in an inner office, where Tom leaped out of his city suit and into morning dress, then vanished to find the Yeomen of the Guard and carry out the traditional search of the buildings.

This turned out to be a very quaint ceremony, with Tom holding the key to the great door in his hand for all to see, and the Yeomen of the Guard carrying paraffin lamps. It was a fairy-tale procession of scarlet uniforms, Beefeater hats, square-toed shoes and red-and-white cross-bows. Shakespeare would have felt quite at home. At the sight of all this fancy dress, I was irresistibly reminded of Sir Alec Guinness playing Malvolio in *Twelfth Night*.

After a welcome cup of tea provided by a member of Tom's staff, we flew down to the basement to see the very last of the search conducted in the very bowels of the Mother of Parliaments. Pipes ran everywhere, overhead and underfoot, carrying water, heat and light, and it seemed the strangest setting from which to watch, away at the far end, the approaching feet of the Yeomen, with Tom in front, and then the twinkling light of the lanterns. Somehow Guy Fawkes and the plotters seemed very real at that moment. Every movement was steeped in history.

When we went upstairs and into the Royal Gallery to find a place where we could watch the proceedings, I was astonished to discover that, apart from about a score of crimson leather seats with the Royal Insignia impressively tooled on the backs, reserved for personal guests of the Queen, it was standing room only for the rest of us. Then when I consulted the leaflet describing the timing of the proceedings, I practically collapsed on the spot when I realized that the Royal procession wouldn't pass until almost *two hours* later. Two hours standing on our feet, and we'd not sat down since we entered the building around nine o'clock.

We were to arrange ourselves on three long shallow tiers, which ran the entire length of the gallery on both sides of immaculate carpeting, so that we spectators faced one another across a very narrow divide. There was nothing so vulgar as pushing or jostling, just a discreet opportunism to get nearer and nearer the front as we made way for new arrivals. Rose positioned herself beside a tall policeman in plain clothes, leaving a gap for the newcomers to get through, a gap which I would fill when the doors were finally closed. Meantime I leaned against the wall behind the policeman to take advantage of a restful position while I could.

The discreet hum of a carpet sweeper spoke of workers doing last minute cleaning, and there was an amazing amount of coming and going of well-known personalities recognized from TV appearances. Dame Pat Hornsby-Smith's glorious mane of red hair was unmistakable, as were the distinctive features of Lord Elwyn Jones, the Lord High Chancellor. A slim austere figure was identified as the Gentleman Usher of the Black Rod, as Admiral Sir Frank Twiss was impressively named, and somehow seen against his serious dignity it seemed incongruous to find bare arms and shoulders at such an early hour. For the ladies were in full fig. There were visions in complete evening dress, others in sequins, bead bodices, diamond tiaras, long gloves, unbelievable necklaces which dazzled all the more because we knew that every piece of jewellery we were looking at was real. Not a bit of paste or costume jewellery within miles.

Suddenly the film lights sprang into blinding brilliance, for the scene was being filmed for the first time since 1964, in colour, and would surely be a splendid dollar-earner when sold abroad. Everybody loves to see our Royal occasions, and such films are a guaranteed sell-out. No sales pitch required!

The beautiful gilded ceiling was vanquished by this sudden light, but the portraits of Edward VII and George III were revealed impressively and attractively, and at the far end of the gallery we could now see the portraits of the Queen and the Duke of Edinburgh in all their bright beauty. These flanked the great door through which they would enter in an hour's time. Goodness! I could scarcely believe an hour had already passed, but there was so much to see, and so much movement, that every minute was packed with interest.

The timetable was so finely calculated, that an exact

twelve minutes were allotted for the Royal party to get from the Royal entrance in Westminster to the robing room, and change into the robes and crown and all the necessary impedimenta, ready to enter through that great door at the appointed second. I shuddered at the mere idea of having to work to such a minutely measured timetable, remembering times backstage when fingers were all thumbs as one leaped out of one outfit into another. And I didn't have the whole world judging me when I made my re-appearance. Nor did I have streets lined with people gazing intently at my first outfit, which therefore must be perfect.

Heralds, looking exactly like animated playing cards in their mediaeval crimson and gold tabards, marched up the centre of the gallery, gravely eyed by all of us. Yeomen of the Guard marched in and took up positions in front of us, mercifully not exactly in front of me or I wouldn't have seen a thing. Even in a Royal Gallery you're up against the hazard of a giant suddenly appearing to block the view! Tall Gentlemen-at-Arms complete with white-plumed helmets and carrying axes, even wearing spurs, moved solemnly towards the great door. They were followed by a procession of the Queen's judges, with sober, clever faces.

No sound of the outside world reached us. We might have been taking part in some strange rite known only to ourselves. It seemed impossible to believe that the streets outside were thronged with people, and that TV cameras and cheering crowds were everywhere.

And then, almost before we had time to realize it, the first batch of Royals had come through the great doors. The Duke and Duchess of Gloucester, the Duke and Duchess of Kent, Lord Snowdon. The Duchess of Kent, as always, was elegance personified, hair immaculately dressed round her tiara, white crystal-pleated chiffon dress with the bodice oversewn in criss-cross gold bugle beads; she glided past like a fairy-tale beauty, sweet and remote.

Then sounded a fanfare of trumpets to signal the entrance of the Queen and her entourage, the great door swung open once more, and the Royal Party came into view.

Gentlemen-at-Arms, stiff and erect marched towards us. Two gloriously-clad gentlemen walked backwards, facing Her Majesty (What an ordeal! Suppose they stumbled?). The Queen walked as though in a dream, left hand held high by Prince Philip, who gazed sternly ahead. The pearl-embroidered satin gown was perfect, the vivid blue velvet crown striking a note of colour, and the diamonds in the crown flashed a million sparks under the film lighting. She was very pale, and detached as though in a trance, with an expression that was almost stern and very solemn. The Prince of Wales, in his crimson uniform, was equally serious. Not a hint of the twinkling modern young man anywhere. Princess Anne and husband Mark Phillips followed, Anne slim as a reed in her dazzling white silk dress with its high pearl-encrusted mandarin collar, hair bouffant and beautifully dressed round her tiara.

The most impressive feature of the whole occasion was the silence. I longed to shout, 'God Save the Queen!' or even 'Hip, hip, hooray!' But nobody so much as sighed, whispered or even coughed. It was truly like a dream. It was unreal. We were in a wax-works, watching wax figures. Not a smile, no human warmth lit those beautiful features, or ruffled this lovely scene.

Pale and distant, they swam into view and disappeared through the door at the other end. It was almost like a cremation.

And yet, with all the strangeness there was a familiarity. It was like one's own wedding, which seems unreal because one is taking the leading rôle for the first time and yet is familiar because of all the weddings attended in the past.

So it was now. Seen on TV and film so often, it was a recognizable experience in spite of its strange surrealism.

We listened in silence to the voice of the Queen coming to us through the loudspeakers as she made the speech from the Throne. How intimate it felt to be hearing it from the room next door and not through the loudspeaker at home. I had the irreverent thought that it would be glorious to hear some personal feeling in the voice over passages with which she disagreed. 'Pay-beds?' I wanted to hear her say, in the tones of Edith Evans, 'why shouldn't there be pay-beds, you envious lot?' No private schools? You'll abolish them over my dead body.' 'Library payments for authors? Goody, goody, it's time they had it!'

As my thought struggled for utterance, the Gentlemen-at-Arms appeared and ranged themselves alongside the Yeomen. One powerful nose like Wellington's carried a tiny dew-drop which had to remain suspended, glittering in the light, because both hands were engaged with sword and axe.

Another face, lean and dark, with black beard and piercing eyes, might have stepped from a portrait from the times of Charles I. It was perfect in this setting of crimson and gold. Impossible to believe this Knight lived in the twentieth century, and wore a lounge suit, and caught trains and taxis.

Even as I mused, the Royal procession was returning, and once more glided between our silent ranks, no hint of relief evident in those pale distant faces that it was all over.

The film lights dimmed. The Royal Gallery returned to its quiet subdued beauty and we went our ways.

I was invited to a delicious lunch in a magnificent flat within the Palace of Westminster which was the very essence of gracious living. The hostess had attended the ceremony with us, and I couldn't even begin to speculate how she had managed to offer such food and such elegance, and still have been able to be out from nine o'clock that morning. I would have died of fright at the mere idea of having to entertain a dozen or so to lunch at the end of such a morning, but this slender member of the aristocracy took it all in her stride. Truly there are some 'hostesses with the mostest', as the song goes, and she was an eighteen carat example of the breed.

When we came out into the work-a-day world and made our way home, we knew we were heading back to 'auld claes and parritch'. But we had brushed shoulders with Royalty for a brief hour or so, and had played our small part in Britain's history. It was an unforgettable experience, but it was one I wouldn't want to repeat. I would rather cling to that first wonderful impression, to savour it as a unique, once-in-a-lifetime occasion. The most lasting memory I took away with me was the silence. Impenetrable, unreal, dream-like.

So like a dream in fact that I wondered if that was what it had been. But no, when I was putting my finery away, the programme and the ticket in my handbag proved it had all really happened.

Quietness and silence were to become a way of life for me when I started to write my first book. I'd never wanted to do such a thing, not even when Lady

Georgina Coleridge asked me for first serial rights if ever I put my memories between hard covers. I liked the life of a literary butterfly, writing articles and scripts and little stories just when the white heat of inspiration burned, but the discipline of a whole book! That was something else. And how would I find time for a book if I suddenly had TV or radio or filming or a play to do?

Then I had to go to Glasgow to do some TV with Renee Houston, and one day there was a message for me at the desk, asking if I would ring Andrew Stewart's office (he was head of Scottish radio at that time) and make an appointment to go up to see him.

I instantly thought I was to be offered my own series. The girls at the desk were quite awe-struck at my having been invited to visit the great man in his private office. So was I!

His first words shattered my hopes of a series. 'Have you ever thought of writing a book?' he asked. My heart sank. It wasn't a series, it was a blooming book. I sighed patiently. 'Well, I have been asked quite a few times,' I said. 'In fact I sought the advice of a writer friend and she told me not to write a word until I had a publisher, so I mentioned the idea to the company who produced my cookery book. They weren't interested, and I decided not to do anything more about it.'

He smiled. 'Molly, there is more than one publisher in the world. You must try someone else.'

I opened my mouth to protest that I didn't really fancy writing a whole book, when I so much enjoyed writing articles and scripts, but he silenced me by telling me that his wife had listened to me on *Woman's Hour*, and she had urged him to encourage me to put all those memories of my childhood and of my grannie

307

between hard covers. He said, just as Dorothy Laird had said at the Ladies' Press Club, 'You write with such warmth, and you have no chip on your shoulder. You must put on record the story of the Glasgow you knew, before it all vanishes under the demolishers' sledge-hammers.'

I was fairly stunned by all this, and for once couldn't think of a thing to say to oppose the suggestion.

He went on to tell me that obviously *he* hadn't heard my talks on *Woman's Hour*, because he was busy on other things in the day-time, but he trusted his wife's judgment. He laughed, 'She won't give me any peace until I can tell her that I have asked you.' And then he added, 'It will be a social document of a Glasgow which no longer exists.'

That sounded quite enticing. But where would I find the time?

'Collect all the articles and talks which are relevant to your childhood,' he said. 'Let me have them, and I'll go through them and select the best. And then I would suggest Hutchinsons should see them, with a view to publication.'

I followed his advice to the letter.

In due course, when the bundles had passed back and forth between Pinner and Glasgow, and then Hutchinsons in London, I had a call to present myself in Dorothy Tomlinson's office in the Hutchinson building, and so began my writing career almost without my being aware of it. Dorothy Tomlinson was friendly, but cool and business-like. She held up the bundle of talks and articles. 'As they stand,' she said, 'they haven't a hope in hell of being published.' Then she picked up one, and held it out, 'But this convinces me you can write. If you can produce a book on those lines, we would be interested.'

I seized the article she was holding. 'But this is one I've never been able to sell, either as a talk or a newspaper article.'

She smiled serenely, 'Shall I tell you why? Because it is pure literature. Now go away and write a book in the same style. The ball is in your court. Give me a ring when it's ready, or if you need any help.'

The article which had so impressed her and which started the whole literary life was the story of our downstairs neighbour in the tenements who had died at her sewing machine, her long black hair hanging to her knees like the heroine of a story-book.

I took my bundle of scripts and articles home, and on our wedding anniversary on 13 October I followed Bernard Shaw's dictum and applied the seat of the trousers to the seat of the chair, and started writing. And I wrote every single day until the book was finished.

When I rang Dorothy Tomlinson to tell her, she said, 'My word, you *have* been quick.' 'It didn't seem all that quick to me,' I said. 'I've worked a full writing week for months, only surfacing each night in time to put the potatoes on for our dinner.' She laughed. 'Eight weeks is still very fast,' she said, 'but let me have two copies, and you keep one in case the place goes on fire.' I shuddered in horror. 'Don't even *suggest* such a thing,' I said. 'Where will I keep my copy to be safe?' 'Under lock and key,' she said.

Then her next remark fairly rocked me on my heels. 'How many chapters are there?' she asked pleasantly. 'I don't know,' I said, 'I thought *you* divided it up into chapters.'

She was horrified. 'Oh no we don't,' she said smartly. 'That is your responsibility.'

What I had done, in fact, was to write a book

consisting of one chapter of 194 pages! Which proved, if proof were needed, that I knew nothing of the technicalities of writing a book.

Now I had to divide this mass of writing into more or less evenly spaced chapters, which meant altering endings to bring a chapter to a close. And then altering the next paragraph to indicate a new beginning for the next chapter. I ground my teeth with frustration. I could have thrown the whole thing out of the window. I was quite fed up with it. I was getting ready for Christmas, and here I had to start all over again with something I thought I had finished.

And that wasn't the worst of it. I had had to punch holes down the sides of the pages, and thread them with string, as per Dorothy Tomlinson's instructions, and as I'm not the most technical female in the world, the holes didn't exactly match. Undoing them and re-threading became a nightmare as I detached pages to alter the chapter endings and beginnings. The string unravelled at the ends and I couldn't get them through again. Pages swung out of line. Even Sandy grew impatient at the amount of fiddling work we had to do. But at last it was done, and Sandy delivered two copies to Hutchinsons, and I neurotically hid my copy in a different place every night in case of fire or theft!

Strangely enough, Hutchinsons' building did have a terrible fire, but much later, and thank God not with my manuscript in it, but Dorothy's fears were well-founded. It was a very old building, and all those papers must have made it go up like a torch.

It was a glorious relief not to have to worry about that book any more, and I went off to Scotland after Christmas to do a broadcast, and to spend a day or two with Tommy and Rhona to exchange presents and catch up with all the family news.

One night in Tommy's house the telephone rang. It was Sandy. His voice fairly quivered with excitement. 'You'll be pleased to hear Hutchinsons like your book,' he said. I let out a whoop of joy, which was quickly quenched when he said, 'But they want you to change the title. They don't like your title.' I was absolutely indignant. 'They don't like my title?' I echoed. 'What don't they like about it?' I think it's dead right.' 'Well,' said Sandy, 'you have to change it, so think about it.'

Tommy and Rhona were full of congratulations about this acceptance. As a writer himself, Tommy knew only too well the sweat and tears which go into the work of producing any sort of literary work. He was undismayed about the criticism of the title. 'Hutchinsons know what they're doing,' he said. 'You'll easily think of a better one.'

I had called it *A Tenement Childhood*.

All the way down in the train to London next day, I jotted down titles. Mentally I went through all the chapters, and tried to think of something which encapsulated the whole spirit of the book. I would write down a title, mouth it to myself, gaze at the roof of the compartment, gaze out of the window, sigh and start again. There were only two people sharing the compartment, a youngish pair, who sat silently watching my antics. At last the woman could contain her curiosity no longer. 'I'm sorry to seem nosey,' she said, 'but what *are* you doing? Are you writing poetry?'

'Well,' I said, smiling with relief at being able to take my mind off those blessed titles, 'I've just had my first book accepted. You're the first people to know, outside of my own family, but the publishers want me to think up another title. That's what I'm trying to do.'

They were agog with excitement. 'Oh, isn't that *marvellous*,' the woman said. 'Fancy us being the first

311

to know.' Then, turning to her husband she said, 'We'll have to buy it as soon as we see it in the shops.' Encouraged by their interest and enthusiasm, I said, 'If I read out all the titles I have, will you tell me which one you like best?'

Slowly I went over the list:

A Tenement Childhood. ''Mmmm, quite nice.'

Springburn's Child. 'Oh that's good.'

No Silver Spoon. 'Too like Galsworthy.'

Grannie's Wee Lassie. 'I like that.'

Shoes Were for Sunday. '*That's the one*!'

As soon as I said it, I knew it was the one. Hutchinsons agreed, and so did the whole country.

I don't know how the world of publishing operates, but I was astounded to find that before I had even put a foot on the train to go to Glasgow for the launching of *Shoes*, the first edition had already been sold out! Apparently the book grapevine is very accurate, and the moment there is a hint of success, the booksellers rush in with their orders so they won't be caught napping.

The whole publicity campaign started out in hilarious fashion because Sandy decided that snow and strikes might delay things, and that I ought to catch an earlier train on Sunday to make sure of arriving in Glasgow at a time which would give me a decent sleep before Monday's marathon interviews with Press, radio and TV.

I had had no idea of the excitement this book would generate. I had hoped my childhood memories might please some folk, but never in my wildest dreams did I expect that everyone in the newspaper world would greet it with such loving enthusiasm. In fact when I held the first copy in my hands (a magic moment!), and started to read it as a real book with hard covers,

312

I thought everybody would think I was daft writing about the kitchen range, and the baths, and grannie and me cleaning the brasses. But it turned out that these were the very things everybody pounced on, and it seemed I had truly written 'a social document of Glasgow'. I hoped Andrew Stewart and his far-sighted wife would be pleased, for between them they had prodded me into the action which had ended in this success. They would receive their own very special copy.

Because it was the week-end and he was away, I couldn't contact the publisher's representative to let him know I'd be arriving in Glasgow earlier than we had arranged, so of course he would meet the later train I should have been on. I hoped, however, to be able to get a message over the station loudspeaker telling him to contact me at the station hotel. That was where I met my first snag. There were no loudspeaker operators working in Glasgow Central Station on the Sabbath! I couldn't believe my ears when they told me. It was as bad as the Welsh pubs!

Next, I tried to coax them to chalk a message on a board. Not a hope!

By the time I had discovered the conveyance of information was going to be impossible, I was already changed into natty black silk evening trousers and black wool and sequin jacket, ready to dazzle the station dining room! I wasn't at all keen on strolling through the station in this outfit, but time was now pressing and I had to go in search of a man whose appearance was a complete mystery to me. Calmness deserted me and I flew across the forecourt without even taking time to put on a coat. Douce Glaswegians, well wrapped up against the cold, stared in amazement at the sight of my evening outfit, and a couple of

313

cleaners said, 'My Goad hen, are ye no' hauf frozen?' They looked at me with the disbelief usually reserved for University students walking about half naked on Charities' Day. I hoped I wouldn't have the same effect on the unknown representative.

A man at the barrier detached himself and headed towards me. He seemed a bit stunned at my approaching from the opposite direction and dressed for dinner at that, but he had obviously recognized me and introduced himself as being indeed the publisher's representative. After a swift bit of explaining, he sent my spirits soaring when he pushed two Sunday newspapers under my nose, both containing half-page glowing reviews of *Shoes*. He had arranged interviews with the rest of the Scottish papers at half-hourly intervals next day, as well as two live TV programmes in the afternoon. So, although Bob and I got on like a house on fire from the word go, and he was a tower of strength in every way, I decided it was high time I headed for bed, to gird my loins for what the morrow would bring.

The newsmen were the first outsiders to tell me in person how much they had enjoyed the stories of my childhood, and one paper even brought along two of Sandy's boyhood pals, both still living in Springburn, who were photographed standing watching me as I played peever on the pavement outside the Central Hotel. Grannie's training dies hard, and I couldn't believe I was actually being encouraged to chalk ball-beds and peever-beds outside this famous hotel, and was sure I'd be arrested. Passers-by joined in the fun when they realized who I was, and the police discreetly turned their eyes the other way.

That night, when a friend and I went along to Jimmy Logan's Metropole to see the opening of *Sailor Beware*, starring old friends Renee Houston and Walter Carr, with Paul Young and his dad John Young, the whole theatre rose and cheered when Jimmy Logan's dad, Jack Short, told them I was in the audience. The book had been in every shop that morning, alongside huge photographs of me, and it seemed they approved what I had written of dear old Glasgow town. Wouldn't it have been awful if they hadn't! If I had known how impossible it was to be to hide from failure, or to avoid the exhaustion of success, I would have been even more apprehensive of stepping into the world of books. Ignorance was bliss, and I was so lucky in my timing. People were disillusioned with high rise flats, and the demolition of familiar backgrounds, with communities broken up and scattered to alien areas. They hungered for reminders of the days of the wash-house, and the closes, and the church kinderspiels, and Sunday school trips, and my book provided all of those things. They were amazed to find names of familiar streets and districts within the covers of a book which not only could be bought but would be stocked in libraries, and delighted to discover that somebody whom they had known on the radio and on television felt exactly the same as they did, and had shared the same experiences. We were all Jock Tamson's bairns, and it was a magic discovery.

If I had written it five years earlier or five years later, I doubt if it would have had the same impact. In the case of *Shoes* the time, the loved one and the opportunity had coincided with stunning effect, and I was deeply thankful that I hadn't let anybody down.

I was deeply touched by the number of people who brought the book for signing, because they wanted their children to read how they had enjoyed themselves when they were young, with nothing laid on to help them. How the dykes were their adventure playground, the back-courts the venue for playing shops, and the 'wally-money' had been dug up by their own hands to provide the 'cash' for buying and selling.

During the Glasgow signing sessions, I was quite overwhelmed by the number of old friends who had taken the trouble to come in to see me and to get a signed copy of the book. There were colleagues from the Pantheon Club, from the BBC, people met on holiday, the stage manager of *Dear Octopus*, the play I had appeared in before leaving for London after the war. The niece of one of my school-teachers turned up, just to check up on the female her auntie used to hold up as an example, she told me! Friends of Sandy, from the Boys Brigade came too, and even office friends from Stewarts and Lloyds where I used to work.

Most staggering of all, though, was the moment when a well-dressed, good-looking man laid a tiny photograph on the table and said quietly, 'I've carried that in my wallet for over fifty years.'

It was a picture of my mother!

For once in my life, I was quite speechless, and had to clench my fists to stop myself from bursting into tears in front of the queue. Apart from the shock of seeing my mother's young face at such a moment, my heart was moved to wonder at such a romantic attachment. First love is truly a lasting thing with some faithful souls. If one were to see such an incident in a film or in a TV play, it would seem a bit far-fetched. But it happened. In a Glasgow shop on a grey Monday morning. And I knew I would never forget it. How I wished I could have let my mother know.

The signings went on and on, and so did the travels. Aberdeen, Dundee and Edinburgh. In shops, in radio studios, and on TV until I felt quite punch drunk with all this attention. In Edinburgh, where I did a TV guest appearance in a quiz show, I took away a lovely souvenir in the shape of a large cartoon drawing of myself in colour. It was done by that talented artist, Emilio Coia, who had to do it in about five minutes, for as usual everything was in a mad rush. I had been smuggled in at the back door so that none of the panellists would catch sight or sound of me, and Coia had to sneak into my dressing room and work like lightning while I drank a cup of tea and tried to make some sort of a job of tidying my hair.

I was enchanted with the result, which also pleased Sandy and everyone who saw it. I had it framed and it hangs in the dining room, and is a reminder of the heady days of that first launching of my very first hardback book.

I actually thought I had finished with the world of autobiography and books with the publication of *Shoes*, and was happily resting on my laurels, reasonably pleased by all the interest which had been shown, but above all glad that it was all over.

One day the telephone rang, and it was Hutchinsons. It was Dorothy Tomlinson to be precise. After the usual exchange of polite nothings, she practically knocked the feet from under me by asking sweetly, 'When are we going to receive the next book?' 'The *next* book?' I echoed. 'What next book? I'm not writing another book. That's me finished with books.'

'Oh no it's not,' she said firmly. 'If you read your contract you will see we have an option on the next two books, and after such a success as *Shoes* you must follow up with the next one, with the least possible delay. You must strike while the iron is hot.'

I put down the receiver and groaned. Another book!

Another dive down that mine which would hide me from the light of everyday living for weeks and possibly months. All those wee holes to be punched down the sides of the sheets. The string. The printers hieroglyphics to be mastered all over again when it was time to correct the proofs. I knew now that my head was stuffed with book material. It was the sheer grind of translating it from thought to the reality of the printed page which I again resisted.

But I have always done what I was told, so after a bit of mutinous sighing, I reminded myself of what my mentor Bernard Shaw said about applying the seat of the trousers to the seat of the chair, and plunged into volume two. In three months it was finished, and although I was fearful of invidious comparisons with *Shoes*, it also took off like a rocket. I called it *Best Foot Forward*, for I now had a little superstition about having some connection with feet in the title.

As each book followed, for now I was well and truly committed to being an 'author', my foot fetish became quite a game with the newsmen. 'What's the next one to be called, Molly?' they would ask, wondering what angle I would find for a following book. Smilingly I would shake my head. 'You'll know when it comes out,' I would tell them. For now I also had another superstition and that was *never* to announce a book title until it was ready for the publisher. (A superstition which the publisher of the present volume refused to pander to, I may say!)

Best Foot Forward was followed by *A Toe on the Ladder*. Then came *Stepping into the Spotlight*, *Walking into the Lyons' Den*, and a year or so ago *One Small Footprint*.

They all went into paperback editions, and then into large print. How enormous they looked on the library

318

shelves in large print. I could believe the hours and days and weeks I had laboured over them when I saw them taking up such a lot of space in the large print editions. I read them in the Talking Books for the Blind tapes, and I was so touched when I discovered that one of them had been sponsored by our own fine comedian Johnny Beattie and his wife, and another by a Highland ladies' organization from the islands. I recorded *Shoes* on cassette, and I serialized it on *Woman's Hour* for the BBC which is where it all started.

I've had letters from every corner of the world, from exiled Scots who shared every moment of my early life because a hard-up childhood and caring parents are the same in whatever part of the country they were spent.

Nowadays, when I am asked my profession, I honestly don't know whether to say I am an actress who writes, or a writer who acts. What I do know is that both are essential for my happiness. I think it is because I am a Pisces, with those two wee fish swimming in opposite directions, that there will always be two strong and competing interests in my life and I've been so lucky in being able to indulge both.

CHAPTER FOURTEEN

Ever since I was a wee girl, I've had a continuing love affair with films, and although I take a delight in every aspect of show business, there is something about being in a film which has a special appeal. For one thing, I have just happy excitement about my work before the cameras, and none of the nervous fears which are too often present with other forms of acting. So, when the telephone rang one morning, and I found my agent wanted me to go along to be seen by an American movie director, I was agog with interest.

The film company were considering me for a small part in *Tam Linn*, set in the Scottish Borders, and with Ava Gardner in the lead it had more than a touch of Hollywood glamour. The director, an erstwhile juvenile Hollywood star who was having his first 'go' at direction, had seen me in the *Brodie* film and decided I had the sort of face he wanted for the character of a wee Scots widow. Sandy, I may say, took a less than enthusiastic view of my playing a recently bereaved lady. He doesn't like to see me in sad parts, but I was prepared to weep from here to Kingdom come to be in a film with the fabulous Ava, and to play a sombre graveyard scene with that lovely Irish actor, Cyril Cusack.

I had been told they wanted a Geordie accent, and all the way to town in the train I was mouthing every paragraph in the newspaper in what I fondly hoped was the right rhythm and intonation. It's a notoriously difficult accent to imitate. It's very like our Scottish accent, but just different enough to be confusing.

The director and his producer welcomed me graciously, and handed me a script. I launched into my reading with the full Geordie accent. The two Americans stared at me, brows knitted in perplexity. It was obvious they hadn't understood a word I had said.

'Can you tone down the accent a bit honey,' one of them said. 'It would be tough for them to understand you in the Middle West.'

'I can lose it altogether,' I said with relief, 'I'm not a

Geordie. I've only used that accent because you specified that was what was wanted.'

'Why doesn't she just use her own accent,' the other man suggested. 'It's far prettier.'

And far easier, was my unspoken thought!

I read the whole thing again with my usual Scottish lilt. They liked it far better, and the part was mine.

So I packed my bag and headed for Peebles. It was truly 'Peebles for pleesure'. I was billetted in great style at Cringletie Hotel, a four-star hotel in anyone's book, with thirty acres of grounds and lovely views over the green rolling hills to Peebles. The others were at the Peebles Hydro, and during 'resting' periods or while waiting to be called for rehearsals, I swam in the hydro pool, and I sunbathed, and enjoyed the gossip of the other actors. Cyril Cusack was more interested in my writing than in my performance, and when I would throw out a wee hint about going over our lines, he would tug his lip and gaze at the distant horizon and say, with wonder in those blue eyes, 'And you've written a book or two, have you? Now isn't that wonderful. I would like to do that very thing myself.' Incidentally, I was interested to observe that he spoke with his familiar soft Irish brogue, and I wondered if he'd had a shot at Geordie before it was decided to leave him as he was!

There were two days of resting, swimming, chatting and generally revelling in the flesh-pots before the location telephone rang to tell me I'd be wanted next morning and would be collected at 7.45 A.M. It was lovely driving the twenty-five miles through the fresh cool countryside at that hour in the morning, and as we neared the Ettrick Kirk where the scene was to be shot, I wanted to get out of the car and walk up the hill. The driver was scandalized at the very idea of not delivering me straight into the hands of the director, and was so busy arguing that that was what he was paid to do, that he drove the car straight into the middle of the scene that was being filmed at that very moment, and ruined it! I was sure we'd both be sacked. But the wrath fell upon the posse of watchers whose duty it was to keep intruders at bay, and I fled to wardrobe and make-up while the going was good.

Ten minutes later I emerged with every bit of my face masked with a greyish pancake make-up, clad in widow's blacks. I'd aged twenty-five years in that ten minutes, and was the living proof that not all film work is flattering and glamorous! But who cared? It was a great day and I was working.

When we reached the cemetery, we found a party of Hollywood top brass had flown in to see how the film was progressing, and I was so pleased Scotland was showing its fairest face for them. It was a marvellous day, sunny and bright and beautiful, and as one of them surveyed the blue skies and the emerald rolling hills, he threw out his arms and said, 'All it needs is for Julie Andrews to appear over that crest singing, "The Hills are Alive with the Sound of Music."' He was right. It had that sort of magic.

In the afternoon, things were considerably enlivened by the arrival of Sean Connery. James Bond in person! Powerfully built and deeply tanned, I found him as truly Scottish as a sprig of heather, and within minutes we were deep in discussion about *Macbeth* as an all-Scottish production, and I was applying for the part of first witch! Lee Remick then turned up, and while we waited for the cameras to be set up for the next shot, we all lay in the kirkyard in the sun, as much at home as though we'd known one another all our lives. That is the wonderful thing about show business. Actors take to one another like ducks to water. There is an instant friendliness, a shared humour, and a sort of secret language. When I took the little 'Geordie' job, who in a thousand years would have dreamed it would mean rubbing shoulders with such film luminaries as Sean Connery and Lee Remick?

Alas, though, the one star I did *not* meet was Ava Gardner. She wasn't due to arrive until my scenes were finished. Och the pity of it.

I was highly entertained by the outrage expressed by the local villagers they were using in the film, at the amount of time everything took. They had been engaged to sing half a hymn, and in their innocence thought it might take about an hour or so. Instead they had been called on Wednesday. On Thursday. On Friday. And, worst of all, on Saturday! 'What about the sheep shearing?' one asked indignantly of the assistant who was telling her she was called for the following day again. 'Aye,' chimed in another, 'and what about the messages I should have got in by this time?' 'And the outing we had planned for Saturday,' said a man defiantly. 'We have our own lives to lead, you know.'

'Oh no you haven't,' I said. 'Not when you're in continuity. Once you've been seen in background shots, you have to be in position for every scene where the camera just might catch sight of you.'

One old lady sent me into giggles by calling out to me, right in the middle of a shot, 'And it's Ettrick Kirk, mind noo Molly, no' church!' She was completely oblivious to calls for 'silence' while shooting was in progress, and ruined several shots before it was realized she was deaf!

When the villagers were asked to recite the Creed in the church scene, there was a general hubbub, then

323

point blank refusal. 'We don't say that in this part of Scotland,' they said. 'It wouldnae sound right.' In the end, they were persuaded to read this litany which was not part of their faith. It didn't sound right at all, as they knew full well it wouldn't but I don't suppose they would notice that in the Middle West!

I also noticed, with interest, the ingratiating cunning of film people. There was a caretaker's house by the kirk, and the first item which was coveted was the telephone. After only a little arm-twisting, that was made available to the *Tam Linn* unit. Then bedroom one was required, to accommodate both sexes during a complicated scene change. Next the toilet was declared out of bounds to everyone, including the owners, when this was roped in for the camera crews to work on technical problems as they arose.

In the end, the couple who owned the house sat outside on deckchairs, and were fed by the film unit, and queued up with the rest of us for toilet and other facilities!

I'd never seen a more convincing example of the fable which warned of the folly of letting the camel put even the tip of its nose inside your tent.

On the last day, as I prepared for the final 'take', I looked around the cemetery and took in the plethora of cameras, lights, generators, tracks, sound booms, technicians and the army of production assistants.

Locals from the church scene stood about watching, occasionally dodging over for an autograph, and the visiting VIPs were scattered about the lawns and between the grave stones.

There could never have been a livelier churchyard. If the last trump had sounded the risen dead would have been in for a great surprise!

It was a lovely film to have been in, even in the

smallest capacity, and it was such a pity that after all that work, and all the money spent on it, it vanished without trace.

Could it have been because Sean Connery and I invoked the dreaded name of *Macbeth* in Ettrick Kirkyard? I wonder?

It certainly didn't shed its unlucky shadow over me, for almost at once I was booked for a nice little part as a frightened stall-holder in *Scrooge*. True to his word that I was his little lucky mascot, Ronald Neame had written in this part for me, which of course included Helena Gloag as my big sister. It was to be done at Shepperton, a ghastly journey from Pinner, involving a drive across London and skirting the industrial route round London Airport, and when Sandy and I did a 'dummy run' to time ourselves, we got hopelessly lost. We did this three times before we found the studios, and even when we did arrive at our proper destination, it had taken us two hours. I knew perfectly well I could never add four hours to my working day, for film calls start at 7 A.M. and finishing time is around 5.30 to 6.00 P.M. So I made up my mind to look for digs, as there were to be six weeks' work for me, involving a great deal of singing and dancing.

My finding of the digs was pure pantomime. I knew a director's wife who lived in Shepperton, and I rang her number, merely to ask her if she knew of any local guest houses, or private people who rented rooms to film artistes.

A man's voice answered the telephone, and the accent told me at once I wasn't speaking to Liz's husband. I learned that the house had changed hands, and Liz now lived in London. 'Well,' I said, never one to be put off by small difficulties, 'perhaps you can help me. I'm looking for digs for a few weeks, while

I'm filming at Shepperton. Do you know of any guest houses, or locals with rooms to rent? I'm perfectly willing to look after myself, but I start very early in the morning, so it would have to be someone who understood the film working hours.'

His voice quickened with interest, 'Am I speaking to an actress?' he asked. 'Yes, you are,' I replied. 'You wouldn't be that Scots lady who was in the Lyons, would you?' 'The very same,' I replied. 'Coo,' he said, 'listened to you for years, I have. You come and stay with us. We've got a spare room. You're welcome to have it.'

'Wait a minute,' I said hastily. 'Have you a wife?' 'Course I have.' 'Well, don't you think you'd better ask her first? She might not like to have a lodger.'

'My wife will love it,' he assured me positively. 'Tell you what, you come along tomorrow and have a look at us, and see the room. My wife's out shopping now, but come along tomorrow morning anyway.'

I put down the receiver, and shook with laughter as I retailed all this conversation to Sandy. 'Goodness knows what his wife will say,' I giggled. 'And goodness knows what sort of folk they are, but I do know it will be a nice house for Liz and her husband are very established show business people.'

When we arrived at their house on the Sunday forenoon, husband Peter threw open the door, with a welcoming 'Come in, come in,' and roared upstairs 'Leopolda, here they are. You wouldn't believe me when I told you, but here's Molly Weir and her husband.' There was a scurrying and scuffling from upstairs, and a face leaned over the bannister, hair still in rollers. She was dark haired and foreign-looking, and was wearing a pale blue dressing gown. Her hand went to her mouth in dismay. 'I did not believe Peter

326

when he told me,' she said. 'He is always teasing, and so I did not get up. I am a nurse, and I was having a good rest, since it is a Sunday.'

And that was my introduction to a pair who welcomed me into their home, made me a part of the family, and said, when I left at the end of the film, 'It is like losing a daughter.' Leopolda was Greek, and she used to come upstairs to the bedroom where I was lying, flat out, exhausted after a day's dancing in the studios, and sit quietly chatting. She found my Scottish enunciation very easy to follow, and enjoyed improving her vocabulary, she told me, and was altogether delightful both as a friend and a landlady. I had the freedom of the kitchen, and whoever arrived home first at the end of the day lit the fire. Peter had trays and trays of plants he grew from seed, and as an enthusiastic gardener I handed out advice and assistance when required! We couldn't have been more compatible, we three, if we'd been picked out by computer dating. And it all happened by the merest chance. I had put in my thumb and pulled out a plum!

The film itself started off in great style, with the news that Maggie Smith had won an Oscar for her performance in *Brodie*, and Ronald Neame, now about to direct us in *Scrooge*, was naturally cock-a-hoop, for of course *Brodie* was his film.

Scrooge had the starriest of casts, but I didn't meet many of them. Our scenes in the market and the streets of London were concerned with Albert Finney as Scrooge, Anton Rodgers as a swash-buckling cockney, and Roy Kinnear and other actor friends in bit parts. I was longing to meet Dame Edith Evans, and Alec Guinness who was a marvellous Marley, but alas I wasn't involved in their scenes. When we did the scenes with David Collings and Frances Cuka, as Mr and Mrs Cratchit, all their hungry children forgot their screen misery as soon as they spied the 'lady from the advert', and they rushed over to the window and yelled out to me, 'Hey Mrs M. gonna do our floors?' It wasn't exactly in the script, but it sent them into peals of merriment.

If the children were astonished to see me, I was absolutely rocked on my heels when a lady came over to me in the canteen one day and said, 'I wonder if you know who I am?'

I saw an oldish woman with fair hair, worn short, gentle blue eyes, pink cheeks and a very warm smile. There was something vaguely familiar in the expression, but I couldn't put a name to her, not even a background.

'I'm Auntie Bella Ross,' she said.

It was my mother's old friend from Springburn, and I hadn't seen her since I was ten.

I remembered the last time we'd met as though it had been yesterday. I had been sent over on a Sunday morning with a message from my mother, and Auntie Bella Ross had given me the biggest chunk of milk chocolate I'd ever held in my hand, so thick and solid compared to our wee penny bars that I had never forgotten it. I boasted about it to my school chums for weeks afterwards.

She was now the matron looking after the children on the film, and she told me that for twenty years she had kept looking for me on every production, and couldn't believe it when one of the children pointed me out in the canteen. Oh if only my mother had been alive, and I could have told her of this exciting meeting! It was somehow fitting that we should have met on a film which showed 'the ghost of Christmas past'. My meeting with Auntie Bella Ross was truly 'the ghost of childhood past'.

Later, long after the film finished, I had a letter from relatives with whom she was staying in Jersey, telling me that she was very ill and asking me to write to her to cheer her up. I sat down and wrote at once, and it was just like writing to my mother again. She had been my mother's one 'posh' friend from Springburn days, and my mother really only knew her through Bella's brother's friendship with my young father, so I could write of a link which stretched back to the mists of very early childhood, and to a time when Bella's own mother was alive. I had a reply from a granddaughter telling me how much pleasure my letter had given. And then silence.

The work on *Scrooge* was absolutely exhausting. The music sessions lasted for hours, and were an impressive display of the musical director's brilliance. Everyone was recorded separately, and then all the various voices were 'married' to the orchestral backing, on separate recording bands. Each note had to be sung at exactly the right tempo so that every voice was in unison, and that director could tell to within a thousandth of a second whether or not we were synchronizing perfectly. It was nerve-racking, but the results were astounding when we heard our voices played back to us complete with orchestra.

Later when we came to the dancing sequences, this method of recording allowed the camera to flash to any face it chose, and be quite certain to find each of us singing our own parts.

It was a marvellous moment when principals and 135 extras erupted into joyous song and dance, and filled the narrow snow-bound streets with movement. We looked like a mob of revolutionaries as we surged down towards the square, an impression that was emphasized when we were told to 'relax' and sank thankfully to the ground to rest, heedless of the 'snow' on our petticoats. It was like the retreat from Moscow, with exhausted bodies dropping everywhere.

We were at it from half-past-eight in the morning till half-past-five at night for two whole days, with breaks for tea and lunch, and we wore clothes which felt as if they weighed a ton. What with four petticoats under a thick tweed skirt, an apron, a woollen pinny, a thick blouse, woollen scarf, short shoulder cape and long shoulder cape with hood, woollen mittens and boots, lined cap topped by a black bonnet, they were so heavy that we were provided with a car to get us from our dressing rooms to the stage. If we'd had to walk carrying all that weight, we'd have been exhausted before we'd done a stroke of work. Helena and I took up so much room with all our petticoats that we had to get into the car from both sides, and once in our seats, we had to be pushed from the outside to get the doors shut, because we couldn't move ourselves an inch! When I took them all off at night, I leaped into the air like a shorn lamb! I was deeply thankful I hadn't to face a two-hour drive to Pinner at the end of each day's stint. Back at the digs, I used to flop down on the bed, weariness pressing down on me like a blanket, where I lay unmoving until Leopolda gently wondered when I would like to come down to cook my egg.

Albert Finney was marvellous in the 'Ghost of Christmas Future' sequences, and so touching that in spite of his being such an old skinflint as Scrooge, I couldn't bear the thought of his heartbreak when he realized we were cheering the news of his death.

I was highly diverted one day when the director asked him to use a bit more voice in one of our singing

330

sequences, when he had to speak lines over the music. He was right behind Helena and me at this point. 'I'm being drowned out by the Dagenham girl pipers,' he called up to the director. Everyone enjoyed the joke. Finney was so easy, so lacking in any displays of temperament, that he was a constant joy to work with. This, I may say, is not always the case with a big star.

I took Sandy down to the studios one Saturday morning when I had a dancing rehearsal, just to let him see what was then the biggest stage in Europe. He always says I exaggerate wildly when I'm telling a story, and I'd been boasting for weeks that the whole of Pinner High Street and Bridge Street could be accommodated on our set with its little Dickensian shops, its long streets, its houses with windows edged with 'snow', its overhanging balconies and high roofs, and its great square, which itself was large enough to accommodate a beautiful real chestnut horse and elegant carriage, with two liveried chaps sitting high on the box in front.

I had to sneak him in before the director arrived, for there was a 'strictly no visitors to the set' rule, but it was worth the risk to see Sandy's face. As soon as we reached the set, I rushed him up one street, across the square, and down the other street, and had to drag him away from the shop windows crammed with everything from hobby horses to cottage loaves. As the director walked in Sandy walked out! Afterwards, *he* was the one who told visitors to our house of the astonishing re-incarnation of Dickensian London under one vast roof, and he it was who finished his description with the comparison 'The whole of Pinner High Street and Bridge Street could have sat inside it.' As he is the master of under-statement, they believed him!

After all this film work, on top of the launching of

my first book, we decided we must have a really special holiday to mark such a wonderful year, and we chose Portugal. I don't like flying, we both love ships, and so we decided to use a cruise ship as our transport to Lisbon. It was quite idyllic. White-coated stewards to see to our luggage at Southampton, the band of the Royal Marines to play us out, and in the space of the two days it took us to reach Lisbon we attended the captain's cocktail party, saw *Butch Cassidy and the Sundance Kid* at the cinema, went to church next morning, played deck quoits, table tennis and shuffleboard, enjoyed a variety of delicious meals, and felt we had been on a first-class mini-holiday. And the holiday hadn't even started!

Portugal had been described as always having a cool breeze, and tourists were recommended to take a coat and cardigan for what could be chilly temperatures, especially in May and June. So I bought lightweight wool and heavy linen slacks, and at the last minute, just in case of a heat-wave threw in an old pair of cotton Bermuda-length pants and a sleeveless cotton sun-top. Portugal that May enjoyed its hottest summer for over one hundred years, and in every photograph I am to be seen wearing threadbare cotton Bermudas and an old sleeveless cotton sun-top!

But it was a wonderful holiday. The hotel and food were excellent, the sea-bathing utter bliss in all that heat, and we were so lucky to see such a beautiful country quiet and peaceful before the revolution destroyed so much. All the tiredness of the busy year sloughed off like an old skin, and we both returned with golden tans which showed us satisfyingly healthy faces when we looked in our mirror. Sandy looked like that advert for 'Digger Tobacco', and I was entranced when a passenger on the returning ferry said mine was the most dazzling complexion he had ever seen! Mind you, he was from darkest Africa!

While we were away lotus-eating, builders were carrying out one of my happiest notions, which was to have a sun-lounge added to the back of the house. Sandy took some persuading, for he felt he would never have time to sit in this expensive white elephant, and then a very good friend of his and brother Tommy's died, and I said, 'Sandy, Matt can never have a sun-lounge now. I have waited twenty years for one, and with my Flash savings I can.' He looked at me steadily, and then said, 'You're quite right. Go ahead.'

I chose the builder with the same care I might have shown in selecting a husband! I knocked on the door of a house where I had seen a sun-lounge of a quality streets ahead of the dozens of others I had studied, and the lady was agreeably charmed to find Molly Weir of the telly on her doorstep. She warned me that her treasured builder would be hard to find, and she was sure he had gone bankrupt and had given up. It appeared he was a superb craftsman, but an innocent abroad when it came to cash concerns. I wasn't to be put off though, and I started with a 'last-known address'. Hot on the trail we went from one clue to the next, and finally found a house and then a caravan, and then our quarry!

I was captivated at once. Like the Chinese philosopher Lin Yu Tang, who believes that the seat of the emotions is in the stomach, I know that when my stomach registers calm content, all is well. And my stomach positively purred at first sight of a slim, gentle, country-looking man with golden brown eyes, and a humorous smiling mouth. He *had* given up, he told us, but when he heard of how I had tracked him down, determined to have him and no other, his eyes crinkled with laughter and he said, 'Well, it looks as if it's got to be me, doesn't it?'

When Sandy saw the drawings our Mr D. brought along with him when he came to measure up, and the expert way he ran over the measurements, he said 'How about a cup of coffee?' and I knew he too had been won over.

The day the foundations were laid was as good as a circus. It was a lovely sunny Saturday morning when six men turned up, one to go down the trench, the other five to keep him supplied with the sloppy concrete mixture. Side doors were wedged open, planks laid across the open 'ditch' and across the intervening terrace. Then an enormous cement-mixing machine arrived, to the great delight of the children in the lane. It was like the Pied Piper, as children ran from every house to form an audience. One little boy was visiting his grandparents, and he thought the whole thing had been organized for his special benefit, and of course grandad did not disillusion him. He talked about it for months.

Five men with wheelbarrows formed a queue. The man in charge of the mixer dialled something, pressed a button, and from the chute attached to the machine, out shot a mixture like instant porridge! Non-stop!

A barrow was thrust under the open end of the chute, filled up, and the man *raced* to the side entrance, tipped the stuff into the ditch, ran across the planks, round the side of the house, and back to the mixer again.

They were like an army of busy ants. I've never seen men work so fast, for the stuff set so quickly and the machine worked so fast they just had to keep up with it. I was terrified the man in the foundations would find himself trapped, for in no time he was up to his knees in the stuff. But he knew what he was doing and escaped in good time! Round and round the house they ran, for almost an hour, sweat dripping off them. It was a superb piece of organized teamwork.

Only when they had swept down the side paths and terrace with plenty of cold water to remove all the wee blobs which had been spilled, would they relax sufficiently to enjoy a cup of tea. The children gave them a round of applause, and followed the cement mixer to the end of the lane. It had been a splendid Saturday entertainment for them.

As for Sandy and I, we both felt if the rest of the extension was as enthusiastically carried out as the 'foonds', we would have nothing to worry about and could depart for Portugal with an easy mind.

Mr D. said it was the pleasantest job he had ever done. It was a summer of endlessly sunny days, and he and his mate used to sit under the malus tree, dreamily enjoying the quiet of the garden and the welcome shade as they sipped their tea and munched their sandwiches. When we got back from Portugal, the framework was up, and to Sandy's great joy the view from the house hadn't been spoilt, as he had feared, for the design took account of the angle to be seen from the kitchen window. It was at that moment he began to show real enthusiasm, and Mr D. and I used to wink privately to one another at each casually offered compliment. For I had told this fine craftsman about Sandy's reservations about the whole project, and he took the greatest pains to ensure that the aesthetic aspect of the building was considered at every point.

To effect some economy, and because he is an excellent painter, Sandy undertook to do the painting of all the woodwork, which was pretty extensive, for I wanted the lounge to be like a real room, with a solid roof, and the huge windows were fitted into strong heavy frames, all of which had to be painted. Sandy enjoyed playing his part in the final touches, and his work matched Mr D.'s.

We had blinds fitted to all those windows, for I knew very well that if we had any sun at all, the problem would be to keep such a large place cool. I tracked down just the perfect flooring for such an extension, and the man who laid the tiles was just as expert as Mr D. A small machine like a miniature tar-boiler was whirred into activity, hot black asphalt bubbled and boiled, and was then slapped on the concrete floor, and the tiles set into position. I had drawn a colour sketch of exactly how I wished them placed – they were a mixture of beige and burgundy tiles – and when the man stopped for a bite of lunch less than three hours later, the floor was complete, and matched my drawing to a T.

They stopped making that flooring shortly afterwards, and I felt so lucky to have been just in time to order it. For there wasn't a soul who saw the lounge afterwards who didn't want to know where we had bought the flooring. Not a word in praise of the lovely proportions of the sun-lounge itself, it was the flooring that riveted them!

It reminded me of one of our advertisements where we started off with people sitting round the breakfast table, and just to be ultra-fashionable the buyer had 'dressed' the table with a double-egg-cup newly on the market. Not a viewer wanted to know about the product which was being advertised, but *hundreds* wrote in to ask where they could buy the double-egg-cup! The advertiser was furious, for he had spent a vast sum on the commercial, and the egg-cup-man nothing!

Similarly, when I was featured on the front cover of a gardening magazine, nobody showed the slightest interest in the plants we discussed, but everybody wanted the pattern for the tabard I was wearing. As it was my own, and I had no pattern, I had to lend it to their 'home' expert, who had to try to count the stitches and the number of rows to a pattern, and publish her findings to satisfy their readers. Verily, the world of advertising is fraught with pitfalls! Like life!

When relatives in Scotland saw a photograph of our completed sun-lounge, Rhona's mother said sadly, 'Oh Molly, you'll never come back to Scotland now. You could never leave such a bonnie extension.' I do love it. And so does Sandy. As Mr D. truly predicted, we sit there now more than in any other room in the house, and even in the depths of winter friends love the sense of being in the garden while enjoying the warmth of sitting indoors. It has been the most rewarding 'souvenir' of my years as Mrs Flash, and almost compensates for the complete loss of privacy thereafter. It was worth every penny spent on it, and is a lasting tribute to the excellent work of a true craftsman.

I had hardly time to sit and admire the view from the windows before I was asked to go up to Glasgow again to do another Bill Tennant *Dateline* show, this time with my old friend and 'boss', Ben Lyon. I was staying with Rhona's mother, but went along to the Central Hotel to dine with Ben. It was comical to see the diners doing a 'double take' when they caught sight of us, followed by a furious whispering as they obviously wondered what we were doing together in Glasgow.

Ben had news for me. I had spoken to him many

times on the telephone since Bebe died twelve months before, and I knew how appallingly lonely and heartbroken he had been. Every day can be a lifetime after suffering a bereavement. He seemed very diffident, very tentative when we met, and then he told me of his plans to marry again. I knew that Bebe had begged him to remarry if anything happened to her, and to be happy again. She had a generous heart, and she knew how bereft he would be, but he was terribly afraid people would think it was 'too soon'.

It was no autumn and spring mating this. The lady of his choice was the Hollywood starlet to whom he had proposed marriage long before he knew Bebe. She had refused him then and had married a top Hollywood director, and both she and Ben had found great happiness with their chosen partners. Now she too was lonely in her widowhood after thirty-seven years of marriage, and when fate threw them together on each of Ben's visits to Hollywood to sort out Bebe's affairs, they recalled their first strong attachment for each other. With so many shared memories they felt they could comfort each other in their loneliness, and they had decided to marry and spend their declining years together.

'Ben,' I said, 'every year is a bonus after the age of seventy. You had a lifetime of happiness with dear Bebe. Yours was an eighteen carat marriage in a Hollywood of crumbling values. Anyone would understand your need for companionship and comfort, and realize you have made the best possible choice in a lady you have known since 1927.'

I think I reassured him. In fact I know I did. But it was strange to be playing the part of Ben's confidante after years of teasing from him. We had a deep and true friendship, and I think we could honestly say

338

anything to each other. Indeed he always used to say, when telling me a secret, 'Well of course honey, I had to tell you. You're family.'

Rhona's mother was very sympathetic when I got back after I'd said good-night to Ben, and she felt I had said all the right things. I was so glad, for Mrs Dickson was very wise, and very balanced in her judgments. 'Och there *will* be some folk who'll say a year is gey short to think of marrying again,' she said. 'But a man who's been used to a wife for over forty years needs a woman about the house. And 365 empty days and nights are an eternity to the lonely bereaved who have to live through them.'

Before I left for London, while waiting for the taxi, on an impulse I dialled Meg Buchanan's number. I usually tried to see Meg when I was in Glasgow, but there had been no time on this visit. She was an old and valued friend, of whom I was very fond, and I treasured the little gold thistle she had given me for luck when I left to find fame and fortune in London. She played Sarah McFlannel in *The McFlannels* and before that had been one of the shining lights of the Scottish National Players. It was Meg who used to quote to me, marvelling at my non-stop activity, 'Aye hen, a gaun fit's aye gettin'.' When she answered the telephone, her voice was very weak. She seemed to have no strength at all. I tried to rouse her by telling her all about Ben and the show we had just done for Bill Tennant, and I could hear little laughs as she responded to my tales. When I asked how she was, she said, 'Och no' very weel. I haven't been out for ages.' 'Have you seen a doctor, Meg?' I demanded. 'Are you taking a tonic?' 'Och I'm fed up with doctors,' she said. 'If I send for him again I think he'll just say "Dig a hole fur her!"'

That was to be my last conversation for all time with my good friend Meg. She died shortly afterwards. It was a sad loss. But I was so glad I had spoken to her, and renewed the bond of our friendship, and we had shared a few laughs on a grey sleety day in Glasgow.

Incidentally it was on that Glasgow visit that a bookseller told me that somebody had pinched the last copy of my *Shoes Were for Sunday* from his shelves! It was quite a compliment in its own way!

And when I got back to Pinner, I discovered that a Great Dane had eaten one of my books when the owner was out for lunch! I hope it digested all my tales, as well as the paper they were written on! The owner was livid, because it was a hard-back copy, and she would have to buy another to complete her set.

A nice little assortment of parts now came my way, and to my amazement none clashed. I had been shattered to have had to turn down a lovely part in *Dr Finlay's Casebook* which I just couldn't accept because I felt both Sandy and I needed a holiday far too much to cancel our plans for Portugal. I had waited five years for it too, but there comes a time when health and happiness are more important than anything else.

I felt sure future offers were doomed to follow this pattern, but I was wrong. Everything fitted like a jigsaw, and my only worry was trying to work brightly and breezily through a pulverising bronchial cold. For *Looks Familiar* with Denis Norden, my head felt like cotton wool, my chest like jagged glass, and my mind just refused to focus. It was lovely to be working with Ted Ray and Greta Gynt, and dear old Sam Costa, but my performance was wobbly in the extreme. I felt too shaky to make wild guesses, and was mad with myself for not coming out boldly with a name which turned out to be correct! However I slightly redeemed

340

myself with the mystery voice, for even in my woolly state I recognized the lovely singing tenor of Alvar Liddell. We were all entertained to supper afterwards, and Alvar was quite concerned because I couldn't touch a morsel of food. I tried, but it was no good. When that beastly virus attacks the Weir tubes, all food tastes like Dead Sea fruit.

I was right as a trivet again for the Hammer Production of *Hands of the Ripper*, and it was worth getting up at six o'clock in the morning to find myself sitting next to Eric Porter in make-up. Eric Porter, over whom the entire nation had fumed and fretted in *The Forsyte Saga*. We all felt Saturdays would never be the same when that series ended. Like Celia Johnson, Eric was great fun, and nothing like the saturnine Soames of the series. He put on a comical Scottish accent when he introduced me to Angharad Rees, the lovely little Welsh actress (later superb in *Poldark*), when he said, 'Aye Molly, this yin's a bad wee besom, so she is. She stabs a lady in the breist wi' shears.' It was a revelation to find such larkiness in an actor noted for the sombreness of his characterizations, and a great start to the day.

Margaret Rawlings was the victim destined to be done in by the little Welsh charmer, and I played Margaret's maid demure in black dress and a little Victorian cap. Hammer specialized in blood and thunder melodramas, with fairly 'over the top' performances, but *Hands of the Ripper* received excellent notices, and was generously received everywhere as an enjoyable example of its kind. It's always good to be in a success, even if in a part so small you could have missed me if you'd sneezed! It was repeated last Hogmanay while we were feasting at the house of Scottish friends, and we all missed it!

341

I had a meatier part in an episode of a popular TV series, *The Fenn Street Gang,* and was cast as a 'medium', a lovely Margaret Rutherford type of part, complete with one of Margaret's flowing capes. When I went for clothes fitting, I found, to my amusement, that the location was a courtyard in a block of flats at the far end of the very lane where we live! I had to go all the way to Wembley Studios to be made up and dressed, and then had to navigate the driver and cast back to Pinner, for nobody else had the slightest idea where the flats were.

I had fondly imagined I would be able to pop home for my meals, but I wasn't allowed to leave the location, and had to queue up with the others at the 'chuck wagon', and eat my pork chops and potatoes inside the parked bus which had been converted to a temporary restaurant for us. It was funny to think of Sandy sitting before his solitary meal not five minutes away, at the other end of the lane.

The whole neighbourhood was enthralled, for we filmed at midnight and the bright floodlighting kept everybody awake. On the night the episode came over on TV, all Pinner was watching, and there was great admiration for the artistry of the camera crews in making the scene one of such ghostly beauty in the artificial moonlight. The occupants of the flats kept telling everyone next day, 'It was filmed at our flats, you know. Didn't the gardens look beautiful? Oh yes, they wanted something which looked really striking.' They dined out on it for weeks.

A more distant engagement took place when *Woman's Hour* decided to go outside London for some of their summer broadcasts, so that audiences in other parts of the country could participate, and meet some of the regular contributors. Elizabeth Beresford and I were delighted to find ourselves travelling together for the same programme, and there was a hilarious incident at the ticket barrier. We had discovered there would be no refreshments on the train, and had rushed back to the station buffet to collect tea and biscuits. Balancing my plastic container, I rummaged in my bag and handed the ticket collector what I thought was my ticket. He unfolded it, put on his spectacles, pursed his lips, and said, 'I'd gladly do so, Madam, if I knew who she was.' I seized the 'ticket' back. I had handed him a note sent to me by a fan of *Woman's Hour*, with a message for another contributor, which read, 'Give my love to Ann.' I almost dropped my tea laughing, as I found the right ticket.

With all this hilarity we nearly missed the train, but quickly settled down to exchange all our news. Elizabeth's big news was that she thought she had had a good idea accepted for a children's TV series. I was so pleased for her, because so many terrific suggestions from her in the past had come to naught.

'Oh that's great,' I said. 'What is it called? Have you got a title for it yet?'

'Yes,' she said, '*The Wombles of Wimbledon.*'

Now normally I have quite a good instinct for the smell of success, but I had no 'pricking of the thumbs' at all, and wondered what on earth could I say to sound encouraging, without sounding false. I truly hoped it would do well, but it sounded a bit of a nonstarter to me! How wrong could I be?

The rest is television history. *The Wombles of Wimbledon* filled the screens and the imagination of children and their parents for many a series and many a year, and there were toys and books and all sorts of spin-offs. Elizabeth had triumphantly hit the jackpot.

But in spite of my lack of instinct for what was to

343

come, the name itself must have made an impression on me, for why should I remember so vividly the exact moment when I first heard it on that train?

CHAPTER FIFTEEN

There was a sad journey to Scotland before the year was out, when we lost Sandy's younger brother Jimmy. There had been a nightmare of standing by the telephone for thirty-six hours, but there was really no hope from the start.

Sandy, Rose, Tom and I travelled to Glasgow together on the train, and because I was still suffering from a virus and my stomach was most unhappy, I packed sandwiches and took thermos flasks filled with fresh coffee. Whatever the others decided, I knew I couldn't face train meals. In the end, none of us had appetite for more than the sandwiches, and Tom kept me supplied with antacid tablets to keep tummy pains at bay.

We had booked into the quiet little hotel near the Botanic Gardens where I usually stayed when I was working in Glasgow, and because they knew the reason for our visit, they were kindness personified. Tea and small meals were supplied at all hours, without a penny extra being charged.

But I was shocked by the evidence of the vandalism of the Glasgow hooligans. We went to my mother's grave before crossing to the Chapel of Rest for Jimmy's removal to the crematorium, and not only had those mindless morons painted their crass gang slogans on gravestones, they had actually used broken glass to prise out the lead lettering on the headstones. What

344

sort of people were they, I wondered, who could derive satisfaction from such cruel ugly behaviour. I completely rejected the argument that it was because of social conditions and lack of proper playing fields. We had ónly back-courts to play in, and we hadn't two pennies to rub together, but we did have a sensitivity to the feelings of others and a wholesome fear of the laws of God and man.

With a fortune spent on education, with psychiatrists to probe every difficulty, and help offered in directions undreamed of when my mother brought up the three of us, *and* kept grannie, unaided, we seemed to have bred a type of ignorant vandal with no respect for other people's sorrows or property. Not all, possibly, but far too many for comfort.

I wished I had the powers of those witches I played, and could put a proper curse on them!

On reflection, though, it would be best to leave them to God. As a fellow-journalist quoted in a similar context, 'With God and oneself, there's a majority!' And in my heart there was still the comforting feeling that there were more good folk than the other kind.

One of the strangest things which happened during those two heartbreaking days in Glasgow, was when we got back to the hotel on the night of the cremation. We were all feeling quite drained, and on our way upstairs we met a lady coming down who was carrying some large paintings. I could see a strikingly painted head and shoulders through the transparent wrapping of the top picture, and I happened to comment on its excellence.

Discussing the artist's work, we learned that she was a faith-healer, one of those people who 'lay hands' and cure apparently hopeless cases. To my surprise, in the middle of the conversation, she closed her eyes, stretched her hands out towards the four of us, found mine, and began to tremble violently as she told me I was full of tension and aching pains. With her eyes still closed, she said, 'This person whose hands I am holding is having a lot of pain and discomfort just here,' and she laid her hands across her stomach.

We all looked at one another, and I said, 'You're absolutely right. I've had a great deal of recurring pain for weeks now.'

Next minute we were all in the lounge, and she was laying her hands across my back and my stomach. It was quite extraordinary. Like an electric heater vibrating and yet her hands were icy to the touch. Whether or not it was coincidence, my stomach did really feel soothed and quiet after her ministrations, and she told me that she would put me on the 'distant cure' list and it could help me over the miles! It all seemed quite incongruous, like a scene from a Pinter play, and as Rose said, 'It's not many hotels you visit where the day ends with a spiritual cure.'

The journey home seemed much longer than to Glasgow, for we all ached to get back to ordinary everyday things and to be quiet, and not to have to speak too much. Jimmy was dearly loved by all of us, and we knew we would have to face the complete sense of loss in the days which lay ahead.

By the strangest coincidence, there was a letter from Katie Boyle waiting for me. She had enclosed it with a note acknowledging my letter of sympathy on the death of her husband.

The letter said:

Death is nothing at all. I have only slipped away into the next room. I am I, and you are you. Whatever we were to each other, we are still.

346

Call me by my old familiar name. Speak to me in the way which you always used. Put no difference in your tone. Wear no forced air of solemnity or sorrow.

Let my name be ever the household word that it always was. What is this death but a negligible accident? Why should I be out of mind because I am out of sight?

I am waiting for you, for an interval, somewhere very near just around the corner. All is well.

What a wonderful consolation.

Katie's letter confirmed something I have believed for a long time, that we must not shut out from our conversation those whom we have loved and lost, but should carry them with us through all our continuing experiences. So in a sense they are always with us and are part of us. It doesn't stop me hungering at times, with piercing longing, for the sight of their faces and the sound of their voices, but it does help.

Rose too came to feel this way. When she read the words of my dedication to Miss Chree in one of my books, 'To Live in Hearts we leave behind is not to die,' she said, 'That's quite true. I never feel Jimmy is dead when we speak and laugh about him and his witty words and ways.'

But it took us some time to reach that state of mind.

It was Katie who sent me to another faith healer, who also 'laid hands' back and front of that aching centre of my body. For a whole hour I thought I was cured. I went skipping down Baker Street, absolutely free of pain for the first time for months. It was marvellous. I was on winged feet, but in bed that night I wakened again to the familiar knife twisting close to the breast-bone. 'It's the doctor for you in the morning, my girl,' I vowed, and with the decision came sleep.

Several appointments later, followed by a series of X-rays, I learned the unexpected truth. I was nursing in my bosom, not a viper, but a duodenal ulcer! All those butterflies and nervous traumas over years of show-biz challenges had done their stealthy work, and the shock of Jimmy's death had been the last straw. Surely they must have made a mistake. Everybody knew women had the babies, and men had the ulcers. Not so, said the doctor, struggling with laughter.

When surgery was recommended, Sandy was horrified. So was I. I still had vivid memories of those wild eyes of his when he panted with thirst after his ulcer operation, not to mention those clips holding a fearsome wound which ran from breast-bone to stomach.

So what was I to do? Well, knowing the devil you are unwittingly entertaining in your vital parts is a tremendous help. If it could be controlled by disciplined eating, there was nothing to lose in seeing if this would work. If it didn't work, then surgery it would have to be. I reckoned that practically everyone in the Western world is on some sort of a diet. If it wasn't to lose weight, it was to keep the heart healthy by cutting out cholesterol. Or it was for the gall-bladder, or hiatus hernia. I was no worse off than any of those sufferers. So I would just find out the dos and don'ts of living with an ulcer.

It didn't take long to sort out the things I could eat and the foods I mustn't touch with a barge pole. And, as all the medicos emphasized, 'The life style is more important than the diet,' so the candle mustn't be burnt at both ends. One job at a time from now on, early to bed when this could be managed, and when humanly possible the old Scots advice would be followed, 'Aye mind and keep a calm sough'.

I never was much of a drinker, only sipping the conventional sherry or Cinzano, so that was no problem. I wasn't much of a smoker either, and when the next bout of bronchitis laid me low, I joined the growing ranks of non-smokers, and so banished another possible irritation to the little pest within.

The hardest thing to give up was onion. I used to be the pin-up girl of the Onion Johnnies who came round selling those strings of beautiful Brittany onions, and if I happened to be out when they called, I've been known to pursue them through Pinner, leaping out of the car at the first sight of a bicycle festooned with the beauties I coveted. Now, never no more! It was the one thing which *all* medical opinion agreed upon, however much they varied with their other advice. Onions in any shape or form were absolutely forbidden. And that includes leeks, syboes (or spring onions as they are called in England), not even chives. Oh that was a real 'heart'. How was I to live much less cook without onions? I turned to onion salt, and found that a very acceptable substitute. 'And where do you think they get onion salt from?' demanded Sandy, as if I was cheating. 'I don't know and I don't care!' I replied. 'And I don't intend to enquire too closely into it.' So far, I've been doing fine, and the surgeon and I parted the best of friends!

It was wonderful to start feeling well again, and to enjoy some refreshing sleeps. I began to feel, cautiously, that I might with a bit of luck survive! And if I needed any sort of encouragement to believe that 'old doctor greasepaint' is the best physician of all, it was the sight of Dame Sybil Thorndike having her ninetieth birthday celebrated at a star-studded gala performance at the Haymarket Theatre.

The queue of stars making their way down the

Haymarket to the theatre practically started at Piccadilly Circus, and everyone encountered on that busy pavement was a famous face. The first pair I bumped into were Gordon Jackson and Rona, but we had barely time to say 'hullo' before we were pressed apart by the watching crowds. Joyce Grenfell was right behind us, not 'stately as a galleon', but forced into a trot by the throng of eager sightseers.

Everyone wore full evening dress, which gave a lovely sense of occasion, and I was glad I hadn't listened to Sandy when he told me I was daft to wear a long skirt just to go to a theatre.

The stalls fairly buzzed with 'Hullo darlings', and 'What are you doing these days?' or *loved* your last play, darling'. Sandy winked and cast his eyes to the ceiling. He always affects a slight deprecation of the extravagance of actors' conversation, but it never ceases to amuse him when he is in their company. I think he feels we're just a lot of children. Which is true in a way, I suppose.

All chatter ceased when Dame Sybil entered her stage box with Princess Alexandra and husband Angus Ogilvie, and with one spontaneous movement the entire audience rose and applauded her. Positive *waves* of emotion flowed like a torrent, until I thought the roof would almost lift off.

Then, without a moment's delay, it was on with the show. Sir Laurence Olivier strode to stage centre, and opened the evening with a prologue by Emlyn Williams. He was followed by a galaxy of talent. Sir Ralph Richardson, Sir Alec Guinness, Peggy Ashcroft, Celia Johnson, Margaret Leighton, Joyce Grenfell, Peter Ustinov, Edith Evans, Wendy Hiller, Irene Worth, to name but a few! All doing their party pieces.

There was a change of mood with a magnificent

ballet set-piece danced by Margot Fonteyn and partner, so exquisite that it brought shouts of 'bravo!' from all over the theatre. I love the enthusiasm of show business audiences. They are so warm and generous in expressing their appreciation, for they know only too well how tough it is.

As the cheers died away, a parade of stars swept on to bow and to curtsey to Dame Sybil, before taking their places among those already assembled on stage. It was like an animated *Who's Who* in the Theatre, and a game for us watching from the stalls to recognize them as they moved swiftly in and out of the spotlight. The Attenboroughs, Jack Hawkins and his wife, Ann Todd and Michael Wilding, Deborah Kerr, Peter O'Toole, Sian Phillips, Paul Scofield, Nigel Patrick, Coral Brown, Joyce Redman, The Hulberts, Lady Redgrave. All of them were actors who hadn't performed on the bill, but who wanted to be included to pay their own personal tribute in this way, happy for once to be merely 'walk-ons'.

At the end, Dame Sybil took the centre of stage, and an easy chair was provided so that she could sit comfortably while she accepted a scroll containing the epilogue written by J. B. Priestley, and a gleaming golden goblet donated by an admiring organization.

When she stood up to thank artistes and audience, at ninety years of age hers was the clearest and most carrying voice of all! She had an obsession about voice projection, and did vocal exercises every morning of her life, and it showed!

'Look well at that stage Sandy,' I whispered, 'for you'll never see such a line-up in your life again, not if you live to be a hundred.'

'I know,' he whispered back.

Everyone seemed to realize this at the same moment,

for the applause swelled and exploded, and the throat tightened with emotion. It was a second or two before we realized that the National Anthem had started,. and as we were already on our feet the applause died away and the music took over. Dame Sybil stood erect and her voice took up the words. Soon the entire theatre was singing, 'Send her Victorious, Happy and Glorious,' with Dame Sybil's voice soaring up like a lintie.

It was a most memorable occasion, and I felt very proud to be part of it.

She lived for another four years, and died on a summer day when England looked at its most beautiful. There was a Service of Thanksgiving held in Westminster Abbey for her life and work, and every seat was filled. Not only the reserved places where we who had shared her profession sat, but the seats for the public too, right to the very doors of the Abbey.

Organ music by Bach sighed softly as more and more people came in, and I remembered that Dame Sybil had followed daily piano practice as part of her self-imposed discipline. Wherever the eye rested, well-known faces were recognized. In front of us sat Evelyn Laye, pale and serious in lavender blue chiffon, and behind was Dame Wendy Hiller, very regal. Two rows ahead of us sat Andrew Cruickshank, and Robert Morley and his son Sheridan came in, behind Joyce Grenfell.

The British are marvellous at observing these rituals. There wasn't a hitch. Sir Ralph Richardson read, in ringing tones, the Lesson from the Psalms, palm upturned in the unconscious gesture of the actor.

Paul Scofield followed and spoke without notes, the beautiful lines from *Cymbeline* which begin, 'Fear no more the heat o' the sun,' and the first verse of which finishes with the moving words, 'Golden lads and girls all must, as chimney-sweepers, come to dust.'

Sir John Gielgud's tribute was undoubtedly the highlight. He spoke with affection and with the humorous honesty of a loved colleague. He had us rippling with soft laughter as he recounted Dame Sybil's sometimes extravagant style of acting. She always excused any over-enthusiasm with a light laugh, and the plea that it was 'so much more fun' doing it that way.

When we stood to sing *All people that on earth do dwell* and came to the phrase, 'O enter then His gates with praise, approach with joy his courts unto,' a beautiful silver cascade of trumpets sounded thrillingly. It was spine-tingling and moving at one and the same moment.

And when we reached the last verse, there was a final, full-throated trumpet accompaniment as if all the heavens were ringing with the joyous sound.

John Casson, Dame Sybil's son, then read a piece from Bunyan's *Pilgrim's Progress*, and it was evident that he had inherited the splendid voice of his parents, both of whom were devoted to the pursuit of excellence in the human voice.

Dame Sybil is the first member of the acting profession to be accorded the honour of being buried in Westminster Abbey since the great Henry Irving.

It is easy to understand why. She had devoted her whole life to the theatre, and by so doing she had enriched the lives of all of us, actors and public alike, and so on a very hot morning, in London's great Abbey, we had gathered together to say 'Good-bye, and thank you.'

The cloisters were cool and beautiful when we came out to a London blazing with heat. The tourists gazed and sucked their ice-creams and we headed for home. It had been a wonderful and uplifting morning.

Following this enriching experience, I was in just the right frame of mind to play the part of a nun. I was delighted to be offered this part, for I always think I have a somewhat old-fashioned type of face, and as the little timid Sister Cecilia who never speaks above a whisper I was playing a character entirely different from my own chatterbox ways, but who could *look* the part. Gaye Brown played the other nun, a big six-footer to my 4ft 11½in and we presented the most comical sight as we stood together. Derek Nimmo was the cleric, and *Oh Father* promised to be a lot of fun. At the first rehearsal when I whispered, with a sibilant rush of esses, 'Sister Cecilia', when I was asked my name, Derek Nimmo looked up startled, 'Was that it?' he asked. As the episode ended with me changed into the most raucous of bingo-callers who teaches Derek how to conduct this game, the contrast between that and my whispering start was most effective. In fact we kept having visitors to the rehearsals, just to watch our performances, which always ended in gales of laughter. It was too good to last! We were just about to move into the studios to record this episode, when a drivers' strike caused the whole thing to be postponed. It was maddening. I loathe strikes, which always seem to me to hurt most those who have nothing whatsoever to do with them. With a more educated work-force nowadays, it should surely be possible to find better ways to settle our grievances. So there we were, all keyed up to give of our best, and left high and dry with the most miserable sense of anti-climax. It felt as if Christmas had been cancelled. It was many weeks before we managed to get into the studio, and by that time some of the cast had to be replaced because they were no longer free, and it felt very strange to go through dialogue which was familiar by this time, and yet unfamiliar because the reactions of the new cast were different.

When we came to the recording, it was most astonishing to see the effect Gaye and I had on everyone in the TV Centre, when they caught sight of us in our nuns' habits. Every detail of our clothes was perfect, and we looked so gentle and demure that men held doors open for us, stopped shouting, held their cigarettes behind their backs and generally behaved as though we were recording angels! One of the actors said, 'But you look so *pure*, Molly'. I always thought those nuns' habits were highly effective in entirely changing anyone's appearance, and *Oh Father* certainly confirmed this. The show went beautifully, the audience loved it, although I think a lot of my Presbyterian friends north of the border were a bit shocked to see me playing the part of a nun so convincingly!

Later, Sandy and I had a great trip to Scotland when I was booked to appear in Andy Stewart's Hogmanay programme from Edinburgh. We hadn't been in Scotland for Hogmanay for years, and we had two splendid days with Tommy and Rhona at Loch Lomond before having to worry about rehearsals. Helensburgh was gale-lashed on the Saturday. We had never seen the gentle little holiday resort so wild and storm-tossed, and my mink coat was like a drowned rug by the time we had finished our shopping. Like the good-tempered garment it was though, it eventually dried out as good as new, and gleamed like a healthy head of hair after a wash in soft Glasgow water. Rhona had been amazed by my lack of concern over the soaking the coat had, but when she saw how harmlessly it recovered, she realized I was speaking the truth when I told her that mink, like diamonds, is virtually indestructible. Costly to acquire, certainly, but lasts a lifetime and keeps its looks.

Sunday morning was worth the trip to Scotland itself. Bright blue skies, strong sunshine, and sparkling frosts on pavement and in hedgerow sent us busily preparing for a picnic. Then with Sandy and I wearing borrowed anoraks, we set off in a blizzard to climb 1000ft over the track where Rob Roy used to rustle his cattle. Tommy is a mine of information on such matters, and we had a running commentary with practically every step. It was fairly strenuous, but I was helped over swiftly-running burns, yanked out of boggy marshes, and hoisted atop slippery stones, and in no time we had left the blizzard behind. The snow-capped peaks were dazzling in brilliant sunshine, and the foreground was unbelievably colourful with vivid bracken and bright green fir. I was so glad for Sandy's sake that the day had turned so glorious after the dark storms of Saturday, for this was his first New Year in Scotland for fifteen years and his first ever winter visit to this part of the Trossachs with Tommy and Rhona. We had a picnic at 1000ft, with Scotland's icy beauty spread out before us, but before we'd finished our snack another blizzard swept over and soaked into the bread we ate. We looked like something from Scott's Antarctic Expedition, sitting munching our sandwiches in whirling snow.

Pinner seemed a lifetime away, and I had almost forgotten that I had really come north to do a TV show. I laughed and said to Rhona there couldn't be many in the company who had climbed a wee mountain the day before, and dined in a blizzard!

Tommy and Rhona took us through to Edinburgh next day for my 2.30 P.M. rehearsal call, and they enjoyed a peep at the ballroom scene before we went to lunch. Everybody loves a peep behind the scenes, and they were very impressed with the glimpse they had of the Alexander Brothers who had had to have an early rehearsal to allow them to get back to Glasgow for their pantomime. There's a general belief that actors are pale and not too healthy because of all the time spent wearing make-up and working under hot lights, but the two brawny Alexanders quickly dispelled that idea.

I had a great piece of luck with my room-mate. There were only we two females performing solo work in the entire programme and naturally we shared a room, and when I was wondering when on earth anybody would find time to do my hair, she said cheerfully, 'Don't worry about it, Molly. I was a hairdresser. I'll do your hair for you.' So not only was the charming Elaine Simmons a delightful singer with a bonnie face, but a first-class hair stylist into the bargain! Sandy, who had returned to tell me he'd booked in at the hotel, was fascinated to watch her transform my wind-blown locks into a swirling graceful shape which perfectly complemented the Victorian dress I was wearing.

Elaine told me she had shattered her first TV make-up girl by asking for a pair of scissors, and there and then expertly snipping and shaping her own hair for the performance! I'm pretty independent myself at times when it comes to arranging my hair, but Elaine was truly in the 'stylist' class.

There was plenty of time to chat with Fyfe Robertson, whom I was meeting for the first time, and we got on like a house on fire. Tall, quiet and courteous and a fine talker of course, I found he had the true journalist's interest in other people and in everything around him.

I told him I hoped I would be able to stay awake until it was time for my contribution, for I'm normally in bed around eleven o'clock, but Roy Kinnear, calmly smiling, told me not to worry, they'd waken me in good time for my part in *The Four Craws*.

A few supposedly lesser-known artists had been booked to entertain the audience until twelve o'clock, but they wouldn't be seen on television. At midnight they would vanish like Cinderella, and we others with 'weel-kent' faces would take the floor. I noticed a man in a black kaftan, with multi-coloured long hair and beard, carrying a guitar, waiting to go on for the earlier part of the show and wondered where on earth they'd found such a strange-looking character for a Scottish Hogmanay party. I discovered when Russell Hunter came in from his pantomime in Glasgow, that the kaftan-clad singer was somebody called Billy Connolly! 'He's one of the funniest blokes I've ever heard, Molly,' whispered Russell, whom I was also meeting for the first time. 'Just you wait till he comes on. He'll tear them apart.' Russell was right. He did, and I'll bet that was the last time Billy Connolly was part of the 'warm-up' of any audience anywhere in the country. It was to be 'top of the bill' from then onwards.

Russell had slipped into his seat beside me as we waited for midnight, and gripped my hand. 'Tell me what we have to do, Molly,' he whispered. I pushed my script in front of him and swiftly explained the routine. I was flabbergasted that Russell could take this in his stride after two performances in the theatre. I'd never been out of the building since half-past-two, and even so was quite jittery to be taking part in such an important piece of nationally net-worked live television.

At a few minutes to twelve Andy Stewart moved to

the centre of the floor, and was picked up by a spotlight. Then came the countdown. Five, four, three, two, one, and we were on vision. The moment the bells chimed midnight, Russell rushed over to his father, who was in the audience, and wished him 'A Happy New Year'. The Scots have a great sense of priorities and sentiment when midnight chimes. Russell introduced us and I had Pa Hunter's company till it was time for me to leap on to the high stool to take part with my solo in *The Four Craws*. Almost before I knew it, it was all over and we were singing *Auld Lang Syne*.

Sandy and I strolled through the cool night air to our hotel, where the proprietrix welcomed us with open arms. She was introducing a party of Americans to their first Hogmanay party, and when we walked in, apparently straight from the television screen, they were enchanted. 'But we just saw you a minute ago,' they kept exclaiming. 'How'd you get here so fast?' 'Gee it was a great show.' 'Isn't Hogmanay in Scotland quite something?' and I was nudged in the ribs, and had to sign autographs for all of them. The proprietrix had found another two glasses, and after a few toasts to 'Edinburgh', 'Glasgow', 'New York' and 'Washington', we managed to escape, and I went down, down, down into a beautiful sleep. Almost the best part of a performance is when it's successfully over!

I was hardly back from Scotland, when the telephone rang and it was Thames Television on the line. It was highly confidential and they didn't want to speak on the telephone, but could I come in to discuss something with them, or if necessary they could come out to see me. What on earth could it be, I wondered? I had to be in town for something else, so I popped along to solve the mystery. I was quite impressed with their integrity and caution, for what I was being asked to do was to take part in Deryck Guyler's *This Is Your Life*! There must be absolute secrecy, I was told. I must inform nobody, apart from Sandy who would be given a ticket for the show and who must also be sworn to silence, and I would be collected by car and taken to the studios, to arrive around 2 P.M.

By the most curious coincidence I was actually to be working with Deryck on a broadcast about five days before this surprise packet of *This Is Your Life* would take place, and I had to be so careful not to let the cat out of the bag. When we parted, we exchanged all the usual pleasantries, 'Lovely to be working with you again', 'Give my love to Paddy and the boys', 'Give my love to Sandy'. All this acted out to the full by me, knowing full well I'd be prancing on stage to greet him five days later!

You wouldn't believe what a cloak-and-dagger affair this turned out to be. The car collected me, as promised, and when I reached the studios I was ushered straight into the 'green room' where dress, coat and bag were deposited, and from where I wasn't allowed to move without permission, and without being accompanied by a programme assistant.

We guests spent hours gossiping together in our little 'prison'. We all knew one another, or had worked with one another at various times, and the only actor I hadn't met and was delighted to see in person was John Alderton, who had had such a success in *My Wife Next Door*, and *Please Sir*. He was much taller than I had expected, and was a serious, sensible, interesting chap. The others were Eric Sykes, the Fenn Street Gang and of course Deryck's family whom I hadn't seen for years. I hadn't seen some of my colleagues in the flesh for years, and it was a great chance to catch up on what we were all doing or hoped to do.

I kept looking for food, for I was absolutely starving, and with my innards demanding sustenance every few hours I couldn't believe that a sandwich at least wouldn't be forthcoming at tea-time. How wrong I was. We had one biscuit apiece, and not another thing, and the meal wasn't scheduled till 9.45 P.M. That would be nine hours after my poached egg lunch!

I sent for crisps, which never came. I sent for more biscuits which didn't arrive. We were truly under lock and key, with no remission to nip up to the canteen, in case we would be spotted and the secret out. I would just have to starve. Security was all important.

At last we were rounded up and smuggled through to the room beside the stage. Then it was on with the show. 'DERYCK GUYLER, THIS IS YOUR LIFE.'

My heart was hammering. I'm always terrified the 'victim' will be so shocked he'll have a heart attack before our very eyes.

Deryck, although shaken at the start and white as a sheet, sailed through it all with great charm and affection.

It was the warmest, happiest show, with the perfect ending when a baby grandson, flown all the way from Bahrein, cuddled close to Deryck's tear-damp cheek.

As soon as the large red book had been handed over, and the camera had faded us out, there was a stampede for the room where the party was being held. We 'witnesses' fell upon the buffet as though we hadn't seen meat for a week, and not a word was uttered until we had assuaged our hunger. 'If I'm ever asked to one of those things again,' I said to Eric Sykes, 'I'll know better, and I'll bring a Thermos flask and a box of sandwiches with me.' Little did I know

361

that by the time this happened, all memories of Deryck's *This Is Your Life* would have vanished into thin air, forgotten like a dream.

It seemed to be the season for honouring personalities, for I was also invited up to Scotland to appear on the *Mainly Magnus* programme, which turned out to be a sort of *This Is Your Life* to do honour to that delightful producer of BBC children's programmes, Auntie Kathleen, or to give her her full name Kathleen Garscadden. This was great fun from start to finish.

Gordon Jackson and I fell upon each other with cries of gladness, not having worked together since *The Prime of Miss Jean Brodie*. We instantly broke into 'Lord behold us with Thy blessing', sending Howard Lockhart into appreciative chortles, and when Rikki Fulton joined us later at dinner, it was a typical animated Glasgow table, although it was in the beautiful surroundings of Stirling University, with non-stop talking and laughter all the way.

I was a bit taken aback to find that practically everyone had prepared a party piece except Gordon, Moira Anderson and me. What on earth would I do to grace this special occasion? In the end Willie Joss and I did a lively little duet of our old signature tune for *Down at the Mains*, words to suit our characters, tune that of the *Dashing White Sergeant*, and then I was interviewed by Magnus centre stage before a packed and welcoming audience. Moultrie Kelsall, my old friend and BBC producer was in great form and gave a vigorous sparkling rendering of *The Wee Cooper o' Fife*, and Ruby, his wife, who is a dazzling pianist, put the final gloss on the song with her rippling accompaniment. Ruby was always a great strength at the piano. She it was who first realized I was being asked to sing in a key which was wrong for me, away

362

back when I sang in revue, and actually transformed me into an acceptable singer of some confidence, instead of a nervous performer with a tentative soprano.

I hadn't realized that Father Sidney McEwan came from Springburn, like me, and he was brimful of ideas that we must one day do a programme together on that colourful part of Glasgow. As for Magnus Magnusson, his easy manner and smooth interviewing made it all so simple that I kept saying to myself, 'I've no right to be enjoying myself so much on a TV programme.' It didn't seem natural, somehow, not to be beset with nerves!

It was very funny to see us all on the stairs in a sort of 'celebrity' queue, hiding out of sight until Auntie Kathleen had been manoeuvred into the studio, there to be confronted by us one at a time, or in duet, as we paid our tributes to her. Her blue eyes lit with pleasure and surprise, but she kept her end up with the right pithy comments at appropriate moments, and the whole show went with a happy swing. It was so exciting that we couldn't bear to break the party up when the programme had finished, and kept milling around and laughing, sipping a celebration drink, and talking nineteen to the dozen. We had a group photograph taken as a record of a show which was for us, and I hoped for many a viewer, a memorably happy experience.

Next day in Glasgow, judging by the number of times I was shaken by the hand in the street, I think the whole of Glasgow must have looked in at the show. That's the marvellous thing about doing a performance in Scotland, everybody gives you a reaction. Not for them the laconic, 'Saw you on telly last night,' and then silence. It has to be either, 'Oh Ah saw you last night on the telly, it was great so it wis.' Or, 'Ah saw you last night on the television. You hadnae much tae dae, hid you?' In either case, you're left in no doubt of the impression you made. That's my Glasgow, and I wouldn't have it any other way.

Auntie Kathleen's tribute was actually the opening of a week of celebrations marking the BBC 50th anniversary exhibition. I think the queues really stunned the BBC. They'd never imagined there would be such widespread public interest when they planned it. I was practically mobbed when I went on to the celebrity stand one night with that fine singer Peter Morrison, to sign autographs. Youngsters pressed on every side until I could hardly breathe. They cracked bubble gum in my ear, pushed the table against my knees, thrust books under my nose, and breathed down my neck.

To give my lungs a chance to breathe, and to create a bit of air space round my back, I kept calling out, 'Not round the back, please. I won't sign anything if you push me from the back.'

The youngsters instantly appreciated my objections and started shouting, 'No' roon' the back. She disnae like you roon' the back.' Peter and I were helpless with laughter at this chorus.

Then there was a recording for *Autograms*, which seemed to give a lot of pleasure to people who enjoyed my musical memories, and much autograph signing at another public session, followed by a very grand VIP lunch at the Central Hotel. This was a bit like Parliament with its tiny gathering of women, only seven of us all-told, to assert ourselves among hundreds of important men.

The distinguished guest was Sir Robert Grieve, whom I'd last seen in leisure kit in Tommy's house at

Loch Lomond, and he proposed the toast, 'The BBC in Scotland', as well as enlivening the occasion with a splendid speech. He's a great conservationist is Bob Grieve, and always well worth listening to.

I met the legendary Wendy Wood, famous Scottish patriot, and had my photograph taken with her, Auntie Kathleen and Baillie Jean Roberts. A grand souvenir for the archives! I'd have liked to have had the opportunity for a proper conversation with Wendy Wood, but we were goldfish in a bowl, at the mercy of photographers and journalists and it just wasn't possible.

Remembrance of Wendy Wood's fierce patriotism reminds me of the time when a friend who had charge of some public buildings refused to be brow-beaten by unofficial strikers and pickets. One of the jobs usually undertaken by a member of the striking Union was to hoist the Union Jack daily, and to take it down each night. On the first day of the picketing, our friend was told by a picket that the flag would not be flown.

'Oh no?' he said. 'Then I'll fly it myself.'

The picket was aghast at such defiance.

'You can't do that,' he gasped.

'I certainly can,' came the reply. 'If you won't allow me to engage outside contractors, then I and my assistant will climb up to the roof and fly the flag ourselves.'

'You wouldn't have the nerve,' the picket scoffed.

'Look,' said our friend, with what I think was admirable and patient logic, 'I fought for four years to keep that flag flying, and no striker, official or otherwise, is going to keep it furled.'

Next morning, long before the pickets arrived, he and his assistant climbed up to the right spot, and the

Union Jack was fluttering from its pole in patriotic defiance by the time the pickets came on the scene.

And it flew unchallenged until the strike was over.

And it was floodlit when the building was floodlit.

And the little episode, told to me by the friend who did it, made my week.

Oh for such courage to spread and spread, so that people with 'muscle', as tyrannous Unions are called, would come to realize that bullying days were over.

Once upon a time people went on strike to put boots on their children's feet and food in their stomachs, and they themselves suffered more than anyone.

Today hardship is inflicted on people in high-rise flats, in hospitals, in old people's homes, on the bereaved, on those who have to walk great distances for water, and on the urgent traveller, by workers in pursuit of the sacred 'differential', or to keep up a standard of living which must include colour television, cigarettes and cars. Very very few strike from need. And if the innocent suffer, so much the better. I remember going up to Edinburgh for a Burns' dinner, and I climbed the Scott monument on a day when not a train moved because of a strike. As I looked down on the silent station, and at the empty lines, I threw my arms wide and cried to the frosty heavens, 'Man's inhumanity to man makes countless thousands mourn', and I felt that Rabbie would have turned in his grave.

On my way back for lunch, I met a posse of railwaymen who had obviously dined well. 'Oh it's wee Molly,' one of them cried out. 'Gaunny gie's yer autograph hen.' They had just been to a Union meeting, they told me!

'Is it you lot that are keeping me from getting home?' I said.

'Aye, it's us hen,' a Glasgow voice replied.

366

'Do you realize I had to come up here a day earlier because you wouldn't drive your trains today?' I demanded.

'Ach well, that gie's ye a day mair in Scotland,' the wee dark one said.

'And you've got the cheek to ask me for an autograph,' I said. 'I've just had a word with Rabbie when I was up the Scott Monument, and it was folk like you he had in mind when he wrote "Man's Inhumanity to Man" – and that includes woman!

'Och you're a wee warmer,' the oldest chap said, and he turned to his pals. 'Isn't she a wee stotter?'

'You'll get an autograph if you promise to get back to your work tomorrow,' I said.

They roared with laughter as if I'd cracked the biggest joke. 'Oh we canny promise ye that, hen,' they said. 'We hiv tae wait tae see whit the Union says.'

'Vote to get back to your work then,' I said as I signed their autographs, 'and tell them I said it.'

'Ach you're juist magic,' the wee Glasgow voice said, putting his autograph carefully in an inside pocket.

That is the special thing about being able to speak to your own folk in a common language. You can get it off your chest without the risk of getting thumped, for you speak in the voice of their own wives and mothers. And there is no lasting bitterness.

CHAPTER SIXTEEN

That Hogmanay programme with Russell Hunter was a good omen for me, for I was booked for a great little drama series for Grampian Television, to be done from Aberdeen. Three plays were to be written specially for five of us, because between us we had a fairly wide range of characters and could 'age' up or down as the story demanded. There were Colette O'Neill, Derek Anders, Callum Mill, Russell and me. Watt Nicol was to write the plays and John Sichel would direct them.

The first immediate need was to find digs, for I like looking after myself if I'm to be away for any length of time, and this series would take at least five weeks. Remembering the ghastly Glasgow digs with the noisy neighbours, I determined to take great care this time, and by a splendid piece of timing I was able to obtain the help of a delightful lady whom I had seen as a 'fan' on previous visits to Aberdeen for book-signing sessions. It appeared she had bought a copy of my latest book, and she wrote asking me to get in touch if ever I was in granite city on other ploys, so that she could have it autographed to match the others she already had.

An unexpected broadcast from Aberdeen meant a sudden trip north, and when I invited her for coffee so that I could sign her book and have a proper chat, we took to one another immediately, and the moment I asked her to put out a few feelers for digs where I could have the use of a kitchen, she was off on the search without delay. She in turn roped in the aunt of another friend, and between them they solved my problem, and found a lovely little room with use of kitchen, views of the sea on the distant horizon, and only ten minutes walking distance from the studios. Bliss!

If I was slow to spot any oil magnates with gold teeth, the Aberdonians were quick as lightning to spot me in their midst. Smiles and nods met me in every shop, my hand was shaken till my fingers stung, and there were lots of 'wee speaks' as they call a chat, with people who had heard the recent broadcast or had read my books. It's the most friendly feeling to receive such a warm welcome in another city, and never to be regarded as a stranger.

I felt very lucky.

And what a law-abiding city it seemed. There was a comfortable feeling of safety and security, and even the public telephones were in working order. It didn't surprise me that the Glasgow girl to whom I spoke, serving in a supermarket, had been so impressed with this quality in Aberdeen that what was supposed to be a two weeks' summer holiday had turned into a stay of over a year. To me her decision just to stay on and find a job when her holiday was over, was equally impressive, and a perfect example of the roving quality and freedom of the younger generation compared with our own serious sense of responsibility at the same age. My mother would have sent out a search party if I had simply disappeared and failed to come back from a holiday. But of course the question would never have arisen, for I would never have contemplated doing such a thing. To have met a young girl who did obey such an impulse without turning a hair was a revelation.

Within days I had returned to the routine of my early days in London, when I lived in my room in Clapham, with my tray, my kettle, and my small radio for company. I went to bed early, slept like an infant, and had nightly talks with Sandy to make sure all was well with him. He liked me to suggest menus for his dinner, and he became so skilled in the kitchen that one night I found I had rung at the exact moment when he was making fudge and wondered at what point he should add the walnuts! 'You *must* be well organized,' I said, 'when you have time to make fudge. That's great.'

We rehearsed the plays in a church hall, whose kitchen was staffed by the members, and home-made biscuits, shortbread and other goodies were on offer non-stop. These coffee lounges raised funds for the churches all over Aberdeen, and were enthusiastically patronized by the locals. My good friend 'fan', Helen, husband John and her two sisters had a weekly rendez-vous in the one near the studios each Friday when they came into Aberdeen to do their shopping, and I sometimes joined them *en route* to my rehearsal if I had time. We were fast friends by this time, and I had a glorious week-end with them when they introduced me to the grandeur of 'The Bullers of Buchan', great headlands of vivid red rocks rising from heaving seas, where we found an artist battling to get her canvas erected. A trio of rocks, jagged and sculptured against the waves were being captured on canvas, and looked very promising.

Not only did they take me to Collieston, where Sandy's mother and his Aunt Jeanie used to drool over the speldings, but later Helen took me to the cemetery to see Tom Patey's grave. He was the great climbing friend of my brother Tommy. His death from a fall from a sea-stack was a shattering blow to all his many mountaineering companions, and hit Tommy very hard. The inscription on the stone was very apt.

I to the hills will lift mine eyes, from where
doth come my help.

Helen said she hadn't noticed that the old-fashioned bible words 'from whence doth come mine aid' had been replaced by more modern working until I pointed this out. I have little liking for the modern English bible, for I love the language of the King James edition, which we know as the authorized version. I was very touched to see the words below the inscription, 'A loving husband, father and son.'

He was killed tragically early, but his name will long be remembered and spoken by people who never knew of his skill on rock and sea-stack, because one of the roads on the local estate is called 'Patey Road'.

I found our rehearsals stimulating and very good fun, and both make-up and wardrobe were towers of strength. Betty, the wardrobe mistress, put her entire personal wardrobe at our disposal if we couldn't find the right things in wardrobe or in the shops. She could run up a blouse or a bonnet faster than a bus could take us into town, and yet could still find time for little personal jobs. She it was who transformed the cut-off ends of a too-long pair of trousers of mine, into a natty little skipped cap.

As for Liz, our make-up expert, she sent me into gales of laughter by wearing one of Russell Hunter's wigs for a whole day just to get it pulled into shape. Russell was a delight. He never stopped joking. He sang and he clowned, but the moment we started working his concentration was absolute.

Colette and Derek enjoyed the social scene, I noticed, and enjoyed dining out, but Callum Mill and I were the 'straight home' characters. I used to stride out along the beach, drinking in great breaths of frosty clear air, learning my words, and revelling in the quietness of miles of sea-shore out of season.

It was a really happy little company, and there was great enthusiasm from the powers-that-be when we had put the first two plays 'in the can' and they could judge the results. I had to employ my 'La Strada' technique to produce floods of tears for the cameras, and I reduced the studio and the director to startled silence by my stormy emotions! I was thankful I hadn't to do it too often!

With the last play safely recorded, we had three parties to celebrate the end of a successful experiment in drama for that station. There was one given by us for the Grampian top brass, wives, and husbands, then one for us by Jim Buchan, the head of Grampian who was due to retire the next day. And a third one by us for all the back-room boys and girls, the camera crews, the sound-boom expert, the lighting man, art man, props, carpenters, make-up lady, secretaries, wardrobe, all of whom combined the quiet humour and enthusiasm which made the work such a pleasure, and made me feel specially proud of them.

We all rushed about exchanging presents, washing our hair, packing for the last time. Mr Mair, the new head of Grampian, generously presented all of us with Grampian travel rugs and a drop of 'the craitur' as souvenirs of our five weeks' work with them, and there were also ties for the lads. John, our director, who normally worked in London, was amazed by all this generosity, and in Aberdeen at that! 'But they make up all those jokes about meanness themselves John,' we assured him.

I was touched to the heart when the boys in the production team presented me with a beautiful bouquet at the end of the final day's shooting. And amazed to receive a most unexpected compliment from a tall quiet lad who used to help with props at rehearsals. On that last day, he looked at me thoughtfully and said, 'When I think of you now, I'll remember a neat little lady, who always wore the most beautiful jerseys and woollens.' I was really startled, 'Do I wear specially beautiful woollens?' I said, 'I don't think so.' 'Oh yes you do,' said Colette emphatically. Now of all the descriptions of me I might have guessed at, that was surely the most surprising. But as one who loves good quality knitwear, I was secretly charmed!

Helen and John came to see me off at the station, and to help with my luggage, for I had added so many things that I had to buy another suitcase. They were thrilled to meet Russell, who arrived at the station just as I was waving good-bye to them. It had been a great five weeks, with time to visit Sandy's Auntie Nellie and Cousin Maisie, whom I hadn't seen for years, and also to drop in on fans who had written to me over the years as a result of my newspaper articles in the *People's Journal*. One of them, Jimmy Wright, a talented writer of poems and ballads, could hardly believe his eyes when he opened the door in answer to the bell and found me standing on his doorstep. Although relatives were expected for a meal, I was drawn into the family circle, a place found for me at the table, and as my mother would have said, 'we talked the minutes into hours.' I had a poem from Jimmy every Christmas, as well as a holiday postcard in verse, and on a later visit to Aberdeen I took Sandy along to meet him and his wife Jean, and there was never an awkward pause as we all had a good 'speak', and then a visit to beautiful Duthie Park.

Sandy's mother was born in Aberdeen, and it is like a home from home for us.

The sequel to this Grampian season was hilarious. We discovered that one of the plays was to be nationally networked, around lunchtime, when Sandy would be in the city, where he worked. He thought he had nothing else to do but to pop down to Thames Television in Euston Road and ask if he could watch on

373

one of their sets. Unknown to him, it was a day for a *This Is Your Life* recording, and the viewing room was out of bounds for everyone, and especially for a suspicious-sounding stranger!

Time was ticking past, and the nearest store was Bourne and Hollingsworth in Oxford Street, so he flew like the wind, not pausing to wait for bus or tube, tore up the stairs, arrived panting in the television department which was completely empty of people but *packed* with television sets. He rushed and switched every one of them on to the commercial network, and stood surrounded by screens showing our play, so that whichever way he turned, we were acting for him. I was fascinated by this enterprise, for normally Sandy is very quiet and wouldn't dream of taking liberties with other people's property. He was equally fascinated to find himself in a completely empty department, with not a soul to say him nay. In fact, he said, if the sets had been easy to carry, he could have walked out of the shop with any one he fancied under his arm! He was appalled by such laxity in such a store. But he enjoyed his free show, and thought it worthy of a prime time slot. Praise indeed! Almost worth our long separation to achieve such a result!

So often after working so closely with one's colleagues, one doesn't see them again for months and sometimes years. But John Sichel, our director, quickly found parts for four of us in his *Thriller* series which was filmed at Elstree, and we all greeted one another like old friends. John Carson, with whom I had worked in *Ghost Squad* years before, was also in it and it was like one big happy family. Only Russell was missing, and that was because he was already busy on another production.

374

I was highly amused by the leading lady, an American beauty, who had come all the way from Los Angeles to do this television film. She was riveted when I produced my knitting from my bag. '*Knitting!*' she yelled as if I'd performed a miracle. 'Oh, will you teach me to knit? I never learned, and I'd love to know how to do it.'

I laughed at this unexpected reaction, for usually everyone laughs at my busy needles. But this girl thought it the greatest of skills, and I found her sitting beside me at every spare moment watching how it was done.

I only knit at rehearsals, for I'm far too busy to sit at such a task at home, and John our director couldn't believe it was the same piece I had been working on when we were in Aberdeen.

I informed him that this was my 'John Sichel jumper', and when I wore it it would forever be associated with the productions I had done for him. I always do this with my handicrafts. I have my *Prime of Miss Jean Brodie* turquoise sweater, now fit only for gardening chores. There is my *Scrooge* striped jersey. My *Oh Father* sleeveless waistcoat, my *Enchanted Castle* striped coat, and my *Life with the Lyons* firescreens.

It gives every garment a personal memory and brings back all the details and the fun of the shows each time I look at them or wear them. Sandy always says, 'Every garment tells a story!'

Incidentally, on the day of the recording, the breakfast scene required six takes, and I ate an egg at each one! Six eggs devoured in an hour! Plus toast and butter and tea. No wonder I wasn't fit for any lunch, or wanted to look an egg in the face for weeks afterwards.

Before I left the studios, I had a great piece of luck, for they were having a sale of garments used in previous series, to make a bit of space for their newer clothes. I only had about fifteen minutes to spare, and raked through a wild assortment of things from evening coats to pure silk dresses, which I didn't even have time to try on. I just held everything against me, judging my own size by the eye alone, and in the end acquired an enviable selection for about £25, including a heavy silk model evening coat which reached my feet and had been worn by Millicent Martin. How lucky I was to be in the right place at the right time. The coat looked like a million dollars when I wore it to the Dorchester to attend a literary cocktail party thrown by a publishing group, and I was thrilled to the marrow to meet James Herriot, the vet, who has written all those enjoyable books which culminated in the TV series, *All Creatures Great and Small*. We had a great old chat, for he too is from Glasgow although he is now established in Yorkshire, and I ended the evening by joining his literary agency! My Hutchinson's lady said I was mad, for I was already an established author, and it was a waste of commission, but it seemed a good idea at the time. I did it mainly, I think, because I thought they might perform the magic of selling *Shoes* and *Best Foot Forward* as a TV series or a film, but they were no more successful in this than I had been myself. They did, however, introduce me to an American magazine editor who commissioned a humorous article, for which I earned a fistful of dollars. All else I could have done for myself!

I had written to tell Rhona about my television clothes bargains, and as she had a few days' holiday left, and Tommy was away on a climbing expedition, she decided to accept my invitation to come down and see my glamour goodies for herself. Rhona is headmistress of a country school, and I thought it might be a good educational titbit to pass on to the children if I could arrange for us to visit the Mother of Parliaments, while she was down, and attend one of the debates.

I was able to suggest this with some confidence because Tom at that time had the distinction, shared with Chaucer among other past Clerks of Works, of caring for the fabric and safety of Westminster. If tickets were available for anyone, they would certainly be available for my brother-in-law.

As a prelude to this treat, it was arranged we would climb the spiral staircase to the belfry which held the mighty Big Ben. The views from the top were magnificent, with an amazing amount of grassy lawns dotted among the fine houses, and I became so absorbed in spotting the famous landmarks that I completely forgot the time, and nearly jumped out of my skin when the first note signalling twelve o'clock boomed forth. I got such a fright, indeed, that I threatened our amusing and highly-informative guide that I'd give him a similar shock by leaping to the microphone which was transmitting the twelve chimes live to the entire country, and shouting out 'Home Rule for Scotland'. He was slightly scandalized, but relieved that I was only joking.

That, I thought, was the worst possible outrage I could have committed during the course of the visit. But I was wrong!

We showed our special tickets which allowed us to get into the House of Commons gallery, and were docility itself when we submitted our handbags for official inspection. The French family behind us, on the other hand, were highly incensed at being suspected of being terrorists, and were most reluctant to hand over cameras, huge hand-grips and books.

I was wishing I had something to write on, when Tom slipped into a seat beside us and whispered to ask if we had a copy of the *Guide for Visitors to the Galleries*. On learning that we hadn't, he left, collected one for each of us, and brought them back with him. The public galleries were very full, which was more than could be said for the rest of the House. I could count only six members spread thinly over what looked like acres of empty benches.

I seized my *Visitors Guide* with delight, although I had no intention of reading it just then. I wanted it because of the blank half-page which would be perfect for jotting down my impressions of the climb up Big Ben while they were fresh in my mind.

I was fascinated by the relays of shorthand writers who took over from one another, sometimes singly, sometimes in pairs, with all the skill of runners handing over a baton, before disappearing to transcribe their notes. I felt almost part of their team as I jotted down my own outlines.

As I wrote, I could follow the speed of their pens as they slid over the sheets of paper.

Suddenly I became aware of a concentrated gaze in our direction. On a side bench, almost at eye level, sat a figure resplendent in black tail-coat, wearing the gold badge of the office of messenger. He was shaking an admonitory finger in our direction. We all three turned and looked behind us to see who was misbehaving himself and offending gold-badge. We knew from the printed notice that it was an offence to shout, cause an interruption, or generally interfere with the smooth running of the business of the House.

I couldn't see anyone doing anything other than

listening, more or less attentively, so I went back to my shorthand jottings.

Suddenly, to my amazement, Rhona dug me sharply in the ribs. 'You've to stop writing,' she hissed. It was like being back at school.

'Stop writing?' I whispered. 'Why? How do you know? Who says so?' I couldn't for the life of me think of anything less offensive than the quiet gliding of my biro over the half-sheet on my knee.

'*He* says so,' whispered Rhona, indicating gold-badge. I stared across at the man disbelievingly. The eyes which met mine were sorrowful and accusing. I curved a finger towards my chest and mouthed, 'Is it me?' I couldn't really believe it could be. Even Tom hadn't realized I was the culprit.

Gold-badge's eyes now filled with laughter as he nodded, and mouthed 'Yes'. He slowly wagged a finger in reproof, as he imitated the movement of my writing. It was true. It *was* my writing which was the offence.

My face slowly crimsoned, while at the same time I had the strongest desire to burst out laughing. It was exactly like the old Bateman cartoon where an entire orchestra and audience gaze at a man accusingly, causing him to shrink to half his size, with the caption underneath making his sin clear to all. 'The Man Who Coughed at the Proms.'

I was the wife who had written at the Debate!

Who, in her wildest dreams, could have believed that the pen could be as reprehensible to the Mother of Parliaments as a shouted interruption?

I had to finish my notes in the train going home. London Transport, for all its faults, had no bye-laws which forbade the capture of the fleeting experience with pen and paper.

Nevertheless, I was impressed by the watchfulness

shown by gold-badge. I could, after all, have been penning an insulting dart to hurl at a member. But where was he, I wonder, on the day when that protesting female threw a bag of manure down on the luckless heads of the members below? Truly the price of freedom is eternal vigilance. I wonder who wagged a finger sorrowfully under *his* nose at the post mortem which surely followed the manure explosion!

The whole episode made a great story for Rhona to tell when she went back to her school by Loch Lomond.

Sandy and I had a glorious holiday in the East Neuk that summer, and when we came back one morning with the milk and rolls, it was to find a telegram lying on the doorstep of our holiday flat. A telegram! Who on earth wanted me with such urgency? It was from my agent and I was to ring her without delay, in connection with a film part. My stomach did somersaults as I anticipated Sandy's wrath if we had to cut our holiday short. But he knew how much I love films and he also knew that there weren't so many British films being made that one could afford to sneeze at an offer to appear in one.

I hadn't taken my diary with me, for I had firmly determined that *nothing* would bring me back to London before our holiday came to its planned end. So thoroughly had I put London and show-biz behind me that it took me a good ten minutes to remember my agent's telephone number! She, quite naturally, hadn't thought it necessary to include it in her telegram. The next problem was to find an empty telephone box. There was but one in that wee village and a couple of long-haired youths seemed to have taken up permanent residence. I circled it. I gazed in at them, doing my best to hypnotize them with my basilisk stare to exit, and let me in. It was no good. They were obviously there for the day.

We were going to St Andrews that day anyway, so we jumped in the car and headed for the golfing mecca, certain that there would be a choice of telephone kiosks there. We found one by the first tee, and as I waited to get through to London, I was treated to the most magnificent aerobatic display overhead by the Red Arrows. They dived, zoomed, twisted, tumbled and displayed their flying skills so breathtakingly, that when my agent came on, I opened the door of the kiosk so that she could hear the thrilling sounds in her office in London. It seemed far more exciting than any film at that moment!

The good news was that I was wanted for a lovely little part as a nannie in a prestigious Walt Disney production starring Peter Ustinov and Helen Hayes, the great American actress, *One of Our Dinosaurs is Missing*. The bad news was that I would be wanted for the following Monday morning at 7.00 A.M. and we hadn't planned to return on the motorail until Sunday night, and weren't due to arrive in London until around 9.00 A.M. Monday morning. It was the middle of the holiday season – would we be able to change our booking at this late date? My agent urged me to accept, which I did, and Sandy and I decided, if the worst came to the worst, that I would travel back alone by ordinary train, to reach home by Sunday, and he would use the Sunday motorail as booked.

It would only be a difference of one day to our holiday, but it would be an expensive nuisance if we couldn't change our motorail booking. Sandy was very good about it. He is a great admirer of Peter Ustinov, and he thought it would be a great pity to miss a chance of working with him.

381

I was in that kiosk longer even than those long-haired lads back at our village 'phone-box. First I had to get through to motorail. I told them the whole story, which had them jumping with excitement. They promised faithfully to try to re-jig some bookings, and I was to ring them back later. They felt fairly sure they would be able to do something. The man at the other end had read my books, and announced himself as my number one 'fan', so that was a good start!

Then I had to ring the studios, and dictate my measurements so that they could look out a nannie outfit which would require minimum alterations when I arrived to do the filming on Monday morning. They were enchanted to be speaking to somebody ringing from St Andrews, and as the Red Arrows were still diving overhead, I held the door open to let them too hear the engines roaring. They were thrilled. It was vastly different from their usual telephone conversations, and that was putting it mildly. Fortunately I know my measurements down to the last millimetre, so there was no worry on that score.

Another call to the motorail 'fan' brought the good news that they had been able to change our booking to Saturday. We did a little dance of joy, Sandy and I, parked the car, and turned our minds to making the most of the rest of our holiday.

The moment I arrived at the studios on Monday morning, I was whisked along to wardrobe and fitted into the nannie outfit they'd found. It only needed tiny alterations for a perfect fit and while they got busy with needles and thread, I had every scrap of make-up removed from my face, and my lovely holiday tan was completely blotted out with a pale pancake powder. My hair was arranged in a wee old-fashioned bun at the nape of my neck to fit into the back of my nannie's poke bonnet, and I was now free to go back to my 'film-star' dressing room with its comfortable divan, where I lay down and drifted off to sleep.

A knock on the door announced wardrobe with my altered costume. My mother would have loved it, with her passion for good gaberdine. It was a navy gaberdine two-piece suit of excellent quality, with three-quarter length jacket over a mid-calf skirt and under it a plain white blouse. When I'd added a pair of black gloves, black handbag, and poke bonnet, I was a living doll of a 1920s nannie, and looked about a hundred!

And yet, when I met the great American actress Helen Hayes on the set, she paid me the unforgettable compliment of saying, 'You look exactly as I have always wanted to look. Hair, figure, everything, perfect!' Such words from anyone would be hard enough to accept without a feeling that they were after the loan of a fiver, but from someone of such theatrical stature, I was struck completely dumb. I think it must have been the gaberdine costume, which was so well cut that it emphasized my slimness, which intrigued Helen Hayes, for by then she was a little round plump figure and had lost the slenderness of her earlier days. I told her how much I had loved her performance in *The Glass Menagerie*, and had seen it at a matinée before going on to do my own performance in The Apollo in *The Happiest Days of Your Life*. Who could have believed the day would dawn when I would be sitting chatting with the first lady of the American theatre like this? When I see her on the screen nowadays, I feel I am meeting an old friend.

It was a hilarious day altogether. Joan Sims played the supporting lead to Helen Hayes, and I was nannie number three. Derek Nimmo and Deryck Guyler were instantly recognizable as their own selves, but I hardly recognized Peter Ustinov at first in his guise as a Chinese gentleman complete with jet-black wig. Bernard Bresslaw, that amiable giant, played a Chinese spy.

The set was a handsome replica of the National History Museum and we worked there all day. The action called for Joan Sims and I to launch a violent attack on Bernard Bresslaw, and even the director, Robert Stephenson (who directed *Mary Poppins* among other successes) laughed aloud when we both flew at Bernard and began walloping him with our bags and umbrellas. We must have looked like a couple of corgis attacking a mastiff!

There was a glorious 'free for all' when the cameras started turning. I got a kick on the shins from Bernard as he struggled to his feet, then an uppercut from the Chinese spies who rushed to his aid, and a thump on the back from the 'museum attendants' who raced to throw everybody out. I was covered in bruises for days afterwards. But it was marvellous. The cameras kept turning, and we yelled and attacked and reacted perfectly naturally, which resulted in a wildly comic piece of filming.

When we sat on the side waiting for the cameras to be set up again for the next shot, Peter Ustinov joined us and had us hiccuping with laughter with his brilliant impersonation of a Scottish councillor whom he'd once met who couldn't get over having to pay three-and-sixpence for his bus fare! There was nothing malicious about it, just a perfect appreciation of someone else's dialect and sense of values. What a sensitive ear Ustinov has. There wasn't a syllable which could be faulted, and that's praise indeed from someone like me who's heard more awful attempts at Scots than I care to remember.

I found Joan Sims a bundle of fun, and when we weren't actually working we sat with Derek Nimmo, Deryck Guyler and Helen Hayes, and swopped stories which had us erupting with laughter the entire day. Actors are great company on occasions like this, and I felt so thankful I had been able to get back in time to fulfil this engagement. I wouldn't have missed it for the world.

With my next engagement, there would have been no possibility of dictating my measurements over the telephone, because I was to be dressed as a nineteenth century German *hausfrau,* and fitting had to be so accurate that they were sending over an expert from the Continent to take the measurements. Such glamour!

To save this august gentleman from having to visit each of us in turn, I agreed to go over to Bill Fraser's house one Saturday morning, so that he could measure Bill, his wife Pam, and me together. We were all very impressed to be told our costumes would be made in Rome, and would be exquisite. I wasn't so pleased to be told I would be wearing corsets and begged to be excused this torture. I doubted if I would be able to breathe in such a strait-jacket, but I was informed that the period demanded that I looked the right shape, and this could only be achieved by being laced into a corset. Whether or not I could breathe was entirely up to me!

It promised to be a starry production of a play by Graham Greene, with Donald Pleasence, John le Mesurier and Bill Fraser playing husbands and Councillors, and Pam, Jane Wenham and I as wives, plus a few other small part players. Rehearsals were in studios right at the other side of London, and I used to rendezvous with Bill Fraser's car at a given point each morning, which took me two trains to reach. The journey took two hours each way. Who says it's all frivolity and froth in show business? Stamina is one of the main ingredients for success! Bill Fraser used to say, in his gravelly voice, when we reached the icy rehearsal room, 'Ah the glamour of show business.' It always made me laugh.

When I had to go into London one day for a wig-fitting, I landed smack in the middle of my first bomb scare. I may say it is one thing to see it on television, or read about it in the newspapers, and quite another to be part of it. I had come down a little side street which took me near Piccadilly Circus, and although I noticed there seemed to be quite a few policemen about, I thought they were dealing with the traffic because of some local difficulty with the lights.

As I'm so small, I tend to nip round the back of people rather than forge my way through, so I slid quietly behind a large policeman and into the doorway of a big jeweller's shop to admire the glittering baubles. Next minute a large hand descended on my shoulder, and a voice said, 'Madam, get to the other side of Regent Street immediately. There is a bomb warning.'

I jumped in alarm. And when I looked up the street, I was the only pedestrian on the jeweller's shop side. The place had been completely cleared, but for me!

'Where is the bomb?' I gasped. 'In there,' said the policeman, indicating the shop whose windows I'd been about to examine.

I ran.

Next moment an armoured car drove down, preceded by a motorbike, and a loudspeaker ordered everybody to clear the street without delay, and to make for the side streets leading north. I must confess my legs turned to jelly. I looked at all those acres of

386

plate glass, and shuddered at the holocaust which could follow an explosion in that area.

I prayed it was a false alarm, which indeed it turned out to be. But the waste of manpower, the upset, the nervous tension, filled me with a deep sense of anger. It was senseless. Did those cowards really believe that London, which had resisted everything Hitler had thrown at it, was going to be bombed into submission? There is often a tendency to think of the Sassenach as a bit of a softie. But I saw them in the bombing during the war when I had to come down for interviews, just as I saw them during this later IRA bombing, calmly going about their business, showing no signs of nervousness or panic. And I took off my best bonnet to them.

I was delighted to note that *no* mention of this false alarm was made either on radio or TV or in the press, so the 'bomb-happy' morons were robbed of any publicity and consequent satisfaction. Denied publicity, there was just the possibility that they might realize that a solution must be found by sitting round the table. If indeed a solution could be found at all.

Their antics certainly shattered me that day, and I was glad I hadn't to go into town again for further fittings of wigs or anything else. The clothes from Rome for the TV play were exquisite. So elegant, and of such beautiful materials, I couldn't believe anyone would have put such fine workmanship into clothes to be worn for a television performance. The blouses were fully lined, and the little rows of buttons were fastened with hand-made loops. The petticoats were dainty and hand-sewn, and we had short kid lacing boots as fine as glove-leather, and lovely brooches at the neck. My 'Best Sunday outfit' was chocolate brown fine pure wool gaberdine (it was my year for gaberdine!), with full skirt to my feet, pale beige lace vestee trimmed with chocolate braiding, and little waisted jacket with wide chocolate velvet lapels and velvet cuffs. And I was only seen sitting at the table *knitting* in that splendid outfit!

We 'wives' ooohed and aaahed over such haute couture elegance, but decided that we would never have the patience to get into such layers of intricately fastened garments for work-a-day living. I don't like big lunches when I'm working, and with the crack of dawn rising, I was more than happy to subside on to the bed after a sandwich lunch, first removing all my fancy trapping and getting into a dressing gown. When Pam and Barbara (two of my 'neighbours' in the story) returned from the restaurant, they found me asleep. So they sat down, slippered feet up on the bed for comfort, and when I wakened we gossiped most of the afternoon away before we were called.

No wonder the producer said later that the scenes with the wives were so friendly and natural he could believe we had known one another all our lives.

With my hair having been under a wig for two days it was a bit of a mess, so I made an appointment to have it washed and set in one of the local shops, to look my best for Sandy's birthday celebrations. I had also quite a bit of shopping to do, for the card, the cake, a present, and other odds and ends. When I came out of the hairdressers I found to my disgust that it was fairly pelting with rain, and I hadn't a thing to cover my brand-new expensive hairdo. I was determined that it wasn't going to be ruined as I dashed from shop to shop, so I took out the plastic shopping bag I always carry as a spare, rolled it down to manageable size, with the handles over my ears to secure it, and popped it on my head. It looked just like one of those 'Mammy' hats worn by the black servants in the Old American films. The bus queue did a 'double take' and exploded with suppressed giggles. The lady in the baker's shrieked with delight, especially as the name of the shop was written all over the bag. Between peals of laughter, she told me I made a great walking advert.

In the supermarket, selling came to a standstill while I explained to the laughing staff and shoppers that I was protecting my hairdo.

The Post Office saw more hilarity than it has witnessed for years, as each queue looked up, gazed in wonder at my 'hat', and then started laughing. Even more amusing to all of us, one woman was so convulsed with laughter that she walked out wiping tears of laughter from her face, leaving her own beautiful mink hat on the counter!

It was quite marvellous to hear laughter wherever I went, and almost worth being considered either mad or eccentric to be able so effortlessly to chase the anxious look from people's faces. I began to feel that if only we dared to behave like this more often, we would have a lot more fun.

CHAPTER SEVENTEEN

Because I wanted to share the joke of the plastic bag hat with my old sparring partner Doris Rogers (Florrie) of *Life With the Lyons*, I sat down and wrote her a cheery chatty letter. I knew she had had a heart attack and wasn't allowed long tiring telephone conversations. But it arrived too late. I had written to her on the very day she died. She had been on her way to have her treatment, with the ambulance men actually in the house, when the tired heart stopped. No drama, no fuss, no pain as far as could be judged; a wonderfully peaceful ending to a long, full life.

She had actually been doing children's television almost to the end, and when we spoke on the telephone earlier in the year, she had been be-moaning the rush-hour traffic night and morning getting to and from rehearsals. Like the seasoned trouper she was, Doris died in harness, working up till almost the very last moment, which is the fulfilment of an actor's dream.

One of the fascinating things she told me was that she had once understudied Dorothy Ward as principal boy in Glasgow, in those far-off days when I was taken to the pantomime as a child, and it was very touching to see the legendary Dorothy Ward at Doris's funeral service. She looked lovely, and had the same light, musical tone of voice which I remembered so well. She told me she had been nineteen in that Glasgow pantomime and she had never forgotten the reception she got. She actually remembered the little girl who had jumped up, and exclaimed with such rapture, 'Oh Mother, isn't she beautiful?' and she laughed when I told her how affronted my mother had been at my piercing interruption of the show. I could almost hear my mother's voice, had she known of this amazing meeting, saying, 'Ah hope ye tellt her whit a showin' up ye gied me shoutin' oot like yon wi' yer Sergeant-Major voice!'

Our script-writer, Bob Lock and his wife Madeleine were at the service with us, but nobody else from show business. Barbara Lyon sent a wreath, and there was a magnificent cushion of white arum lilies, chrysan-themums and carnations from Mary Ellis, a famous star in musicals, who had been a life-long friend of Doris.

Ben Lyon must have been so glad he had rung Doris when he was in London a week or so earlier for Ted Ray's *This Is Your Life*. We had spoken on the telephone, and I had given him the hospital ward number, knowing how bucked she would be to hear his voice. It must surely have been a great comfort to him to know he had taken time for such a friendly chat when, all unknowingly, that was all the time there would ever be.

One of my best discoveries around this time was the BBC World Service. I had always been an erratic sleeper, and when my head buzzed like a bike of bees with all the excitements of the working day, I was finding it harder and harder to get a decent night's sleep. I didn't want to resort to sleeping tablets, for I knew I would get far too dependent on them, and yet I also knew I must find a solution if I was to be able to re-charge my batteries with restful sleep, especially when there was demanding work to be tackled next day.

And then I heard somebody discussing the World Service, with its all-night programme of news, talks, discussions, occasional music and repeat quiz shows, and I fiddled around with my radio until I had found the correct station. It had exactly the same desired effect on me as on a child being told a bed-time story. Once I had popped in my little ear piece, so as not to disturb Sandy, I was lulled off to sleep under the soothing voices of the readers. It was like being given a passport to a magic land of slumber, and the miseries of tossing and turning hour after hour were over.

When I told my brother Tommy of this, he reacted with horror at the idea of listening in during the night.

'Thank God I never hear it,' he exclaimed devoutly, in the tones of one who accepted sleep as a prize to enjoy every night of his life. Lucky him!

I don't suppose, though, he had much sleep the night before he went to Buckingham Palace to receive his MBE from Her Majesty the Queen. I always tell people he only came to London for this, because the Queen wouldn't go to Loch Lomond! Tommy dislikes London intensely, and can't believe that I find life possible in the capital.

He and Rhona came down to us the night before, and as a reminder of the special treat it used to be when we were children in Springburn, I made a steak pie for them. Tommy's eyes lit up when he saw it. 'Oh, a steak pie,' he exclaimed, 'I haven't had one of those for years.' It sent our minds back to the days when my mother used to send us up to the Co-operative with the steak in an enamel pie-dish, ready to be covered with thick flaky pastry, and baked in the Co-operative ovens. This cost about 1/6d (less than 10p), and was our idea of high living. Now we were eating a pie baked in a house which had its own cooker, as a fitting prelude to a visit to see the Queen!

Tommy, I may say, was appalled to be told that the alarm would have to be set for 6.30 A.M. if we were to breakfast, dress and reach Buckingham Palace by 10 A.M. The breakfast table was set before we went to bed, and in the morning I provided dressing gowns for everyone, leaving just the top garments to be slipped on at the last minute, to avoid accidents with egg-yolk and the like. I felt like the wardrobe mistress dressing the cast for a film. There was quite a touch of the Noel Cowards round the breakfast table, with us all sitting eating and chatting wearing dressing gowns.

It was a gorgeous morning of brilliant sunshine and

bright blue skies, and even Tommy had to admit that London had something to offer in the way of weather, considering he had left Arctic conditions behind at Loch Lomond.

We were all looking forward to seeing our Tommy in his topper and morning suit, not having seen him for years in anything more dressy than his favourite plus fours and wee woollen bonnet with the toorie on top. We were very favourably impressed with the transformation. As Sandy said, a morning suit is the most flattering of outfits, and Tommy looked surprisingly 'right' and really good. Wouldn't my mother have been baffled at the ways of Fate which now sent us, all rigged out in our best, *en route* for Buckingham Palace, with Tommy wearing a tile hat. Actually the hat was in a box in the boot of the car (Sandy was driving), and when we reached the palace quadrangle, Sandy had to open this box for inspection by an army officer, to make sure it wasn't a bomb! Sandy had to wait by the car, while we went into the Palace, for there were only two tickets available, one for Rhona and one for me but he said the time passed most interestingly, for by chance the day of the Investiture was also the final day of the Gurkhas' six weeks' spell of guard duty, and Sandy saw the entire change-over ceremony to the Welsh Guards. It lasted for over an hour, he said, and was a great sight.

Inside the Palace, we spectators filled three long red-velvet covered benches which ran the entire length of the beautifully proportioned room devoted to the ceremony, and the centre space was filled with empty chairs which would be occupied one by one as each recipient returned after receiving his award or decoration. A little orchestra played from a balcony near the entrance, and I wondered if they were the same musicians who had played for us that day in St James's Palace.

There were hundreds of those vacant chairs, it seemed, and the Queen would be on her feet for the duration of this long long ceremony. When she arrived, she looked very slim and informal in a simple green patterned silk dress, a black handbag over her arm, and her bare head. Somebody was very surprised that she didn't have a hat and coat on. 'But she is in her own house,' I said. 'You don't wear your hat and coat indoors, do you?' I did wonder, though, what she kept in that handbag!

Ribbons and medals were pinned on with practised ritual. An equerry handed over each decoration, the Queen took it, pinned it on, had a few words with the recipient, and held out a hand to receive the next medal. I was very impressed with the absolute confidence the Queen displayed that there would be a giving or receiving hand whenever she took or returned a sword or a decoration, and never once had she to turn her head to check that it would be there. That alone spoke of years of reliable service.

When we came out, Tommy and I were interviewed by the newsmen and in front of the TV cameras, and I would have loved it had my mother been alive to see 'her weans' on the television news. As Isa, my old chum from Glasgow, said in her letter, 'How proud your mother would have been. She'd have been up and down Springburn Road telling them about "our Tommy" going to see the Queen at Buckingham Palace.'

There was a lovely warm Scottish reaction when almost everybody saw it from the standpoint of our mother. I always remember Barrie saying of his mother, that whenever she read of any man achieving anything, she had no envy of his wife, but she would sigh and say, 'I'd like to have been that man's mother.' All Springburn seemed to feel the same way about Tommy.

What our English friends found most hilarious was our picnic in the West End. I had packed ham sandwiches and flasks of coffee, for I knew there would be no refreshments in the Palace and that we'd be famished by the time it was all over. But where on earth were we to eat the goodies in London, where parking that day was almost impossible.

We headed for the Covent Garden area to hand back the hired morning suit and the etceteras, which would also allow Tommy to change into his own lounge suit, and the only space near the shop was on a yellow line. 'Och it's the dinner hour,' I said. 'Let's take a chance and we can always scoot off the minute a warden or policeman appears. One of us can go into the shop and tell Tommy where to find us.'

Suddenly the thought of that hot coffee and those delicious sandwiches was too much, so I poured out three cups, handed round the 'pieces', and there and then Sandy, Rhona and I had our picnic. The windows were all steamed up, for it was bitterly cold outside in this sunless street, but I begged Sandy not to wipe them. I didn't want anyone to see in! I felt that if the police came along and found us not only on a yellow line but actually having a picnic in the heart of the West End, we'd all be run in! I didn't fancy the headlines which might greet that little escapade.

Believe it or not, not a soul came near us. If anyone had told me such a snack was possible in a London street in the midst of the pre-Christmas shopping frenzy, I would not have believed him.

To complete the comedy, when Tommy joined us

from the shop, now in his lounge suit, I poured out *his* coffee when we stopped at the lights, and I sat the cup inside one of the picnic boxes so it wouldn't splash his suit. So he had his sustenance on the move, and fairly relished his surprise tit-bit.

The neighbours were aghast at our nerve, and without exception found that picnic the most riveting item of all we had to divulge.

In bed that night I kept thinking of all the fine people who had received awards. Of the little woman in the flat shoes, and porridge-coloured suit, with not even a nod in the direction of fashion, but with a face which shone with a joy which lifted the heart. She was so clearly transported with delight at being in the Palace in the presence of the Queen that we all shared the glorious moment with her, and knew that she would remember it to the end of her days.

There was the wee lance-corporal from Northern Ireland, decorated for bravery, neat as a new pin, with not a hair out of place, his Glasgow accent undiluted even when speaking to a top-ranking military commander.

I saw again the row of Leicester policemen and an ambulance man, heroes of a shooting incident, on whom the Queen smiled radiantly and spoke at length when she gave them their awards for gallantry.

And Andy Stewart, elegant in his dress kilt and jacket, with his bonnie wife, son and daughter.

I remembered the surprise of hearing Mike Yarwood announced as Michael, and was amused to observe his shoulders hunched like Harold Wilson, grin like Edward Heath, and stabbing upward glance like David Frost, as he made his way to the seat near us, there to follow the rest of the ceremony with concentrated attention.

Rhona and Tommy had already left on the overnight train for Scotland, and it would be back to 'auld claes and parritch' for all of us in the morning. But it was truly a day to remember.

'How did the Queen look close-up?' I had asked him.

'A very tired little lady,' he replied.

No wonder, I thought, standing for all that time and having to find something original to say to every single one.

My own wee bit of recognition came that year, when I received an intriguing note from the people who compile *Who's Who in the World*, asking me to fill in details for inclusion in their publication. Not *Who's Who* you will observe, but in the world! If I've to be included among that lot, I thought, I'll surely have plenty to live up to! I sent off the information they demanded, and wondered what they would have said if they had seen their 'illustrious member' five minutes later busy baking a couple of apple tarts, and then cleaning the kitchen floor. But all life is contrast, as I have observed many a time and oft, and that is precisely what makes it so interesting.

Then came my inclusion among the *Great Scots*, a flattering honour, and later my name was to be found in reference books of writers and authors. My grannie would have said, 'Michty Goad, whit wey wid folk want to read aboot whaur ye were born, and whit school ye went to? Surely it wid be of nae interest to onybody?' *My Weekly* was grannie's choice, and to her there would have been no interest whatsoever in lists of names and achievements. The mere thought of grannie's quenching commonsense made me laugh and knocked any conceit out of my head. I was irresistibly reminded of Beachcomber's *List of Huntingdonshire Cabmen*.

I was also reminded of a Scots friend who was so thrilled when she was awarded the OBE that she quickly organized a lunch-party in town with friends to celebrate the honour. She left a note for her 'daily' telling her where she was, and what had happened, fondly imagining the 'daily' would be mightily impressed. When she got home later that afternoon, she found a wee note from the 'daily' which ran, 'Dear Madam, How nice. We're out of Fairy.'

No wonder the Scots keep their feet on the ground. There's a real sense of priorities there! And yet, it's precisely because of this wholesome tendency not to over-praise in case folk get above themselves, that a compliment from a fellow-Scot takes on a tremendous value. When I went to rehearse with Stanley Baxter for one of his Christmas shows, I was quite overcome when Stanley, whom I hadn't seen or worked with for years, told me I must be sure to tell Tommy what a wonderful piece of television he considered the *Chapter and Verse* interview had been, which he had seen from Edinburgh, when Tommy and I spoke of our childhood and of my mother and our upbringing in Springburn. 'It was as enthralling as a well-written play, Molly,' Stanley said. 'I watched it with my producer and we both agreed it was one of the best items we had seen for a long long time.' Well, I ask you! Coming from such a brilliant artiste as our Stanley, is it any wonder I have remembered it word for word? Tommy was fairly bowled over by this praise too, when I told him on my next visit.

The Baxter Christmas show rehearsals were great fun, but the surprising thing to me was that Stanley had forgotten how wee I was. He seemed a bit taken aback by my bantam proportions, especially as I was playing the mother of a large girl who had to pretend to be about nine years old. To look smaller than I am, she had to sit with her knees drawn up practically to her chin, and hunch her shoulders forward to conceal a well-developed bosom! Poor thing, she must have been in torture, and I tried to puff myself up like a frog to make myself look suitably maternal. Stanley played my boozing husband, and it was a lesson in perfectionist characterization to watch him at rehearsal. Every move, every gesture fitted the dialogue and the action, and no detail was too small to demand attention. Not only did he know exactly what he wanted for his own part, he knew it for mine too. In fact he could do my part far more convincingly than I could!

The director thought he'd never get us started though, for the moment we started speaking of Glasgow, we were away on a tide of reminiscences of childhood delights over the tattie scones, the Paris buns, the coffee buns, the fern cakes, and the strawberry tarts. I'm quite sure all Glaswegians must have a sweet tooth, and a passion for bakers' shops, for it's just the same when Janet Brown, or Hannah Gordon, or Moira Anderson and I get together. Janet frankly confesses she is a 'bun-aholic', and has to steer clear of them if humanly possible, or she'd be like a houseside. And even Lulu said it would be murder if she had to be at home all the time taking care of her adored wee boy Jordan, for she'd finish all the puddings he left, and have a job fighting her way into her jeans!

Janet says she thinks it is because a sweet cake was such a treat when we were youngsters, that it became very special to us and irresistible. 'Irresistible' is certainly the word, for when Hannah and Moira and I had tea together at the Savoy, we ate six cakes between us! And we had just come from a VIP lunch! The waiter couldn't believe his eyes!

Stanley was also very intrigued by the way I took down all my acting notes in shorthand. 'Would you look at her?' he demanded. 'There's nae use anybody trying to deny a thing they said, for she's got it all down in that shorthand of hers.'

The hazards of show-biz were well illustrated though, when it was decided to slip in a tiny extra sketch of me as a la-di-da lady, with Stanley as a pink-satin clad fairy who knocks at my door, and when I open it to ask what he wants, he replies, 'Have *you* seen the bottom of your garden lately?' and he holds his nose with disgust, and gives a dainty little 'boke'.

Well, the preparations for that item took all of four hours hanging around for me. I had to go to wardrobe and find a suitable dress (a dinky brown crêpe creation which looked very elegant). I had then to have my hair completely re-set, for I'd worn a wig in the earlier sketch, which had ruined my own hair-style. Stanley had to wait for a break in the rehearsed sketches, before he could go to change into the fairy outfit, which also involved wig and sparkly make-up. And after all that, the sketch was cut from the show! I could never understand why, for to me it was a witty and amusing joke, and everyone to whom I told it later, liked it.

But who was I to complain? It had been a great experience to work with someone for whom only the best was good enough.

But I met my Waterloo when I was asked to play the part of Effie, the old lag with a vicious streak, in the prison series *Within These Walls*. TV people always assume actors can do any mortal thing they are asked to do, and although they had me along for a pep talk about the part, and stressed that I would look a horror with dyed dark hair, and no charm whatsoever, nobody thought to ask me if I could roll cigarettes with convincing expertise.

I found the part very challenging to play, if depressing, and it was awful spitting and snarling and behaving atrociously to the wee soul who shared my cell. To make it all the more realistic, the director commanded everybody to ostracize me so that there would be no hint of a smile or softness, and this would ensure that I would behave like a stag at bay!

That was bad enough, but when he called out one morning, 'Can you roll cigarettes?' I was really startled. 'No,' I replied, 'but I can try.'

His assistant was despatched to the shops there and then, and returned with a packet of Rizla papers, a poke of loose tobacco and a wee machine, and I was shown how to make a cigarette, and ordered to practise all week-end. Which I did. I made cigarettes so fat they wouldn't come out of the machine. Then cigarettes so thin, that they fell to bits as soon as I tried to tap them against a thumb. I couldn't for the life of me think how cowboys managed to do it all so effortlessly with one hand, from a little soft bag, and not even a machine to help them.

On the Monday morning, the director queried, 'Have you been practising cigarette-rolling?' 'I have,' I said.

Came the scene involving my rolling a cigarette, licking the paper, extracting it, and smoking it as I went through quite complicated dialogue. The entire cast stood round to watch. Everyone but myself had known that this was a trick most difficult to acquire in a day or two.

401

The paper stuck to my tongue and all the tobacco fell out. We started again. Too much tobacco, so the fag wouldn't come out. At the next attempt, I was light-headed with the thrill of success when a perfectly rolled cigarette fell into my hand. I tried to light it, and it burned so fiercely that it singed my eyelashes. On the next attempt, I managed one puff, started to speak and found little pieces of stinging tobacco all over my mouth and gums and had to spit out fragments between every other word.

The cast, by this time, were holding their sides with laughter. I was practically in tears over my abysmal failure. The director snapped a finger. 'No cigarettes,' he said. 'Remove the Rizla papers, tobacco and machine.' 'Wait a minute, Brian,' I said, 'I don't think I need smoke them at all. I think the menacing thing about this whole business is the sight of this horrible old lag continually rolling cigarettes, licking the papers with a predatory tongue, and carefully storing them in a box. It could even hint that she had some sort of hold over the others, because she sold them to her fellow-prisoners.'

Brian stared at me thoughtfully. 'Very good,' he said, 'we'll try that.' We did, and it worked. And oh when it was all over, it felt good to wash that ghastly spray dye out of my hair, and change into cool summery cotton after those prison greys. The reactions of friends and neighbours were quite amusing. 'I had no idea you could look such a sight,' said the milkman. 'My you were a bad wee besom to that poor lassie,' said the butcher. 'It was so convincing,' said the paper-shop chap, 'that I began to wonder if Aggie in *Life With the Lyons* was the real you, or that bad little tinker in the prison.' Ben Lyon, who happened to see it when he was over on a trip to London, was amazed.

'That's the stuff you get Oscars for, Molly,' he said, 'not for being a dolly-bird. I've never seen you doing anything like that before.'

I'd never *done* anything like that before, and it certainly caused a stir. One of my *Journal* readers, whose signature was simply 'Your Perth Poet', took the trouble to send me a poem she'd been inspired to write after seeing my performance as the wicked Effie:

I never thocht tae see ye act yon pairt,
Vindictive, cruel, ye seemed tae hae a pebble for a heart.
Ah held my breath, ma temper rose, I coonted tae a hunner.
An' every time yon lassie grat, Ah ca'ed ye an auld scunner,
An' hoped 'himsel' tak's haud o' ye an' puts ye ower his knee,
An' skelps ye till ye squeal wi' pain, an' tears rin fae yer e'e.
Ye seemed sae different frae the lass, wha writes oor weekly letter,
But, mindin' it was juist a play, has made me feel some better.
The pathos o' yon story had ma very heart contractin',
So, Molly, tak' these verses as a tribute tae yer actin'.

After all that, it made a very nice contrast to go up to Glasgow to take part in the celebrations for 'Glasgow 800', and attend the showing of *Floodtide*, which had been chosen for the film festival which formed part of the 800th anniversary of the city charter.

At the Glasgow Film Theatre it was lovely to meet up with many old friends at the pre-film party. It was like old times to be chatting with Jack House, Molly Urquhart, who insisted on telling everybody what 'a nice wee hoose' Molly had, Jimmy Logan's dad, and Ellie Blake, the widow of our famous writer George Blake who had done the script of *Floodtide*. I had been invited to speak before the film was shown, and the audience seemed to enjoy my tales of behind-the-scenes larks with Gordon Jackson and Jimmy Logan.

In the film my voice was heard before my face was seen, and the moment my off-screen voice was heard, a sibilant whisper ran right through the cinema, 'That's her,' followed by, 'Aye, Ah knew that wis her voice.'

What amazed my fellow-actors in Glasgow was my ability to get up and speak off-the-cuff to the audience as I had done. They little knew of the Equity battles which had sharpened my skills in this connection!

I may admit that I was quite apprehensive at being faced with my twenty-six-years-younger self up there on the screen, but it wasn't only *my* young self which was a revelation. There was the younger John Laurie, dark and serious, and the two gangling 'chiels', Gordon Jackson and Jimmy Logan. And the young handsome Molly Urquhart. It was a lovely chance to see them all again, their youth forever fixed on film, and a wonderful experience to see it with a Glasgow audience whose sense of identification with the story and the actors was complete.

In spite of my gained confidence in public speaking, I was a bundle of nerves when I was coaxed to attend the 312th Anniversary of the Royal Scottish Corporation, to be held at the Savoy, to reply to the toast to the guests.

I hadn't really wanted to accept, and was quite frankly terrified to speak at such a high-powered affair, but when they sent me the booklet describing the history of this wonderful Scottish charity which is the oldest in existence, having been formed away back in the early part of the seventeenth century, I simply couldn't refuse. Long before the State gave a thought to the poor in its midst, this charity had been formed to assist widows and orphans and poor children living in London in distress or hardship, who had been born in Scotland, or whose parents or husbands had been

Scottish born. And the money had originally been raised by Scotsmen who had followed James VI to London, had prospered, and who wanted to take care of their poorer brethren.

Today the charity cares for the young, the elderly, the widows and the dependants of Scots in London. It provides flats and hostels and, almost as important as anything they do, it provides company for the old who need it.

So Sandy looked out his dinner suit, and I pressed my Stuart tartan silk skirted dinner dress, and we headed for the Savoy.

When I glanced down the row of faces at the top table, my appetite for the beautiful food vanished in the instant. I was flanked by the Earl of Rosebery on one side and Sandy on the other. Then further down sat the Queen's Chamberlain, Lord McLean, and on Sandy's other side sat the Moderator of the General Assembly of the Church of Scotland, and there were titles and decorations by the score. There were even Clan Chieftains in magnificent tartans, and I had had the nerve to agree to address this assembly of nobles! I must have been mad!

Earl Rosebery seemed as nervous as myself. Mark you, he could have been suffering from jet-lag because he told me that he and his wife had just flown in from the Far East that very afternoon! What stamina world figures have. If I had done that, it would have been straight to bed for me. Suddenly I remembered that he must be the grandson of the Earl whose stately home we had visited earlier in the summer. We had been vastly amused to be told by the caretaker that the old Earl had had three ambitions in life. 'To marry an heiress. To win the Derby. And to become Prime Minister of England.' All this was said with great

405

eloquence by the old chap, before he added with a triumphant flourish, 'And he accomplished all three!' I looked at my dinner companion, the present Earl, with a new interest, and was relieved I had found a topic of conversation so we had a pleasant undemanding chat about the beauty of Ascott House.

The other speeches were on the serious side, although nicely interspersed with a touch of humour, but my mouth was dry with nerves when I rose to speak. It was a bit like that first speech to the Woman of the Year Lunch. Because I stuck to light-hearted topics, and brought in anecdotes of Tescos, and my grannie's economies, and my wizardry with my six-penny nap bone, they responded with enough joyous laughter to reassure me that they had enjoyed my jokes.

The most memorable moment for me was when a wee lady came up to me afterwards and shook me vigorously by the hand. 'You have made history tonight, Miss Weir,' she said. 'You are the first woman in all the 312 years' history of the Corporation to have made a speech from the top table!'

I was flabbergasted. I was heartily thankful nobody had told me this before I spoke or I'd have been even more nervous than I was.

Shaking me by the hand again, she told me, 'I'm very proud of you. And I was a suffragette!'

Well, you could have knocked me over with a feather. Yes, the very feather she had just put in my best bonnet. Never in my wildest flights of imagination did I dream of meeting a suffragette, or have the honour of being complimented by one. That was the second link with the past I had had within a few months. The first was when I had spoken at a Conservative Ladies' Club at Lytham St Annes, and was introduced to a lady in the audience who had just celebrated her hundredth birthday. She was slim, attractive, and very well-spoken and she told me proudly that she had been alive in the times of both Disraeli and Gladstone!

What with that and now a suffragette, the scents and sounds of history seemed very close.

All of this was a seemly prelude to my being asked to take part in the Festive Season offering from STV in Glasgow, called *A Dickens of a Christmas*. We had to work on all sorts of songs and dances as an ensemble, and then each of us had solo numbers based on Dickens' characters and to my joy I was asked to play Miss Haversham in a scene from *Great Expectations*, where I had a lovely ballad to sing, called *Children*.

It was the first time for years I had worked with such a huge orchestra, and I was very self-conscious piping up my sad little ballad with such musicians all round me. But Harry Rabinowitz gave me a true 'ring of confidence' by not turning a hair when he heard my wee voice.

Andrew Cruickshank was as fascinated as I was with the musical side of the production, although he refused to believe I could be as stunned as he was by having to work with an orchestra, and concern himself with pre-recording singing. I know I've sung and danced in musical shows and revues in the past, but I told him truthfully that it is always new and it's always nerve-racking. But it's tremendously stimulating at the same time, after the sober application needed for straight drama.

We had a lovely group of orphans from Quarrier's Homes in Bridge of Weir helping out as Dickensian children, and they were utterly hypnotized by the whole thing. They didn't take long to become friendly and happy with us, and kept telling us in serious tones, 'You're good, so you are!' I was very impressed by their good behaviour. Not a bit cowed at all, just obedient and quiet when they were forming the background to our work, but ready to spring into action and go through their carols the moment they were asked.

They were, in fact, a marvellous illustration of the truth that it's not the modern children who have changed, it's the modern parents. Those children had been brought up in the orphanage in just the same way as we had in Springburn by our grannies and our mothers, and had been taught how to behave in the presence of adults. And, like us, they knew better than to be noisy when they were warned to sit still when other folk were busy.

They were a sheer delight to have with us, and it was very clear to all of us that they had the happiest of relationships with their guardians who came to rehearsals with them.

I had arrived a day late for the rehearsals for this show, because of a previous commitment in Leeds which had been impossible to break, and although I normally stayed at a small quiet hotel further out Great Western Road, this time I decided that as everybody else had booked in at the Grosvenor, I would too. It would be more convenient in all sorts of ways, for transport would pick us up in the mornings and bring us back again at the end of the day, from the far-flung rehearsal rooms dotted around Glasgow.

Studying new songs and learning routines in a very short time cut out any ideas of socializing, and the lovely bedroom would be my refuge for the week, with all comforts greatly appreciated. Kettle, tea and coffee indicated I'd be able to have refreshing brews any time I wished. There was colour TV, a radio, and fresh

fruit to nibble if one felt hungry during the wee sma'
hours and couldn't sleep. I was definitely in clover.

When I rang through to Bonnie Langford's mother
to see if there was anything I might usefully catch up
on before the next day's rehearsals, she assured me
that apart from studying the words, there was nothing.
All the big numbers would be tackled next day when
everyone would be present. Then she riveted me by
telling me how lucky I had been in *not* being in the
hotel the night before. There had been a fire alarm,
and all the guests had had to scamper downstairs and
into the street in night-gowns and curlers, and were
left standing in the freezing cold for half-an-hour until
the building was declared safe by the fire brigade. She
herself had only taken time to thrust her feet into her
evening shoes, and one man who obviously slept in his
birthday suit had pulled on his evening trousers and
nothing else!

A hotel fire is one of my nightmares, and although
Sandy assured me when I told him about the false
alarm on the telephone, that it was unlikely to happen
twice, I followed a nightly regime for the whole of my
stay in that hotel!

Each night I laid out my 'Survival kit' on the other
single bed. First my bag with my cash, papers, return
ticket to London, hotel bedroom key (one girl had
dashed out without hers and had had an awful job afterwards finding someone with a pass key), my warm
boots, jersey, cape, and my favourite gold chain.
Whether or not I'd have taken the time to grab all
those things is another matter, but it was a good
discipline. I didn't intend to be caught in my bare feet
and 'nichtie-goon' if I could help it!

I also made it a little exercise to find where the
nearest fire exits were, and I timed myself to see how

quickly I could reach the street door, and checked the direction so that I wouldn't run the wrong way.

In the morning, everything had to be restored to its proper place. It was a bit of a nuisance, but for my peace of mind I stuck faithfully to this routine.

I grew to love that room where I spent each evening working on my songs and my script. I discovered that if I left the bathroom door ajar I could lie soaking and watching the TV play at the same time. How sybaritic could one get, I giggled, and the others laughed when I told them, especially when I added that of course the one touch of 'hardship' was that it meant lying with my head at the tap end of the bath!

I left safely at the end of the week. Just as Sandy promised, lightning hadn't struck twice.

Less than a fortnight later, I switched on the television news and even before the picture came on I could hear the clanging of fire engines, and hear the newsreader's voice telling us of a terrible fire in Great Western Road, in Glasgow, and fire brigades were arriving from every area within miles. Even before he got the length of saying which hotel it was, I knew it was the Grosvenor. I was transfixed as I watched the flames roaring through that lovely hostelry. I could picture the inferno devouring all those colour television sets, the electric kettles, the fitted carpets and the oh-so-comfortable beds. I could visualize my very own room perishing in the holocaust and I thanked God I wasn't in it at the time.

There is a particular poignancy in the loss or destruction of a person or a place which has just become of special significance for you alone. A long friendship or intimate knowledge builds up very different memories. But in a strange way, someone known only briefly, or a place enjoyed for a short time, leaves a sharpness of impression which seems too vivid to take its place among old experiences.

The memory of a train guard who spoke to me minutes before he leaped to the track and was killed, lives with me still. Young Prince William of Gloucester, who smiled at me at the Savoy when we were at a private dinner party became a real person, over whom I grieved when he was killed shortly afterwards in an air crash.

So now with the Grosvenor Hotel. I felt very close to that tragedy. It would forever be associated in my mind with Christmas, with Dickens, and with a very happy company. In a sense I was almost in at the dress rehearsal of the destructive force of that consuming fire. Thanks be to God I missed the actual performance!

CHAPTER EIGHTEEN

I think the only original contribution I made in the television world was when I devised *Tea-Time Tales*. I had the strongest conviction that such little 'couthy' five-minute stories would be a boon for a commercial network, which would have odd corners to fill before matching up with the net-worked programme times, and I knew in my bones that everyone loves a story. Years of experience writing for *Woman's Hour* told me that it was the little homely tales people remembered. So I tried to get STV interested. Not a chance. Again and again I put up the idea, and each time the idea was tossed out.

Then a new broom arrived in Glasgow to sweep away all the old conventions, perhaps, and as luck would have it I had heard him speaking at an Oxford Debate on Television. I used this as my introduction when I wrote to him, and I urged him to allow me to record half-a-dozen stories. All I required was the studio with facilities for recording. If he didn't like them, nothing was lost. If he did like them, he could pay me. My enthusiasm impressed him, and so, on my next visit to Glasgow, when no extra fares were involved, I arrived with my batch of tales, recorded them, and almost at once their usefulness was recognized. And the public appeared to welcome them. 'Ah love your wee stories, hen,' people would say to me in the street, 'an' the weans enjoy them too. They canny believe Ah played in the back-courts just like you, and they actually sit and listen tae me.'

At a dinner, a Rangers football-player turned to me and asked, 'Are thae wee stories o' yours a' true, Molly?' 'Yes,' I said, amazed that he knew a thing about them and must have listened and watched. 'Aye,' he said with a smile, 'Ah thought they were. They ring true.'

Railway guards call out to me, 'Up tae dae mair o' your wee stories then?' and letters pour in from viewers, anxious to tell me how much they enjoy them. It's the oldest form of entertainment in the world, storytelling, and I now write and record them twelve at a time, and leap in and out of all permutations of tops and trousers and skirts to ring the changes, and I have the greatest sense of fulfilment that something I suggested has proved such a success. And not only to me. Others have come along with their own little stories, and because we are all different, with our own individual memories and experiences, it makes a satisfyingly varied feast for viewers. And provides a great little stock of odd items for STV, even if I did

412

have to do a bit of arm-twisting before they saw it my way! It is a continuing tribute to the late Anthony Firth, who had the foresight and the flexibility to make it all happen. Although I only met him once, I will never forget him.

With anniversaries of various shows and personalities taking place almost monthly, it seemed, I began to find it a bit unnerving to be asked to come along with my memories because, in the words of the producers, 'You're one of the few still surviving!' Deryck Guyler and I used to pat ourselves all over, checking that we were still in good working order when we would find ourselves yet again recalling how we started in *ITMA*, or our work in *The Charlie Chester Show*, of my years in *Life With the Lyons,* and even on one unforgettable occasion being rushed to the *Nationwide* Studio to tell of my enjoyable experiences in working with Compton McKenzie. His death had been announced while I was on the air doing a live performance with Pete Murray, and I happened to mention that I had appeared with Sir Compton in Glasgow, and someone from *Nationwide* heard me, and seized upon me to add my tribute.

But the *pièce-de-resistance* came when I was invited to be guest of honour at a celebration of local writers in Middlesex. I was staggered when I saw the list of writers who had lived in the area, for they included Sheridan, Goldsmith, Trollope, Charles Kingsley and W. S. Gilbert, to name but a few! With cheerful honesty it was announced to the assembled company that the only reason I had been asked to fill the honoured seat was because I was the only person who was still alive! A qualification not to be sneezed at, and one which I trusted I would continue to enjoy with zest undimmed!

So with all such signs that the years were flying past

with unseemly haste, I ought to have been more aware than I was that the date of Sandy's retirement was almost upon us. I always knew somewhere in the back of my mind that life would be a bit different when he laid down his pen and briefcase for good, but in spite of all the splendid advice ladled out by newspapers and magazines about preparing for this traumatic event, somehow I couldn't really believe it when the actual day arrived.

To make it even harder to adjust, his firm cut off their employees' working life on the actual birthday, which in Sandy's case happened to be a Tuesday, so there wasn't a tidy 'end-of-the-week' finish, but rather a sensation of anti-climax as though the curtain had come down half-way through the play and stuck there.

Till that Wednesday morning following Sandy's farewell to city life, I had been used to having the house to myself from early morning till seven at night. If I felt like it and was in creative mood, I had been known to spend the entire day writing in my gazebo in the garden, free of all interruption, apart from the telephone. The locked side door told neighbours I was busy, and only an emergency would have brought them to the door.

On that first changed morning, I vanished into the gazebo with the mail, as usual, and announced I'd be in for coffee around half-past-ten. Out of the corner of my eye I could see Sandy standing on the terrace, gazing thoughtfully up the garden. He drifted over and pressed his face against the glass of the gazebo, observing with distaste the chaos which is the usual state of my writing background. 'Shouldn't we tidy up all that mess?' he suggested helpfully. '*No*,' I shouted. 'Don't *touch* it. I know where everything is. I like it this way. Wash the windows if you want something to do.'

Poor Sandy. He gave me a wounded look and disappeared in the direction of the compost heap.

For days I couldn't work, I was so aware of him circling the gazebo, his face turned in my direction to see how I was getting on. I remembered Lillian Beckwith telling me she had had to move her office to the top of the house, because when her husband was permanently at home, and wandered about outside where her eye caught his every movement, her concentration completely vanished. So I didn't feel quite such a monster that this was just how it was affecting me.

As for Sandy, it seemed he hadn't made any of those recommended mental preparations either, for all those little jobs which had been so pressing during our precious week-ends, now somehow lacked urgency, because there was all the time in the world to do them.

I despaired of being able to write another word. 'A writer *needs* peace and solitude,' I kept repeating to myself, to stop feeling guilty. But how could I hurt Sandy's feelings by insinuating he was in the way?

Very very gradually we fell into a routine. By mutual consent, Sandy took over the shopping and found, to his surprise, that he began to enjoy it. People he'd never spoken to in his life now stopped to ask what he was doing, and to check if Molly were ill, and in no time at all he knew far more neighbours than I did. Once in a blue moon I went with him, just to let everybody know he hadn't buried me at the bottom of the garden! I had disappeared from the shopkeepers' lives as if I'd left the district.

At tea-time I downed tools, stopped writing, and we went walking in the country for at least two hours every day. It cut down the writing hours of course, but

415

it made a rare focal point of our day and was great exercise for both of us. In no time at all, the whole of Pinner grew used to us striding past their houses, whatever the weather. We didn't have to take up jogging when that fad started, our legs and stamina were in great shape with all these regular outings. We have always loved walking of course, for it's an exercise which can be adapted to your own pace, and which can be followed to the end of one's days, barring accidents. It was my old mentor Bernard Shaw who said, 'The legs go first', so it's a good idea to keep them in good fettle.

By the time summer arrived, with the long golden days of that marvellous year, Sandy was blissfully basking in the freedom to sunbathe whenever he felt like it, to turn to gardening chores without rush, and to be able to consider holidays without having to arrange dates with anyone else in the office. He was no longer at a loose end, and I found I could settle down to the writing without worrying about him.

But if that part was working well, the domestic side was now under constant scrutiny by his lordship! At the sight of a mop in my hand, he would demand, 'What are you doing? Leave that alone. The floor is perfectly clean.'

'Put on your specs,' I'd retort angrily, amazed at my own fury, 'and you'll *see* it's filthy.'

How could I ever bring a casual visitor into the kitchen if I wasn't to be allowed to clean the place? I developed great cunning! As soon as Sandy disappeared to do the shopping, I flew around with mop and duster as if I were indulging some secret vice.

He soon discovered that cleaning windows was not the piece of cake he had imagined, in spite of all the brave promises that this was now *his* job. Pay a

416

window-cleaner when he was there to do them? Nonsense. Quite. Except that he considered that such a boring job shouldn't be tackled in one go, and it would be a far better idea to do one window a week and leave it at that. So that there was never a point when all our windows were clean at the same time. I only achieved clean panes everywhere when visitors were expected from Canada, and I hinted that it would be a pity if they came all that way and then found they couldn't see out of the windows!

The flex leading from the food mixer was wound into a neat little coil, tightly fastened, which I now had to undo every time I wanted to use the mixer. Neatness was all to my man about the house.

Food smells drifted around the house and bedrooms, because Sandy didn't mind them, and he was deaf to my pleas to *shut the kitchen door* when the pots were boiling. As for the smell of burning toast! That permeated every corner of the house several mornings a week. The toaster had developed a temperamental habit of popping up the finished toast just when it felt like it. I suppose if it had always burnt the bread he would have learned to keep a watchful eye on it. But because it sometimes worked, suspicion was lulled, and he would be deep in his newspaper, back turned to the toaster of course, and only my anguished cry from upstairs, 'Sandy, the toast is *on fire*' made him jump guiltily and save the kitchen from being burnt to a cinder. He liked bringing me up my breakfast on a tray, so I daren't stir so much as a toe to venture downstairs.

If I was observed too often with a duster in my hands, he suspected I'd broken something and this was my way of playing the over-zealous housewife! He refused to believe that while he was at the office, and I was working in the house unsupervised (!), the house was dusted daily and the kitchen floor cleaned regularly.

Neat and well-organized, the trouble was that the man in my life was now doing a full-time job of organizing me!

Everything became economically related to the stark reality of the state pension. Unless it was actually blowing a gale, two bars of the electric fire became practically out of the question. If I meekly requested a bit more warmth, I was invited to put on a warm pullover! I felt sure I must be the only housewife in Pinner who wore more indoors than outdoors. I seriously considered nominating him Minister for Energy.

I couldn't believe I had exchanged my quiet gentle husband for this energetic sparring partner. It was a marvellous recipe for keeping a marriage lively! Blood coursing through our veins, we argued and acted as the mood and the moment seized us and life was far from humdrum. Every decision for a while became a battle of wills, and the only words *never* spoken by either of us were, 'Whatever you think best, dear.'

But once the smoke died down, we laughed constantly over our domestic frays. It became a game, ruefully played by me sometimes I must confess, when I had to use devious means to get the floors cleaned and the house dusted, but Sandy looked younger every day. He had found his niche in life. Foiling me, protecting me. Stopping me doing too much domestic work. Running the house to *his* satisfaction. With never a dull moment for either of us.

And on those occasions when he went out for a morning or afternoon's golf (I persuaded him to join a golf club!), and he was away for hours, the silence became a reproach, and I found my heart turning over

418

at the fearful thought of this peace and quietness becoming permanent. It was at such moments I knew to the depths of my soul that floors, windows, toaster, open doors, were simply the pin-pricks of life which kept us on our toes. They were nothing at all. 'The man's the gowd for a' that', as Rabbie said. And as I reached for the floor mop, I would murmur to myself, 'Oh King, live forever.'

Mark you, in spite of such pious sentiments, deeply held, it didn't stop me enjoying tales of the trials and tribulations of other wives of newly retired males. At a 'social studies' group one afternoon, everything came to a halt when one of the wives innocently asked another if her husband had got back from a scientific study trip to America. Her lips tightened. 'Yes he has,' she said. 'And do you know what was the first thing he did when we had our first cup of tea together? He lifted the lid of the teapot, examined the pot, and said, "I don't believe you've scoured the inside of this teapot since the day I left!"'

I dissolved in helpless laughter. 'The inside of the teapot,' I echoed. 'I don't believe I have consciously actually *cleaned* inside of a teapot. I've shooshed it round with hot water, but I haven't got down to really scraping or scouring it.' Nobody else in the room had either!

The lady beside me said, 'She's lucky that her husband goes away on those long trips. Mine is with me day and night since he retired, and I can't get near my sink now. Apart from the half-hour of *Gardeners' Question Time*, which he loves, I dare not wash a dish in our house. During that single half-hour in the week, I stand over the sink and wash dishes and pots and pans, and dream of the days when I was boss of my own kitchen!'

A little quiet soul at the end of the room said, in hushed tones, 'Mine's a compulsive gravy-stirrer!' Even the rather grand lady by the door laughed uproariously at this. It sounded like the worst sort of vice!

A youngish woman said despondently, 'Gosh, is that what it will be like?' 'Yes,' came the chorus. I wondered if it might be a good idea to form a group on the lines of Alcoholics Anonymous for 'Wives-of-retired-men-anonymous'. I'm sure we all felt better after that little unburdening of our private griefs! When I told Sandy, he said accusingly, 'What did you say about me?' 'Not a word, darling, not a word,' I assured him. Well, there really wasn't time, and besides the little idiosyncrasies of the other husbands were so much more hilarious.

One of the most exciting occasions we were able to lend a hand with together after Sandy retired, was the Garter Day celebrations at Windsor Castle. This would be the first time Sandy's sister Rose would be expected to play her part as wife of a senior official. I hadn't realized what a hectic time faced the wives of officers of the Crown and of the Royal Household, for they were all expected to give parties for the staff and their wives. The public purpose of the day might be the celebration of the Most Noble Order of the Garter, founded by King Edward III in 1348, but as far as the hostesses were concerned, it was a sort of midsummer Hogmanay, with everybody going mad trying to have all in readiness for the first arrivals around half-past-eleven in the morning for drinks, followed by the provision of lunch for from thirty to sixty guests.

Sandy and I had gone over the night before, laden with items requested by Rose. Half-opened rosebuds from the garden for her vases, extra lettuces, a cucumber, and a pint of milk 'just in case', extra cutlery to eke out Rose and Tom's, for who would have sufficient to accommodate over thirty folk from their own canteen?

We leaped up and down on chairs and ladders to collect ashets and big containers from every corner of the kitchen and larder, and then set to work slicing cucumber, washing lettuces, shelling eggs, slitting radishes, and slicing tomatoes. Then it was into the deep freeze to remove the chicken breasts in aspic, the turkey mousse, and the pâté, and a word of encouragement to Sandy and Tom to start slicing the whole turkey so that we could arrange the food attractively on the serving dishes, and cover everything with clear-wrapping film. The marvellous thing about living in a castle is that there are acres of spacious shelves on which to arrange everything, many of them of lead which keeps everything cool and fresh.

We were dizzy with rushing around, and after a cup of tea, while Sandy and Tom sat down to watch television, Rose and I headed for their private garden for a breath of fresh air and to take a look at the changes there since our last visit. The weedy neglected plot was now filled with brilliant annuals, as though a fairy had waved a magic wand, and I was genuinely impressed.

On our way back to the Castle to resume our chores, we had a lively encounter with an Irish Guard who gave us a friendly grin, and asked, 'Do you two work in the Castle then?' Clearly he took us for a couple of domestics, and no wonder, with our flushed faces and working slacks. Rose drew herself up to her full five feet and said, in slightly outraged tones, 'I *live* here.' 'Is that so,' said he, without turning a hair, 'I might see you sometime then.'

I couldn't wait to get back to tell our spouses we had been chatted up by one of the Queen's guardsmen!

In the morning when I drew back the curtains, the thought crossed my mind that the Queen was maybe gazing at the self-same view from the windows of her private apartments nearby. But there wasn't time to stand there dreaming, for all the last-minute things had to be done. Cream to be whipped, sweets to be made, all the food to be set out on the buffet table. Outside bands marched, playing briskly. Detachments of soldiers tramped past our front door, on their way to take up their positions. A solitary guardsman was marched past, with a corporal in command. What could he have done? Then Rose's sharp eye spotted a six-inch slit in the back of his otherwise perfect trousers, revealing a most unceremonial flash of bare flesh! Banished for the duration of the ceremony, we wondered? Or just being handed over to a capable tailor?

Rose flew upstairs to get dressed, while I carried on checking all the dishes, making sure we had enough butter containers, and transferring more food from the shelves to the dining room.

In the middle of all this, just as if it had been Springburn, the doorbell rang and it was the insurance man! I could almost hear my mother's own voice, 'It's the man fae the Prudential!' I tried to persuade him to come back another day, as thirty guests were expected within the hour. Not a hope.

Forgetting I was in a Castle where modulated tones were expected, I yelled upstairs to Rose, 'What am I looking for?' and prepared to rifle a packed box-file.

'This, madam,' said the man at the door, not wasting a word or a minute, realizing this was a crisis. He held up the little red book. I found it – tucked at the very back of the box. Saved!

Outside, the gardener was snipping away any faded blooms from the geraniums in the moat. A huge suction cleaner picked up every odd leaf, matchstick and crumb on the long walk leading to St George's Chapel. A detachment of the Household Cavalry swung past, breast-plates glittering in the sun, plumes rising and falling, and everyone stopped to admire them. Somebody remarked that when the Household Cavalry were stationed in London in pre-decimalization days, people used to drop half-crowns down those long thigh-length boots. It was pretty uncomfortable, but they 'bravely' endured it for the small fortune they could empty out later!

As the first guest arrived, Rose whipped off all the plastic wrappings from the food and I headed for the bedroom to don my glad rags. In no time we were all chatting and sipping our sherries as though we'd been at ease all morning. At the last minute, somebody delivered a magnificent bouquet from the Royal gardens which, normally, I'd have drooled over and taken an hour to arrange properly. There was no time for such frivolities. I merely snipped the binding tape, placed the loosened bouquet in a big crystal vase and sat it in the fireplace and it looked superb.

The buffet lunch vanished like snow off a dyke under the enthusiastic attack of the guests, and we were just starting our coffee when the first notes of music alerted us to the fact that we ought to be heading for the balcony reserved for members of the Royal Household. That's the great thing in being on the inside. No queueing. No standing on tip-toe to try to see over the heads of six-footers or the soldiers lining the route. A ring-side seat, as though from a Royal box, with views of the chapel, the walking Royals in their Garter Day velvet tammies, and the crowds.

I was so glad we had decided to stay out of doors, and not avail ourselves of tickets to go inside the Chapel, for the day was magnificent, and the tourists in their summer outfits made a background like confetti for the scarlet uniforms of the soldiers. In the English manner, there was continuous applause for the Knights and the Royals, not cheering, and only the specially invited schoolchildren raised lusty 'hurrahs'.

The service was relayed to us by loudspeakers, and everyone listened with quiet attention, and followed the words on their programmes. When the open carriages brought them all back up the hill, nobody walking this time, there was more applause, and hundreds of cameras were held high to record the scene. It was quite hard to see who was who, for those big velvet tammies make a terrific disguise. I was amazed when the Queen Mother and Prince Charles had almost passed before I realized who they were. And me standing there watching for them!

So many little things you notice when you're actually there. The unexpected whisper of the air escaping from the long boots of the Household Cavalry as they were marched off. The little bursts of extra applause in appreciation of certain favourites among the Royal Family. The pale serene beauty of the Queen. The reluctance of people to move away, even after the last carriage had disappeared. The sight of every balcony filled with elegant guests, and glazed-eyed hostesses!

I found it to be a tremendously happy occasion, with something of the fun of the fair, combined with the gaiety of a garden party. But absolutely exhausting in the preparation of it all.

I can tell you we didn't have to rock the cradle when

we got home that night! We fell into bed, and slept the sleep of the just who had earned a night's repose.

There was one comical postscript to all this. I had been so staggered by the amount of work involved that I wrote a pretty full account of the occasion for a very popular magazine. All the guests who read it were so impressed by the sheer extent of the sort of catering required for such an occasion, that the following year Rose was inundated with offers of help! Even in a Castle, all hands are welcome when a mountain of dishes have to be washed, dried, and put away. It seemed to take hours when there were only the four of us.

After this rubbing shoulders with Royalty, there came a nice little assortment of television jobs. A very enjoyable one was when I was cast as the landlady of the honeymoon hotel in *All Creatures Great and Small*, for James and his bride after their marriage. Because the lady's name was Mrs Burns, the director decided she would be a Scot, and so I found myself rehearsing and working with the much-loved Siegfried, and Tristan, and James and of course the new bride. Carol Drinkwater has a most marvellous head of hair – a real mop of curls in everyday life, which had me lost in admiration and not a little envy! I love a good head of hair. Speaking of which, I had to wear a little 'twenties' wig for my part, a 'bobbed' effect, Marcel waved, with a side parting. I can't tell you the number of people who told me afterwards, 'Oh I thought your hair was far nicer in that *All Creatures* show – you should wear it like that all the time.' 'It was a *wig*,' I had to tell them, through slightly gritted teeth! And here was I, fondly imagining that my own hair looked pretty good. I know better now.

There was a very funny little episode when I played

the part of a woman who works in a fish and chip shop in the series *Doctor in the House*. We had to go to the other side of London for this, to a working-class district, where the TV people had found a great little fish and chip shop which was dead right for the cameras and the plot. I had a marvellous time shovelling fish and chips, rehearsing under the instruction of the owners, and within the hour I was reaching out for the correct wrappings, dishing out the right quantities, wielding the salt-shaker and the vinegar bottle to the manner born, and finally handing the parcel over the counter.

A 'watch-dog' from the TV team kept outsiders at bay while we prepared to shoot the scene. But, rather as I had done during the bomb scare in Regent Street, a wee old wifie had slipped round the guard's back, and I knew she hadn't the slightest idea that we were filming. Up she came to the counter, 'Ten-pennyworth of chips, love,' she said. I looked round desperately to see if anybody else would deal with her, but they were getting the marker-board ready, and making last-minute adjustments to the lighting.

I leaned forward and said to her, 'I'm sorry, I can't serve you . . .' I got no further. 'Why can't you serve me?' she said truculently. 'The shop's open ain't it? You got chips there, 'aven't you? Why can't you serve me?'

'Ten-pennyworth of chips,' she repeated.

I leaned forward again and said slowly and clearly, 'I'm sorry, I can't serve you because we're making a film. And you're right in the middle of it!'

She jumped as if I'd shot her. With a wild look round the shop, she took in the camera, the lights, the crew, and then rushed from the place shouting, 'Oh my Gawd. They're makin' a fillum, and 'ere I was

426

askin' fur ten-pennyworth of chips.' Suddenly she leaned against the door, and laughed and laughed. 'Och,' I said, 'give her one of those parcels we rehearsed with. They're still hot, and they're delicious.' She was delighted, and so was I. I must really have looked like the real thing to one customer at least!

I still get repeats for that *Doctor in the House* episode. Twenty pence from Malaysia, fifty pence from Zambia, forty pence from Australia, hardly enough to buy one of those mouth-watering fish suppers, and I never see the title on the invoice but I remember the ecstatic face of that wee customer who gate-crashed the set, and won a free fish supper.

But there were no prizes for me the day Sandy and I decided to go into town and enjoy London like a couple of tourists. The capital was choc-a-bloc with visitors. It looked like the cross-roads of the world as Arabs, Indians, French, Scandinavian, Germans, Italians and Americans strolled, or sat in deck chairs or lay back on the grass of St James's Park. I was so glad I'd decided to wear my favourite sparkling white dress with the Madeira embroidery, and when we found an empty bench for our picnic, I carefully laid a napkin on my lap, and reached for a sandwich. Next minute, disaster struck! My arm caught the full cup of scalding coffee and splashed the whole lot over my dress from neck to hem. You'd have thought I'd spilt six cups not one! I leaped to my feet, and held the dress away from me as much as I could to avoid being scalded. I certainly couldn't yank it off, much as I'd have liked to, with the 'League of Nations' gazing at me with polite dismay. It was a complete mess of huge stains.

We had intended going on to a theatre later, but there wasn't a hope of that now. We headed for Baker

427

Street, and I reasoned that everyone who looked would just say, 'Oh look at that poor soul. She has spilt something down her dress,' and then they'd forget both it and me. I was thankful to be mature enough to think like this. I was nagged by the thought, though, that I'd never get the stains out once they'd been sun-dried right into the material. I glanced down at my dress for the one and only time since the spillage, and held it up, saying to Sandy, 'How on earth will I ever get this mess out?'

Suddenly I heard a voice in the traffic calling from a car driving past, 'You'll easily get it out with Flash!' From the open car window David Jacob's face grinned at me, and my laughter over this marvellous piece of timing blew away the last of my vexation.

When TV work quietened down a bit, the publishers suggested I ought to get busy with book five of the autobiographies. Book four had just come out in paper-back, and they wanted the next book in the spring, so I concentrated on tackling the sequel to *Stepping into the Spotlight*. I had the odd broadcast and advert between times, but nothing seriously interrupted my writing schedule.

One day the telephone rang and it was my agent to see what I was doing in February, round about the first or second of the month, or possibly even the end of January. She always had to check with me, because as well as my acting performances which were booked through her, she knew I had dates for Associated Speakers and with Flash. I looked at my diary, and said that as far as I could see, there was only a possible Flash commercial which could always be rearranged if they knew early enough. It appeared that the Scottish Tourist Board wanted me to go up to Scotland in May, to make a film to promote tourism for them, but at this stage they merely wished to check if I was free, if I was interested, and if I would be prepared to do an opening shot for them either at the end of January or early February, showing me leaving from Euston Station. Because Euston was a working station, they had to take whatever date was most convenient for them, and it was suggested by British Rail that January or early February would be best. We would just pretend this was me leaving in the merry month of May, for inside a station nobody would know what time of the year it was.

I was agog with excitement. Putting my hand over the mouthpiece, I said to Sandy, who was hovering by the kitchen door, 'Sandy, they want me to go up to Scotland in May, isn't that great? You come too, and we'll have a holiday out of it, for my fares will have been paid.' Always the prudent Scot, I seize the chance of a holiday the moment somebody pays my fares to any enticing location.

My agent came back again, having checked her own diary, and told me that she would be in touch with the firm date later. She couldn't say exactly where I was going to do the filming in Scotland; all that would be arranged in good time. It was merely the preliminary shot from Euston they were concerned about, so that they could go ahead and make their plans with the Railway authorities.

That winter Sandy seemed much more content to whizz about on his own doing the shopping, disappearing for hours to the library, and cycling far afield for fruit bargains. He even went into town one day and bought himself a dinner suit at a sale in Moss Bros. I was quite bemused, for normally he likes me to hand out a bit of advice when he's buying major items like this, but when I offered to go with him, he said, 'No,

429

no, I'll manage fine. You get on with the book, that's far more important.'

So I settled down to the writing, and was amazed to find what a surprising amount of time I was able to devote to this book, without having the slightest feeling of guilt that Sandy was finding time hanging heavy on his hands.

My agent rang again within a week or two, to tell me that the date had been definitely fixed for 2 February. I was reminded to wear clothes appropriate to the merry month of May. Nobody looking at the finished film would guess that the shot of my departure had been done months before. The important thing was to look suitably summery when I was filmed getting off the train in Scotland at the other end, when it would actually be May. I wondered how I was going to disguise my red nose on a freezing February day in light weight skirt, a jacket you could have 'spat peas' through, and fine shoes. I decided I'd take my cape along to keep my legs warm, even although they'd said they would send a car.

It was bitterly cold and there was a fall of snow in the morning. When I looked out of the window I said to Sandy, 'I think I'll ring the Tourist people and tell them I'll go in by train. It's far more reliable than risking being held up on snowy roads.' 'Och I wouldn't do that,' said Sandy. 'The train might be held up and they wouldn't know where you were. Just you take the chance of a comfortable warm ride into London.'

'Och aye, you're quite right,' I said. 'I'll let them do the worrying, and it's only a short sequence after all. It shouldn't take long.'

I spent the whole morning in the gazebo, writing, and was slightly irritated by the way Sandy kept hovering around, asking me when I'd be coming in for lunch;

430

what I'd be wearing on my feet, and whether I wanted to take perfume and make-up with me.

'Sandy,' I said, 'a quarter to one will be time enough to come in. They're not coming with the car till two o'clock and I want to delay as long as possible taking off these warm trousers.' I sighed slightly impatiently, 'And of course I don't need to take perfume with me. I've got it on, and it'll surely last for the hour I'll be at Euston.'

That's what I thought!

When I was ready, Sandy suddenly decided to inspect my shoes, and gave it as his opinion that my flatties weren't very elegant to travel into London with a movie director. 'Sandy,' I said, 'they'll not see my *feet*. It's my head and shoulders they're interested in, I'm just to be seen waving from the carriage windows.' I had put warm insoles into the flat shoes, and nothing was going to part me from their comfort on this icy day. 'Just try on your court shoes,' Sandy coaxed, 'I think they look nicer with your suit.' To humour him, I put them on, privately amazed at the interest he was taking in this quite small engagement. '*Far* nicer,' he beamed. 'I'd wear those if I were you.' 'All right,' I said, 'but I'm going to wear the insoles with them even if they cripple me.'

I found there was just time to varnish my nails, and Sandy flew back and forward to the front window like a hen on a hot girdle watching for the car. 'Sit down and keep warm,' I said. 'The man will ring the bell, and he'll just have to wait till my nails dry anyway.' I was just at my pinkie when the bell rang, and on the doorstep stood a tall man in a white suit, looking every inch a movie director. 'Will these clothes do?' I asked him, after he'd introduced himself as Maurice George. 'Will they look right for the later shot showing me

431

getting off the train in May?' He hardly even glanced at them, and me 'chittering' with cold just to please him. 'Yes, yes,' he said, 'they're fine.'

I turned to Sandy, 'Just take the tripe out of the fridge about four o'clock,' I said, 'I'll cook it when I get back. I should be home about half-past-five at the latest.' I turned to the Tourist Board man, 'It won't take longer than that, will it?' 'No,' he said, 'that should be all right.'

He was most attentive. When I wanted the car stopped to drop some letters into a pillar-box, he seized them and posted them for me. Again, when I asked if I could drop some letters into the BBC when we were passing, thriftily taking the chance of saving about a dozen stamps, he wouldn't let me budge out of the car, but leaped out and did this little task himself. 'Nice man,' I thought, 'typical filming spoiling!'

We chatted about writing, about books, and of course about the film, and I was slightly surprised that he didn't seem to be too certain about exactly what poses we'd strike when we actually got down to taking the pictures at Euston. For I now discovered that it was 'stills' we were taking, and it was not a filmed sequence at all.

'But why do we have to go to Euston to take still photographs?' I asked. And then, before he could answer, I said, 'Oh of course, where else could we find an inter-city train but in a station?' I make life very easy for deceivers!

To my delight, he suggested that as we were a bit early for the railway people, we should go and have some tea. We actually went into the newly refurbished Ritz. The Ritz, indeed! This was spoiling with a vengeance. Even as I was preparing for an orgy of cucumber sandwiches, we were told we were too early for

432

tea. They didn't start serving for another hour, so we headed for a French pâtisserie where I devoured a huge chocolate meringue, and made a fine old mess of my lips and teeth, and drank a whole pot of tea.

It was the last bite of food I was to enjoy for two whole days, I may say.

We reached Euston at exactly 3.55 P.M. We were due at four o'clock.

'My word,' I said, 'you're very exact. Suppose the car had been held up?'

We went through the ticket barrier with the words, 'We're the Scottish Tourist Board,' and were nodded past. This made me laugh. 'I like our cheek,' I said. 'Just the two of us. *We* are the Scottish Tourist Board.'

As we strolled down the ramp, I saw a crowd standing at the bottom. 'Oh,' I said with some excitement, 'the Queen must be coming. There's a crowd gathered down there.' Never for one moment did I think that that crowd had anything to do with me.

Then to the right of the ramp, near the crowd, I spotted a pipe band. 'Oh,' I said, 'maybe she's come from Balmoral.'

The next moment, as I wondered why the director wasn't pushing through the crowd to reach the train for our photography session, lights blazed, there was a skirl of the pipes, and from somewhere, like a Jack-in-the-box, out jumped Eamonn Andrews with the famous red book, and said, 'MOLLY WEIR, THIS IS YOUR LIFE'.

'But I'm here to do a film for the Scottish Tourist Board,' I said indignantly, and I turned to the big director who had brought me. 'Will you ever forgive me?' he said.

My stomach turned over, my legs turned to jelly, and I realized this big man was all part of the plot.

I covered my face with my hands, and said, 'Oh Eamonn. Oh crikey!'

Then in sudden awareness, I said, 'Am I not going to Scotland in May at all?'

The man shook his head.

'And there's no Scottish Tourist job?' I asked.

Again a shake of the head.

It was such a disorientated feeling, that I was pulverized and my mind became a complete blank.

I was whisked away to a hotel with the big man, but I have no recollection of how we got there. By this time I was shaking so much and felt so sick with fright that I had to ask for my ever-reliable Phosferine tablets. I could have had practically anything else in the way of food, drink or sustenance, but not a Phosferine tablet was there in the entire place. In desperation I searched through my purse, found a 'stoury' squashed one which had been there for weeks, and washed that under the tap and then sucked it feverishly to see if it would give me some strength, and control of my shaking limbs.

Then a thousand questions. 'What about clothes? Oh can I ring Sandy? He'll die of fright if you spring this on him for he won't know anything about it. Can I ring my sister-in-law?'

'No, you can't ring anybody.'

I was persuaded to take a tiny drop of champagne and nibble at a sandwich, and then, with my teeth still chattering with shock, was taken by car to the Thames studios.

I was smuggled through a side entrance, passed from hand to hand, and locked into a make-up room. When the girl saw my hair was long, she said, 'Oh I can't do long hair very well. Would you like to do it yourself?'

It was at exactly that moment that I decided the

whole thing was simply a very vivid dream. It all fitted. Make-up girls didn't suggest you did your own hair. They *loved* doing hair. That was what they were paid for. And nobody kept champagne on ice in make-up rooms, except in dreams. Why was there no tea, but plenty of champagne? They didn't even have an elastic band for my topknot of hair. In a make-up room in the heart of London! Of course, I was dreaming.

There was no doubt about it.

The clothes which were hanging up confirmed it. There was my long dress. There was also a top but no long skirt. There was a tiny short petticoat. And there was a fur coat. And gold shoes. And an odd belt. It had all the daft irrelevancies of a state of dreaming, and suddenly I became as calm as a cucumber and thought I must remember as much of it as possible so I could tell Sandy when I wakened up.

CHAPTER NINETEEN

Until Sandy walked on to that TV stage, I didn't know that he had been in the plot since *Christmas*. I could not believe it. I would never have thought him capable of acting such a part for so long.

Later, much later, those mysterious telephone calls, the disappearances to 'get the paper', or 'go to the library', fell into place. When there is perfect trust, there is no suspicion. But it wasn't deceit on his part, he was just keeping a confidence. He told me later he absolutely hated it, and at times he couldn't believe that I could be so naïve, and so unquestioning. I've always said I would be the easiest person in the world to kidnap, for I never believe anyone would do me any harm, and if a car arrives for me I step into it, confident I will be taken where I am supposed to be going.

I always said, too, that I would never do a *This Is Your Life*, for I was far too emotional and would be in floods of tears from start to finish. In the event, I never shed a tear, for I was too caught up in my dream.

Another of the things I 'always said' was that I would *never* be caught, for I would know at once if anything was phoney. And I *was* well and truly caught. They couldn't have thought up a better trap if they'd thought for a hundred years. For, having already done work for the Scottish Tourist Board, and having a long-standing love affair with trains, it seemed the most natural thing in the world to be asked to take part in a film for them, and to be photographed in a railway station.

The rest of the show, and the party, and the pipers, were unforgettable.

Those who know my volatile temperament were amazed when they looked in and saw how happy and composed I was. They couldn't know that the shock had been so complete that it had frozen all my normal emotions, and I had given myself up to my vivid dream.

How else could I have leaped up in front of an audience of over *nine million* and sung a song I hadn't thought of for years, without giving a thought that I might not remember a word?

How else could I have remembered without the slightest hesitation the names of people I hadn't seen for years?

How else accepted the fact that my brother Tommy disappeared from the scene afterwards without a word to me? Actually he had had to fly back to Scotland for his own TV filming the next morning, but I didn't even question the reason for his leaving.

The pipers came to the party, and we danced and we sang, and I did a Highland Fling, and played the drums. The whole thing was the most exciting madness.

And then, suddenly, the dream was going on too long. I felt exhausted and said, 'I want to go home.'

A car arrived, and Sandy collected the flowers and the champagne, and we dropped Rose and Tom off at Charing Cross Station, and we went home.

Sandy had arranged tickets for them to be in the audience, but I questioned nothing at that time. I was coasting along with the very tiring dream still.

It was only when we reached our own house and the telephone started ringing after midnight, and we read the notes which were lying in the hall from the neighbours, that I wakened up, and realized with a dazed sense of shock that it had all actually happened.

It wasn't a dream. I had really seen all those friends and colleagues. Willie Joss, and Jack House from Glasgow. My brother Tommy. Moultrie Kelsall and Ruby Duncan from Edinburgh. Janet Brown and Moira Anderson. Deryck Guyler. And Ben, my old boss Ben Lyon, all the way from Hollywood. Isa from Springburn. How did she get there? Where had she stayed?

I never slept a wink all night. Each time I was on the point of drifting off, I re-lived that frightening moment when Eamonn Andrews had leaped out at me with the big red book, and I shot up wide awake, as if I'd been hit over the head with it.

All next day I talked and talked, trying to unwind. Things I had never noticed at the time suddenly became significant. Sandy's interest in my shoes, for of course he knew I'd be seen full-length walking down that ramp towards the cameras. His persuasiveness that I ought to let them take me by car while I had the chance, and not change my plans and go by train. He said that when he told Eamonn this during their rehearsal, Eamonn had said, 'Thank God nobody told me. It would have ruined everything.' The director's lack of interest in my clothes, and his keeping me safely in that car until he could deliver me at the right spot at just the right time. Those 'wrong' numbers when I would pick up the telephone – they had been from Thames of course. My agent's confusion when I answered the telephone one day when she had expected me to be out. I had changed my hair appointment without telling Sandy! Sandy's insistence that he bought the dinner suit without taking me to town! That had been the day, he told me, when he had met the man I knew as Maurice George (he was really Maurice Leonard) to hand over some photographs. It all made sense bit by bit, and I wondered how I could have been so blind.

Next day the letters started coming. Scores of them. People wrote whom we hadn't heard from for years. The telephone went non-stop. There were the telegrams and the bouquets and the poems. There were even letters from dozens of people who hadn't seen the show, apologizing for having missed it, and wondering if I could possibly have it repeated!

The common theme of many of the letters was that the writer had just been on the point of going out, or hadn't had the TV switched on, and that the telephone had rung umpteen times, with the voices of friends shouting down the 'phone, 'Molly's on – switch on *This Is Your Life*,' before banging down the receiver.

One of the funniest was from a vicar to whose parish

my dear old Blackpool landlady had retired. Olive and her sisters had taken good care of me when I was in Blackpool with *Life With the Lyons*, and now she lived alone. The vicar knew I kept in touch with her, and what a valued friendship ours was. He had been out delivering the church magazines that evening when suddenly, waiting at the door of one house, he heard Eamonn's voice announcing the famous words, 'Molly Weir – This is Your Life'. He told me he simply threw the magazine in his hand through the open door, picked up his cassock, and *ran* non-stop through the village street and catapulted right into Olive's sitting room. Before she could draw breath to ask what was the matter, he had switched on the TV, and they both watched the show to the end, without a word being spoken. He was out of breath anyway, and Olive was speechless with joy in meeting on television all my friends and family. She especially loved seeing Ben Lyon again, for she was a great fan, and she was thrilled they had brought him all that way to be on my programme.

It was the top show nationwide that week, and it won the Bouquet of Roses from the *Sunday Mail*, a bouquet awarded by the readers and viewers by popular vote.

It was the most staggering thing that had ever happened to me in a life packed with challenges and surprises, and I thanked the good Lord from the bottom of my heart that it could not happen twice. I could never again be so lucky to be protected from making a fool of myself with tears and terror, because of my absolute certainty that I was dreaming. It was a wonderful accolade, but it was also the most tremendous shock, and it took me a long long time before I could eat or sleep properly.

439

Alas, my temperamental teeth, which are the most accurate barometers of my state of health and nerves, at once set up a perfect storm of jangling in their sensitive roots, and two of them formed raging abscesses and had to be whipped out! That was the price I was most reluctant to pay for *This Is Your Life*.

Although I didn't know it, that public occasion was to be the last time I was to see my dear old boss and colleague Ben Lyon, in the flesh. We did speak on the telephone when he came to London with Marion, his wife, and they actually made a date to come out to Pinner for tea. Then Marion thought she would like to visit Stonehenge and as there wouldn't have been time to do both, we left Pinner for another time. It was a strange situation for me, knowing so much of what was in Ben's heart, and yet seeing him on former visits taking such tender care of this immaculately groomed little blonde lady who was his second wife. Ben was the sort of man who needed to look after someone. Yet, at the same time, he told me he knew the years were passing and so he had made all the necessary arrangements on that last visit to London, that Bebe's ashes would be taken to Hollywood and buried with his when the time came.

I think it was I who put the idea into his head to take up celebrity lecturing. I had suggested that he join Associated Speakers when he lived in London, but he was much too nervous at that time following Bebe's death. Later, in Hollywood, he assembled a wonderful collection of old film clips and accepted an invitation to join the company of celebrity lecturers on board the QE2. Moira Anderson told me he was tremendously popular, and a first-class performer, for she went on those cruises as an entertainer too. I knew Ben would be a 'natural'. Anyone who had ever watched him 'warming up' an audience realized what a warm rapport he had with his public, and his new career aboard the luxury cruise-ship was tailor-made for him. He could take Marion with him, they could live in the style to which they were both accustomed, and he was able to exercise his talents as an actor. He quickly graduated to become entertainments officer of the QE2, and had the time of his life. He always said the BBC was so 'cheap' in providing only second-class travel! He was born to travel first-class!

And he died travelling not only first-class, but state-room too, and almost with his boots on. He took a heart attack in the middle of the night, after a successful and happy evening, and knew no more.

My 'phone started ringing before eight next morning. It was Barbara, telling me 'Daddy's dead.' She had rung me only the night before and joked as she told me, 'Daddy is in Japan. He's working the boats.' This was her humorous way of telling me he was off on one of his lecturing tours aboard the QE2.

'You'd better get up,' Sandy said, 'for you never know if you'll be wanted to go into the BBC to be interviewed.'

He was already dressed and went out to get his bike to go down for the newspaper, and to his amazement there was a huge BBC van drawn up right outside our front door. 'Do you happen to know where Molly Weir lives?' called out the man at the wheel. 'I do,' said Sandy. 'She's in there – she's my wife.'

They waited until I was bathed and dressed, and then they moved the furniture around on the very carpet Richard had fitted and which I had bought from their antique shop when our *Life With the Lyons* series came to an end. I was interviewed at length, and I found family photographs for them, and after an hour they left. That night I was seen on television paying my tribute to Ben, and to Bebe. They showed a clip from one of our TV shows, and I felt the deepest sense of loss that never again would I hear that deep rich voice calling down the telephone, 'Hi there Aggie. When are you coming to have tea with me at the Dorchester.' It had been a long and lasting friendship.

Bebe's ashes are now with his in the Hollywood where they met, wooed and married.

Marion survived him by four years, and sent me a card each Christmas. She was a sweet little lady, but it always seemed strange to me to see her notepaper headed 'Marion Lyon'.

That year when I was featured in *This Is Your Life* was a year of tremendous happenings for me. If I had ever wondered in the past whether a particular year was my prime, I must have enjoyed a second one in 1977.

Unlike the Woman of the Year event in London, which nominates no one woman but regards each and every woman who is invited as 'Woman of the Year' in her own right, Scotland does name its top woman. She is chosen by public ballot by the readers of the *Glasgow Evening Times*, having first been nominated by accredited organizations and put on a short list.

I had found myself on the short list on several occasions, but that was as far as I got. However, four months after the *This Is Your Life* programme, I had custody of the magnificent silver rose bowl at last! But, funnily enough, for the first time in the history of the award, it was a tied vote. Neck and neck the votes poured in for me and for Agnes Hoey, a charming and talented musician, who was conductor of the 300-strong Glasgow Youth Choir, and because there's no such thing as a casting vote for this award, it was decided I should keep the rose bowl for six months, and Agnes would have it for the second six months.

This brought a neat little poem on a lovely card from a reader:

> From radio to 'big' screen
> You've gied us mony laughs,
> But I'll wager it's the first time,
> You've done a thing by 'halfs'.

By coincidence they had invited my brother Tommy to present the rose bowl, so on Jubilee day while the Queen rode in state through London town, Tommy was handing me the bowl as joint Scotswoman of the Year. It was a lovely memento of a very special year, but it was of such a size and weight that I was quite thankful it had to be left behind to have our names inscribed. The wee silver trophy was easier to fit into my case, and was mine for keeps.

Because of the clashing of the dates, though, I saw nothing of the London Jubilee celebrations and had to get Sandy's account of it second-hand. He had gone into town to enjoy being part of the millions of happy revellers who lined every route to cheer on our beloved Queen.

So there he was in London celebrating, and there I was north of the Border, being fêted by my fellow-Scotswomen.

In the evening, in Tommy's house by Loch Lomond, it was a curious feeling to be watching on TV the bonfire being lit in Windsor, where Rose and Tom were, and then looking out of Tommy and Rhona's window and seeing the beacon blazing on top of the nearby hill.

We had actually been invited to the Windsor celebrations, but with the best will in the world 'ye canna be in two places at once!' Except via the magic of television!

STV interviewed Agnes and me 'live', with our bouquets, and our silver goblets, and the viewers who had voted for us were delighted to see us wearing our best hats and dressed to kill! I was thankful it was our Tommy who had presented the cup and could wait for me to take me down to Loch Lomond by car. I would have felt a real daisy walking through Glasgow or travelling on the local train in a cream dress with emerald satin waistcoat and matching hat, carrying an enormous bouquet and brandishing a cup. Shades of Wembley!

When the inscribed rose bowl did reach Pinner, the garden was ablaze with roses, and we filled it, and Sandy took transparencies of me standing by it in the garden, just to have a souvenir of the occasion for the 'archives'.

And when our own roses were finished, and it was almost time to hand the lovely bowl back, lo and behold the *Sunday Mail* readers voted my TV appearance on the Joan Bakewell interview programme as the winner of the Bouquet of Roses award, and three dozen red roses again filled the bowl with their beauty and scent.

Then came one of the most enjoyable dates that year, all the more so for being utterly devoid of nervous fears, and that was when I was invited to be Roy Plomley's guest on that famous desert island. I'd listened to it so often, for it is a favourite programme, that I felt I'd rehearsed it for years, so I settled down happily to choose my eight discs, my luxury object, and that 'one book apart from the Bible and Shakespeare which I would already have on the island'. When I was asked the question, 'If you could only have one disc, which would it be?' I unhesitatingly chose Sir Hugh Roberton conducting the Glasgow Orpheus Choir in *All in the April Evening*. This would remind me of dear Miss Chree and Sandy, and the memorable Christmasses we spent together, when that particular record had been her delight. The choice of my luxury object presented no problems either. It had to be a typewriter with an inexhaustible supply of paper, for if I have the tools for writing I am never lonely. And for that 'one book' which would enrich my mind and provide escape into another imagination, I chose Compton McKenzie's *Four Winds of Love*. As I'm almost as garrulous as he was (no disrespect, Sir Compton!), and am bidding fair to follow in his busy footsteps as far as numbers go, with this seventh book of autobiographical writings (he reached ten!), it seemed an excellent idea to take him along for company. I've always loved his writings, and although I knew only too well I wasn't in his league, I felt I could profitably learn from him during my stay on that island.

That year too, *Stepping into the Spotlight* was published in paperback, and although rehearsals cut short some of the launching excitements of interviews and lunches, I managed to finish *Walking into the Lyons' Den* for the hardback edition, and to enjoy the fun of the usual launching parties.

That was a year that was, and I felt it could only be downhill all the way from then on!

There might have been a wee omen, though, of other things ahead when I went to Skegness one Saturday evening to speak to a ladies' club. Because there were no trains from there on Sundays, I had to be taken by car next morning to a station some distance away where I could pick up a connection. My hostess driver brought along an old lady for company, and we

445

had a hilarious episode when we reached the traffic lights which were close to the house where Margaret Thatcher had lived as a girl. 'We'll just stop the car here,' said the old lady, tapping the driver on the back. Obediently the car drew to a halt.

'Now,' said the old lady, as if she had all the time in the world, 'you see that corner over there? That's where Margaret Thatcher's father's shop was, and in that house above it is where she lived as a very small girl.'

The traffic lights, meantime, had changed to green, but the old lady completely ignored them, *and* the traffic which was now behind us.

'Now just look across the road there. Do you see where I'm pointing?' 'Yes,' I said, nervously glancing at the queue of cars. 'Well, they moved there later on, and she lived there till she went to her other school.'

The lights had gone from red to amber and were back at green again.

'I think the lights have changed,' I said, risking her wrath in my attempt to get us moving.

'Och,' she said, as if explaining some simple truth to a backward child, 'you don't *have* to go when the lights change to green. That's just to let you know that you *can* go if it suits you.'

I had never heard such comical reasoning conveyed in such commonsense tones, and I simply couldn't stop laughing. Strangely enough, in a recent interview with Mrs Thatcher, she herself spoke of those self-same traffic lights, so they must have meant a lot to her too.

It said much for the patience and good nature of the drivers in that area that they never even tooted their horns as they waited for us to move. Maybe they thought we'd stalled, or were disciples at the shrine of the home and shop once graced by their local heroine

Margaret Thatcher, but it is a fact that they seemed quite content to allow us to take all the time we needed to mark the spot on that lovely Sunday morning.

I had only heard of Mrs Thatcher as a very able politician on the Opposition benches at that time, but when the momentous decision was made that she would stand against Edward Heath as leader, we all realized that here was a lady of courage and enterprise. Truly a lass of many parts.

Then came the election fever, and one day when I answered the telephone I was very surprised to be asked by an actor friend if I minded, as an actress, being identified with the Conservative Party. In the world of the arts, it is very unfashionable to be right-wing! All the trendies and the militants are for Labour or Communism, and are very anti-establishment. This actor had heard me many times denouncing the extremists at our Equity meetings and he knew my politics, but didn't know if I would be willing to be identified in public as a Conservative.

'Of course I don't mind,' I said. 'I'm not ashamed of my politics, but what do you want me to do?'

It appeared there was to be a huge CTU rally at Wembley Conference Hall, and they'd like me to appear on stage with Maggie and other celebrities. CTU, I learned, meant Conservative Trade Unionists. This was to demonstrate that there were many trade unionists who were also conservatives.

'All right,' I said, relieved that I wasn't to be asked to speak, but just to appear, 'I'll come. Let me know what time you want me.' I'd never been in Wembley Conference Hall and it would be interesting to attend a political conference for once in my life.

The place was seething when we got there, and Sandy went into the body of the hall while I was taken round a perfect maze of corridors until I reached a private back room where I joined my other 'celebrities'. There were Nigel Davenport, Maria Aitken, Pete Murray, Sebastian Breaks, Vince Hill, and one or two others. Lulu was to join us later. We would have Willie Whitelaw and Jim Prior, and our own local MP Jack Page on the platform with us, and possibly other top Conservative men as well.

After about half-an-hour, an official took us through to the hall and on to the stage, and we were introduced one by one to a vast audience. It was absolutely riveting. The seats were packed, and each trade or profession was indicated by huge banners held high in front of their particular section. I had chosen to wear my kilt and black velvet jacket, and there was a roar from the Scottish contingent the moment I was introduced, and a huge Scottish flag appeared. I felt like Muhammed Ali going into the ring, holding my arms high and walking round the front of the platform to greet all sides of the house!

It was all quite spontaneous and suddenly tremendously exciting. Sandy told me afterwards that I actually seemed quite sedate in my demeanour, but happy and cheerful looking, and quite at home. It's not too difficult to give that impression, of course, when that is all that is expected of you. It's the ordeal of addressing huge audiences which weakens the sinews and sets the heart skipping a few beats.

Vince Hill sang, the organist played, and there were speeches from Pete Murray (excellent), and from the politicians, and as everybody in the hall had been handed leaflets with the words, we all sang to the tune of 'Hello Dolly':

Hello Maggie, Well hello Maggie,
Now you're really on the Road to No 10.

You're going strong Maggie, won't be long Maggie,
Till you turn that key, then Mrs T. you'll see Big Ben.
All wreathed in smiles Maggie, in the aisles Maggie
They'll be dancing on that very special day.
So here's to you Maggie, give them old one-two Maggie,
Maggie we're right behind you all the way.

Lulu had slipped in at the back, and she and Vince
Hill sang together, and then just when I was wondering
when Mrs Thatcher would appear, the audience were
rising to their feet, banners waving, cheering, and
she was walking across the platform and taking her
applause. I whispered to Lulu, 'This is when we should
have sung "Hello Maggie".' And as though reading
my lip movements, a man's voice, with unmistakable
Glasgow accent, shouted out from the crowd, 'Whit
aboot the song? We should have the song noo.'

Vince Hill and Lulu signalled to the organist, who
had sat down by this time, we on the platform rose to
our feet, handed the bewildered Mrs Thatcher a leaflet,
drew her along with us to stand round the organ, and
lustily we all sang, audience, Maggie and platform
party, 'Hello Maggie', till I thought the roof would fly
off. The TV cameras had a field day, for it certainly
made great television, and from later reports I think
the whole of the country saw it. It had all the razzama-
tazz of American elections, and was very different
from the usual Conservative Conferences.

Mrs Thatcher spoke well when the time came to
address the conference, and we were introduced to her
and to Denis and all the others afterwards, and then
she disappeared into the body of the hall to do a sort
of miniature 'walk-about'. I thought that was the end
of it, as far as we were concerned, but suddenly she
was back again among us and somebody said she
wanted to meet me. As we were speaking, another

voice asked her what she was doing next, and she said, 'The thing I like least – just me and the TV camera, addressing the potential voters.'

I hesitated for a moment, and then I said, 'If I can be of any help, please ask me. Speaking directly to the camera is something I am very used to, for I have been telling stories on STV for some time now.'

She took both my hands in both of hers, looked at me with immense concentration and said, 'Tell me.'

My goodness, but she can listen. When you are speaking to her, her eyes never leave yours and her attention is complete. I swallowed nervously and plunged in. Speaking from my own experience, I suggested that during the 'count-down' she gave herself something to do, such as picking up a tissue, or a handkerchief left lying nearby. Anything but sitting staring at the camera, waiting to speak. However experienced anyone is, it's like posing for a photograph. Even ten seconds can 'fix' the expression in an unnatural stare. 'Get the floor manager to give you a low hand-signal,' I said. 'Your eye will catch it, even if you're not looking at him. And when you get that, swing round to the camera as though someone had come into the room, and your eyes will be alive and welcoming, and so will your first words.'

I gave a slightly embarrassed laugh when I'd finished, 'Mind you that's if your producer will allow you to do all that. But I always do it with my stories, and it seems to achieve a natural effect.'

As she squeezed my hands and said 'thank you,' I suddenly thought with a tremor of alarm at my own daring, 'My goodness, I'm having the nerve to hand out advice to somebody who might well be the Prime Minister of the United Kingdom next week.'

Which she was.

Between the Conference and that victory, I was roped in to campaign for her. Again, this was something I'd never done in my life before. I took along a packet of Flash, stood outside factory gates and said, 'Get Maggie in in a *Flash*!' to the workers as they came out. Even if they didn't agree with my advice, they recognized me from television and it made them laugh. My little 'prop' packet also made me feel less self-conscious.

I went to a few districts with the campaigning MPs and knocked on doors, chatted to the occupants, and if we talked almost as much about *Life With the Lyons* and Flash as on Conservative policies, at least I was welcomed and not chased for my life!

Two of the MPs I campaigned for got in. The third one didn't, so two out of three wasn't too bad a score for a novice! I was really only the tiniest cog in the machine which worked for both MPs, but it was fun being associated even in a small way with the winners.

It was quite amusing to have to go into Broadcasting House the morning after the election to do a broadcast, and find myself rubbing shoulders with several Conservative MPs and Ministers who had also been there recording some interviews, and finding myself on nodding terms with them. Norman St John Stevas, whom I had last heard addressing us on the subject of the Arts, giving us his plans for all sorts of projects, was now devouring a banana with all the fervour of a man who has had to miss his breakfast.

I was tempted to greet him with the old Glasgow query, 'Are your jaws goin' the way you want them?' but refrained. It would have made a marvellous 'candid camera' shot for some lucky photographer! I like St John Stevas. He's a nice 'chiel' with a witty turn of phrase, very human and very sincere, and natural

451

enough not to be in the least put out to be seen enjoying a sustaining banana tit-bit in the foyer of the BBC on the morning after such a famous victory.

Always when I have had a new and interesting experience like the election capers, I look out at the garden and say to myself, 'Well, I wouldn't mind having a nice wee quiet spell for a while to plant the bulbs, and really tackle all that tidying I resolve to clear up every New Year's Day.' And always something unexpected happens. That year it was an invitation to take part in a new radio series starring Tim Brooke-Taylor, Patricia Hayes, John Graham, Kenneth Connor and myself. It was a long time since I had been a regular member of a radio series, and it was great fun to be working at the Paris Cinema again, the scene of all those *ITMA* recordings, and of years and years of working in *Life With the Lyons*. Alas, in the age of television, radio comedy was to prove very tricky, and it was almost impossible to predict what would capture the public imagination. Success proved elusive, in spite of such an experienced team of players, and the series only lasted a short six weeks.

It was, naturally, very disappointing for all of us, but for me it wasn't the end of the world, for I was now doing so much writing that I just heaved a sigh for our dashed hopes, and settled down once more in front of the typewriter.

I had been exceptionally lucky in the long runs I had enjoyed in the theatre, on radio and on television, and if I never had another name part in another series, it was still stimulating and enjoyable to go into various successful series for a single show, as a guest artist, and I loved meeting old friends and new talent whenever such opportunities arose. The North Acton studios were particularly exciting, for all the BBC shows rehearsed there, and I used to say if a bomb had fallen on it, it would have wiped out practically the entire acting profession. I was still sufficiently star-struck to enjoy sitting having coffee with Ronnie Barker, and I used to shake with silent laughter when I would observe Ronnie Corbett balancing his coffee cup in the canteen, standing at his big partner's elbow, in just the same manner as at those hilarious cocktail parties which formed part of many of their sketches.

I loved sharing jokes with the *Last of the Summer Wine* cast, and I was secretly very amused on the day when I was sitting alone at a table, and my old friend and colleague Patricia Hayes came rushing over to join me for a quick coffee. Our shouts of laughter drew every eye, for Patricia is quite as much of an extrovert as I am, and within ten minutes practically every well-known name had found an excuse to pass our table to say 'hullo' and 'congratulations', for it was within a few days of Patricia having won the television award for her brilliant performance in *Edna, the Inebriate Woman*, and everybody wanted to meet her. Thanks to Patricia, that was truly a star-studded coffee break!

I had quite settled down to the rhythm of this 'guesting' existence, when out of the blue came an invitation to lunch with a director of children's television. A soft Dublin voice was telling me where and at what hour I should meet him at the Television Centre. It appeared they were considering me for the part of the Witch Hazel in the children's TV series called *Rentaghost*. I had never met Jeremy Swan, although I knew he was producer/director of this successful children's series, whose scripts were written by the same talented and inventive writer who had collaborated with Bebe Daniels in *Life With the Lyons*. I had known Bob Block for years, of course, when he worked with Bebe, and now it seemed he had written this part of the witch with me in mind. It only needed Jeremy Swan's approval to make it happen. I hoped fervently that my face would fit, for I have always loved working for children, and I particularly adored the thought of playing a different sort of witch.

The moment I saw Jeremy, I knew I wanted to work for him. The eyes were bright with humour, the manner was warm and welcoming, and if I had to be let down I knew he would do it kindly. In appearance he was like a slimmer, younger, Irish version of Paul Newman, and I can't remember a thing we ate during that interview, I laughed so much. We both decided it was a great idea that I should come into the series as a visiting witch to help out with a magic spell which had gone wrong, and that was how I became Hazel the McWitch.

I was only supposed to be in that one episode, but it became two, and then in the next series I found I was in three of the stories. In the next one, I was included in four of the episodes, and eventually I was in all of them.

It's one of the never-failing delights of show business that there is always something new to learn, and for me it was an absorbing exercise adapting to the techniques required to perform 'witchcraft'. I had to teach myself to watch a monitor screen as I 'flew', so that I would know exactly at what angle I should hold my body in relation to the broomstick. I didn't even know that CSO meant Colour Separation Overlay, and I was entranced by the trick photography. I was sitting watching a monitor when suddenly I saw a tiny witch about four inches high on the screen. 'Oh,' I thought, 'they've made a wee model of me – what a good likeness.'

As I stared, I raised my hand in wonder, and so did the wee 'model'. Only then did I realize I was looking at myself reduced to the size of a doll.

I loved my costume, with its layers of materials to form a flowing cape over a cream 'nightdress', and a grey skirt, pointed hat and black mittens, and wee striped socks. But with the perversity of life, my hair stayed so neat and sedate under the pointed hat that Jeremy decided I would look wilder with it down, and so at last my long hair was right for a witchy part. This time it didn't have to be hidden under a balaclava as in that Derby production of Shakepeare's story! I was so glad I hadn't had it cut off.

When I read Bob's script, I decided to make Hazel a sort of *Blithe Spirit*, with silvery sparkly make-up, long eyelashes, green fingernails, and gold-dust round my lips. A glamorous fairy-tale witch in fact, who wouldn't frighten the children, and the hair streaming down my back added just the right final touch.

It would take another book to describe the fun and the jokes we enjoy making *Rentaghost*. One of the early ones which had me helpless with laughter was when they produced a live tortoise for one of my tricks. I had thought it would be a toy. It looked up at me inquiringly, and when I let out my shrieking 'spell', it promptly drew its head inside the safety of its shell and the unexpected reaction made me dissolve in helpless giggles. We had to re-shoot that!

The series has eight million viewers, and the children love it. I adore playing Hazel, and working with such imaginative people, and it is a sort of magic for me that I am helping to entertain a whole new generation of children so many years after my start in children's radio in Glasgow with Auntie Kathleen. And with my character as Hazel another little piece of magic happened. The children no longer ask me if I'm the Flash lady! To them now I'm McWitch, and they're both fascinated and slightly scared. They're not *quite* sure whether or not I might just put a spell on them.

I think it was surely due to Hazel's witchcraft that I won a long-standing battle with the local Council. For years I had had a lively correspondence with them on the subject of the traffic using our long, winding, highly dangerous lane. It is also very beautiful, and actually attracts walking parties from various societies in the autumn to admire the rich colouring, the gardens, the grass verges and the almost rural aspect.

All of us who live in the lane are well aware that it is used as a by-pass by far too many heavy vehicles intent on avoiding the High Street with its double-parking. Our verges are scarred with their heavy wheels as they mount recklessly to avoid head-on collisions with oncoming traffic. To add insult to injury, their speeds are excessive and terrify the old ladies from the homes in our lane.

To all my pleading, Harrow Council turned a deaf ear. Worse, they informed me that a 'study' of the traffic had revealed only two heavy vehicles in the space of an hour or thereabouts, and as for speed, I must be imagining things!

I sarcastically replied that I was quite certain that if they used a stop-watch, they would come to the conclusion that all traffic proceeded down our lane with the grace and dignity of a sedan chair!

I tried another tack. I begged them to erect a sign to alert users of the wide lane leading from the busy main road that they were approaching a side-road – ours – and to slow down accordingly. Without some warning sign, drivers tearing up the wider lane had no idea they were likely to meet us emerging from our lane, and so were unable to slow down while we were only half-way across with our right-hand turn. It could only be a matter of time before there was some ghastly accident. Did they want to wait until that happened, I enquired, before they would take action?

The Council informed me it would be a retrograde step to add to the 'street furniture' by yet another sign. As to my other suggestion for ramps as 'sleeping policemen' to slow everything down – out of the question on the grounds of cost alone.

Well, that seemed to be that. Until we had *three* accidents in a row in our lane. One of them involved our close neighbours, and resulted in the husband having to spend some time in hospital with a recurrence of heart trouble. Nothing to be proved, of course, but it didn't take a genius to realize that a speeding vehicle smacking into you with teeth-rattling impetus isn't going to keep you in a very healthy condition.

So into battle waded Weir once more. With evidence presented sharply and clearly, *and* truthfully, I requested a junction sign in that wide lane, with a *Slow* sign painted about twenty to thirty yards ahead, so that we might all drive in safety through both lanes. The first crack in the opposition came when I received an acknowledgment, not opposing my hare-brained suggestions, but telling me that my letter was receiving careful consideration! I wondered if they had been influenced by my advising them to check with the police, to whom all three accidents had been reported, so that everyone was aware that this was not all in my imagination.

And now for the fairy-tale ending! One day, as I walked down the wider lane, *there* was the Junction sign. Success! It took several months, of course, before the electricians realized it was there and managed to wire it up for lighting, but light it up they did in the fullness of time.

I positively *glow* with triumph every time I pass that illuminated junction sign. All achievements seemed to pale into insignificance beside the fact that I triumphed over bureaucracy and managed to convince a reluctant Council that safety was more important than parsimony.

I have a tender, proprietory interest in this monument to my persistence. I feel that it is almost mine.

As Churchill truly said, 'Say not the struggle naught availeth.'

I wonder if the Council feared the 'Witch Report'?

CHAPTER TWENTY

When I had to go into the BBC on 5 November, I groaned when I pulled the curtains back in the morning. Fog swirled down and blotted out the end of the garden, and it was obviously going to be a raw horrible day. I drew on my warmest trousers, heavy sweater, and thick boots, and headed for the West End. It was bliss to get into the warmth of Broadcasting House, and to spend the day with Phyllis Robinson, recording a long interview with her and playing over the gramophone records I'd chosen for her programme *Be My Guest*. I had had no idea how difficult it could be to choose just the right section of a long playing record which would give the mood of the piece without spoiling the composer's dream. Fascinating work, which took us the whole day, and when I came out the fog was icy and penetrating.

The tube entrance sucked us all in, hundreds of us,

and whirled us down on the escalators to our various platforms. Trains rushed in, picked up shivering commuters and rushed off with them again. Except for the platform where I waited. All was silent there, to everybody's irritation. A train was standing with all its lights dimmed, and it was clear there had been an electrical fault and it could be stuck there for hours. We stamped our feet to try to keep warm, and faces were pinched with tiredness and cold. Suddenly I thought I heard the noise of the bagpipes. 'Och you're imagining things,' I thought. 'It's all those records. They're still echoing in your head.'

The thin wail rose again, and all at once everybody seemed to hear it, for there was an instinctive movement towards the sound and we all drifted down the platform. We joined the knot of people already gathered there, and sure enough, when they parted slightly, I caught sight of a set of bagpipes. The owner was obviously well on the road to being 'fu''. Not really drunk, but arguing solemnly with a Cockney friend who was very drunk indeed. Neither listened to the other, and Jock waved the pipes to emphasize every point he made. I decided he was from the West Highlands with his dark eyes, moustache and hair, that tell-tale pale clear skin, and fine physique.

The English commuters were cheered by the thought of some unexpected entertainment to enliven the dull wait, and someone called out encouragingly, 'Come on, Jock, give us a tune.' Jock took not the slightest notice. Then somebody threw down a penny, and there was a general laugh. He tantalized them a while longer, putting the mouthpiece to his mouth and then, as the crowd grew silent, taking it out again and continuing his argument. Groans of good-humoured disappointment followed each feint and at last, obviously feeling he had teased them long enough, he clapped the bag smartly, took a deep breath, and played.

My, how he played. My heart swelled as he broke from strathspey into reel, and there were yells of merriment from the Sassenach audience as he threw his shoulders back and marched with graceful dignity up and down the platform. The crowds parted, but their eyes never left him, and it was as though he were really the Pied Piper come to lure us all away, not to our doom, but to some better place.

A relief train was shunted in from the other platform, and we all marched towards it, Jock leading the way, playing without pausing. Now that he had the bit between his teeth, it was impossible to stop him. The faces of the people already in our relief train were a joy to behold. Heads jerked incredulously from papers and magazines. Churlish faces broke into wide delighted grins. The train was absolutely packed, and there were people swaying from every strap. The noise was deafening for Jock had come into the compartment with us, but not one voice was raised in protest. When we came to a station he marched along the platform, still playing, and marched into the next compartment, to give the whole train a treat.

The girl next to me said, 'Gosh, if that's how he behaves on Guy Fawkes night, I wouldn't like to see him at New Year.' I turned to her in amazement. 'But it's nothing to do with Guy Fawkes night,' I said. 'It's because he's had a wee drop too much and he has pipes with him. He's not celebrating anything but being happy.'

When I got out at my station, I left a train where people were sitting laughing and talking together in a way I'd never seen in all the years I'd lived south of the Border. Commuters hardly open their mouths in

460

the London area, but for that one journey, thanks to the skilful fingers of a rather tipsy Scot, they were discovering what fun it was to be 'a' Jock Tamson's bairns'.

When I told Sandy all about it, he said, 'Nothing like that ever happens in the trains I travel on. I wish I'd been there.' I think he thought I'd made half of it up, just to cheer him on a foggy night, but I hadn't. Every word of it was true, just as I described it.

I thought that was the most fantastic episode which could happen and be enjoyed by me on a wintry London night, but I was wrong. One night, just when I was thinking it was high time I was getting busy with the Festive preparations, the telephone rang shortly after six o'clock.

For some reason, I imagined it would be Rose on for a wee chat while the potatoes boiled. 'Miss Weir?' a voice enquired. 'It is,' I replied, thinking Rose was putting on an act for my benefit. We often did this, because of her ringing me from Windsor Castle.

'This is the Prime Minister's Office in Downing Street!' the voice said.

I burst out laughing. I was absolutely sure now that it was Rose.

'Oh yes?' I said. 'How *nice* of you to call. What can I do for you?'

There was a little cough at the other end of the line. 'Mrs Thatcher would like to invite you to a reception,' the voice said primly, 'And she would like to invite your husband with you, so may we know your married name?'

My stomach did a double somersault. It was *true*. It was the Prime Minister's Office. The girl must have thought she was dealing with a real fruit and nut case.

There was nothing else for it but to go on in the

same light-hearted tone, so I said, 'And what do I wear for a "do" at the Prime Minister's official residence?' 'Oh just the usual sort of dress you'd wear to a party around six o'clock-ish.' 'And the boys?' I asked. 'What do they wear?' I heard a stifled giggle, and then she said, 'A dark suit will be very suitable.'

When I put the receiver down I still wasn't absolutely certain that the whole thing wasn't a complete hoax. 'Well,' said Sandy when I went through to tell him of this dramatic telephone call, 'we'll soon know if no invitation arrives, that somebody has been pulling your leg.'

A day or two later, on the breakfast tray was a thick white envelope from the Prime Minister's Office, 10 Downing Street (I hope the postman was impressed!), and inside were two cards, one inviting us to the cocktail party, and another to allow the policeman on the door to let us through.

Then began a wild rake through the wardrobe for a little 'something' suitable for the most famous cul-de-sac in the world. Sandy had no such problems. His best dark suit, new shirt, and dark tie, would fill the bill admirably.

That night we had a hilarious dress rehearsal, with me fleeing up and downstairs a dozen times to parade various garments for Sandy's inspection. My neighbour across the lane said, 'If you had as few glad rags as I have, you wouldn't be so spoilt for choice.' But, as I told her, I was asked to open so many fêtes and bazaars, and to speak at so many events, I had collected a wardrobe of what I called my 'public appearances' clothes, and I just mixed them around as the occasion demanded. What I never did was to go out specially to buy an outfit for a particular occasion. I picked up things as I saw them, and by the time I came to wear them they were old friends which had hung in my wardrobe sometimes for months. For the Downing Street 'do', I ended up with what I knew from the start I'd wear, my Mary Farin crunchy beige and cream silky knit dress, with a pale coppery crêpe-de-chine blouse underneath, with wide Cavalier-style collar and double circular cuffs.

It turned out to be a horrible day of black skies and pouring rain, and we decided to go by train, as we knew we'd never find a parking place on a wet evening in London, and we would either walk down Whitehall or get a taxi. Even taxis would be as scarce as hen's teeth. Londoners are terrified of getting wet. So I carried my peeric-heeled fancy shoes in a crochet bag something like a carrier bag, together with my hair brush and gold evening bag, and I wore my sensible wee boots for the journey just in case there would be no taxis and we'd have to walk from Trafalgar Square tube station.

Well, in the event we did have to walk. There wasn't a taxi to be had for love nor money, and I was thankful to be able to stride out swiftly in my comfortable boots. It was exciting to turn into Downing Street, although because of the rain there wasn't so much as a single sightseer to observe us hand over our first card to the policeman standing in front of the famous door. In view of my headscarf and boots, it was probably just as well!

I had expected that, once inside, I would be directed to an impressive ladies' room where I could change into my shoes in decent privacy. That was the first shock. Once inside the door, we found ourselves in the wide chequered hall, off which ran the staircase leading to the reception rooms, and far from there being an impressive changing room, there wasn't one

463

at all! There were merely three clothes-rails and two middle-aged ladies taking the guests' coats.

When I asked where I could change my shoes, I couldn't believe my ears when one of the clothes-rail ladies pointed to a wee chair behind the front door, in full view of everybody coming in, and said, 'I'm afraid that's all there is.'

A detective sat on another chair, at least I presumed he was a detective, and watched me with great interest as I removed my boots, (praying the while that my walk hadn't pushed my big toe through the nylon!), and I wondered if he suspected me of being in possession of a pair of those exploding boots, so beloved of the Beachcomber column in the *Daily Express*. I had a job stifling my laughter as this thought struck me, and I was further convulsed with giggles when each arrival looked down with amazement at me sitting pushing my wet boots into a crochet bag!

I still hadn't seen what my head-scarf and my curlers, which I'd removed at the last moment from my side-tendrils, had done to my hair, and there wasn't a mirror in sight. By this time the clothes-rail ladies were laughing almost as much as I was myself. They could identify with me completely, and when I whispered to them 'Where can I find a mirror?' they advised me to have a word with one of the guides upstairs to see if I would be allowed to use a dressing room.

Oliver Twist asking for more couldn't have caused more amazement than my modest request. The girl I asked was guarding a corridor against wanderers, and was obviously petrified to leave her post for more than thirty seconds, so she darted with me to another corridor, pointed out four doors along, and said, 'If not in there, try round the corner.' As she rushed back to her allotted spot, she called back, 'Try not to get lost.'

It was a beautiful dressing room, with warm pinky-bronze mirroring all round, and I was relieved to find there wasn't a hair out of place, for I hadn't carried any hair lacquer in case it might be suspected as a bomb. With all the drama of actually finding this dressing room, I was terrified to use the toilet or to stay a moment longer than was strictly necessary. I was sure they were timing me.

I joined Sandy on the upstairs landing, and we were just behind Sir Billy Butlin. Next moment we were being announced and greeted by Mrs Thatcher and Denis, her husband. She was in black chiffon, three-quarter length I think, and in spite of all the stresses over Rhodesia, and all those shouting matches at question time, looked amazingly cheerful and relaxed. And very good-looking. She seemed to me to be one of those Englishwomen with the enviable facility of always looking well-groomed. I think the fine beautiful skin and lovely hair have a lot to do with it, and I couldn't imagine her being ever less than squeaky clean from top to toe.

The surprising thing about the house in Downing Street is its size. It is huge. Sandy and I admired the beautiful pale blue satin wallpaper, and managed a quick glance at the photographs of previous Prime Ministers which lined the walls leading to the reception rooms. We were allowed to wander about those main rooms, as we sipped our drinks and ate our little bits and pieces, and Richard Briers advised us to have a look at the small dining room and the Cabinet Room nearby. The company was a most enjoyable assortment of show-biz personalities, Government ministers and Trade Union officials.

While we were enjoying this hospitality, Lord Car-rington was battling out the future of Rhodesia, later to be Zimbabwe, with Nkomo and Mugabe, and when he arrived dramatically in the middle of the proceedings, Mrs Thatcher slipped away from us for a few moments to hear the momentous news that a settlement had been agreed. History was being well and truly made while we tucked into the canapés and toyed with our wine glasses.

I was delighted to meet Donald Sinden and his wife. He is an actor whom I greatly admire, and we had a most enthusiastic discussion of a play I'd seen him in years before, *London Assurance*, with lovely Judi Dench, and he seemed quite surprised that I had remembered it so vividly. I could see by the thoughtful look his eyes took on, that I had maybe given him the notion of putting it on again.

His wife pounced with cries of envy on my necklace of coloured stones set in silver-gilt. 'Did you get that in Brazil?' she asked. 'We saw them out there, and I wanted Donald to buy me one, but we were running short of cash because it was the end of our stay there, and we daren't risk it.'

She couldn't believe that I had actually bought it in a little shop off Baker Street! That was one of those little items I spoke of, that I just picked up in passing, and it was in fact an early Christmas present from Sandy who had been with me when I spied it. He never knows what to give me, and when he saw how much I admired it in the window of a favourite shop he had said, 'All right, if it's not too expensive, I'll give it to you for Christmas.' Now every time I wear it I think of Downing Street and of nice Mrs Donald Sinden.

Bryan Forbes and his beautiful wife Nanette

Newman came over, Nanette looking quite gorgeous in a deep red velvet suit. But, as my grannie would have said, 'A bonnie face suits a dish-cloot,' and that dark-haired stunner put us all in the shade.

Well, maybe not all of us, for Lulu in a black shimmery trouser suit looked very bonnie, and I met her nice husband for the first time, the popular and trendy top hairdresser, John Frieda. I had a feeling I was possibly the only female in that august gathering who had washed her own hair, and I hoped he wasn't casting a professional eye over it, for the most fashionable heads in theatrical London knew the touch of his skilled styling.

Just as we were reaching out a hand towards the dish of delicious savouries which were being offered, a wee dark-haired major-domo in a black tail-coat came up to me. 'Will madam follow me to the other end of the room, where Mr Askey would like to have a word? He apologizes for not coming to madam, but he has injured his leg and has to sit down.'

'Oh,' I said, 'where is Arthur? Yes of course, I'd love to see him.'

'Follow me, madam,' said the courteous little waiter.

Lulu nudged me, and winked at the waiter's back. 'See the wee yin?' she said, 'he's fae Possilpark!'

Somehow at that moment, the very word Possilpark in that setting brought my mother's face vividly before me and I could almost hear her say 'My Goad, fancy oor Mooly hob-nobbin' wi' the Prime Minister. An' fancy a wee fellow fae Possilpark workin' there tae! Ah wid hae thought it wid have been a' gentry.'

Jean Rook and her husband were talking to Arthur when I reached the sofa where he sat perched on the edge. 'Don't get up now, Arthur,' I said. 'I know you injured your leg rehearsing for pantomime, so rest it while you can. How is it?'

He said it was improving, and told us that he had seen Prince Charles at some charity affair the day before and when the Prince had asked him how old he was, he had told him he was in his eightieth year. 'Oh,' said Charles, 'you came in with the century?' 'Yes Sir,' Arthur had said, 'just like your grandmother.' At that Charles had smiled broadly and said, 'That must have been a *very* good year!'

By a strange coincidence, both Mrs Thatcher and Sandy and I had been on holiday on Islay that summer, and I was telling her that we had met the artist who had made a beautiful seaweed picture for her. When we were out walking, Mrs Owen had actually been on her way to deliver the picture to the 'big hoose' so that the laird could deliver it personally to No. 10 and confirm that the contents were safe. (All parcels to Downing Street are treated with caution.)

Mrs Owen had been so tickled at seeing us on the island that she stopped the car and took us back to her house where she opened the parcel, and gave us a preview. Unless I had seen them with my own eyes, I wouldn't have believed that coloured seaweeds could convey the delicacy of an exquisite water colour painting of carnations, roses and ferns. Certainly when I was shown that picture, I little thought that before the year was out I would be chatting to Mrs Thatcher in her official residence, with the Islay picture hanging in her bedroom not far from where we were standing.

I didn't mind a bit sitting on the hall chair and changing into my boots again for the walk back to the Tube. It had been a lovely peep behind the scenes, and an enjoyable mingling with the powerful. 'Aye Sandy,' I giggled as we went up Whitehall, 'from 310,

468

Springburn Road to 10, Downing Street isn't a bad leap, eh?' 'No sae bad at a',' he said. 'Christmas will seem a bit of an anti-climax after this.' He was right. It was really the Downing Street visit which brought the year to its climax, just as it now surely brings me to the end of this chapter of my life.

And yet, as I finish this seventh volume of what started out originally as a modest autobiography, with *Shoes Were for Sunday*, there is still so much I have left unsaid. Not a word of that tribute to Jack House on his seventieth birthday, when we his friends and colleagues did our party pieces for him on BBC television. My 'present' was a poem *Where is Glasgow*, for Jack is truly Mr Glasgow, and that poem became one of a selection which featured on an LP of ballads I recorded, called *Down Memory Lane*. It has been sent to all corners of the world where nostalgic Scots foregather.

And what of that unforgettable day in London? The day before the wedding of Prince Charles to Lady Diana Spencer, when we wandered with the crowds along the Mall, and had a picnic, with hundreds of others in St James's Park.

The happiness, and the quiet yet radiant joy of the populace was so tangible as it spilled over in soft laughter and sweet secret smiles, you could have stretched out your hands and gathered it to your heart.

I actually delivered my newly re-issued book of recipes to Buckingham Palace, and hoped a 'clootie dumpling' might one day be served to our Prince for his birthday. The man in charge was delighted I'd had the good sense to leave it unwrapped so that they didn't have to undo the paper and string to check the contents. I had rung first to make sure it was possible to deliver wee presents from ordinary folk like us, and

469

the official who spoke said to me, 'Don't waste your time and money with fancy wrappings or ribbons, for we'll just have the trouble of opening them.' As a prudent Scot, I followed this good advice, and got my wee pat on the back when I handed the book over.

Will there ever again be such a feeling of spontaneous rejoicing and enjoyment of the London scene as took place on that magic day, and the day of the wedding itself which followed? I doubt it. The time, the loved one, and the opportunity had coincided with blazing happiness and we all knew it.

For a brief spell we were a united nation again. People stepped aside with the greatest good nature to let others pass. Children were handled tenderly. The old were helped to the best places. Smiles were exchanged by strangers as they surveyed the exhausted sleeping bodies, and heads were shaken in wonderment as to how the sleepers would last out another twenty-four hours.

Photographs were taken of everyone in sight who could add a touch of extra excitement to the day. I was so glad I had chosen to wear that favourite white Madeira dress with its turquoise and green accessories (the coffee stains had completely vanished), for I had to pose again and again for pictures, with policemen, and without policemen. Standing in the middle of the Mall with the flags waving behind me, and walking along the Mall towards Trafalgar Square. Those who took them just wanted to prove they had been there when someone recognizable from Television had been part of the crowd, just like themselves. Nobody was more special than anybody else – some faces were maybe a bit more recognizable, but we were each and every one of us members of a family out celebrating a wedding of which all of us thoroughly approved, and

470

there wasn't a cross word to spoil the jollifications. Grateful I was on that fair day to be alive.

And what of those other 'flooers o' the forest' whom I haven't yet mentioned? Those friends and colleagues who so enriched my life, and were now 'a' wede awa''? Peter Sellers, with whom I shared that cartoon commercial for Lyons' ice cream, whose little ditty Ben Lyon used to make me sing when he wanted to start rehearsals with a laugh. Ronnie Waldman, who was so encouraging in every way when I first came to London to seek fame and fortune. Arthur Askey, who always greeted me so warmly and who always had a joke with me and whose memorial service, to my grief, I wasn't able to attend because I wasn't free. Renee Houston, one of the 'greats' in entertainment, who used to say when anybody swore backstage or at rehearsals, 'Don't use thae bad words in front of ma wee Molly, she disnae like them!' And dear, dear Moultrie Kelsall, my drama producer and friend, whose pawky coolness hid a heart as vast as a cathedral, and whose wit was diamond sharp. Moultrie had a passionate concern for all good causes, and he made an enormous contribution to all that was best in Scottish entertainment, from radio to films. He was a huge part of my early professional life, and I had great affection both for him and for Ruby, his talented musical wife. It was a shattering loss for Ruby, for theirs was one of the lasting, truly happy show-biz marriages.

I wrote to Ruby after Moultrie's death, and in her reply she told me that because the Keeper of MSS from the National Library of Scotland was coming to the house to look over Moultrie's papers, she had had a quick glance through some letters, and she sent me copies of two letters which she thought might amuse me. He never forgot his law training and he kept every

471

scrap of correspondence, and I was both amused and touched to the heart to see this typical example of his humour.

I had wanted to open a bank account with Lloyds when I first arrived in the capital in October 1946, and far from coaxing young people to open an account with them as is the case today, banks then required references before they would consider one as a client. So I had given Moultrie's name.

The two letters Ruby enclosed read thus. The first one was to Moultrie from the Clapham Branch of Lloyds, and it was dated 8 October 1946:

Dear Sir,
                    Private and Confidential

Miss Molly Weir is desirous of opening a Banking Account and has given your name as a reference. I shall be glad to know whether you consider her a suitable person for this purpose. A stamped addressed envelope is enclosed for your reply.

                    Yours, etc

To this letter Moultrie had replied:

Dear Sir,
  Miss Molly Weir has been known to me for six years, and I have always found her to be sober, industrious and serious-minded. Other than the language difficulty I can see no reason why she shouldn't be an eminently suitable person to open a bank account with you.

                    Yours, etc

I couldn't ask for a better reference, or a more apt reminder of the pawky humour of a great Scot, who was my friend.

And there was Hattie Jacques, who had followed me into *ITMA*, to give the newspapers their headline

472

Out goes Tattie, in comes Hattie'. When she telephoned me she used to speak in a tiny breathy whisper like a little girl, 'Hullo darling, this is Hat.' I never called her Hat, always Hattie, but she always called herself Hat, just as Eric Sykes did. Her memorial service was a joyous celebration, and the actors' church in Covent Garden was filled with her friends and colleagues. A choir of soloists and choristers from the Players' Theatre, where Hattie had worked a great deal at the start of her career, sang gloriously, starting with *The Battle Hymn of the Republic*, in which we all joined, the music soaring to every corner of the lovely church. Then the Players' choristers sang a lovely potpourri of all Hattie's special numbers. Quietly and gently they slid into *My Old Man said 'Follow the Van'*, the first song I ever heard Hattie sing at the Players. Then followed *There was I waiting at the church*, *The saucy little bird on Nellie's hat*, *Always have a little of what you fancy*, *The Old Bull and Bush*, and finally from a coloured singer, *Swing Low Sweet Chariot*. I was sitting next to Deryck Guyler and when it had finished we both whispered, 'Beautiful, simply beautiful.' And it was.

Later most of us went on to the Players' Theatre bar, for drinks and sausages, cheese and biscuits and we spoke of Hattie and of all the shows we had shared with her. There was an ambience of friendship and shared remembrance, and I somehow felt Hattie would have approved.

Worst of all, was poor Lady Barnett. Isobel, lovely, elegant and such fun, her tragic death was a contradiction of all she stood for in life. I had wanted to ring her on that Sunday night, but I didn't know her number and I didn't want to break into the precious Sunday of the only person I knew who would have it. This friend was to be at a lunch next day which I was attending and I thought I would get the telephone number then Her first words to me, before I could even ask for i were, 'Isobel is dead'. My heart gave a great lurch o pain. Too late, too late to call her with my support Would my words have made any difference? I wil never know.

Yesterday, when I was tearing the date off the calendar, it occurred to me that one of those calenda blocks was very like life. It looks so thick and solid a the beginning of the year that you wonder how or earth, tearing off a leaf a day, it will ever be finished And then, suddenly one day you find you are within the last dozen or so leaves, and you've scarcely realized it.

I was just chewing over this bit of philosophy when I switched on the radio, and there was the voice of long-departed brilliant Bernard Shaw exhorting the boys of his old school to make the most of every minute for they'd find they had no sooner learned to grow up than they would be old men. So, he urged them, live life to the full while you can. How I agreed with him.

Once, after I had opened a fête, when I was racing round the stalls buying home-made cakes and honey, and bric-à-brac, I heard a lady say to her friend, 'Doesn't Molly really enjoy life? Isn't she always fairly fizzing?' What a marvellous compliment I thought, and I hoped and prayed that I would continue to do just that as long as I lived. For joy is the grace we say to God.

If I could pass one single law, with any hope of it being carried out, it would be for the medicos to invent and administer an annual pill or injection to *all* people over sixty which, like the doggy advertisement, would really PROLONG ACTIVE LIFE, so that the population would remain self-supporting, fit and energetic till the moment the ticker stopped. Sandy thought it would be awful to drop down dead when you thought you were full of life. But to me that would be a consummation devoutly to be wished.

Think of it. No need for home helps. No more geriatric wards required. Perhaps a few meals on wheels for the elderly who craved company. But everybody 'fairly fizzing' with enjoyment of the quality of life.

What couldn't we achieve with this release of energy?

And what couldn't we do with all the money we might save?

I would dearly like this to be the epitaph of every one of us:

'She (or he) lived every minute of every day of her life.'

I certainly mean it to be mine.

For still I write.

And still there is the excitement of never knowing what I'll be asked to do when the telephone rings.

It is clear, in the words of Eileen my producer at Grampian Television, I am still 'spinning like a peerie'.